Programming in the OSEK/VDX Environment

Joseph Lemieux

CMP Books
Lawrence, Kansas 66046

CMP Books
CMP Media LLC
1601 West 23rd Street, Suite 200
Lawrence, KS 66046
USA
www.cmpbooks.com

Acquisitions Editors:	Berney Williams, Robert Ward
Editor:	Rita Sooby
Manging Editor:	Michelle O'Neal
Cover Art Design:	Robert Ward

Distributed in the U.S. and Canada by:
Publishers Group West
1700 Fourth Street
Berkeley, CA 94710
1-800-788-3123
www.pgw.com

ISBN: 1-57820-081-4

RAGHU CHEJARLA

To my parents, Henry and Joan,
who recognized my love of technology early in my
life and supported me throughout.

Table of Contents

Foreword

In May 1993, several German automotive manufacturers — BMW, Bosch, Daimler-Chrysler, Opel, Siemens, VW — agreed to collaborate on the specification for a common, real-time distributed operating system tailored for automotive applications. The project was coordinated by the University of Karlsruhe in Germany and was to be called "Offene Systeme und deren Schnittstellen fur die Elektronik im Kraftfahrzeug" or OSEK for short. Roughly translated this means "Open systems together with interfaces for automotive electronics."

Meanwhile in France, PSA and Renault were developing a similar system called VDX, or Vehicle Distributed eXecutive. The two projects merged in 1994, and a year later OSEX/VDX was presented to the world.

OSEK/VDX sets out to address vehicle manufacturers' requirements on both the technical and commercial levels. By providing an appropriate feature-set, it can speed the development of the many Electronic Control Units (ECUs) found in a modern vehicle. Code and expertise can be re-used in different projects, and the external economies of scale could be realized by an industry using a common interface standard. The idea is attractive, and every major car manufacturer in the world is evaluating OSEK/VDX for the next generation of products.

Unfortunately OSEK/VDX has some way to go if it is to achieve its original aims. The committees defining the standards can't ignore the wishes of the project's sponsors, but producing a specification that accommodates every requirement inevitably leads to implementation-specific features, inconsistencies, and vagueness.

Environments like this ferment de facto standards as system users demand features they need from system suppliers, whatever the published specification says. The challenge for OSEK/VDX is now to formalize the de facto standard, and this will take time. Until this project is complete, OSEK/VDX is an exciting melting pot of ideas for the world's vehicle electronics community.

To be useful, such an environment needs order, but the official specification cannot match the standards used in the field, which leaves a terrible void in the documentation for anyone wishing to actually learn and use OSEK/VDX. I am delighted that this book is now addressing the problem, in such a well-researched and comprehensive manner. OSEK/VDX has now come of age.

Frank J. Leonhardt
Independent OSEK/VDX Working Group Member and consultant based in Europe

Preface

I was first introduced to the OSEK/VDX set of standards in 1998. During a meeting at my employer's European technical center, I mentioned that I was redesigning the division's software architecture in the United States. A European engineer asked if the new architecture would be OSEK compliant. Not knowing anything about OSEK/VDX, I did what any good engineer would do — I dodged the question by responding that many options were being investigated. When I returned stateside, I immediately spoke with the software engineer responsible for the new software architecture, and I began my journey into discovering what OSEK/VDX was and, more importantly, what it was not.

The OSEK/VDX standards, like many specifications, were difficult to read and understand and were written primarily by committee members who were not native English speakers. I had to read many of the phrases three or four times to understand what was intended. In addition, feature functionality was sometimes defined in many different sections. From this effort, I wrote two articles for Embedded Systems Programming Magazine that provided an overview of the specifications. These articles, *The OSEK/VDX Standard: Operating System and Communication* and *OSEK/VDX Network Manager and Implementation Language*, appeared in the March and April, 2000 issues. Next, I expanded the articles into a class, which I still present for the Embedded Systems Conferences. The result of these articles and classes is this book, which I hope will shorten the time it takes you to implement the OSEK/VDX standard.

What is OSEK/VDX?

OSEK/VDX is a set of standards for a distributed, real-time architecture that was developed by a consortium of European automobile manufacturers and suppliers in conjunction with the University of Karlsruhe, Germany. It is primarily comprised of four standards: the operating system (OS), communication (COM), network management (NM), and the OSEK implementation language (OIL). Three additional standards are in progress: the OSEK/VDX real-time interface (ORTI), the OSEK/VDX Time-Triggered Operating System, also known as OSEK-

Time, and the OSEK/VDX Fault Tolerant Communication specification. ORTI defines a real-time interface for application development with the use of third-party tools. OSEKTime is an extension of the existing standards that address the specific nature of time-critical applications, such as stear-by-wire and brake-by-wire in automobiles. The OSEK/VDX Fault Tolerant Communication specification is also intended for time critical applications that include time critical communication. Because I am not involved in either of these efforts and because they are still evolving, I cannot comment on them at this time.

What is OSEK/VDX Not?

Although developed by the European automotive industry, OSEK/VDX is not just a real-time OS for automobiles. Systems based on this standard can and will arise in applications that are statically defined and require a compact, distributed, real-time system that must fit within minimum resources. Ideal applications will be in the control field (manufacturing, process, automotive, aerospace) in 8-, 16-, and 32-bit microcontrollers with 8 to 512Kb ROM and 1 to 32Kb RAM. However, other applications, such as small consumer electronics and electronic toys, can benefit from this standard as well. I have seen implementations advertising a basic kernel size as small as 800 bytes.

OSEK/VDX also is not just an OS. Although the OS is a part of the standard, there are applications based on OSEK/VDX that do not use an OS at all. They implement the COM and NM standards with a round-robin scheduler. That is why I titled this book Programming in the OSEK/VDX Environment instead of Programming in the OSEK/VDX OS.

Acknowledgments

First I acknowledge the loving support of my family: my wife, Jennifer, and my two darling children, Megan and Kyle. I have noticed in many books that the family is acknowledged first. I always thought that this was a very nice gesture, demonstrating the love of one's family. It was not until I wrote this book that I understood the tremendous sacrifices a family makes while a family member is writing. The support that my wife gave me while I focused on the book, instead of assisting in the maintenance of our home and family, was tremendous. Thanks a lot Jennifer!

The second major contributor has been Wind River Systems, Inc., who provided all the software and some of the hardware that I used to develop the applications in this book. Included in this software was the Tornado Development Environment, the OSEKWorks implementation of the OSEK/VDX standards, the Diab toolchain for the Motorola Power PC MPC555 processor, and the EST VisionProbe Debug Interface with VisionClick software. The development of the example program provided an opportunity for me to increase my understanding of the actual operation of each service. Wind River Technical Support was extremely responsive in answering questions on the workings of OSEKWorks and on their interpretations of the standards. They also corrected some of my misinterpretations of the standards. In particular, I would like to thank Michael O'Donnell, the Business Development Manager for Wind River in the Detroit area, Gary Bourdon, the Product Marketing Manager for OSEKWorks, and Venkat Viswanathan and Thomas Yu from the Wind River Technical Support team. Their support in making sure that I had the right software and equipment and knew how to use it was critical in the success of this book.

The hardware on which this book was written was provided by Axiom Manufacturing. I thank them for providing this equipment at a discount so that I could get up to speed rapidly. Axiom Manufacturing develops a line of low-cost development boards for various processors that are ideal for evaluation and prototyping of both hardware and software systems.

I would also like to thank Frank Leonhardt, who has been a member of the OSEK/VDX Technical Committee since 1997 and who provided significant insight into the background of the standards, in particular the communication standard. Mr. Leonhardt also reviewed the entire book to ensure the technical accuracy of the statements, and provided valuable additions in many areas.

Finally, and not least, I thank the Applied Engineering Solutions organization of Electronic Data Systems (EDS), my employer. As crunch time came, they provided me with the time I needed to finish the book. In particular, I thank Mohamed Ashmawey, my direct leader, for his support and encouragement while I was writing this book, and John Huth, our Client Delivery Executive, who supported my assignment to an in-house project so I could maintain my focus on writing this book.

Introduction

The number of embedded microcontrollers in automobiles has grown rapidly over the last 20 years since the first microcontrollers were embedded in electronic engine control modules. Today, some automobiles contain over 70 microcontrollers. The result of this growth is higher quality, safer, and more efficient automobiles and a dilemma: The need for embedded software engineers is growing faster than universities can produce them.

To resolve this dilemma, major automobile manufacturers and suppliers in Germany and France investigated ways to increase the productivity of current software engineers. The investigators discovered that an extensive amount of effort was spent in developing and debugging software for the operating system (OS), network communication and management, and input/output (I/O) to the detriment of application development. Out of this investigation grew the OSEK and VDX consortia, which merged to develop the OSEK/VDX open standards for operating systems, communication, and network management. These three standards are mutually exclusive, and the use of one does not require the use of either of the other two. However, most network management implementations are intricately linked to an OSEK/VDX communication implementation.

Although the OSEK/VDX standards were originally developed for the automotive industry, the resulting specifications describe a small, real-time OS ideal for most embedded systems that are statically defined—dynamic loading of tasks is not supported. These standards are now candidates for standardization by the International Standards Organization (ISO) under standard number ISO 17356.

This book describes each of these standards from a programmer's perspective. The reader is assumed to have some knowledge of embedded systems, real-time operating systems (RTOSs), and objected-oriented design. I do not describe how to write an OSEK/VDX-compliant system. The application programming interface (API) for each standard is described in detail with a description of the operation of the system.

Throughout the book, I develop an example that illustrates the use of the API. This example is intended to illustrate the function of each API service and allows the reader to play with the software and the service. It is not intended to, and frequently does not, illustrate the best way to implement the intended function.

Although an I/O standard was not developed by the OSEK/VDX committee, it is strongly recommended by the committee that the user develop a standard method. This topic is out of the scope of this book and is not covered.

History of OSEK/VDX

OSEK, a German acronym for Offene Systeme und deren Schnittstellen für die Elektronik im Kraftfahrzeug, which translates roughly to Open Systems and their Corresponding Interfaces for Automotive Controllers, was initiated in Germany in May 1993 by the automotive companies BMW, Daimler Benz (now DaimlerChrysler), Opel, and Volkswagen; the major automotive suppliers Bosch and Siemens; and the Institute of Industrial Information Technology at the University of Karlsruhe, Germany. VDX, an acronym for Vehicle Distributed eXecutive, was initiated in France about the same time by the French automotive companies PSA and Renault. In 1994, the two consortia merged to form the OSEK/VDX Consortium and created the OSEK/VDX Steering Committee. Since that time, other companies have joined as members of the Technical Committee to assist in developing the technical standards.

The original motivation for the standards was to resolve the problems of increasing software content in automobiles, duplication of effort in the areas of operating systems and communication networks, lack of qualified software engineers, and a desire for high-quality products. The goal was to develop a standard API that could reduce the amount of duplicated effort and increase the amount of code reuse within the vehicle. The result was the three standards in existence today: Operating System (OS), Communication (COM), and Network Management (NM). Although originally intended for the automobile environment, the specifications have been carefully developed to meet the requirements of a small embedded system with interprocessor communication.

Definitions and Conventions

The following terms are used frequently and are best predefined here. The terms that start with OSEK/VDX can be confusing because there is a slight difference between what is defined in the standard and how it is implemented in a commercial version.

- **OSEK/VDX standard or OSEK/VDX** refers to the standard as published.

- **OSEK/VDX implementation or the implementation** refers to a particular implementation of one or more of the standards. The standards tend to define the minimum requirements for a compliant system. Individual implementations can vary because of variations in processor requirements, processor capabilities, or both.

- **OSEK/VDX application or the application** refers to an application that was developed using a particular OSEK/VDX implementation.

- **OS** is the OSEK/VDX operating system standard.

- **COM** is the OSEK/VDX communication standard.

- **NM** is the OSEK/VDX network management standard.
- **OIL** is the OSEK/VDX implementation language standard.

Throughout the book, an API service has the format `ApiService()`; references to operating system tasks will have the form `TaskName`. Although a task is typically a function in C, I have eliminated the parentheses to illustrate the difference. All other OSEK/VDX objects, such as alarms, events, and messages, are in capital letters (e.g., `ALARM_OBJ`).

Flow of Book

Each of the three OSEK/VDX standards was written to stand alone and can be implemented independently of each other. This book follows that format and is written in parts, with each part corresponding to one of the major OSEK/VDX standards. The reader can choose to read the parts in any order based on which components of the standard are being implemented. However, because the example program uses all components of a complete implementation and builds on previously developed concepts, I recommend that you read the book sequentially. The OSEK/VDX standards do not explicitly cover I/O in any standard. The Technical Committee does address I/O by strongly encouraging each company to develop a standard hardware abstraction methodology to allow for maximum portability of application components within the company. Figure 1 shows a typical application, with each standard identified as a separate block, and the relationships also shown.

Figure 1 Typical OSEK/VDX application.

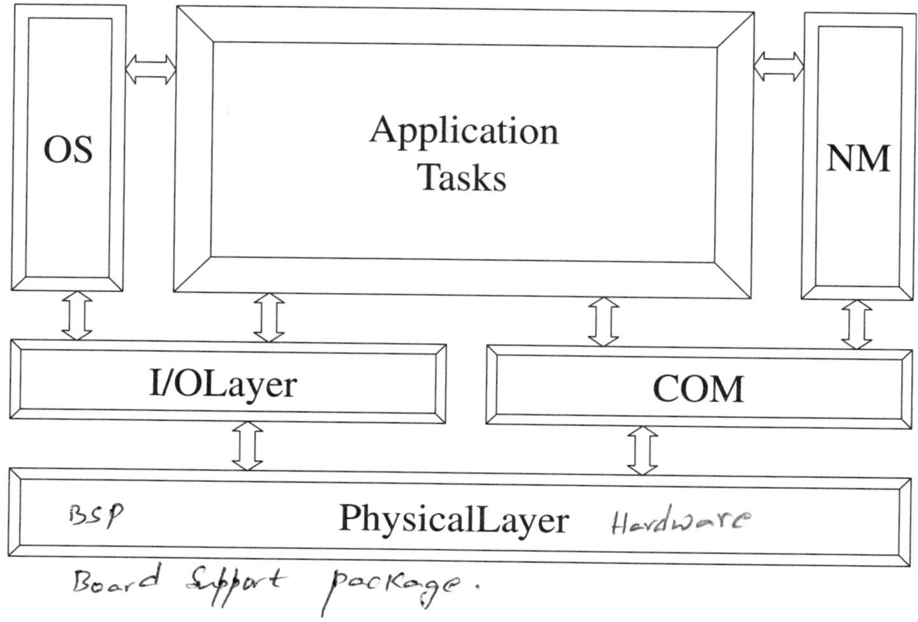

Part 1: Operating System

This part describes the OSEK/VDX OS standard. This standard defines a scalable OS using the concept of conformance classes. An application written for one conformance class is upwardly compatible with higher conformance classes. Objects such as tasks, alarms (a type of timer with greater flexibility), resources, events, and internal messages are defined in the standard and discussed in detail in this section.

The standard also defines a method of system development using two types of error handling: standard and extended. Because an OSEK/VDX application is statically defined, most potential errors should be identified and tested during development so that they will not occur at run time. To reduce code complexity, an OSEK/VDX implementation removes the code to check for some errors, such as undefined tasks, events, and so on.

Part 2: Communication

The communication standard is covered in the second part of the book. Interprocess and interprocessor communication is specified in this standard. Communication conformance classes also are introduced, along with the different types of messages. This standard works with an OS that provides certain services, but it does not have to be an OSEK/VDX OS. It also works in systems that have minimal OS support, such as simple round-robin schedulers and time-sliced executives.

The COM standard defines three layers: interaction, network, and data link. This book focuses primarily on the interaction layer because it is the only one visible to the application. However, knowledge of the other layers is required to some extent to understand how the system works and to enable message configuration. Therefore, a high-level discussion of these layers is provided.

Part 3: Network Management

The third part of the book describes the OSEK/VDX network management standard, which describes two methods of managing a network: direct and indirect. Each method describes the transient operation of the network during startup of nodes, the management of the network during a steady-state operation, and the shutdown of the network.

The network management standard defines the method of identifying the state of each node on the network but does not define how this information is used in the application. This part expands the published standard with a further discussion and examples of how the status of each node can be used by the application.

Example Program

I develop the example program, an electronic blackjack game for 1 or 2 players, throughout this book. It is intended to demonstrate all aspects of the standard without focusing on the automotive origins. The requirements of the card game are defined in Table 1.

Table 1 Blackjack game requirements.

Requirement Number	Description
1	System plays one game — Blackjack.
2	If no other systems are connected, the system defaults to a single-player game against the dealer.
3	When another player connects, the system allows either player to start a head-to-head game.
4	The program only allows the player to request a head-to-head game between local hands.
5	The system allows players to send messages while connected. The players do not have to be playing head-to-head.
6	The dealer in a single-player game must hit at 16 and stay at 17. Five cards under 21 automatically wins.
7	The dealer in a head-to-head game is not limited to the previous requirements.
8	In head-to-head play, the deal rotates between two players when fewer than 10 cards remain in the deck at the beginning of a new hand.
9	When a player drops out of a game, the system immediately terminates the current game and returns to a single-player game against the dealer.

Each chapter includes snippets of code from the example application, and the final section in each chapter describes the code for the entire example application using the API routines described to that point. Exercises provide hands-on practice. The application was developed using Wind River System's Tornado for OSEKWorks and two Axiom Manufacturing CME 555 development boards incorporating a Motorola MPC555 Power PC microcontroller. The example code included on the CD can be used as-is with these two systems. However, if you use another system, some code changes will be needed. In keeping with the goal of OSEK/VDX, these changes are primarily in the I/O layer and the configuration files. The location of these changes are clearly marked in the code, along with the interface requirements. It is left to the reader to make the modifications.

The accompanying CD is described in more detail in Appendix B, including installation and modification of files for different OSEK/VDX environments. Included on the CD is the entire source code for each chapter to enhance learning while studying this book. The complete OSEK/VDX standards are also included for reference. Because the standards are copyrighted material, the following copyright notice is included in the documents and reproduced here at their request.

> "This document is an official release and replaces all previously distributed documents. The OSEK group retains the right to make changes to this document without notice and does not accept any liability for errors. All rights reserved. No part of this document may be reproduced, in any form or by any means, without permission in writing from the OSEK/VDX steering committee."

Updates and Contact

Throughout the book, the example program is developed using the current version of OSEK-Works, which supports OS v2.0, COM v2.1, and NM v2.5. However, the text and the listings have been written for the latest versions of the standards: OS v2.1r1, COM v2.2.2, and NM v2.51; consequently, the code on the CD was written for the earlier releases. This will affect the COM-based examples primarily. When the new version of OSEKWorks is released, I will update the code and release the changes to my web site at http://www.osekbook.com. Wind River informs me that the new version should be released around the time the book is published, so check the web site first. As with all things on the internet, this web site could move. CMP Books (http://www.cmpbooks.com) will keep a link to the current site. You might have to select R&D Books first in order to search, then search by title, and the link will be in the description. You can also contact me at author@osekbook.com or through the contact link on the web site.

PART 1

Operating System

The OSEK/VDX operating system (OS) defines a small, scalable, real-time operating system (RTOS) that is ideal in embedded systems with high memory constraints and dedicated functions. A system with as little as 8Kb of ROM running on an 8-bit microprocessor up to a system with 512Kb of ROM running on a 32-bit microprocessor can use this OS. The operating system manages real-time tasks, enhanced timer functions (referred to as alarms), shared resources, task synchronization using events, and interprocess communication. This part of the book also describes an OSEK/VDX-compliant operating system from the standpoint of the application.

1

Chapter 1

Implementation Startup

After you have decided on the OSEK/VDX operating system (OS), you must choose which implementation to use. An implementation refers to how a development company realizes the OS standard. Unlike many other OSs, OSEK/VDX is an open standard, and many companies have created implementations for different processors. This differs from Linux, which is an open-source system; only one implementation of the kernel exists, which is controlled by Linus Torvalds' team. Implementation features and capabilities vary from those that just meet the standard to full-blown systems that include the integrated development environment (IDE) with an OSEK/VDX-aware debugger.

To determine which implementation to use, you should analyze many factors. Appendix A lists some questions that may help you analyze these factors. This book uses examples that can be used immediately if you already have an OSEK/VDX OS implementation and have installed it per the instructions. If you have not yet chosen an implementation, this book can help you make the best choice. After obtaining an implementation, return to the examples in this book to help you get up to speed.

This chapter shows you how to get your system running and ready for the OS. This includes the system boot, the C entry point main(), and the first OS interface, StartOS(). Finally, you'll learn about the OSEK/VDX implementation language (OIL). By the end of this chapter, your system should be up and running and doing absolutely nothing! Don't worry, you will add features and functions later.

1.1 System Boot

Embedded systems differ from other computing systems by hardware designs that result in unique system boot codes for each system. Most OSEK/VDX implementations, like most other RTOSs, provide startup code that is generic to the target microcontrollers. However, this code usually only provides the necessary configuration to get the OS running.

The first step in bringing up an OSEK/VDX OS is to create the system boot code. You can do this in two ways: Either modify the vendor-supplied code or create your own code. The easiest way to get started is to use the vendor example startup code. However, some OSEK/VDX users will have legacy boot code, in which case, your best option probably is to create your own code. The rest of this section addresses factors required to create the boot code and get the system going. If you either have an operational implementation or can use the vendor-supplied code, then you may skip this section and go directly to the "Main Module" section.

You must take the following actions to create boot code.

- Initialize the microprocessor registers. These critical registers must be initialized for the processor to operate properly and access memory. Most vendor-supplied OSEK/VDX implementation boot code includes this step. The stack pointer and any other standard pointers used by the system are included in these registers.
- Initialize the peripheral registers. This puts the processor into a certain configuration based on the unique hardware design of the application. Some registers, such as memory map registers, must be set before others for the system to operate. Typically, this is not included in vendor-supplied code.
- Initialize memory. Two types of memory initialization occur: initialization of all memory (usually set to `0`) and initialization of variables (usually using `cinit()` for C programs). This is also usually part of the vendor-supplied boot code.
- Call `main()` to start the application.

These actions might be performed differently in a boot code program, and some optional actions, such as those listed below, might be performed.

- Determine the source of the processor reset. This could be a hard reset (i.e., reset line asserted), a power-on reset, an internal watchdog reset, or another exception that forces a reset.
- Modify hardware register initialization based on the type of reset.
- Identify a startup mode — such as a system test, reprogram, and so on — and set the microprocessor and system registers differently based on the mode.
- Determine whether memory has been compromised. This usually includes some kind of checksum or checkbyte that is analyzed on reset. Memory is initialized only if it fails.

For the example program, I have performed the minimum required actions. Listing 1.1 shows the boot code that initializes the critical MPC555 registers, other registers, then the system memory. This source code is found in the `startup.s` module. Because this book focuses on the OSEK/VDX OS, I have not included any of the optional actions described in the previous list; you might want to explore these options as exercises.

Listing 1.1 Example boot code.

```
_cstart:
_START:
;#-------------------------------------------------------------------------------
;# Initialize some general-purpose registers required by the Motorola EABI
;#-------------------------------------------------------------------------------
    lis   r2,%hiadj(_SDA2_BASE_)   #Initalize pointer to read-only SDA
    addi  r2,r2,%lo(_SDA2_BASE_)
    lis   r13,%hiadj(_SDA_BASE_)   #Initalize pointer to read/write SDA
    addi  r13,r13,%lo(_SDA_BASE_)
    lis   r1,%hiadj(__SP_INIT)     #Initalize stack pointer
    addi  r1,r1,%lo(__SP_INIT)
    li    r0,0                     # r0 is assumed to be 0
    stwu  r0,-16(r1)               # Terminate stack in preparation for
                                   # C routines.

;# Initialize Critical Memory Registers

    lis   r4,%hiadj(_MEMORY_BASE_ADDR)  # Load base address of registers
    addi  r4,r4,%lo(_MEMORY_BASE_ADDR)
    lis   r5,%hiadj(_MEMORY_MAP)        # Load address of content table
    addi  r5,r5,%lo(_MEMORY_MAP)
    li    r6,0x1C                       # Counter of addresses
    li    r7,0x04                       # Constant for math

_MemMap:
    lwz   r3,0(r5)        #Get next register value
    stw   r3,0(r4)        #Store to register
    add   r4,r4,r7        #Update pointers
    add   r5,r5,r7
    sub.  r6,r6,r7
    bne   cr0,_MemMap     #Continue if not complete

;# Init SPR registers
    bl InitSPR

;# Init 16 bit registers
    lis   r3,%hiadj(InitResetRegs16)
    addi  r3,r3,%lo(InitResetRegs16)
```

```
    bl     InitReg16

;# Init 32 bit registers
    lis    r3,%hiadj(InitResetRegs32)
    addi   r3,r3,%lo(InitResetRegs32)
    bl     InitReg32

;# Initialize Memory to 0x00000000
    bl     InitRAM

;# Initialize C variables
    bl     cinit

;# Jump to main() with argc=0
    li     r3,0
    bl     main
```

In this code, I first initialized four internal registers — R0, R1, R2, and R13 — to point to the small data area that contains constants (SDA2 to R2), to the small data area that contains variables (SDA to R13), and to the compiler stack (R1). These register to data area mappings are defined in the Motorola Embedded Application Binary Interface (EABI) and are common to all compilers that support these requirements. The stack is then initialized per the EABI requirements.

Next, the memory registers are initialized in the MPC555. This is critical very early because this area usually contains the application executable code. The memory registers are initialized by writing the values contained in the _MEMORY_MAP table, defined in the source module, into the memory registers. I have defined an external _MEMORY_BASE_ADDR variable in the linker file, which can be changed there if the memory registers move (which is highly possible in a PowerPC processor).

Finally, I call InitSPR(), InitReg16() and InitReg32(), and InitRAM() to initialize the MPC555's specific special-purpose registers, the 16- and 32-bit peripheral registers, and the RAM, respectively. These routines can be found in the source code, so I do not discuss them here.

After the system is initialized, main() of the primary application is called with argc set to 0. This parameter can be changed to a value calculated by the boot code based on one of the optional actions defined previously.

1.2 Main Module

The main module is found in the source code file main.c. The first routine in this module is the C entry point main(). On entering main(), the control of the application passes to the user. At this point, only minimal microcontroller initialization has occurred, and nothing has been initialized in the OS. The application now has control and can perform the remainder of the system initializations. At the minimum, `main()` (Listing 1.2) should perform the following activities.

- Initialize the application-specific microcontroller registers.
- Perform application initialization.
- Determine the desired application mode (`APPMODE`).
- Start the OS.
- Process the shutdown of the OS and switch the `APPMODE`s. When the OS shuts down, it usually returns from the API (Application Program Interface) service that started the system. The shutdown of the OS might not occur in `main.c`; rather, it could require a different module, which is described later.

Listing 1.2 Example application `main()`.

```
void main(long argc)
{

   InitReg16(InitHardwareRegs16);
   InitReg32(InitHardwareRegs32);

   InitSystem(INIT_RESET);

   while(1){
   StartOS(SINGLE_PLAYER);
   }
}
```

The first step is to initialize the application-specific microcontroller registers, which typically control the I/O ports. The example application uses `InitReg16()` and `InitReg32()` to perform this initialization. I wrote these functions to assist in register initialization; they are not part of an OSEK/VDX implementation. Because MPC555 registers are two different lengths — 16 and 32 bits — two functions allow you to create an efficient routine that fills the registers from a table constructed with 16- or 32-bit values. With just one function, the table would have to include the size of the registers, the routine would be slower and not much smaller, and the tables would be much larger. The argument for each function is a pointer to a table of register description structures, which the routine navigates and which are defined in the `init.cfg` configuration file. At this point, the lists are empty because I have not defined the hardware functions. These lists are filled in later.

Now the application has to be initialized. At this point, it is put into a state in which it is ready to be run by the OS. Because the OS is not functioning yet, no OS calls can be made. The application-specific initialization functions are invoked using `InitSystem()`, which I developed to aid in system initialization. This function accepts an argument that defines the type of initialization to be performed and navigates a predefined table of initialization function calls. Each application has only one table of function calls defined in `init.cfg`. At this stage in the application, only the INIT_RESET type of initialization is performed. (You will see other types of initializations throughout this book.) The application developer is responsible for ensuring that the initialization functions do not call OS API services.

The application can use the APPMODE of an OSEK/VDX OS to modify its operation. This concept is discussed in detail in . The current APPMODE is defined by the application when the OS is started. At least one APPMODE must be defined, but the OSEK/VDX standard does not define a limit for the maximum number of modes. However, each implementation sets a limit based on the size of the memory variable used to store the mode. I have defined just one APPMODE, SINGLE_PLAYER, to enable the system start.

The start of the OS is performed using the API call StartOS(), which is described in more detail in Chapter 2. Because the OSEK/VDX OS is capable of being started and stopped without a reset, this interface is enclosed in a while(1) loop, which can be expanded in the future to include more processing outside of the OS execution. The argument to StartOS() is the default application mode SINGLE_PLAYER.

The final routine in the main module of the example is ChangeMode() and is specific to a particular application. ChangeMode() is responsible for changing the APPMODE of the system based on requests from the user. In the example application, this routine first checks that a valid mode is requested then shuts down the OS using the API call ShutdownOS(). Because this routine is specific to the application, it can be modified to ensure that a shutdown can occur safely. If not, the routine should return an error. The OSEK/VDX OS then usually returns from the previous StartOS(), where main() restarts the OS using the default APPMODE. This might seem like a lot of code to do nothing, but as you will see in later chapters, these functions will be expanded extensively. The ChangeMode() routine is shown in Listing 1.3.

Listing 1.3 Example application ChangeMode().

```
ApplicationErrorType ChangeMode(AppModeType mode)
{
  if((mode == SINGLE_PLAYER)){
  ShutdownOS(E_OK);
  }
  return ERROR_INVALID_MODE;
}
```

1.3 OSEK/VDX Implementation Language

OIL provides a method of configuring the objects in an OSEK/VDX implementation for a specific application. The system is configured by using an OIL configuration file that contains the definition of the application. Throughout this book, I will introduce the OIL language as necessary to configure the system up to the current level of discussion. Most OIL files have two parts: that specific to the implementation and that specific to the application. The implementation-specific portion is supplied with the OSEK/VDX implementation and should not be changed. Some implementations, such as OSEKWorks, include this information in the OIL generator file, which simplifies the actual OIL application-specific configuration file. The application-specific portion of the OIL file is defined by the user during application development. I will develop an application section for the example in this book.

The method of generating the OIL configuration file varies with each OSEK/VDX implementation and ranges from hand-coding the file to the use of an intuitive GUI (graphical user interface) with context-sensitive help. I strongly recommend purchasing an implementation that includes a GUI unless you enjoy debugging so much that you actually look forward to debugging the OIL file!

The Wind River OSEKWorks GUI is shown in Figure 1.1 as an example. Some of the key features that can be found in other OSEK/VDX GUIs as well are

- a list of OSEK/VDX objects in a Windows Explorer format on the left,
- a graphical and tabular display of attributes for each object on the right (both standard and implementation-specific attributes are shown), and
- a log window on the bottom.

Figure 1.1 OIL setup screen.

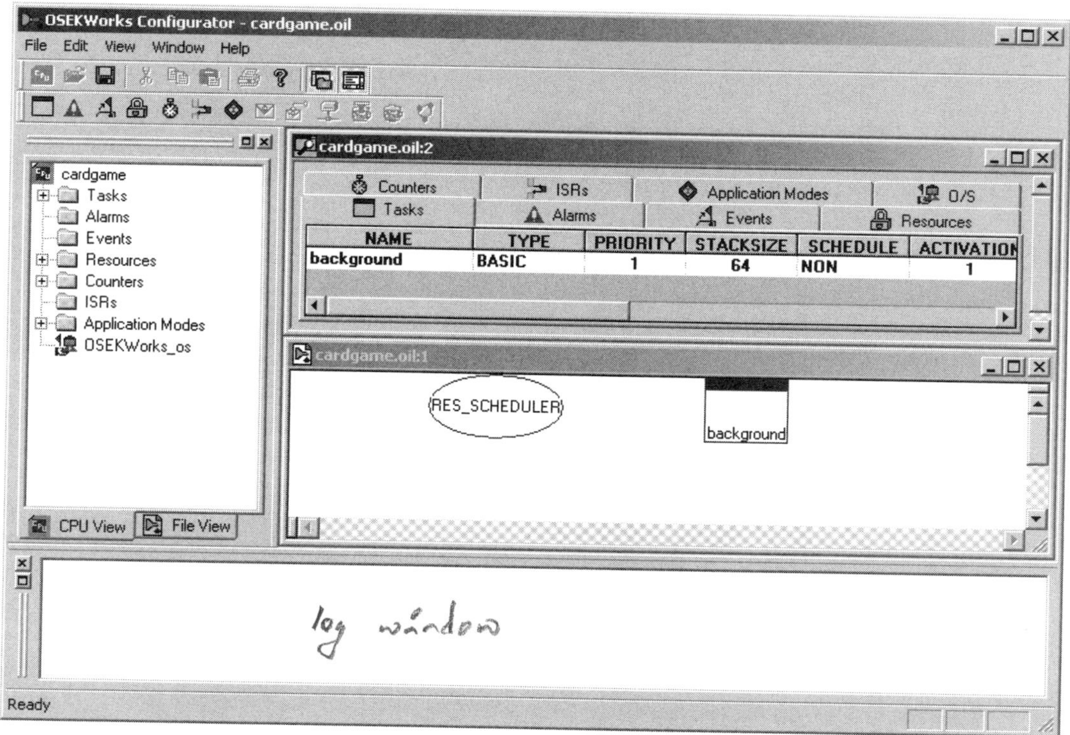

The OIL configuration file appears similar to a C structure definition. It consists of objects that correspond to the objects in the OS, with a minimum set of attributes that are defined for each object. An attribute can be required (mandatory) or optional. Because the OIL standard only defines the minimum attributes for each object, an actual OSEK/VDX implementation may define additional attributes. Because these attributes are not portable, they should be avoided. A GUI is helpful when porting to a new implementation because undefined attributes are ignored and implementation-specific attributes are readily apparent.

At this point in the development of the application, three objects in the OIL need to be defined: CPU (central processing unit), OS, and APPMODE. The Wind River OIL file also contains two standard objects that are required in all applications. One is the RESOURCE object RES_SCHEDULER, and the other is the COUNTER object SYSTEM_COUNTER. These can be ignored for now; they are discussed later in the appropriate sections.

At least one CPU must be defined in each OIL file. Some implementations allow all applications to be configured in one OIL file if the application consists of multiple identical CPUs with some type of interprocessor communication, such as a Controller Area Network (CAN). Listing 1.4 shows the application-specific portion of the OIL configuration file for the example.

Listing 1.4 OIL definitions for initial application.

```
CPU cardgame {
/************************************************/
/*              Tasks                           */
/************************************************/
    TASK background {
            TYPE = BASIC;
            SCHEDULE = NON;
            PRIORITY = 1;
            ACTIVATION = 1;
            AUTOSTART = TRUE;
            STACKSIZE = 64;
            SCHEDULE_CALL = FALSE;
    };
/************************************************/
/*              Resources                       */
/************************************************/
    RESOURCE RES_SCHEDULER {
            /* No attributes defined */
    };
/************************************************/
/*              Counters                        */
/************************************************/
    COUNTER SYSTEM_COUNTER {
            MAXALLOWEDVALUE = 65535;
            TICKSPERBASE = 100;
            MINCYCLE = 5;
    };
```

```
/*************************************************/
/*              Application Modes               */
/*************************************************/
   APPMODE SINGLE_PLAYER {
           VALUE = AUTO;
   };
/*************************************************/
/*              O/S                             */
/*************************************************/
   OS OSEKWorks_os {
           CC = AUTO;
           STATUS = EXTENDED;
           SCHEDULE = AUTO;
           SYSTEMSTACKSIZE = 1024;
           StartupHook = FALSE;
           ErrorHook = FALSE;
           ShutdownHook = FALSE;
           PreTaskHook = FALSE;
           PostTaskHook = FALSE;
   };
};
```

The CPU object is defined first in the OIL file and is a container object for all other objects defined for the configuration. In this example, the CPU object is called cardgame because there is only one CPU in this application. The CPU object has no attributes.

Within the cardgame CPU object are five additional objects. The first is a TASK object. Most implementations require that at least one TASK is defined to operate. To compile the program, I defined a do-nothing task that immediately terminates itself. This task is included in main.c and is shown in Listing 1.5. It is probably a good idea to add this task as a sanity check when the system is started. Place a breakpoint at the entrance to this task to verify that the OS has started properly.

Listing 1.5 Startup background task.

```
TASK(background)
{
   TerminateTask();
}
```

The next two objects, RESOURCE and COUNTER, are discussed later. The fourth object is APPMODE. A system must have at least one APPMODE object, although it usually has many more. At this point in the example, there is only one: SINGLE_PLAYER. Other APPMODEs will be added throughout the book.

The final object, OS, defines the parameters of the OS configuration used on the cardgame processor. Only one OS object can be in each CPU; consequently, I have chosen to leave the name as OSEKWorks_os, which is the default name in the Wind River system. Other implementations will have different default names. Six required attributes are in this object: STATUS, STARTUPHOOK, SHUTDOWNHOOK, PRETASKHOOK, POSTTASKHOOK, and ERRORHOOK. STATUS defines the return status of each OSEK/VDX OS API service and is either STANDARD or EXTENDED. The return status is discussed in more detail in later chapters. The other five attributes define the existence of each of the hook routines within the application and are either TRUE or FALSE. The application provides the hook routines, which are introduced in later chapters. At this time, the OS operates in EXTENDED status and the application does not define any of the hook routines.

The provider of the implementation usually adds many attributes in the OS object. Because each microcontroller has its own quirks, the OS object is the most likely section in which to add attributes that configure the microcontroller-specific features. The added attributes in Wind River OSEKWorks are defined in Table 1.1. Similar attributes can exist in any implementation; unfortunately, a naming standard for these attributes does not exist, so names will likely be different between implementations.

Table 1.1 Attributes specific to OSEKWorks.

Attribute	Description
CC	Conformance class for the application. With this attribute, the configurator can force a conformance class of AUTO, BCC1, BCC2, ECC1, or ECC2 and can generate an error if the class is violated.
SCHEDULE	Like CC, can force the scheduling policy for the application. Valid values are AUTO, NON, FULL, or MIXED with respect to preemption.
SYSTEMSTACKSIZE	Reserves a set amount of system stack space that can be set by the application developer.

1.4 Example Program

Now the fun begins! At the end of each chapter in this book, I describe the example program that appears on the accompanying CD. Each source code module is described, and the functions and major structures of that module are defined. This is your opportunity to play with the source code, modify it, and even break it. Refer to the actual code as you read this section for clarification. If you do not have an OSEK/VDX implementation available, you will not be able to play with this code, so you might want to skip this section. If you do proceed, make sure you have read Appendix B, which describes in detail the structure of the development tree that I use and how the system is built. This appendix describes which files can be used as they are and which files might need to be modified if you are not using Wind River OSEK-Works.

At this point, the application can be built using the tools associated with the OSEK/VDX OS implementation. This usually consists of a two-part build. First the OS is built and configured based on the information in the OIL file. Next, the entire application is built and linked into the OS. The example application is very simple at this time, but it is a complete application that can be built and run on the target. This small application operates rapidly, doing absolutely nothing at all! If you were to stop the software and observe where it is running, you would find it operating in an idle task provided by the OS implementation. Unless the watchdog is operating, it will continue in this tight loop forever.

1.4.1 Modules

The "Modules" section, included in all chapters, describes each of the source code modules found in the src directory.

startup.s The startup.s module contains the startup assembly language code that is entered when the microcontroller is reset. Its only function, _cstart, is entered when the system is reset; trap vectors also are used in case other exceptions occur. This module is specific to the microcontroller being used and needs to be modified extensively if you use this code on anything other than an MPC555-based system. The good news is that this module is the same throughout the book.

initspr.s The initspr.s module contains the assembly language code that sets the special-purpose registers of an MPC555 microcontroller. Its only function is InitSPR(), which is called from startup.s. It is required because of the inherent nature of addressing special-purpose registers in the PowerPC type of processor. This module is not required in systems using a different microcontroller, but a similar module might be required.

cinit.s The cinit.s module contains two functions, InitRAM() and cinit(), which initialize RAM to a known value as well as all the C initialized variables. The cinit() function is usually provided by the supplier of the compiler and might have a different name or be integrated into a startup module. I developed InitRAM() to initialize memory. Both of these assembly language functions use registers alone and do not require that any memory is initialized or available.

init.c The init.c module contains the routines that support initialization of the microcontroller registers and the application. At this point, only three services are available to the application.

void InitReg16(InitReg16ListType const *list); This service initializes the microcontroller registers defined in the null-terminated list referenced by the parameter list. This list is an array of structures of type InitReg16ListType, which is defined in init.h. Each entry in the list consists of the address of the register and its initial value. The null terminator is identified when the address of the register is at zero, which can never occur in an MPC555 microcontroller. The construction of each list uses configuration macros defined in init.h and used in init.cfg. When constructing the table, the name of the register is defined as a member of a structure defined in register.h in the format <register set>.<name>. I have chosen the same name found in the Motorola documentation for the processor. The register set value is the name of a set of registers that are both logically related and reside in the same block of memory. The available values can be found at the end of register.h.

`void InitReg32(InitReg32ListType const *list);` This service is identical to `InitReg16()` described previously but initializes 32-bit registers instead.

`void InitSystem(InitType type);` This service invokes a series of functions that are registered by the application in `init.cfg` and that allow the application to initialize itself based on a specific application-wide event. This event is defined in the parameter `type`, and can be any of the values defined in the `InitType` enumeration that appears in `init.h`. This routine invokes all of the functions in the list `InitFunctionList`, regardless of the value of the parameter type. `InitFunctionList` is defined using the macros in `init.cfg`, which create this constant array. The initialization function defined in this list is responsible for determining the actions to be taken based on the initialization type, which is also forwarded as a parameter to each function. As the example application is developed, initialization functions will be added to new modules to ensure that the application is in the proper state.

`main.c` The `main.c` module contains two functions and one OS task. This module will be expanded throughout the book to include functions and tasks that are applicable to the entire application. The two functions are described below.

`void main(long argc);` This is the C entry point that is called from `startup.s`. For my particular startup system I allow the startup code to pass one argument defined as a long integer. At this point, the startup code always passes a `0`, but it can be modified to pass information that indicates the type of startup that occurred, such as a hard reset, a watchdog timeout, or another exception. This routine performs all functions required outside of the OS function for the application and invokes the service that starts the OS. It does not return to the startup code in the OSEKWorks implementation, but it may on other systems.

`ApplicationErrorType ChangeMode(AppModeType mode);` This function enables a running application that is operating within the OS to change the `APPMODE` of the system. Because the OSEK/VDX standard does not allow the `APPMODE` to be changed while the system is running, this routine shuts down the application and restarts the system in a different `APPMODE`. It also verifies that the `APPMODE` is valid and returns an error if an invalid `APPMODE` has been sent. The `ApplicationErrorType` enumeration is defined in `main.h`. In the following chapters, this function is expanded to handle more `APPMODE`s.

The only task included in `main.c` is the `background` task: a do-nothing task that is expanded in future chapters.

1.4.2 Configuration Files

In addition to the module files found in the `src` directory, a number of files used to configure the application are in the `cfg` directory. They are header files, into which the application programmer puts application-specific information to tailor the standard operations.

`cardgame.oil` This is the OSEK/VDX OIL configuration file that is produced by the configuration utility. It contains all the information used to generate the specific implementation of the OSEK/VDX OS. Do not edit this file directly if you have a GUI-based configuration utility.

`init.cfg` This file contains the configurations for the register initialization tables and the function initialization table. These tables are constructed by macros that start the table, add a new entry to the table, and close the table at the end. Refer to the comments in the configuration file for a description of how the macros are used.

1.5 Exercises

Now that you understand the modules in the example program, it is time to change them. The best way to learn a new OS is to start using it. The exercises at the end of each chapter are intended to allow you to play with the software and become more familiar with how the system operates. At this point, you will become most familiar with your development tools, such as your compiler and debugger. However in later chapters, you will make changes that use the services of the OSEK/VDX OS.

1. Determine the source of the reset that put you into the `startup.s` module. Pass this value to `main()` as the argument, then within `main()`, save this value to a global variable.
2. Modify the RAM initialization routine to check whether memory has been compromised before initialization. If memory has not been compromised, skip memory initialization and C initialization. Pass this information, combined with the type of reset, to `main()`. Hint: The MPC555 has a register that indicates whether memory integrity is questionable. Other microcontrollers will require a different algorithm.
3. Expand the definition of the `InitType` enumeration to include possibilities based on the type of reset and the integrity of the memory after the reset. Pass this information to `InitSystem()`.
4. Add some registers to the initialization lists to put the system into a different state than the default state on reset. For example, switch some digital ports into output mode and set them to a default value of either on or off. You might want to add an LED to a port to observe the initial values.
5. Modify the `background` task so that it immediately calls `ChangeMode()` with the requested mode of `SINGLE_PLAYER`. Then use the debugger to observe what happens as the application enters and exits the OS.

1.6 Summary

This chapter has defined the items required to get an OSEK/VDX OS implementation up and running on a specific target hardware system. The boot code provides the method to get the hardware functioning and then enters the C startup function `main()` with the proper parameters. The purpose of `main()` is to provide any further application-specific initialization of the hardware and to start the OS.

`ChangeMode()` was added to allow the application to change mode at any time because OSEK/VDX does not allow the `APPMODE` to be changed directly without shutting down and restarting the OS. `ChangeMode()` verifies that the new mode is valid before shutting down the OS and allowing `main()` to restart.

Finally, the OSEK/VDX implementation language (OIL) was introduced and the objects required to get the system up and running were defined. The result is a fully operational OSEK/VDX application that can be used to set up an implementation when it is first purchased. This book will now expand upon this application to include more of the OS services.

2

Chapter 2

Starting and Ending

Chapter 1 focused on getting the system up and running and verifying that all of the tools operated properly. At this point, your system runs rapidly, doing absolutely nothing! The next step is to configure your application startup and shutdown. So far, the example application, a blackjack game, has a minimal startup capability and only one application mode (APPMODE). This chapter expands on the system startup, adds APPMODEs, and introduces the interfaces that shutdown the operating system (OS).

OSEK/VDX services allow the OS to start in different APPMODEs and to shutdown from any point in the application. The methods used to startup and shutdown the OS with the use of APPMODEs are expanded in this chapter. The various interface services provided by the OS API are discussed in more detail, along with examples using these services.

2.1 Application Mode

The first concept to understand in an OSEK/VDX OS is the use of application modes (APPMODEs), which are used by the application to define the current operating environment. The OSEK/VDX standard for the OS does not specify how the OS functions based on the APPMODE; rather, the purpose of APPMODEs is purely to provide another level of information and control for the application. In some OSEK/VDX implementations the user can define certain tasks that are allowed to execute in a given APPMODE. If an undefined task is activated, an error occurs.

When beginning a new application, you should first define the APPMODEs in which the system can operate. Examples of APPMODEs might include a normal operating mode, a fail-safe mode, a manufacturing mode, a diagnostic mode, and so on. These APPMODEs are then used to design the individual application modules and to define their functions. In the example here, the only APPMODE defined to this point is the SINGLE_PLAYER mode.

Three modes will be defined in this example program: a single-user mode (SINGLE_PLAYER), a multiplayer mode (HEAD_TO_HEAD), and a test mode (TEST). The single-user mode is a single user playing a card game against the computer and is the default mode after a reset. The multiplayer mode will be added at a later time when discussing the communication and networking portions of the OSEK/VDX standard. The test mode is based on communication over a serial port and is intended to be used at the end of the manufacturing line to test and diagnose the display and the keypad. This mode is not implemented in this book, but you can implement it as a way of developing your skills. The OSEK/VDX implementation language (OIL) configuration for the APPMODEs is shown in Listing 2.1.

Listing 2.1 OIL description of the APPMODEs.

```
/******************************************************************/
/*              Application Modes                                 */
/******************************************************************/
   APPMODE HEAD_TO_HEAD {
           VALUE = AUTO;
   };
   APPMODE SINGLE_PLAYER {
           VALUE = AUTO;
   };
   APPMODE TEST {
           VALUE = AUTO;
   };
```

The OSEK/VDX specification does not define attributes for the APPMODE object; however, the OSEKWorks implementation has an attribute that allows you to set the value of a particular APPMODE. Because this is a nonportable attribute, it should be set to the default value AUTO. The OSEK/VDX API service that supports APPMODEs is called GetActiveApplicationMode().

```
AppModeType GetActiveApplicationMode(void);
```

An application uses this service to determine the active APPMODE and then uses this information to modify its operation. ChangeMode() is expanded from a previous example to include a check of the requested APPMODE and compare it to the current mode. If the current and requested modes are the same, then the function returns with no error. At this point, multiplayer mode is not allowed because networking is not supported. However, the multiplayer and test modes are valid APPMODEs in the OIL file; consequently, if ChangeMode() is called with a request to enter either of these modes, the request is ignored and an error is returned. The resulting function is shown in Listing 2.2. ShutdownOS() is considered later in the section when I discuss shutting down the OS.

Listing 2.2 `ChangeMode()` **including validity check.**

```
ApplicationErrorType ChangeMode(AppModeType mode)
{
ApplicationErrorType error=ERROR_NONE;    /* Default to No Error */

   if(mode != GetActiveApplicationMode()){
      if((mode == SINGLE_PLAYER)){
         SelectedMode = SINGLE_PLAYER;
         ShutdownOS(E_OK);
      }
      if((mode == HEAD_TO_HEAD)){
         error = ERROR_INVALID_MODE;
      }
      if((mode == TEST)){
         error = ERROR_INVALID_MODE;
      }
      error = ERROR_INVALID_MODE;
   }
   return error;
}
```

2.2 Startup

After the `APPMODE`s are defined, the example program must be modified to use them. The updated `main()` is shown in Listing 2.3.

Listing 2.3 Updated `main()`.

```
static AppModeType SelectedMode = SINGLE_PLAYER;

void main(long argc)
{
   InitReg16(InitHardwareRegs16);
   InitReg32(InitHardwareRegs32);

   InitSystem(INIT_RESET);
   SelectedMode = SINGLE_PLAYER;

   while(1){
      StartOS(SelectedMode);
   }
}
```

First, a static variable, SelectedMode, is created. It is used by main() and ChangeMode() to switch APPMODEs. After reset, this variable is initialized to SINGLE_PLAYER, the default. It is changed by ChangeMode() to indicate the desired mode. Next, the OS startup is modified, which occurs in main(). The OS startup uses the API service StartOS(), which is passed the new variable SelectedMode.

```
void StartOS(AppModeType mode);
```

This is the one and only method defined by the OSEK/VDX standard in which the APPMODE is set. In order to change modes, the application must first shutdown and then restart the OS using a different APPMODE, which is accomplished using ChangeMode() as mentioned in the previous section.

When the application calls StartOS(), the OSEK/VDX OS initializes all of the objects defined statically in the OIL file. Once the objects have been initialized, StartOS() checks to see if the hook routine, StartupHook(), has been defined and calls the function if it exists. StartupHook() is created by the application programmer.

```
void StartupHook(void);
```

During StartupHook(), all system interrupts are disabled and the application has limited access to the OS services. The available services are GetActiveApplicationMode(), ActivateTask(), and ShutdownOS(). ActivateTask() is discussed in more detail in Chapter 4. In the example application, I have added StartupHook() in main(). It performs only one task: It calls InitSystem(), as defined in Chapter 1, but with an argument of INIT_STARTUP. The individual initialization routines then can check the current APPMODE and perform any application-specific initialization required. This hook routine is shown in Listing 2.4.

Listing 2.4 StartupHook().

```
void StartupHook(void)
{
   InitSystem(INIT_STARTUP);
}
```

After the hook routine returns, the OS is fully started and executes the highest priority task that is ready to execute. If no tasks are ready to be executed, the OS-defined idle loop is entered.

2.3 Shutdown

The OS is shutdown using the OS API service ShutdownOS().

```
void ShutdownOS(StatusType);
```

When ShutdownOS() is called, the OS first checks to see if the hook routine ShutdownHook() is defined, and if so, it is invoked and the StatusType passed in the original call is also passed to the hook routine. The routine ShutdownHook() is created by the application programmer.

```
void ShutdownHook(StatusType);
```

During ShutdownHook(), the application might or might not return. If the error is severe enough, the application might try to recover from the error by forcing the system into a reset. The only OS API service that can be evoked from this hook routine is GetActiveApplicationMode(). When ShutdownHook() returns, the OS then closes all objects opened during startup and returns from the previous call to StartOS(). Control is now back in the hands of the application in main().

One ShutdownHook() limitation concerns the existence of a new OSEK/VDX specification called OSEKtime OS. It is also referred to as TT (time-triggered). This new specification, which had not been released at the time of publication of this book, is a forced real-time scheduler extension intended for time-critical applications such as drive-by-wire and brake-by-wire. It is possible that an individual application will have both versions of the OSEK/VDX OS running, in which case, ShutdownHook() must return. The ShutdownHook() used in the example program is shown in Listing 2.5.

Listing 2.5 ShutdownHook().

```
void ShutdownHook(StatusType error)
{
    if(error!=E_OK){
        LastError = error;
    }
    InitSystem(INIT_SHUTDOWN);
}
```

ShutdownHook() performs two functions. For diagnostic purposes, it logs the last error that occurred by setting the static variable LastError to the error sent as the argument, if it is not equal to E_OK. The OS never calls ShutdownOS() with a StatusType of E_OK. The hook routine then performs a function similar to StartupHook(), in which InitSystem() is called with an argument of INIT_SHUTDOWN. The called initialization functions can then take action based on the APPMODE being shut down.

The addition of StartupHook() and ShutdownHook() requires a change to the OS object in the OIL file. The new object definition is shown in Listing 2.6.

Listing 2.6 OS OIL definition.

```
/*****************************************************************/
/*              O/S                                              */
/*****************************************************************/
   OS OSEKWorks_os {
           CC = AUTO;
           STATUS = EXTENDED;
```

```
        SCHEDULE = AUTO;
        SYSTEMSTACKSIZE = 1024;
        StartupHook = TRUE;
        ErrorHook = FALSE;
        ShutdownHook = TRUE;
        PreTaskHook = FALSE;
        PostTaskHook = FALSE;
};
```

2.4 Example Program

2.4.1 Modules

The main module skeleton for the application program is now complete. It consists of four functions: `main()`, `ChangeMode()`, `StartupHook()`, and `ShutdownHook()`. The other modules were not modified in this chapter, and no new modules were added to the program. You can now compile this program, load it into the target environment, and analyze it using a debugger to show that the system is operational. I will add to the skeleton extensively throughout the rest of the book.

2.5 Exercises

1. Add an `APPMODE` called `END_OF_LINE` to the application and check for a change in `ChangeMode()`. Do not do anything at this time if the user requests a change to the new mode.
2. In `StartupHook()`, if the `APPMODE` is `END_OF_LINE`, call `InitSystem()` with a new value of `INIT_EOL`.
3. Set breakpoints at the hook routines and the `background` task. Run the program and verify that the hook routines execute properly.

2.6 Summary

This chapter showed how to complete the skeleton of the main module of the application. The functions defined here can be used as a basis on which to build an entire application. The three functions — `main()`, `StartupHook()`, and `ShutdownHook()` — are typical of functions you would find in an OSEK/VDX application. The other function, `ChangeMode()`, was added so that the application could define a new operating environment. Although this function is not required and is not typical of an OSEK/VDX application, it might be helpful in a real-world application.

Chapter 3

Development Support

Two more characteristics of the OSEK/VDX OS need to be discussed before developing the application. Almost all of the functions in the OSEK/VDX API have a `StatusType` return type, which returns an error code based on the results of the API service. The other characteristic discussed in previous chapters is hook routines. This chapter introduces the features that aid the developer in debugging the application. After this, you will be ready to address the meat of the OS and the application.

3.1 Error Handling

First I discuss the return type of most of the API services. As mentioned previously, almost all of the services have a `StatusType` return type. The exceptions are the functions already discussed: `StartOS()`, `ShutdownOS()`, and `GetActiveApplicationMode()`. The first two functions have a `void` return type, and `GetActiveApplicationMode()` returns the active `APPMODE`.

The possible return values for each API service are different and depend on the error reporting status mode chosen during configuration. Two status levels are available: `STANDARD` and `EXTENDED`. The error codes returned from each API service are discussed as the service is introduced throughout the book.

Extended status mode is used during system development. Each API service performs error checks to ensure that the service does not cause system problems. Typical tests include checking that the object on which the service is to operate is a valid object, verifying that the service was called from a legal location, and checking that the value passed in the service is within a valid range. If no error occurs, all services return the `E_OK` value.

When debugging is complete, the system has been tested, and the application is ready for release, standard reporting status is enabled in the OIL configuration file. In standard status mode, most API services only return `E_OK`.

The OSEK/VDX standard defines two types of errors: application errors and fatal errors. An application error occurs when an API service is unable to complete the service because the data or the OS state is invalid. The API service returns the error to the calling function and the service is not performed. Any values referenced by parameters that were passed as arguments to the service are undefined on return. A fatal error occurs when the API identifies that its internal data might be corrupted. In this case, the OS does not return to the calling function; rather, it shuts itself down and returns to the function that called `StartOS()`.

As with system startup and shutdown, the application can define a hook routine that is invoked after an application error is detected.

```
void ErrorHook(StatusType);
```

`ErrorHook()` is called at the end of an API service routine, and immediately before returning to the calling function, if the return is other than `E_OK`. It is also called if an error occurs when an alarm expires or a message is transmitted or received, although OSEK COM might call a different `ErrorHook()`, especially when mixing OS and COM modules from different vendors. `ErrorHook()` is never called recursively.

For the application here, I have defined an `ErrorHook()` that keeps a running buffer of the last 10 errors identified by the system. The complete routine is shown in Listing 3.1 and has been added to a debug module found in `debug.c`.

Listing 3.1 `ErrorHook()`.

```
void ErrorHook(StatusType error)
{
    nextErrorLog->error = error;
    ++nextErrorLog;
    if(nextErrorLog > errorLog + sizeof(errorLog)){
        nextErrorLog = errorLog;
    }
}
```

The debug module is only included in the application during development. At this point, I store just the error value. In the future I will store additional information that is available from the system to assist in debugging the application. To allow for this future expansion, I have defined a structure that contains just one member of type `StatusType`. Additional members are added throughout the book.

3.2 Debugging Hook Routines

The OSEK/VDX OS standard defines two additional hook routines that are intended to be used by the application developer to support debugging.

```
void PreTaskHook(void);
```

```
void PostTaskHook(void);
```

`PreTaskHook()` is called by the OS after it has switched tasks but before passing control of the microcontroller to the new task. This allows the hook routine to query the OS and determine which task is about to run. `PostTaskHook()` is called after the OS determines that a switch is to occur, but before the switch actually occurs. Again this allows the hook routine to query the OS to determine which task has just completed or has been preempted.

Because these two hook routines are tied closely to tasks, I will forego development of the actual hook routines until I have covered tasks completely; however, I include the do-nothing tasks in the debug module along with `ErrorHook()`.

The addition of these three hook routines requires that you update the OS object in the OIL file. The complete object definition is shown in Listing 3.2.

Listing 3.2 OS OIL definition.

```
/**************************************************************/
/*              O/S                                           */
/**************************************************************/

   OS OSEKWorks_os {
           CC = AUTO;
           STATUS = EXTENDED;
           SCHEDULE = AUTO;
           SYSTEMSTACKSIZE = 1024;
           StartupHook = TRUE;
           ErrorHook = TRUE;
           ShutdownHook = TRUE;
           PreTaskHook = TRUE;
           PostTaskHook = TRUE;
   };
```

3.3 Example Program

3.3.1 Modules

In this chapter, I only added one module to the example application — `debug.c`. All other modules are identical to the versions used in the Chapter 2.

debug.c This module contains all routines used by the application to assist in system run-time debugging. At this point, the module only has the three hook routines described in detail in this chapter. Additional debugging functions are added to this module in the exercises presented throughout the book.

3.4 Exercise

1. Set a breakpoint at the entrance to each of the hook routines, including `StartupHook()`. Run the program and observe the sequence of events as the program starts and executes, then terminates, the `background` task.

3.5 Summary

This chapter introduced briefly how an OSEK/VDX OS processes errors and provides debugging capability. In Chapter 4, I will define the basic application building block — the task.

Chapter 4

Tasks

The first and most importing concept in the OSEK/VDX OS is the task. As you might remember from the previous chapters, even the simplest application required defining a small task. The task in the example program, a game of blackjack, was called `background`. It did absolutely nothing except terminate itself on startup; however, without it, the OS could not be built.

This chapter describes tasks as they relate to the OSEK/VDX OS. First I'll discuss the overall task model and the attributes of an individual task. Next, I will discuss each of the interfaces of the OSEK/VDX API that relate to tasks. Finally, I will discuss the scheduling policies of the OSEK/VDX OS.

4.1 Task Model

Tasks within the OSEK/VDX OS have a number of attributes that affect both the operation of the system and the size of the code. A task is either basic or extended, has a statically defined priority, might or might not be preemptive, and might be able to suspend execution while waiting for an event. The combination of these and other attributes creates a conformance class, as defined in the OSEK/VDX specification. Each of these attributes and the definition of conformance classes are discussed in this section.

4.1.1 Basic Tasks

A basic task runs to completion unless preempted by a higher priority task or an interrupt (if enabled). The task, through other API services, can disable preemption and interrupts. Lower priority tasks are inhibited while a basic task of higher priority runs; however, other tasks of the same priority are also inhibited. The OSEK/VDX OS does not allow round-robin scheduling of tasks at the same priority level, as is found in some larger systems. To allow time-sliced scheduling would make the system's performance impossible to predict, which is undesirable in a real-time safety-critical environment.

Basic tasks can exist in one of three states: SUSPENDED, READY, and RUNNING. Transitions between states occur based on four possible events: activate, start, preempt, and terminate. The state transition diagram for a basic task is shown in Figure 4.1.

Figure 4.1 Basic task state transition diagram.

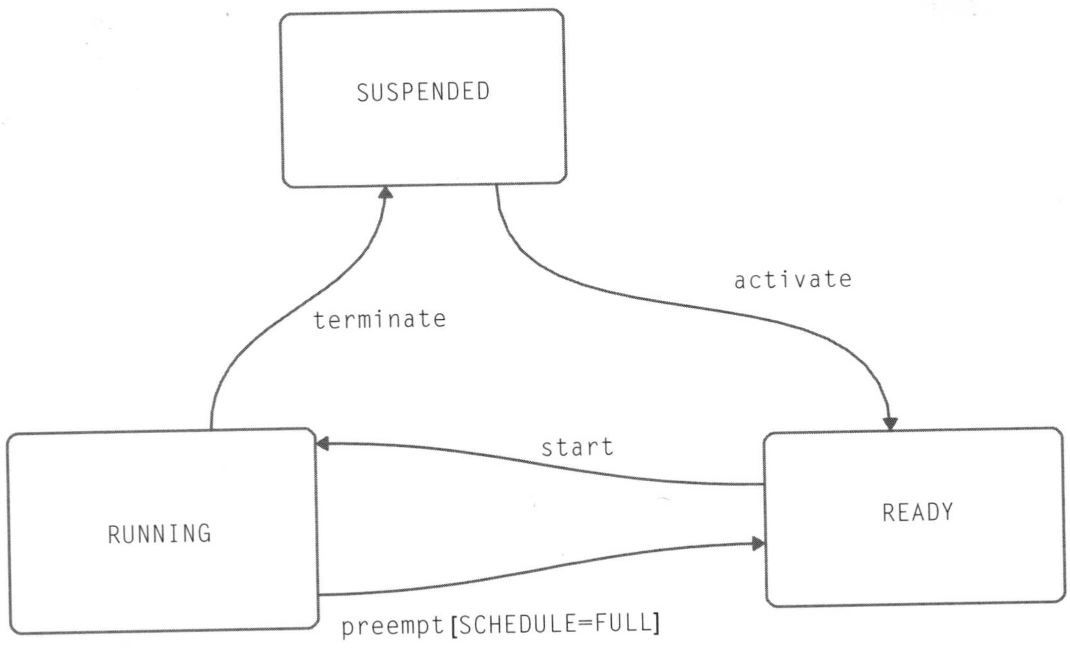

Because OSEK/VDX is a statically defined OS, all tasks must be defined at compile time. When the OS is started by StartOS(), a basic task is started either in the SUSPENDED or READY state, depending on the configuration in the OIL file. If a task is defined as an AUTOSTART task, then it starts in the READY state; otherwise, it starts in the SUSPENDED state. The task then flows through the transitions shown in Figure 4.1 based on the events that occur. More details on task transitions are discussed in the section "Scheduling."

The advantage of a basic task is using the minimal amount of resources required to support it. Because a basic task inhibits not only the lower priority tasks but also other tasks at the same priority, the amount of stack space required is minimized. Basic tasks usually are used in instances where interprocess synchronization is not required.

For the example program, I created a basic task, `IOSampleKeypad`, which samples the keypad, debounces the input, then activates another task whenever a key is pressed. The task is shown in Listing 4.1 and can be found in the module `input.c`.

Listing 4.1 `IOSampleKeypad` basic task.

```
TASK(IOSampleKeypad)
{
UINT32 delayTimer;
BOOLEAN keyState = FALSE;
char tempKey;

  while(1){
    tempKey = HWGetValue(&KEYPAD);
    if(tempKey == lastKey){
      if(keyCount++ == KEY_DEBOUNCE_TIME){
        --keyCount;
        keyValue = tempKey;
      }
    }
    else{
      keyCount = 0;
      lastKey = tempKey;
    }
    if(keyState==FALSE){
      if(keyValue != 0){
        keyState = TRUE;
        ActivateTask(ProcessKeyPress);
      }
    }
    else{
      if(keyValue == 0){
        keyState = FALSE;
      }
    }
    for(delayTimer = 1000;delayTimer>0;delayTimer--){
      Schedule();
    }
  }
}
```

The API services `ActivateTask()` and `Schedule()` found in this task are described later in this chapter. The `HWGetValue()` task encapsulates the hardware interface to the keypad and returns the ASCII code of the key that was pressed. This function is not discussed in this book, but you should be able to understand the source code on the CD.

The task is defined in the source module with `TASK(IOSampleKeypad)`. All OSEK/VDX implementations are required to use this macro to encapsulate the implementation-specific formatting of the task definition. The C name of the function that corresponds to the task usually is created by either prepending or appending the task name with an implementation-specific tag. The function can then be viewed with the debugger using this mangled name. See the implementation documentation for what this tag is and how the task name is mangled for the OS.

This basic task uses a `while(1)` loop, which creates some limitations. The first is that this task must be the lowest priority in the system, and no other tasks with the same priority can exist. The second is that a keypad press could be missed if the higher priority tasks consume too much processor throughput. At this point, the system is still simple, and these limitations are not a concern. As you learn about more features of the OSEK/VDX OS, you can modify this task extensively to streamline the operation. When complete, it will resemble a typical keypad processing routine with a buffer of key presses. The other API services listed in this task are defined throughout this chapter.

4.1.2 Extended Tasks

Extended tasks are similar to basic tasks except they have one additional state in their state transition diagram, `WAITING`, and two additional events, `wait` and `trigger`. Figure 4.2 shows the state transition diagram for extended tasks.

In the `WAITING` state, the extended task waits for an event to occur and continues from the point where it entered the state. (The concept of events will be discussed in greater detail in Chapter 6.) While in the `WAITING` state, the task still consumes resources such as stack space. Because extended tasks can operate out of sequence, they cannot use single stacks, as basic tasks do. Consequently, the resources required are greater.

The definition of whether a task is basic or extended is made indirectly in the OIL configuration file. Within the TASK object definition structure is the optional attribute `EVENT`, which if exists, defines an extended task. Otherwise, it is a basic task. Some implementations might have an optional attribute that is set to the type of the task, but this is not required by the OSEK/VDX specification.

Because extended tasks are intricately linked with events, I will forego creating an extended task until Chapter 6. The other API interfaces work identically with both basic and extended tasks.

4.1.3 Priority

As with any RTOS, tasks in an OSEK/VDX OS have a priority, which is statically defined and cannot be changed dynamically by the application. In one case, however, the OS does change the priority of a task: When the priority ceiling protocol is active, the priority of a task is elevated to the priority ceiling value calculated statically. This protocol is discussed in Chapter 7, "Resources."

Figure 4.2 Extended task state transition diagram.

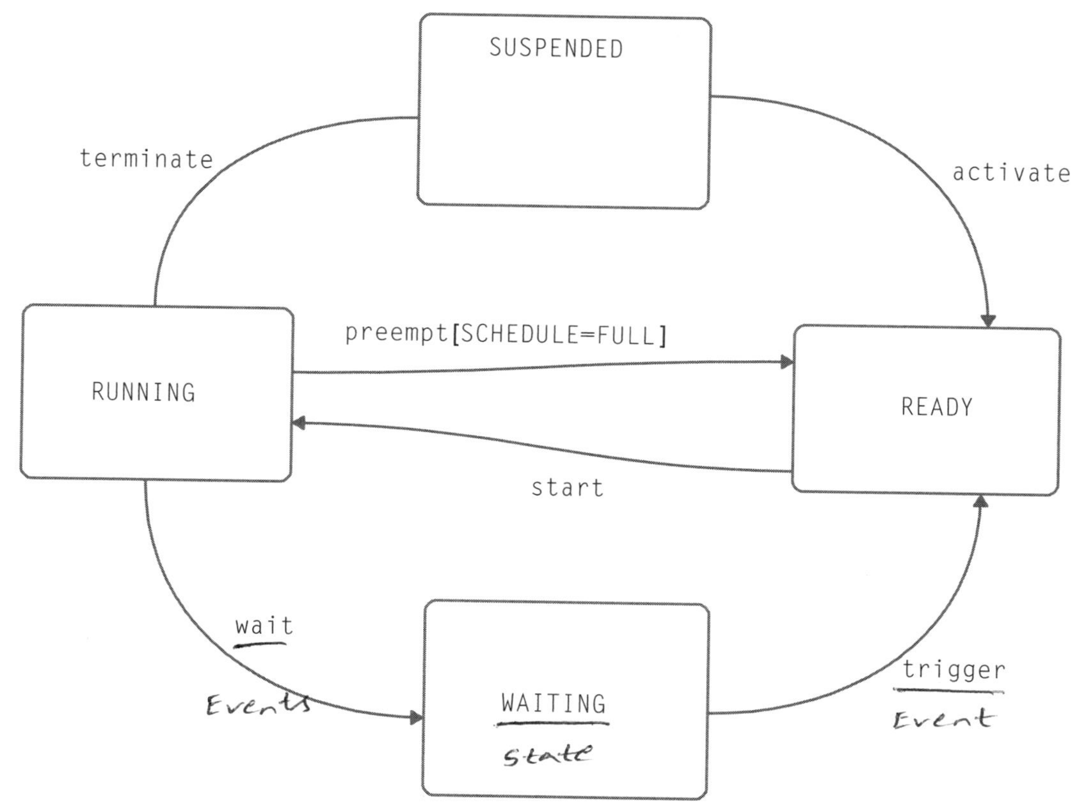

In OSEK/VDX, `0` is the lowest priority, and no maximum is defined in the specification. Each implementation is allowed to define a maximum number of priorities. The specification defines the minimum required number of priorities — eight; therefore, any implementation that uses more risks creating nonportable code. The number of tasks at a given priority can be limited to one. If this is done by the application, and multiple activation (discussed later) is limited to one for every task, the OSEK/VDX OS can minimize the size of the kernel. This is very similar to Jean Labrosse's µC/OS, in which all tasks have a unique priority. This assumption allows the OSEK/VDX OS to perform very efficient task management with minimal resources — in particular, every task can share the same stack.

The `IOSampleKeypad` task, which polls the keypad awaiting a key press, must be defined as a low-priority task. I set the priority to `0` in the OIL configuration file to assure that it is a true background task. In addition, all tasks have unique priorities. The complete OIL file is shown after conformance classes are discussed in Section 4.1.6.

4.1.4 Multiple Activation

Within OSEK/VDX, basic tasks have a unique attribute that the application implements optionally through the OIL file: multiple activation capability. Whenever a task is activated, it is added to a queue for all tasks at its given priority. Consequently, multiple activation allows for a task to terminate then immediately execute again. The drawback of multiple activation is that you must have a queue for all priority levels with multiple tasks defined, thereby increasing the system resources required. In practice, an implementation might choose to use virtual queues rather than physical lists in memory, balancing scheduler performance with memory usage.

In the `IOSampleKeypad` task, only one activation is allowed. Because the `while(1)` loop eliminates the possibility of ever leaving the task, there is no need to have a queue for this priority level, and multiple activations will never be executed.

4.1.5 Preemption

Every task, whether basic or extended, can be defined as having either no preemption or full preemption. A task with no preemption essentially runs until it terminates or, in the case of extended tasks, until it makes the transition into the `WAITING` state. Even with no preemption capability, a task can still perform cooperative multitasking using the API service `Schedule()`.

```
StatusType Schedule(void);
```

`Schedule()` checks for the task with the highest priority that is in the `READY` state and transfers processor control to it. The system only returns to the original task when all higher priority tasks are complete; then the original task again becomes the highest priority task. This service does not allow cooperative multitasking among tasks with the same priority because only higher priority tasks are allowed to execute. The calling task is immediately resumed if no higher priority tasks are ready. This service is not allowed at interrupt level.

In standard API return type mode, `E_OK` is always returned. Under extended status, `Schedule()` can also return `E_OS_CALLEVEL` if called from interrupt level.

The `IOSampleKeypad` task is defined as non-preemptive at this time to better demonstrate the operation of `Schedule()` and `ActivateTask()` when a key is pressed. To allow cooperative multitasking, `Schedule()` is called continuously within a delay loop. This programming device will not be required when the task is defined as preemptive, so the loop is removed in later chapters.

4.1.6 Conformance Classes

The various combinations of the task attributes defined in this section has created a new concept unique to OSEK/VDX: conformance classes. A conformance class is defined as a specific realization of the OS requirements that contain a defined set of attributes for the application. The attributes that define the four available conformance classes — BCC1 (basic conformance class 1), BCC2 (basic conformance class 2), ECC1 (extended conformance class 1), and ECC2 (extended conformance class 2) are shown in Table 4.1.

Table 4.1 Conformance class determination.

Attribute	BCC1	BCC2	ECC1	ECC2
Number of basic task activations	1	≥1	1	≥1
Number of tasks per priority	1	≥1	1	≥1
Basic tasks	Yes	Yes	Yes	Yes
Extended tasks	No	No	Yes	Yes

Tasks are upwardly compatible as follows: Any task developed for a BCCx-level conformance class can be used in an ECCx-level conformance class, and any task written for an xCC1-level conformance class can be used in an xCC2-level conformance class.

For an OSEK/VDX OS implementation to be compliant to the OSEK/VDX standard, it must support at least one conformance class completely. It does not have to support all conformance classes to be compliant.

In the example program, `IOSampleKeypad`, `ProcessKeyPress` (the second task activated when a key is pressed), and `OutputDisplay` (the third task activated) are all basic tasks with different priorities that allow just one activation each. As a result, the system operates in a BCC1 conformance class when compiled. The portion of the OIL configuration file in which these tasks are defined is shown in Listing 4.2.

Listing 4.2 Task object definition.

```
/**************************************************************************/
/*              Tasks                                                     */
/**************************************************************************/

  TASK IOSampleKeypad {
          TYPE = BASIC;
          SCHEDULE = NON;
          PRIORITY = 0;
          ACTIVATION = 1;
          AUTOSTART = TRUE;
          STACKSIZE = 64;
          SCHEDULE_CALL = TRUE;
  };

  TASK OutputDisplay {
          TYPE = BASIC;
          SCHEDULE = FULL;
          PRIORITY = 3;
          ACTIVATION = 1;
          AUTOSTART = FALSE;
```

```
        STACKSIZE = 64;
        SCHEDULE_CALL = FALSE;
};

TASK ProcessKeyPress {
        TYPE = BASIC;
        SCHEDULE = FULL;
        PRIORITY = 2;
        ACTIVATION = 1;
        AUTOSTART = FALSE;
        STACKSIZE = 64;
        SCHEDULE_CALL = FALSE;
};
```

The attributes available for each task and defined in the OSEK/VDX standard follow.

- `PRIORITY` The priority of the task from `0` to the maximum allowed by the implementation (eight priorities must be supported; using more can lead to portability problems).

- `SCHEDULE` Either `NON` or `FULL`. `SCHEDULE` defines the type of preemption allowed for this task.

- `ACTIVATION` A number from `1` to the maximum activations allowed by the implementation. For extended tasks, this number must be `1`.

- `AUTOSTART` Set to either `TRUE` or `FALSE`. `AUTOSTART` defines whether the task is moved into the `READY` state automatically by the `StartOS()` API service.

- `RESOURCE` Defines a reference to a resource that is used by this task. This is an optional attribute that can have multiple instances. I discuss resources in more detail in Chapter 7.

- `EVENT` Defines a reference to an event that is controlled by this task. This is an optional attribute that can have multiple instances. I discuss events in more detail in Chapter 6.

- `ACCESSOR` Defines an optional accessor for a message used within a task. Multiple accessors can be defined for each task. The value of this attribute is either `SENT` or `RECEIVED` and includes its own references. The subattributes are `MESSAGE`, `WITHOUTCOPY`, and `ACCESSNAME`. These subattributes are discussed in more detail in Chapter 9.

These are the minimum attributes required to be supported by an implementation in order to define a task. In addition, OSEK/VDX implementation vendors can add their own attributes when defining a task. To ensure portability, I recommended that you avoid using their extensions if possible. In the case of the Wind River OSEKWorks implementation, you will see the following added attributes.

- TYPE The type of task, either BASIC or EXTENDED.

- STACKSIZE The size of the stack required by that particular task. STACKSIZE is not defined in the OSEK/VDX OIL specification; however, it is discussed in the sample implementation. Because it is not required by the specification, do not expect to see it in all implementations.

- SCHEDULE_CALL Defines whether the API service Schedule() can be invoked from a task. If set to TRUE, a non-preemptive task can use Schedule() for cooperative multitasking, as defined ealier in this chapter.

4.2 Task Activation and Termination

The OSEK/VDX OS provides multiple services through which tasks can be activated, terminated, and queried. The first API service, ActivateTask(), was demonstrated in the prior example IOSampleKeypad. The prototype for ActivateTask() follows.

```
StatusType ActivateTask(TaskType task);
```

The argument passed to this service is the name of the task to be activated as it appears in the OIL configuration file. The OSEK/VDX OS kernel performs the following functions when it is invoked.

1. If the system is operating in extended status mode, the service first checks to make sure that the task being activated is a valid task. If the task is invalid, the service returns the error E_OS_ID.
2. If the task is currently in the SUSPENDED state, the service moves the task into the READY state. At this point, the scheduler is invoked if the OS is in a preemptive mode. Invocation of the scheduler is discussed in greater detail in "Scheduling" later in this chapter.
3. If the conformance class is level 2 (BCC2 or ECC2) and the task is capable of multiple activations, the service ensures that the maximum number of activations have not been exceeded and the task is not in the SUSPENDED state before a request is queued by the OS for later processing. If the maximum has been exceeded and the system is operating in extended status mode, the E_OS_LIMIT error is returned and the activation is ignored.
4. If the task is an extended task, all of its events are cleared.
5. If the system is operating in standard status mode or the service is successful in extended status mode, E_OK is returned.

This API service routine can be called from a task, an interrupt service routine, or StartupHook(). In IOSampleKeypad, shown in Listing 4.1, ActivateTask() is invoked whenever a key is pressed on the keypad, starting the task that processed the key press. The task activated, ProcessKeyPress (Listing 4.3), is in the module cardgame.c.

Listing 4.3 Key press processing task.

```
TASK(ProcessKeyPress)
{
   switch(keyValue){
      case '#':
         if(blankState == TRUE){
            strcpy(displayBuffer,"\f");
            blankState == FALSE;
         }
         else{
            blankState = TRUE;
            strcpy(displayBuffer,"#");
         }
         break;
      default:
         blankState = FALSE;
         displayBuffer[0] = keyValue;
         displayBuffer[1] = 0;
   }
   ChainTask(OutputDisplay);
}
```

This task performs the following functions.

1. Determines whether the display needs to be blanked, and blanks it if necessary.
2. Adds the key character to the global buffer.
3. Stores the desired character to the display by activating the next task.

The first two functions use normal C library functions. The third function uses another OSEK/VDX API service, `ChainTask()`.

```
StatusType ChainTask(TaskType task);
```

This API service performs a function similar to the combination of `ActivateTask()` and `TerminateTask()` (discussed later). When this service completes, the scheduler is run and the next highest priority task is moved to the `RUNNING` state. This might or might not be the task that was requested in this service. If `ChainTask()` is invoked in standard status mode, it never returns to the calling task. If it is invoked in extended status mode, the following occurs.

1. If the task name sent as the argument is invalid, the service returns the `E_OS_ID` error.
2. If too many activations of the task have been requested, the `E_OS_LIMIT` error is returned.
3. If the calling task still occupies OSEK/VDX resources, the `E_OS_RESOURCE` error is returned.

networks for success
SMITH CAREER CENTER

Calendar of Events

Visit the Smith Career Center web site and click on "calendar" for additional information and events scheduled for Fall 2005.

All workshop locations are in the Smith Career Center (Burgess Hall, first floor) unless noted

September

Monday	Tuesday	Wednesday	Thursday	Friday
Looking ahead to October and November . . . Additional workshops for Slane College of Communications and Fines Arts and the College of Education and Health Sciences **Academic Majors Fair** October 13 – 3:00-5:00pm [Michel Student Center Ballroom] **Nursing and Physical Therapy Fair** November 8 – Noon-3:00pm [Michel Student Center, Ballroom] **Multicultural Career Networking Reception** November 9 – 5-7pm [Michel Student Center, Ballroom]			**1**	**2**
5 **Labor Day**	**6**	**7** 4-5pm **Career Compass for Seniors** (BCS, CS, CIS) 5:30-6:30 **Career Compass for Seniors** (EGT) 7-8pm **Career Compass for Senior Student Athletes**	**8**	**9** Noon-1pm **Roadmap to Internship/Co-op Job Search** (BCS, CS, CIS)
12 3-4pm **Dynamic Resumes and Cover Letters** [Student Center, Executive Suite] 4-5pm **Career Compass for Seniors** (EGT)	**13** 2-3pm **Career Compass for Seniors** (*Any Major*) 5-6pm **Roadmap to Internship/Co-op Job Search** (EGT)	**14** Noon-1pm **Roadmap to Internship/Co-op Job Search** (EGT) 4-5:30pm **Interviewing Tips** [Student Center, Marty Theatre]	**15** 3-4pm **Dynamic Resumes and Cover Letters** [Baker, 458]	**16** Noon–4pm **Resume Critique Day** [Student Center, Ballroom] 3-4pm **Job Fair Tips** [Marty Theatre]

networks for success

SMITH CAREER CENTER

Fall Job Fair 2005

September 22, 2005 * 11:00 am - 4:00 pm * Michel Student Center & Baker Quad

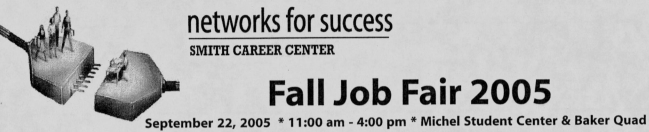

Job Fair Sponsors

AAA Chicago - Gold Star Sponsor

Accenture
Advantage Freight Network
CareerBuilder.com
Caterpillar Inc.
Centex Homes
Cintas Corporation
DICKEY-john Corporation
Enclos Corporation
Enterprise Rent-A-Car
Harris Corporation
Heartland Home Finance
Heinold–Banwart, Ltd.
Liberty Mutual Insurance Co
Linde Gas LLC
OSF HealthPlans
PepsiCo-QTG
Pulte Homes Corporation
SMC Corporation
Verizon Wireless
Virchow, Krause & Co., LLP
Wal-Mart Stores Inc.

Fall Job Fair Participants*

As of September 2, 2005

AAA Chicago**
Accenture
Adams Outdoor Advertising
Advanced Technology Services
Advantage Freight Network**
Aerotek
Aldridge Electric, Inc.
Allstate Insurance Company
Ameren UE/CIPS
American Buildings Company
American Express Financial Advisors Inc
ARAMARK Refreshment Services
Archer Daniels Midland Company
Auto Owners Insurance
Axis, Inc.
Enclos Corporation**
Engineering Enterprises
Enterprise Rent-A-Car
Epic Systems Corporation
F. H. Paschen, S.N. Nielsen, Inc.
F.E. Wheaton & Co., Inc.
Ferguson Enterprises Inc.
Gallagher Benefit Services, Inc.**
George Adamczyk & Company
Gilbane Building Company
Grand Prairie Services
Hallmark Metamora Fixture Operations
Hamilton Sundstrand
Hanson Professional Services, Inc.
Harmon, Inc.
Harris Corporation**
PepsiCo-QTG
Permasteellisa Cladding Technologies
Pizzagalli Construction Company**
Porte Brown LLC**
PricewaterhouseCoopers LLP
PSA Dewberry
Pulte Homes Corporation**
Random House, Inc.
River City Construction LLC
RLI Corporation
Sandvik Coromant**
Sargent and Lundy LLC
Scotts Company (The)
SMC Corporation of America**
State Farm Insurance Companies - Corporate
Stephen Ministries

Becker Professional Review
Black & Veatch
Bovis Lend Lease, Inc.
BroMenn Healthcare
Buckle (The)
Butler Manufacturing Company Inc.
C.H. Robinson Worldwide
CareerBuilder.com
Carus Chemical Company
Caterpillar Inc.
CBT Companies Inc.
Ceco Concrete Construction, L.L.C.**
Centex Homes
Central States Funds
CGN & Associates, Inc.
Chicago Office Technology Group
Cintas Corporation**
Clifton Gunderson L.L.P.
CNH (Case New Holland)**
Compass Group
Congressman LaHood's Office
COUNTRY Insurance & Financial Services
Cowhey Gudmundson Leder, Ltd.
DAXCON Engineering, Inc.
Decatur Police Department
Dept. of Housing & Urban Development
DICKEY-john Corporation**
Dietrich Metal Framing
Edward Jones
Eli Lilly and Company

Heatcraft Refrigeration Products LLC
Heinold-Banwart, Ltd.
Illinois Agricultural Auditing Association
Illinois Constructors Corporation Inc.
Illinois Department of Human Services
Illinois Department of Revenue
Illinois Department of Transportation
Illinois State Police Morton Forensics Lab
Impact Networking LLC
Infogenic Systems
Jackson Hewitt and Sharp Income Tax Service
Korte Company
Kroger Food Stores
L.R. Nelson Corporation
LaSalle Bank
LaSalle County Broadcasting Corp.
Liberty Mutual Insurance Co**
Linde Gas LLC**
Manhard Consulting, Ltd.
MassMutual Financial Group**
Maurer-Stutz, Inc.
MetLife
MultiAd
National City Corporation
Nestle PURINA PetCare Company**
Northrop Grumman Corporation
Northwestern Mutual Financial Network**
OSF HealthPlans
Panduit Corporation
Pekin Insurance

SWF Companies
Target Stores**
TDS Metrocom**
TechniLight
Thrivent Financial for Lutherans
Timken Company
Turner Construction Company**
U.S. Air Force
U.S. Marine Corps Officer Selection Team
U.S. Navy
U.S. Dept. of Labor—Office of Inspector General
U.S. Patent and Trademark Office**
United Parcel Service (UPS)
United States Steel Corporation
University of Illinois - Graduate Intern Programs
Vansco Electronics
Verizon Wireless
Virchow, Krause & Co., LLP
Volt Services Group
Von Maur
W.D. Boyce Council, Boy Scouts of America
Wal-Mart Stores Inc.**
Walgreens
Washington Center (The)
WEEK-TV
Wells Fargo Financial Illinois, Inc.
Zurich American Insurance Company

*For an up-to-date list of employers, as well as links to their Web sites, go to http://explore.bradley.edu/scc.

**Employers building interviewing schedules at Job Fair on September 22 (sign up at their booth).

Employers in **bold** are Job Fair Sponsors.

Sponsored by the Smith Career Center ~ 309-677-2510

19 5-6pm **Career Compass for Seniors** (FCBA) [Baker, B53] 5-6pm **Career Compass for Seniors** (LAS) 6:30-7:30pm **Roadmap to Internship/Co-op Job Search** (LAS)	**20** 5-6pm **Roadmap to Internship/Co-op Job Search** (LAS) 6:30-7:30pm **Career Compass for Seniors** (LAS)	**21** **Career Seminars** 5-6pm **Engineering Careers** [Marty Theatre] 5-6pm **Careers for *All* Majors** [Student Ctr., Executive Suite] 6-7pm **Sales Careers** [Student Center, Marty Theatre] 6-7pm **Design & Photography Careers** [Student Ctr., Executive Suite]	**22** 11am-4pm **Fall Job Fair** [Michel Student Center] (visit the SCC web site for an up-to-date list of participating organizations)	**23** **After Job Fair Interviews** [times and locations scheduled during the Fall Job Fair]
26 6–7pm **Applying to Graduate School** (*Any Major*)	**27** 1pm-4pm **Graduate and Professional School Fair** [Michel Student Center, Ballroom] (visit the SCC web site for an up-to-date list of participating programs)	**28**	**29**	**30**

Career Seminars (times and locations above)

Engineering Careers
- Caterpillar Inc.
- Northrop Grumman Corporation
- Pizzagalli Construction Co.
- U S Patent & Trademark Office

Careers for *ALL* Majors
- Auto Owners Insurance
- Centex
- Enterprise Rent-A-Car
- Target Stores

Sales Careers
Purpose/Audience
- AAA Chicago
- Ferguson Enterprises
- National City Corporation
- PepsiCo-QTG

Design & Photography Careers
Purpose/Audience
- InVision Studios
- Vote Photography

College/Major abbreviations:

CFA - Slane College of Communications and Fine Arts
EHS – College of Education and Health Sciences
EGT – College of Engineering and Technology
FCBA - Foster College of Business Administration

LAS – College of Liberal Arts and Sciences
CS – Computer Science
CIS – Computer Information Systems
BCS – Business Computer Systems

K:\Student Team\Calendar\2005-2006\sep_05_calendar [legal size].doc
Last printed 9/1/2005 3:51 PM

This service can only be invoked from a task and cannot be invoked from a hook routine or an interrupt service routine.

In the example routine, ProcessKeyPress adds the value identified as output to the display into a queue and chains OutputDisplay, which sends the characters in the queue to the display. OutputDisplay is shown in Listing 4.4 and is included in dispdrv.c.

Listing 4.4 OutputDisplay task.

```
TASK(OutputDisplay)
{
    PackDisplay(displayBuffer);
    OutputNewDisplay();
    TerminateTask();
}
```

OutputDisplay is very specific to the hardware used in this example. In this case, I have an 80-character display arranged as four rows of 20 characters, using a Hitachi HD44780 LCD controller. This task calls two specific functions: PackDisplay() and OutputNewDisplay(). PackDisplay() packs the message into the display buffer, blanks and scrolls the display, and moves the cursor. OutputNewDisplay() sends the entire buffer to the display. These functions are also in dispdrv.c, but they are not discussed here because they are specific to the controller used.

When invoked, OutputDisplay flushes the queue filled by the previous task to the display and invokes the API service TerminateTask(), which terminates the task and executes the scheduler to determine which task to run next.

```
StatusType TerminateTask(void);
```

When invoked, TerminateTask() performs the following steps.

1. If the system is operating in extended status mode, it checks to see whether an OSEK/VDX resource is still occupied by the task (resources are discussed in a later chapter). If a resource is still occupied, the service returns the E_OS_RESOURCE error. If the system is operating in standard status mode and a resource is still occupied, the behavior is undefined.
2. The service terminates the calling task, frees the microcontroller resources occupied by the task, then invokes the scheduler to select the next task to run.
3. If the termination was successful, this service never returns to the calling task.

TerminateTask() is only available from within a task and cannot be invoked either in a hook routine or during an interrupt service routine.

IMPORTANT: All tasks MUST end in either ChainTask() or TerminateTask(). If a task terminates using a normal C return, the behavior of the system is undefined and will more than likely cause the entire system to reset.

4.3 Other Task Services

The API services discussed up to this point are the common services that relate to tasks. Two additional services and a declaration function that are used in other areas of an application are also associated with tasks. The prototypes and a discussion of how these elements are used are discussed briefly. Some of these elements appear later in the book.

`DeclareTask(TaskIdentifier)` This declaration function is used by the application to declare a task that is defined externally to the current application module. `TaskIdentifier` is the identifier as it appears in the OIL configuration file. This declaration is used in the C source code on the accompanying CD.

`StatusType GetTaskID(TaskRefType task);` `GetTaskID()` determines which task is presently in the `RUNNING` state. This service can be invoked from the task level or the ISR level and from `ErrorHook()`, `PreTaskHook()`, and `PostTaskHook()`. It is typically used by library functions and hook routines to determine the `TaskID` of the task that invoked the library function or called the hook routine. The argument passed to `GetTaskID()` is a reference to a variable of type `TaskType`, in which the `TaskID` of the currently running task is placed. If no task is running, the value is set to `INVALID_TASK`. In the example program, I updated `ErrorHook()` (Listing 4.5) to store the `TaskID` of the currently running task, in addition to the error that occurred. If `GetTaskID()` is called from `PreTaskHook()`, it sets the variable pointed to by the argument to the `TaskID` of the task that is about to run. From `PostTaskHook()`, the variable is set to the `TaskID` of the task that is being moved out of the `RUNNING` state. This service always returns a status of `E_OK`.

Listing 4.5 Modified `ErrorHook()`.

```
void ErrorHook(StatusType error)
{
   nextErrorLog->error = error;
   GetTaskID(&nextErrorLog->task);
   ++nextErrorLog;
   if(nextErrorLog > errorLog + sizeof(errorLog)){
      nextErrorLog = errorLog;
   }
}
```

`StatusType GetTaskState(TaskType task, TaskStateRefType state);` This API service is intended to determine the state of a given task at the time that the service is invoked. In a fully preemptive system, this service should be called only when the interrupts are disabled. Otherwise, the result might be invalid when it is analyzed. When this service is invoked, the task identified by the first argument is analyzed and the state of the task is placed in the variable of type `TaskStateType` referred to in the second argument. The value placed in this variable will be `RUNNING`, `WAITING`, `READY`, or `SUSPENDED`. In standard status mode, this service always returns `E_OK`. In extended status mode, the service checks the value sent as the `TaskType` and returns the `E_OS_ID` error if it is invalid. This service can be invoked from the task level; the interrupt service routines; and `ErrorHook()`, `PreTaskHook()`, and `PostTaskHook()`.

4.4 Scheduling

Task switching within an OSEK/VDX OS is performed by a scheduler using on sible policies: non-preemptive, fully preemptive, or mixed preemptive. Each one cies are discussed in detail in this section.

As mentioned earlier in this chapter, the scheduler uses task priorities to dete which singular task is in the RUNNING state. Each task is defined with a static priority that cannot be changed by the user at run time. The lowest available priority is 0, and the highest available priority is specific to the implementation.

In the case of conformance classes ECC2 and BCC2, multiple tasks can have the same priority, and individual basic tasks can have multiple activations. To accomplish this, the scheduler uses a first in, first out (FIFO) queue for each priority that has multiple tasks, multiple activations, or both. Tasks at the same priority level are started based on the order in which they are moved to the READY state. The first task in each queue must either complete or move into a WAITING state before the next task can run. If a task is preempted, it remains as the first task in the queue.

4.4.1 Non-preemptive Scheduling

The non-preemptive scheduling policy of the OSEK/VDX OS is invoked in an application in which none of the tasks are configured as preemptive in the OIL configuration file. If a task is not preemptive, it could inhibit a higher priority task from transferring from the READY to the RUNNING state. This was demonstrated in the first example task in this chapter, IOSampleKeypad. When the next task is activated, it is moved by the scheduler into the READY state but is not allowed to run because the calling task is not preemptive. This is illustrated graphically in Figure 4.3, which shows the states of each of the example tasks over time after a key is pressed.

IOSampleKeypad inhibits the transition of ProcessKeyPress to the RUNNING state until the API service Schedule() is invoked by the lower priority task. When a non-preemptive task is in the RUNNING state, the scheduler is only executed when one of four events occurs.

- The task is successfully terminated by TerminateTask().
- The task is successfully terminated, and another task is activated by ChainTask().
- The API service Schedule() is invoked by the task.
- An extended task is moved to the WAITING state.

4.4.2 Fully Preemptive

The fully preemptive scheduling policy is invoked in an application where all of the tasks are configured as preemptive tasks. Modifying IOSampleKeypad to create a preemptive task in the OIL configuration file demonstrates the difference in a fully preemptive system. The task needs one modification: the removal of the API service Schedule(). As a result, the system operates as shown in Figure 4.4, as opposed to the system illustrated in Figure 4.3, in that the higher priority task ProcessKeyPress is not inhibited from running by the lower priority task after it has been activated.

Figure 4.3 Non-preemptive tasks after a key press.

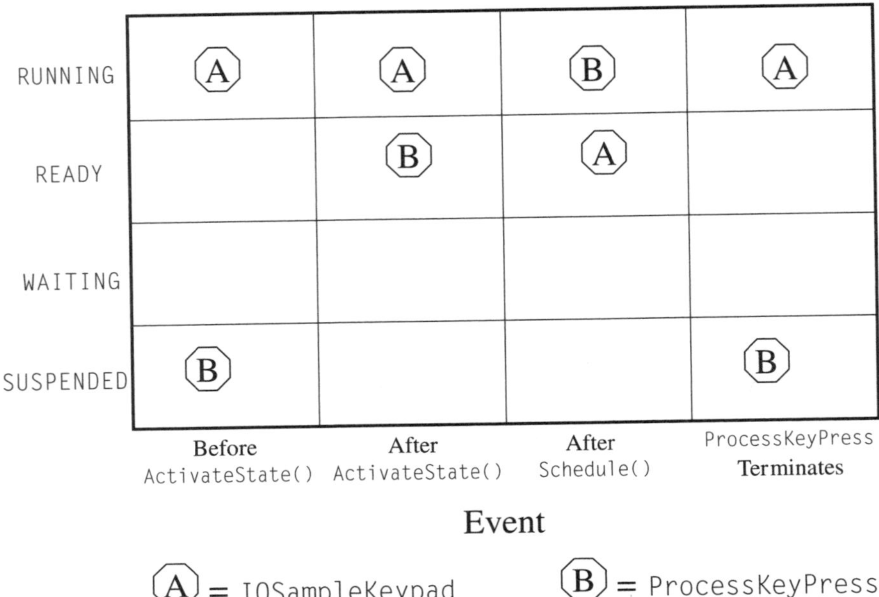

Figure 4.4 Preemptive tasks after a key press.

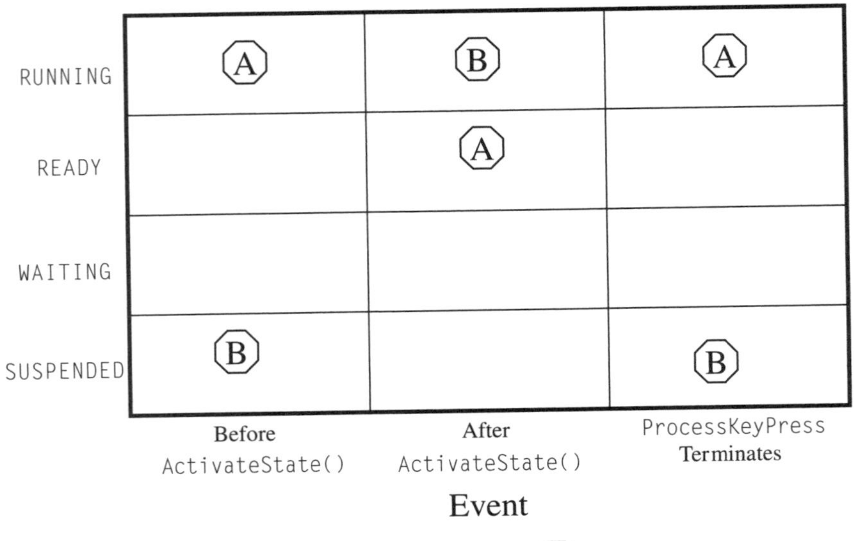

When a preemptive task is in the RUNNING state, the scheduler is invoked when any of the following events occur.

- The task is successfully terminated by TerminateTask().
- The task is successfully terminated and another task is activated by ChainTask().
- A task is activated from the task level using the API service ActivateTask().
- An extended task is moved into the WAITING state.
- An event is set that causes an extended task to move out of the WAITING state to the READY state (events are covered in Chapter 6).
- A resource is released at task level (resources are covered in Chapter 7).
- A return from a category two or category three interrupt to task level occurs. The scheduler is not invoked if the system is running at the interrupt level (i.e., at the return of a nested interrupt).

4.4.3 Mixed Preemptive

The mixed preemptive scheduling policy is invoked in an application in which some tasks have preemption enabled and other tasks have preemption disabled within the OIL configuration file. For example, if the tasks defined in this chapter are set up such that IOSampleKeypad is not preemptive and ProcessKeyPress and OutputDisplay are preemptive, then the system is operating in the mixed preemptive mode. Under this policy, the OS determines whether to invoke the scheduler based on the type of preemption enabled for the currently running task. Typically, an application operates in mixed preemptive mode if most tasks can be preempted safely; however, a few tasks must run to completion without being preempted. An example is a task that must set a series of outputs within a very tight time window — for example, when a serial communication stream is output bit by bit at a very high speed through a single pin on the microcontroller.

4.5 Example Program

If you build the program included on the accompanying CD and program the test setup, the keys you press on the keypad are echoed to the display. When the end of the display is reached, it scrolls up to allow for additional lines. If you press the # key twice, the display is blanked and starts at the top of the display again. To implement the simple functionality, I had to add a number of new modules and a configuration file to support the basic functionality of the card game.

4.5.1 Modules

The modules startup.s, initspr.s, cinit.s, init.c, and main.c were not changed in this chapter. The following modules either were changed or added.

debug.c The only change to this module was the modification to ErrorHook() discussed in section 4.3, "Other Task Services."

`cardgame.c` This new module holds all of the tasks and functions required to implement the game of blackjack in the example application. At this point, it consists of only one task, `ProcessKeyPress`.

`ProcessKeyPress` This is the main task, and it is expanded extensively throughout the book. It consists of one `switch` statement that takes action based on the current state of the system and the value of the key that was pressed. At this time, the only state of the system is after one # key has been pressed that signals the system to await the next key press.

`dispdrv.c` This new module accesses the display driver on the Axiom board, which consists of a Hitachi HD44780 display driver chip and a 20-column by four-row alphanumeric display. This module uses five functions and one task to control the display. If a different display is used, this module will have to be modified. The functions are as follows.

`void InitDisplay(InitType type)` This initialization function is invoked by the initialization routine `InitSystem()` as defined in Chapter 1. It performs three actions. First it resets the display driver and initializes the driver for a particular display. After the driver has been initialized, the special characters for the card suits are programmed into the driver memory. Finally, a welcome message is displayed on the device. This service makes extensive use of the small local service `wait()`, which is discussed next.

`void wait(UINT32 time)` This local service provides a time delay that allows the display driver to react to commands from the processor. It simply takes the value passed in the parameter `time` and decrements at `0`. On the MPC555 microcontroller running at 20MHz, it takes approximately 250ns per count.

`void PackDisplay(char *string)` This function simply packs a display mirror buffer, which is held locally with the information passed in the null-terminated parameter `STRING`, which can contain special control characters. For example, `0x0A` is recognized as the new line character, \n, at which point `PackDisplay()` continues writing the string at the first character in the next line. This is accomplished using `OutputNewLine()`, which is discussed later. The value `0x0C` is recognized as the form feed character, \f, which essentially blanks the display and begins outputting the rest of the string to the first character in the first row. Any character with a value greater than 240 is interpreted as a special character that is one of the first eight characters in the display driver buffer.

`void OutputNewLine(void)` This function moves the cursor to the beginning of the next line. If the cursor is already at the bottom of the display, this routine scrolls the display up one line.

`void OutputNewDisplay(void)` This function writes the local mirror of the display to the display driver. All of the required handshaking is performed by this one routine.

`OutputDisplay` This task is activated by an application after it has written information to the global variable `displayBuffer`. `OutputDisplay` uses the services defined previously to send the application output string to the display. Because there is only one buffer, this is the highest priority task and must complete before any other task that is running and that might corrupt the buffer. In later chapters, I make this module more robust by buffering requests for displays.

hw.c This module provides the lowest level device driver to the system hardware. It is intended to interface with simple external devices such as switches, digital outputs, and analog inputs. More complex devices, such as the display, would have their own drivers. The `hw.c` module has just one function, `HWGetValue()`. If the method of obtaining a key press is changed or a different keypad is used, change this module.

`UINT32 HWGetValue(void *hardware)` `HWGetValue()` is a generic function that gets a value from a piece of hardware. Its responsibility is to translate the information from the hardware to the application device drivers. `HWGetValue()` always returns a 32-bit unsigned value, which the device driver interprets.

The application passes a structure to `HWGetValue()` that contains all of the information needed to access the piece of hardware. The first member in all hardware structures is called `type` and is always of the same type; consequently, no matter what the size of the structure being referenced, `HWGetValue()` is able to access the first member and cast the pointer properly for the structure.

The definitions of all hardware structures are in `hw.cfg`. Presently, the only type of hardware that this application recognizes is a keypad input. The digital port attached to the keypad is read, and the raw value is translated into the ASCII value of the key that was pressed. If no key was pressed, the return value is `0`. The keypad device driver, discussed later, is only concerned with an ASCII value and does not have to change if the keypad changes.

keypad.c This module consists of the `IOSampleKeypad` task.

`IOSampleKeypad` This task is the keypad device driver and has been discussed extensively throughout this chapter, and I will not discuss it here again.

4.5.2 Configuration Files

One additional configuration file was added to support the hardware driver.

hw.cfg Here, the application programmer defines the characteristics of all the hardware inputs and outputs controlled by the low-level drivers with the use of a macro that encapsulates the definition of the structure. The details of these macros can be found in the configuration file.

4.6 Exercises

1. Create a routine in `PreTaskHook()` that counts the number of times a key is pressed since the system has been reset. Hint: One task is activated every time a key is pressed.
2. Create a task that writes a message to the display whenever the * (asterisk) key is pressed. Modify the `ProcessKeyPress` task to start your task instead of chaining the `OutputDisplay` task. Please do not use "Hello World!" as your message :).

3. Modify the `OutputDisplay` task to identify which task sent the message. Hint: The highest priority task that is in the `READY` state would activate `OutputDisplay`.
4. If you enjoy adding hardware to your system, add an LED that is on whenever a key is pressed. Create two tasks, one that turns the LED on and the other that turns the LED off, and activate these tasks whenever the state of the keypad changes.

4.7 Summary

In this chapter, I introduced the most important concept in the OSEK/VDX OS standard: the task. Tasks are the most used item in the OS. The API services `ActivateTask()`, `ChainTask()`, and `TerminateTask()` are probably the most used services in the OS.

5

Chapter 5

Alarms

Now that the concept of a task has been defined, the services available within the OSEK/VDX API can be expanded. The first API service discussed is alarms, which also includes the concept of counters. Unlike other real-time OSs, OSEK/VDX does not have a timer concept; instead, an alarm is defined that covers the functions of a timer and the unique need of an embedded control system to take an action based on the occurrence of a series of events. This is accomplished by creating a counter object that is incremented whenever an event occurs. The alarm is triggered when the corresponding counter reaches a preset value. This counter can be a free-running timer, or it can be another type of input, such as a series of pulses from a sensor.

This chapter introduces the concepts of counters and alarms and defines the API services that manage these objects. The OSEK/VDX standards do not currently define an API for counters. Only the API for alarms is defined. Consequently, the counter API can be different for each vendor-specific implementation of the OSEK/VDX OS.

5.1 Counters

A counter is an OS object that keeps track of the number of ticks that have occurred. Some counter-specific constants are defined in the OIL configuration file. Because a standardized API for managing counters does not exist, I strongly advise that all counter manipulation be kept in a separate file to allow portability between implementations or target processors.

In every OSEK/VDX OS implementation, at least one counter must be based on either a hardware or software timer. This counter is used by alarms as a system timer to accomplish the same function as a timer in other real-time OSs. For example, an alarm based on this counter would be used to schedule a periodically executing task.

In the example application, I use the system counter extensively to generate periodic tasks and delays to implement the card game application. In order to demonstrate the use of counters, I have added a special circuit that allows the user to randomize card shuffling. The circuit is shown in Figure 5.1.

Figure 5.1 Shuffling circuit.

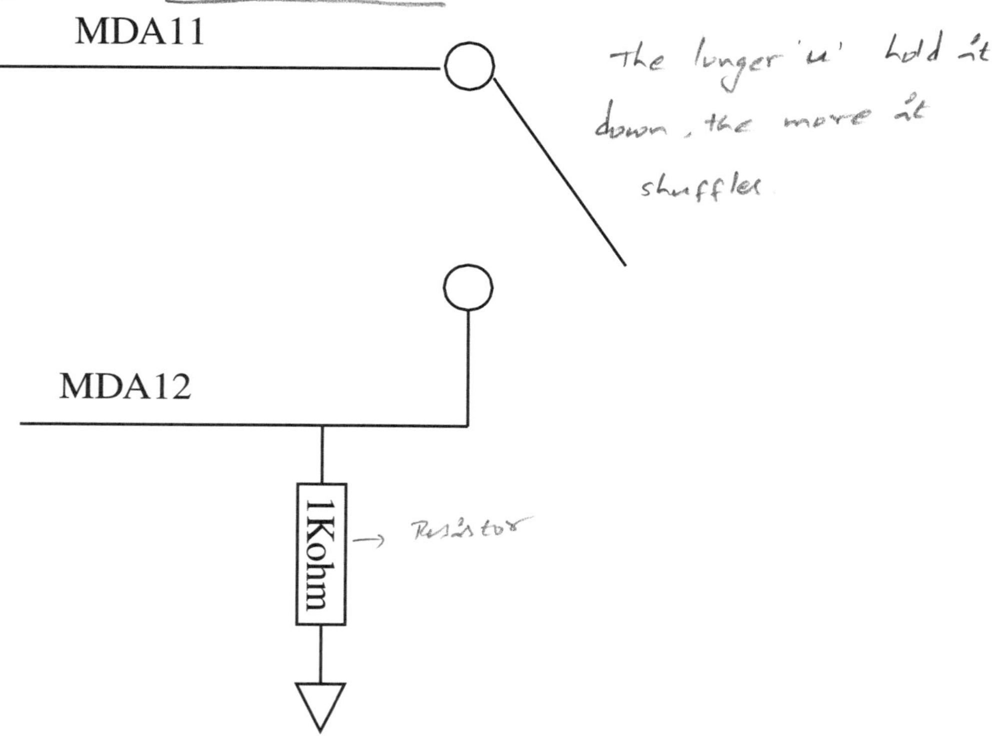

In the circuit, I use an output of the MPC555 to generate a frequency output then feed that back into an input that is sampled periodically to determine when a pulse occurs. I will also create a task that samples the input and updates a counter every time a pulse occurs. Ideally, this frequency output would be fed back into an input that can generate an interrupt whenever a pulse occurs (I make this modification when I discuss interrupts later in the book). By depressing the switch, the user can determine how long the deck of cards are shuffled and thereby generate a random number to be used by the shuffling routine. The portion of the OIL configuration file that defines both the system counter and the shuffling counter is shown in Listing 5.1.

Listing 5.1 Counter configuration definitions.

```
/***********************************************************************/
/*            Counters                                                 */
/***********************************************************************/

   COUNTER SHUFFLE_COUNTER {
          /*@*************************************************************/
          /* Shuffling Counter                                           */
          /*@*************************************************************/

          MAXALLOWEDVALUE = 9;
          TICKSPERBASE = 1;
          MINCYCLE = 3;
   };

   COUNTER SYSTEM_COUNTER {
          MAXALLOWEDVALUE = 65535;
          TICKSPERBASE = 1000000;
          MINCYCLE = 1;
   };
```

Each counter has three standard attributes.

- MAXALLOWEDVALUE This is the maximum value for the counter. When it is reached, the next counter increment is to 0. For example, a sensor on a wheel that sends a pulse every time the wheel turns one degree would have a maximum allowed value of 359 (zero base) if the counter represents the current angle of the wheel.

- TICKSPERBASE This attribute is vaguely defined by the OSEK/VDX standard as being the number of ticks required to reach a counter-specific unit. The standard indicates that the interpretation of this attribute is specific to the implementation. Consequently, you should refer to your implementation documentation for a description of the use of this attribute.

- MINCYCLE This attribute defines the minimum cyclic number of counter ticks allowed for a cyclic alarm. Cyclic alarms are described in the next section.

For the card game example application, the SHUFFLE_COUNTER shuffling counter is defined with a maximum value of 9 and a minimum cycle of 3. In the next section, I use this counter to generate a random number that is used to sort the cards when the application shuffles the deck.

The standard timer counter in OSEKWorks is called SYSTEM_COUNTER and is set up as a free-running 16-bit counter. The minimum number of counts for a cyclic alarm is 1. The name of this timer varies with each implementation, and in some, multiple standard timers might be available. In the OSEKWorks implementation, the TICKSPERBASE attribute is not used by the implementation, but it is available for the application to use as required. The OSTICKDURATION system constant, discussed later, is set to this value for the system counter. The TICKSPERBASE attribute is available to the application as a return from an API service that is discussed in the next section. I have chosen the value of TICKSPERBASE for SYSTEM_COUNTER to be 1000000, which corresponds to 1ms (1,000,000ns).

After a counter is defined, a minimum of two routines must be created: an initialization routine and a handler routine. The initialization and handler routines for the standard system counter that is used as a timer are not only specific to each implementation, but also specific to the individual microcontroller. Refer to the implementation documentation for details on how the standard system counter is initialized and handled. Initialization and processing can be provided by the implementation supplier, or the end user might have to supply these functions. The initialization routine for the example program is shown in Listing 5.2; the handler task is shown in Listing 5.3. Many of the services included in Listing 5.3 will be discussed throughout this chapter, so do not worry if the task is confusing at this time. These routines are found in shuffle.c on the accompanying CD.

Listing 5.2 Shuffling counter initialization.

```
void InitShuffleSwitch(InitType type)
{
    if(type==INIT_STARTUP)
    {
        InitCounter(SHUFFLE_COUNTER,0);
    }
    ShuffleState = SHUFFLE_LOW;
}
```

I must add InitShuffleSwitch() to the table of initialization functions that are called from InitSystem(). In this routine, the shuffling counter is initialized to a set value. In the example case, as will typically be the case for most counters, the counter initializes to 0. The OSEKWorks InitCounter() API service allows counters to be initialized to any valid value. Although this is typical of most OSEK/VDX implementations, because the counter API is not defined, it is not necessary to support this behavior. After initialization, a flag is set to indicate the last state of the input to be used in the sampling routine. Counter initialization should be performed from StartupHook(), and in the example routine, I check this based on the value of the type parameter that is passed by InitSystem().

To handle the counter, I have created an IOSampleShuffleSwitch task that executes periodically and samples the input from the switch. The counter is incremented whenever the input makes the transition from low to high. As mentioned earlier, this will eventually be done by an interrupt service routine. The counter is incremented using the IncrCounter() API service, which is also specific to OSEKWorks. Most OSEK/VDX implementations will have a similar function to increment the counter. In addition, many implementations provide a service that allows the application to query the current value of the counter. In OSEKWorks, this is GetCounterValue(). The rest of the routine is considered later when I discuss alarms in more detail.

Now that the system has two basic counters and the routines to handle them, you can create alarms based on these counters.

Listing 5.3 Shuffling counter handler.

```
TASK(IOSampleShuffleSwitch)
{
static UINT8 timeout;
TickType tick;

   switch(ShuffleState){
      case SHUFFLE_HIGH:
         if(HWGetValue(&SHUFFLESWITCH)==INACTIVE){
            ShuffleState = SHUFFLE_LOW;
         }
         break;
      case SHUFFLE_LOW:
         if(HWGetValue(&SHUFFLESWITCH)==ACTIVE){
            timeout = SHUFFLE_SWITCH_OFF;
            if(GetAlarm(ShuffleAlarm,(TickRefType)tick) == E_OS_NOFUNC){
               SetAbsAlarm(ShuffleAlarm,5,3);
               strcpy(displayBuffer,"\fSHUFFLING -");
               ActivateTask(OutputDisplay);
            }
            ShuffleState = SHUFFLE_HIGH;
            IncrCounter(SHUFFLE_COUNTER);
         }
         else{
            if(timeout!=0){
               if(--timeout == 0){
                  CancelAlarm(ShuffleAlarm);
                  CancelAlarm(SampleShuffleSwitchAlarm);
                  ActivateTask(ShufflingComplete);
               }
            }
         }
```

```
        break;
    }
    TerminateTask();
}
```

5.2 Using Alarms

Alarms are OSEK/VDX objects that are associated with counters. When defining alarms, each alarm is statically assigned to one counter and one task; however, multiple alarms can be assigned to a given counter. Whenever a counter is incremented, the currently active alarms assigned to that counter are compared to the counter value. If the values are equal, the alarm is triggered and it can take one of two possible actions: activate a task or set an event for a task. I have already explained how to activate a task, and I will discuss setting an event in Chapter 6.

For the card game application, I define three alarms at this time: a periodic alarm to sample the keypad, a periodic alarm to sample the shuffle switch, and a shuffling alarm that triggers a random shuffling of the cards after a set number of pulses from the shuffling switch. The OIL configuration for these three alarm objects is shown in Listing 5.4.

Listing 5.4 Alarm definition.

```
/***************************************************************************/
/*              Alarms                                                     */
/***************************************************************************/

   ALARM SampleKeypad {
           COUNTER = SYSTEM_COUNTER;
           ACTION = ACTIVATETASK{
              TASK = IOSampleKeypad;
           };
   };

   ALARM SampleShuffleSwitchAlarm {
           COUNTER = SYSTEM_COUNTER;
           ACTION = ACTIVATETASK{
              TASK = IOSampleShuffleSwitch;
           };
   };

   ALARM ShuffleAlarm {
           COUNTER = SHUFFLE_COUNTER;
```

```
            ACTION = ACTIVATETASK{
                TASK = ShuffleCards;
            };
    };
```

Within an alarm object definition, the standard requires two attributes: COUNTER and ACTION. The COUNTER attribute defines the counter associated with this alarm when active. The name used in this attribute must match the name of a counter object defined elsewhere in the configuration file. The ACTION attribute can be either ACTIVATETASK or SETEVENT. Depending on the value of this attribute, either one or two references to other OIL objects must be defined. If the action is ACTIVATETASK, then one reference, TASK, is required. This references the name of a task to activate, which is also defined in this configuration file. If the action is SETEVENT, then two references are required: TASK and EVENT. EVENT is a valid event for the TASK reference as defined elsewhere in the configuration file. In the OSEKWorks v4.0 implementation, the TASK and EVENT references appear as separate attributes, instead of being associated directly with one ACTION attribute as references. This might affect portability of the OIL file and should be fixed in a later version. The code on the accompanying CD includes the OIL configuration file output from OSEKWorks and will be different from the listing here.

Now that the alarms and counters are defined in the configuration file, I have to update the application to use these alarms. The first item to update is the task previously defined to sample the keypad, IOSampleKeypad (Listing 5.5). This is now be a preemptible task with a higher priority, so I need to remove the delay loop used to allow higher priority tasks to run.

Listing 5.5 Keyboard sampling task.

```
TASK(IOSampleKeypad)
{
static BOOLEAN keyState = FALSE;
char tempKey;

    tempKey = HWGetValue(&KEYPAD);
    if(tempKey == lastKey){
        if(keyCount++ == KEY_DEBOUNCE_TIME){
            --keyCount;
            keyValue = tempKey;
        }
    }
    else{
        keyCount = 0;
        lastKey = tempKey;
    }
    if(keyState==FALSE){
        if(keyValue != 0){
```

```
            keyState = TRUE;
            ActivateTask(ProcessKeyPress);
        }
    }
    else{
        if(keyValue == 0){
            keyState = FALSE;
        }
    }
    TerminateTask();
}
```

Because this task is now triggered by the expiration of an alarm, you must start the alarm at some point with the use of a special initialization task that is run immediately after the OS starts. The purpose of this task, which is not defined in the standards or included in an implementation, is to start the alarms that the application must have running on startup. These are typically periodic alarms that kick off periodic tasks required by the application. The OSEK/VDX standard does not have an autostart configuration for alarms, as it does with tasks, because the state of the counters is uncertain. The task I created to autostart alarms is `InitAlarms` (Listing 5.6, in `init.c`).

Listing 5.6 Alarm autostart task.

```
TASK(InitAlarms)
{
    InitAlarmType const *list = AlarmAutostartList;
    UINT32 currentAppModeMask = ConvertAppMode(APP_MODE_MASK);

    while(list->appmodemask != 0x00000000){
        if((list->appmodemask & currentAppModeMask)!= 0){
            if(list->alarmtype == ALARM_REL){
                SetRelAlarm(list->alarm,list->start,list->cycle);
            }
            else{
                SetAbsAlarm(list->alarm,list->start,list->cycle);
            }
        }
        list++;
    }
    TerminateTask();
}
```

InitAlarms is configured as an autostart task in the OIL configuration file with the highest possible priority. In addition, no other tasks are allowed to have the same priority. This ensures that this task is the first run after the OS starts.

InitAlarms first obtains the current APPMODE and then determines which alarms it needs to start. First, it translates the APPMODE into a bit mask. The AppModeType is not explicitly defined in the OSEK/VDX standard. In one implementation I have seen, AppModeType is a scalar value realized with the use of enumeration. In another implementation, it is a pointer to a structure defining the APPMODE. Consequently, I have created a conversion routine ConvertAppMode(), which encapsulates the format of the APPMODE type. This routine obtains the current APPMODE using GetActiveApplicationMode() and converts it to either a number or a bitmap, which it returns.

When calling ConvertAppMode(), the requested type of return, either APP_MODE_MASK or APP_MODE_VALUE, is passed to the routine as a flag. The return value is always UINT32. If a number is returned, it can be used efficiently in a switch statement; if a bit mask is returned, it can be used efficiently in a table lookup. The details of this routine are found in the source code on the accompanying CD in os.h and os.c. The os files were created to hold any implementation-specific glue routines that might be required to port an application from one OSEK/VDX implementation to another.

In InitAlarms, I traverse a null-terminated list of structures that define the alarms to be started. For each alarm, the structure defines the type and periodicity, the starting value, and a mask of the APPMODEs in which the alarm must be started. The NULL value is the mask of APPMODEs, because there has to be at least one mode in which an alarm starts, or it should not be in the list. The type definition for the startup alarm structure InitAlarmType is shown in Listing 5.7.

Listing 5.7 Alarm autostart definition structure.

```
typedef enum AlarmFunctionTypetag {
   ALARM_REL,
   ALARM_ABS
   }AlarmFunctionType;

typedef struct InitAlarmTypetag {
   AlarmType alarm;
   AlarmFunctionType alarmtype;
   TickType start;
   TickType cycle;
   UINT32 appmodemask;
   }InitAlarmType;
```

For each entry in the table, the APPMODE mask in the currentAppModeMask local variable is compared to an enable mask, structure member appmodemask, for each alarm. If the alarm is to autostart in the current APPMODE, one of two API service routines are invoked: SetRelAlarm() or SetAbsAlarm(), depending on the alarmtype structure member. The C function prototypes for each service are defined below.

```
StatusType SetRelAlarm(AlarmType alarm, TickType increment, TickType cycle);

StatusType SetAbsAlarm(AlarmType alarm, TickType start, TickType cycle);
```

SetRelAlarm() starts a relative alarm, which is an alarm that is set to expire at a value relative to the current counter value. When this service is invoked, the alarm is set to the current value of the counter that is attached to this alarm, plus the value of increment. This increment must not be set to a value less than that in the MINCYCLE attribute of the COUNTER object in the OIL configuration file. If the increment is set to 0, the behavior of this service is defined by the implementation. Because this behavior is undefined by the standard, to enable maximum portability I recommend that increment never be set to 0 by the application.

The cycle parameter is used to create a periodic alarm. If cycle is set to a value other than 0, the alarm is restarted immediately after expiration, with the value of cycle added to the previous value of alarm. This allows a periodic alarm to be defined and to start at a future time defined by increment that might be far greater than the period (cycle), to enable, for example, a large delay that allows the power supply system to settle. If cycle is 0, the alarm is canceled after it expires. They cycle parameter must not be less than the MINCYCLE attribute of the COUNTER object.

SetAbsAlarm() starts an absolute alarm, which is defined as an alarm set to expire at an absolute value of the counter attached to the alarm. When invoked, the alarm value is set to the value of start. If cycle is not 0, the alarm restarts immediately after expiration, with the new comparison value equal to the old alarm value plus the cycle value. This type of alarm is typically used for a cyclic input, such as the crank angle of an engine. For example, a task that needs to fire fuel injectors at 10 degrees of crank angle for the first fuel injector and then symmetrically for each additional fuel injector would set the start value at 10 and cycle at 90 for an 8 cylinder engine.

Both API services have the same return values.

- If the alarm is set properly, the service returns E_OK.
- If the alarm is already in use, the service returns E_OS_STATE.
- In the extended status mode, if the alarm value passed is invalid, the service returns E_OS_ID.
- In the extended status mode, if the value of increment or start is less than 0 or greater than the MAXALLOWEDVALUE attribute for the counter, the service returns E_OS_VALUE.
- In the extended status mode, if the value of cycle is not equal to 0 and is less than the MINCYCLE or greater than the MAXALLOWEDVALUE attribute for the counter, the service returns E_OS_VALUE.

These services can be called from either the task or interrupt level but must not be called by any of the hook routines.

At this point, the only alarm that needs to start automatically with the OS is the keyboard sampling alarm. This alarm is initiated as a relative alarm starting 500 milliseconds after the OS starts. It then samples the input periodically every 24 milliseconds. The other alarms are only required when the system is actually shuffling cards. These alarms are initiated by the task that is activated when the key that determines that shuffling must occur is pressed.

Now that the application samples and debounces the keypad periodically, it is in the OS-supplied idle loop most of the time. In most OSEK/VDX implementations, it is a do-nothing loop. The application remain in this loop until an interrupt occurs that moves a task from `SUSPENDED` or `WAITING` to `READY`. If a watchdog needs petting in order to keep the system running, the application should provide a low-priority basic task that performs this function. This should not be a periodic task unless it is the lowest priority (`0`) task in the system (i.e., it cannot preempt anything). Otherwise, a poorly behaving low-priority task might be masked by the higher priority watchdog task.

To support this in the future, I have reintroduced `background`, a zero-priority basic task that is just a `while(1)` loop, for future expansion. Inside this loop, it is possible to

- monitor idle time,
- manage power to put the processor in a low power state between clock ticks, and
- pet the watchdog.

The `background` task is a placeholder for additional features that might be necessary in the future. The example application, which is not powered by batteries, has no use for power management at this time; however, it could be required in the future, so I recommend that this small task be added in any application.

The next step is to modify `ProcessKeyPress` (Listing 5.8), found in `cardgame.c`, the task that is activated whenever a key is pressed.

Listing 5.8 `ProcessKeyPress` task.

```
TASK(ProcessKeyPress)
{
   switch(keyValue)
   {
      case '#':
         if(gameState != GAME_SHUFFLING){
            DealCard();
         }
         break;
      case '*':
         if(gameState != GAME_SHUFFLING){
            gameState = GAME_SHUFFLING;
            SetRelAlarm(SampleShuffleSwitchAlarm,10,10);
            ActivateTask(ShuffleCards);
         }
         break;
   }
   TerminateTask();
}
```

ProcessKeyPress performs the following functions.

- When the * key is pressed and the system state is NOT_SHUFFLING, the system begins shuffling by starting the alarm that samples the shuffling switch. The ShuffleCards task is activated, which clears the display and shows the message "SHUFFLING -".
- When the # key is pressed and the system state is NOT_SHUFFLING, the next card is taken from the deck and displayed using DealCard(). If all lines are filled on the LCD display, the display is scrolled up.

The alarm that samples the input from the shuffling switch is initialized as a periodic alarm that triggers the sampling task (Listing 5.3) after 10 milliseconds and then periodically every 10 milliseconds thereafter.

IOSampleShuffleSwitch() checks the input and determines when a transition from low to high occurs. If a transition does not occur, a counter is decremented if not equal to 0. When the counter reaches 0, shuffling is complete. Because the counter is 0 until the first pulse occurs, the task will wait forever for the user to press the switch. When the switch is pressed and the first transition occurs, the task sets the timeout counter to a configuration value and starts the shuffling alarm. To initialize the alarm, the task checks whether the shuffling alarm defined earlier has been started using the OSEK/VDX API service GetAlarm().

```
StatusType GetAlarm(AlarmType alarm, TickRefType tick);
```

In this service, alarm is a name of the alarm to check, and tick is a reference to a valid variable of type TickType. The service places the current remaining number of ticks for the alarm in the variable pointed to by the argument tick. The return value from this service is

- E_OK if the alarm is presently running,
- E_OS_NOFUNC if the alarm is not presently running, or
- E_OS_ID in the extended status mode if alarm is not valid.

This service can be invoked from the task level or the interrupt level and from the hook routines ErrorHook(), PreTaskHook(), and PostTaskHook().

If the alarm has not been started, GetAlarm() starts an absolute alarm that is triggered the first time the shuffle switch counter reaches 5 and every three counts after that. This creates some randomness in the shuffling algorithm because the counter is stopped when the switch is released, and the value of the counter when the switch is first pressed will be a random number between 0 and 9. Consequently, the time until the first alarm expiry after the switch is first pressed until the first shuffling occurs is random. The routine also changes the display to "SHUFFLING -".

If the timeout timer has been decremented to zero, the shuffling and sampling alarms are canceled using the CancelAlarm() API service, which cancels an alarm that was previously started — whether single or cyclic — and activates a task to signal that shuffling is complete. The prototype for this service follows.

```
StatusType CancelAlarm(AlarmType alarm);
```

In CancelAlarm(), the alarm parameter is the name of a previously defined alarm that is running. The return value from this service is

- E_OK if the service processes properly,
- E_OS_NOFUNC if the alarm is not in use, or

- E_OS_ID in the extended status mode if alarm is not valid.

This service can be called from either the task or interrupt level and cannot be called by any of the hook routines.

After the shuffling alarm is checked and started, if necessary, the shuffling counter is incremented, using the implementation-specific IncrCounter() API service, and the dash that is displayed after "SHUFFLING -" is modified to look like a clock with the use of the characters "- \ | /". The API service increments the counter object and checks all the alarms defined for the counter. If any alarms have expired, the OS takes the action defined by the alarm. In this case, if the shuffling alarm has expired, the ShuffleCards task is activated (Listing 5.9, in carddeck.c), and one shuffle of the cards occurs.

Listing 5.9 ShuffleCards task.

```
TASK(ShuffleCards)
{
UINT8 count = (UINT8)(((UINT32)rand() * 100u) / RAND_MAX) + 1;
UINT8 location1, location2,tempcard;

   deckStart = cardDeck;
   while((count--)>0){
      location1 = ((UINT32)rand() * 52u) / RAND_MAX;
      if(location1==52) location1 = 51;
      location2 = ((UINT32)rand() * 52u) / RAND_MAX;
      if(location2==52) location2 = 51;
      tempcard = cardDeck[location1];
      cardDeck[location1] = cardDeck[location2];
      cardDeck[location2] = tempcard;
   }
   strcpy(displayBuffer,busyDisplay[busyLocation++]);
   if(busyLocation == 4) busyLocation = 0;
   ActivateTask(OutputDisplay);
   TerminateTask();
}
```

The rand() C library function is used to shuffle the deck every three counts of the shuffling switch. This task is set up with a higher priority than the routine that checks the switch input to ensure that the shuffle is a higher priority than the switch. In Chapter 7 on resources, I consider the deck to be a resource that can be locked.

5.3 Other Alarm Services

In addition to the API services already discussed in this chapter, there are two additional services that are not used as frequently. The first service is a declaration function used to declare an external alarm to a module.

```
DeclareAlarm(AlarmIdentifier);
```

The entry for `AlarmIdentifier` is the name of the alarm as it appears in the OIL configuration file. The second service, `GetAlarmBase()`, determines the parameters of the counter on which the alarm is based.

```
GetAlarmBase(AlarmType alarm, AlarmBaseRefType baseinfo);
```

The `alarm` parameter defines which alarm is being queried, and the base parameters of the counter are put into the `AlarmBaseType` structure referred to by `baseinfo`. The `AlarmBaseType` structure has the following members.

- `maxallowedvalue` The maximum allowed value of the counter in ticks.

- `ticksperbase` The number of ticks required to reach a counter-specific value. The interpretation of this number is specific to the implementation.

- `mincycle` The minimum value allowed when starting a cyclic alarm.

`GetAlarmBase()` can be invoked from the task or interrupt level and from the hook routines `ErrorHook()`, `PreTaskHook()`, and `PostTaskHook()`.

In addition to the services defined above, four global constant values must be defined by every implementation. These values are as follows and might be used by the application.

- `OSMAXALLOWEDVALUE` The maximum allowed value for the system counter that is used as a timer. This is the same as the `AlarmBaseType` member `maxallowedvalue`.

- `OSTICKSPERBASE` The `ticksperbase` for the system counter.

- `OSMINCYCLE` The `mincycle` for the system counter.

- `OSTICKDURATION` The duration in nanoseconds of one tick of the system counter.

These constant values are usually defined in initialization code for the application. The configuration program then uses the values from this counter to define these constants.

5.4 Example Program

The example program now includes the following features.

- When the program starts, a startup message is displayed on the display.
- When the * key is pressed, the system is ready to begin shuffling. The display is cleared, and "SHUFFLING –" is displayed.

- When the shuffling button is pressed and held, the system shuffles the cards. The dash that appears in "SHUFFLING -" on the display behaves like a clock by rotating each time a shuffling sequence occurs using the characters "- \ | /".
- When the button is released, the display is blanked and the first card is displayed.
- Every time the # key is pressed, a new card is shown on the display.

5.4.1 Modules

The modules `startup.s`, `initspr.s`, `cinit.s`, and `debug.c` did not change in this chapter. The following modules were changed or added.

`init.c` The `InitAlarms` task was added. It is set as the highest priority task in the application and autostarts. Its purpose is to start all of the alarms that kick off periodic tasks or are required in other ways by the application.

`main.c` The `background` task was modified so that it no longer terminates but runs continuously in the background. This allows it to perform functions such as petting the watchdog and monitoring the function of the system.

`cardgame.c` The `ProcessKeyPress` task was modified and one additional task was added. Also, this module now keeps track of the state of the game in the `gameState` static variable. The tasks in this module are described below.

> `ProcessKeyPress` This task now provides only two functions. When the * key is pressed, the card deck is reshuffled. When the # key is pressed, the next card is displayed. All other keys are ignored.
>
> `ShufflingComplete` This task is activated when shuffling is completed. It simply changes the state of the card game and then displays the first card on the display.

`dispdrv.c` The initialization of the display that is performed in `InitDisplay()` was modified slightly. A new startup screen was defined to inform the user to press the * key in order to shuffle the deck, and a new special character was added to allow the simulated clock to display while shuffling. The Hitachi display driver does not support the backslash character (\).

`hw.c` The `HWGetValue()` service was expanded to allow two types of input. In addition to the keypad input previously defined, a standard digital input from a 16-bit digital channel has been defined. This supports sampling of the shuffling switch.

`keypad.c` The `IOSampleKeypad` task has been modified extensively to support the change from a background task that is constantly running to a periodic task. It is now a much simpler task that only executes when it is time to sample the keypad.

`carddeck.c` This new module maintains the deck of cards used by the game. The current deck of cards is held in the `cardDeck[]` static array, which is 53 bytes long. The final entry in the array is never used except to indicate the end of the array. The cards are encoded with values from `0` to `51`. The value of the card is the value from this array modulo 13, with `0` equaling an Ace and 12 representing a King. The suit of the card is the value from the array divided by integer 13. Because integer math is used, the remainder is discarded. The suits are taken in ascending order starting with hearts, followed by diamonds, spades, and clubs. The deck of cards is maintained with the following tasks and functions:

`ShuffleCards` This task performs one shuffle of the deck. First it generates a random number from `1` to `100` for the number of pairs of cards to be exchanged in the deck. Then pairs of cards are exchanged randomly. When complete, `ShuffleCards` updates the display to show the simulated clock moving one position.

`UINT8 DealCard(void)` This function deals and displays the next card from the deck. It also translates the value from a single byte into a card value and suit.

`os.c` This new module encapsulates all of the routines that are required to port the application to a new implementation of the OSEK/VDX OS. Each implementation will require some hardware initialization, such as the hardware timer that generates the events for `SYSTEM_COUNTER`. This module has two routines.

`void OSInit(InitType type)` The system initialization function, `InitSystem()`, executes `OSInit()`, which initializes the board support package (BSP) required by the OSEKWorks implementation. At this point, the `RtcInit()` BSP function that starts the timer is the only initialization required. This function initializes the real-time clock for a one-millisecond tick.

`UINT32 ConvertAppMode(ConvertAppModeType type)` This routine translates the current `APPMODE` into either a bit mask or a number, depending on the value of the `type` parameter. This routine traverses a list defined in `os.cfg` and determines a zero-based value for the current `APPMODE`. If a mask is required, this routine translates the number into a 32-bit value with only one bit set and returns this mask. Otherwise, the value is returned directly.

`shuffle.c` This new module is the device driver for the shuffle switch. It consists of an initialization function and the sample task. Both the function and the task were discussed in detail in this chapter and will not be repeated here.

5.4.2 Configuration Files

`os.cfg` This new file provides application-specific configurations for use by the functions in the `os.c` module. For now, it creates a table that translates an `APPMODE` into a zero-based enumeration with the use of macros, as with the other configuration files (`hw.cfg`, `init.cfg`). Refer to the configuration file for a description of the macros.

5.5 Exercises

You can do much more with the sample application now that tasks and alarms are defined.

1. In the IOSampleShuffleSwitch task, replace the timeout counter with an alarm that starts with the first pulse and restarts on every pulse. When this alarm expires, activate the ShufflingComplete task. Modify ShufflingComplete to cancel the other alarms.
2. In the previous chapter, you created a task that output a message to the display when the * key was pressed. Modify this task to output the message when the 0 (zero) key is pressed, and flash the message at a rate of one second on and one second off.
3. Create a timer and a task that stores the hours, minutes, and seconds that the system has been running since the last reset. Display this time whenever the 1 key is pressed.
4. Calculate the amount of time spent in the background task using the time from the clock in the previous exercise and the PreTaskHook() and PostTaskHook() hook routines.
5. Add a switch to a digital input that sends a low pulse every time the switch is pressed using a pull-up resistor to +5V and the switch connected to ground. Create a new counter object and a device driver for the switch that increments this new counter every time the switch is pressed. For every 10 times the switch is pressed, create an alarm that activates a task that sends a message to the display.

5.6 Summary

At this point, the most widely used OS services have been used in the example. Tasks and alarms are the primary objects used by application developers. In Chapters 6 and 7, Events and Resources, I discuss some advanced topics that are used less often but could be required in many applications.

6

Chapter 6

Events

The event, which was introduced briefly in Chapter 4 during the discussion of extended tasks, is the next OSEK/VDX OS object to discuss. Events are owned by tasks in a one-to-one relationship. When a task owns an event, it becomes an extended task. Other tasks refer to the event by both the task name and the event name when accessing the API service.

In OSEK/VDX, events primarily provide synchronization between tasks and between applications that reside on different microcontrollers. Synchronization between different applications is accomplished by the combination of events and external communication messages. (Communication messages are covered in Part 2 on the OSEK/VDX communication standard.) This chapter defines events in more detail, discusses the API services provided to handle events, and expands the sample application to use events.

6.1 Events Defined

Events, as defined in OSEK/VDX, differ significantly from events in other OSs. The OSEK/VDX event is a method of sending binary information from one task to another. In other OSs, an event has a more general definition, such as the release of a semaphore or the reception of an interprocess communication message. These general events could be targeted specifically to one task or could be used by multiple tasks, as is the case with semaphores. The OSEK/VDX event is limited to communicating information to a single task; however, this communication can be sent to multiple tasks in an iterative process.

The primary purpose of events within OSEK/VDX is synchronization between tasks. For example, a task can begin a series of activities by activating a set of tasks and then wait for a

set of events to occur. When each activity completes, it sets an event on which the activating task is waiting. This releases the original task from the waiting mode and allows it to continue with the knowledge that everything has completed properly.

6.2 Managing Events

The API services `SetEvent()`, `ClearEvent()`, `GetEvent()`, and `WaitEvent()` manage OSEK/VDX events. Only the task that owns the event calls `WaitEvent()` and `ClearEvent()`. All other services can be called by any task, including basic tasks and interrupt service routines.

To use events, you must first define an extended task. I redefine the `ProcessKeyPress` task to be an extended task and define three events: `SHUFFLED`, `ABORT_SHUFFLE`, and `KEYPRESS`. Consequently, the OIL configuration file needs to be modified to change the definition of the task and add the events (Listing 6.1).

Listing 6.1 Events and extended task configuration objects.

```
TASK DealCards {
        TYPE = EXTENDED;
        SCHEDULE = FULL;
        PRIORITY = 10;
        ACTIVATION = 1;
        AUTOSTART = FALSE;
        STACKSIZE = 64;
        SCHEDULE_CALL = FALSE;
        EVENT = { ABORT_SHUFFLE, SHUFFLED };
};

TASK ProcessKeyPress {
        TYPE = EXTENDED;
        SCHEDULE = FULL;
        PRIORITY = 2;
        ACTIVATION = 1;
        AUTOSTART = TRUE;
        STACKSIZE = 128;
        SCHEDULE_CALL = FALSE;
        EVENT = { KEYPRESS, SHUFFLED };
};
/***************************************************************/
/*            Events                                           */
/***************************************************************/
```

```
EVENT ABORT_SHUFFLE {
        MASK = AUTO;
};

EVENT KEYPRESS {
        MASK = AUTO;
};

EVENT SHUFFLED {
        MASK = AUTO;
};
```

An additional attribute in the `ProcessKeyPress` task object definition, `EVENT`, links the `EVENT` object to the task. The EVENT attribute for each task object can have multiple event names. At this point, I have defined only two events for this task: `SHUFFLED` and `KEYPRESS`. The OSEK/VDX event is defined as the combination of the `TASK` and `EVENT` objects as defined in the task object definition.

The definition of the `EVENT` object has only one attribute, `MASK`, which is required for the event. The value of this attribute can be either `AUTO` or up to a 64-bit unsigned integer with a single bit set. In most cases, you want to leave this value set to `AUTO` and allow the OS configuration utility to optimize the bit value.

Although the OSEK/VDX event is defined as being owned by a single task, the `EVENT` object defined in the OIL configuration file is only a mask and can be used by multiple extended tasks because the event is defined as a combination of `TASK` and `EVENT` objects. To trigger an event for all tasks that use the event, you must call the API service for each combination of task and event. This is also illustrated in Listing 6.1, where I have added the new task `DealCards`. This task is different from the function `DealCard()`, which was originally created in Chapter 5 to add the next card in the deck to the display. `DealCards` is activated by the `ProcessKeyPress` task when it determines that the cards need to be shuffled. It immediately enters the `WAITING` state until shuffling is completed with the occurrence of the `SHUFFLED` event. After the event occurs, it deals the cards.

Now that the new objects are defined, modify the application to take advantage of the new events. First change the `ProcessKeyPress` task (Listing 6.2) so that it can use the added services provided for extended tasks.

Listing 6.2 Extended task `ProcessKeyPress`.

```
TASK(ProcessKeyPress)
{
EventMaskType eventMask;
BOOLEAN shuffleComplete;
char keyValue;
UINT8 i;
```

```
    while(1){
        WaitEvent(KEYPRESS);
        ClearEvent(KEYPRESS);
        while((keyValue = GetKeyValue())!= 0){
            switch(CheckGameTransition(keyValue)){
                case START_SHUFFLING:
                    SetRelAlarm(SampleShuffleSwitchAlarm,10,10);
                    ActivateTask(DealCards);
                    ActivateTask(ShuffleCards);
                    gameState = GAME_SHUFFLING;
                    shuffleComplete = FALSE;
                    do{
                        WaitEvent(KEYPRESS|SHUFFLED);
                        GetEvent(ProcessKeyPress,(EventMaskRefType)&eventMask);
                        if((eventMask & KEYPRESS)!= 0){
                            ClearEvent(KEYPRESS);
                            while((keyValue = GetKeyValue()) != 0){
                                if(keyValue == '#'){
                                    CancelAlarm(ShuffleAlarm);
                                    CancelAlarm(SampleShuffleSwitchAlarm);
                                    SetEvent(DealCards,ABORT_SHUFFLE);
                                    shuffleComplete = TRUE;
                                }
                            }
                        }
                        else{
                            ClearEvent(SHUFFLED);
                            shuffleComplete = TRUE;
                        }
                    }while(shuffleComplete == FALSE);
                    break;
...
            }
        }
    }
}
```

I have included only part of the entire task because it must handle many key press cases that do not involve events. The complete task is in `cardgame.c` on the accompanying CD. Within the task, I added a `while(1)` loop that invokes the `WaitEvent()` API service (see the C prototype below), which puts the ProcessKeyPress task immediately into the WAITING state for the KEYPRESS event.

```
StatusType WaitEvent(EventMaskType event);
```

When WaitEvent() is called, the service checks the events that are defined by the event mask passed as the argument. If any of the events defined in the mask are set, the service immediately returns to the invoking task, which continues in the RUNNING state. If all of the events defined by the event mask are cleared, then the invoking task is put into the WAITING state, and the scheduler is run to reschedule the system. When any one of the events defined by the event mask occurs, the invoking task is moved back into the READY state. When the scheduler moves the task from the READY to the RUNNING state, the task continues at the instruction immediately following the WaitEvent() service call. The service might only be invoked from a running extended task. Consequently, the service is only available in an application that is operating in either the ECC1 or ECC2 conformance class.

The return values from the service are

- E_OK in standard status mode and when the service is successful,
- E_OS_ACCESS in extended status mode if the calling task is not an extended task,
- E_OS_RESOURCE in extended status mode if the calling task still occupies resources (resources are discussed in Chapter 7; having a resource occupied while in the WAITING state can have catastrophic consequences), or
- E_OS_CALLEVEL in extended status mode if the service is invoked from interrupt level.

WaitEvent() can only be invoked from the task level of an extended task. It cannot be invoked at the interrupt level or in any hook routine.

If one of the events set in the event mask is not valid for the particular task, the standard does not define the actions of the API service. During development, this would make it very difficult to identify an error when one task sets an event and expects an extended task to be moved from the WAITING to READY state.

I configured ProcessKeyPress as a lower priority task because this task dispatches user interface events. It can be preempted by the higher priority events that process the user input, which minimizes the number of tasks that are in the READY state but requires the application to make a decision about which task needs to run first. Consequently, when ProcessKeyPress activates the DealCards and ShuffleCards tasks in the START_SHUFFLING case, it will be preempted. DealCards will return rapidly because it immediately enters the WAITING state. ShuffleCards will return after it has shuffled the cards once. This feature was added to eliminate the "quick finger" of the user. A quick finger event occurs when the player presses the shuffle switch fast enough to get a pulse but does not hold it long enough for sufficient pulses to produce shuffling. Remember, up to 10 pulses are required before the ShuffleAlarm expires the first time. Activating ShuffleCards immediately guarantees that at least one shuffling occurs whenever shuffling is requested. When ProcessKeyPress resumes, it waits for either a KEYPRESS or SHUFFLED event.

Because multiple key presses could theoretically occur between executions of the ProcessKeyPress task, I have modified keypad sampling to create a buffer of key presses. The most recent key pressed is returned from the routine GetKeyValue(). This routine replaces the global value keyValue that was used in earlier examples.

When ProcessKeyPress transitions into the WAITING state, the IOSampleShuffleSwitch task (Listing 6.3, in shuffle.c) begins to execute periodically.

Listing 6.3 Modified IOSampleShuffleSwitch task.

```
TASK(IOSampleShuffleSwitch)
{
static UINT8 timeout;
TickType tick;

  switch(ShuffleState){
    case SHUFFLE_HIGH:
      if(HWGetValue(&SHUFFLESWITCH)==INACTIVE){
        ShuffleState = SHUFFLE_LOW;
      }
      break;
    case SHUFFLE_LOW:
      if(HWGetValue(&SHUFFLESWITCH)==ACTIVE){
        timeout = SHUFFLE_SWITCH_OFF;
        if(GetAlarm(ShuffleAlarm,(TickRefType)tick) == E_OS_NOFUNC){
          SetAbsAlarm(ShuffleAlarm,5,3);
          strcpy(displayBuffer,"\fSHUFFLING -");
          ActivateTask(OutputDisplay);
        }
        ShuffleState = SHUFFLE_HIGH;
        IncrCounter(SHUFFLE_COUNTER);
      }
      else{
        if(timeout!=0){
          if(--timeout == 0){
            CancelAlarm(ShuffleAlarm);
            CancelAlarm(SampleShuffleSwitchAlarm);
            SetEvent(DealCards,SHUFFLED);
            SetEvent(ProcessKeyPress,SHUFFLED);
          }
        }
      }
```

```
            break;
        }
        TerminateTask();
    }
```

The only modification to this task occurs after the counter decrements to 0, which indicates that the player has stopped pressing the shuffling switch. The API service SetEvent() is called instead of activating the ShufflingComplete task as in Chapter 5.

```
StatusType SetEvent(TaskType task, EventMaskType event);
```

When SetEvent() is invoked, it first checks whether the task is in the SUSPENDED state. If it is, then the event is not set. When an extended task is moved from the SUSPENDED to the READY state, all events for the task are cleared by the OS. Consequently, any events that occurred while the task was suspended are irrelevant. If the task is not suspended, then the event or events are set for the task, which is automatically moved into the READY state if it is in the WAITING state. Depending on the scheduling mode of the invoking task, the scheduler might execute at this time.

The return values from this API service are

- E_OK if the event is set successfully,
- E_OS_ID in extended status mode if the value sent as the task is not a valid task,
- E_OS_ACCESS in extended status mode if the task is not an extended task, or
- E_OS_STATE in extended status mode if the task is in the SUSPENDED state.

This service can be invoked from either the task or the interrupt level but must not be invoked from a hook routine.

Two tasks are interested in a SHUFFLED event: ProcessKeyPress and DealCards. Consequently, SetEvent() is invoked twice to set the events for both of these tasks. Because both tasks are in the WAITING state, they are moved to the READY state, and the scheduler runs. Because IOSampleShuffleSwitch has a higher priority than the other tasks, it completes before they move to the RUNNING state.

When ProcessKeyPress enters the RUNNING state, it first checks which event released it from the WAITING state with the use of the GetEvent() API service, which determines the status of all events for a given task.

```
StatusType GetEvent(TaskType task, EventMaskRefType mask);
```

GetEvent() checks the events for the requested task and sets the bits in the variable pointed to by mask that correspond to all events set for the task. You can check the status of the event by ANDing the mask variable with the event as defined in the OIL configuration file.

The return values from this API service are

- E_OK if no error occurs,
- E_OS_ID in extended status mode if the task is not a valid task,
- E_OS_ACCESS in extended status mode if the task is not a valid extended task, or
- E_OS_STATE in extended status mode if the task is in the SUSPENDED state.

This service is available from the task or interrupt levels and from ErrorHook(), PreTaskHook(), and PostTaskHook().

ProcessKeyPress waits for two events during shuffling: KEYPRESS and SHUFFLED. If the task is moved from the WAITING state by a KEYPRESS event, it checks which key was pressed. If it was the # key, then shuffling is aborted by canceling the alarms that sample the shuffling switch then setting the ABORT_SHUFFLE event. This event signals to the DealCards task that shuffling was aborted and it should return to the prior state. If the SHUFFLED event occurs, ProcessKeyPress changes game state to the state of PLAYER_TURN and continues with the normal loop, in which it only waits for the KEYPRESS event. The PLAYER_TURN state is new, and defines how the program interprets key presses.

In both cases, after the event is serviced, ProcessKeyPress clears the event using ClearEvent().

```
StatusType ClearEvent(EventMaskType event);
```

→ Ref Lect 26

If it is not invoked prior to re-entering the WAITING state, the system thinks that the event has occurred and immediately returns from WaitEvent(). ClearEvent() clears the events defined in the event parameter, which is set the same way as mask in WaitEvent(). ClearEvent() is similar to WaitEvent() and can only be invoked from an extended task. It cannot be invoked from a basic task, at the interrupt level, or from an error hook. The possible return values for this service are

- E_OK if no error occurs,
- E_OS_ACCESS in extended status mode if the service is not called from an extended task, or
- E_OS_CALLEVEL in extended status mode if the service is called from the interrupt level.

6.3 Other Event Services

As with tasks and alarms, an event declaration function declares an event external to a module.

```
DeclareEvent(EventIdentifier);
```

The entry for EventIdentifier is the name of the event as it appears in the OIL configuration file.

6.4 Example Program

At this point, the example program is a fully functional game of Blackjack, which plays as follows.

- When the system first starts, the startup message is displayed.
- Pressing "D" shuffles the cards for the first time and deals the first set of cards.
- An "A" key press hits and a "B" stays.
- The dealer must hit at 16 and stay at 17. Aces count 11 for the dealer unless it causes the dealer to bust, then it counts 1.
- At any time, pressing "D" causes a reshuffle.
- When the hand is complete, pressing "C" deals the next hand. If fewer than 10 cards remain in the deck, the deck is reshuffled first.

Although the program is functionally complete, it has not been optimized, and because it is an example program, I have not included betting, doubling down, or splitting as features.

You can add this functionality if desired. There is a remote possibility that a change in the program could corrupt the deck of cards so that a card appears twice. This could occur if the deck is being shuffled and a card is dealt through preemption of the shuffling task. I address this problem by making the deck of cards a resource in Chapter 7. In addition, much time is spent sampling inputs, which I address with interrupts in Chapter 8.

6.4.1 Modules

The modules `startup.s`, `initspr.s`, `cinit.s`, `init.c`, `main.c`, `hw.c`, and `os.c` did not change in this chapter.

`debug.c` I modified the hook routines `PreTaskHook()` and `PostTaskHook()` to measure the time in the background loop. At any point, the system can be stopped and the amount of time that the background task has executed and not executed can be calculated based on ticks of the MPC555 real-time clock. This gives a very good approximation of the amount of idle time in the system. An additional function encapsulates as a 64-bit value the assembly language instructions required to obtain the real-time clock.

`cardgame.c` This module has changed extensively in order to support a true card game. A state machine was defined in which the state of the game is modified based on key presses and other events in the system. The `ProcessKeyPress` task was modified extensively, a number of new functions were added, and the `ShufflingComplete` task was removed.

`ProcessKeyPress` **task** This task was modified extensively to take different actions based on the transition that occurs when a key is pressed. The private function `CheckGameTransition()` determines the type of transition that occurs based on the current state of the game and the key that was pressed. Also, this task is now an extended task and will always reside in memory.

`DealCards` **task** This is the first task to run after shuffling is complete or when a new game starts. It clears the display and deals the first four cards; the first card dealt to the dealer is set up as the hole card and is not displayed.

`DealerTurn` **task** This task is activated after the player presses the B key to end the turn. It displays the dealer's hole card and takes additional cards based on the rule that the dealer must hit at 16 and stay at 17, as discussed earlier in this section. To simulate real play, the task deals one card a time and sets an alarm for two seconds before it deals another card.

- `GameTransitions CheckGameTransition(char keyPressed)` This local function determines which, if any, game transition is to occur when a key is pressed, based on the current state of the game. The transition that is to occur is returned from this function based on the value in `gameTransitionTable`. The table `gameTransitionTable` is defined statically as a table of game transitions based upon the current state of the game and the key that was pressed. If a valid transition is not defined, this routine returns `NO_ACTION`.

- `void EndGame(void)` This local function is executed by the `DealerTurn` task after the dealer's turn has completed. It displays the scores for both the dealer and the player and sets the game state to `normal` in anticipation of the next key press.

`dispdrv.c` This module was modified to add one more special character to the display: the character to be displayed as the back of a card. In addition, the following function was added.

`void SetDisplayPosition(UINT8 row, UINT8 column)` This function moves the cursor to an absolute display position defined by the `row` and the `column` parameters. The next string to be written to the display will start from this new position.

`keypad.c` This module was modified to create a buffer of key presses rather than just holding the last key pressed. The support to obtain data from the buffer and to encapsulate the key buffer was added.

`char GetKeyValue(void)` This routine simply pops the oldest key press from the buffer, updates the buffer pointers, and returns the value.

`carddeck.c` This module also has been extensively modified to provide more information about dealt cards. The `ShuffleCards` task is modified only slightly to initialize the `remainingCards` static variable to `52` when the deck reshuffles. However, `DealCard()` was rewritten extensively, and other functions were added.

`UINT8 DealCard(PlayerType player, UINT8 position, BOOLEAN up)` This routine now deals the next card based on the `player` parameter, which defines whether the next card goes to the dealer or the player, the `position` parameter, which defines which of the five positions of the dealer's or player's hand a card is dealt, and the `up` parameter, which defines whether the value or the back of the card is shown. The return value is now the value of the card that was dealt, from `0` to `51`. This task also invokes `DisplayCard()` to display the card.

`void DisplayCard(UINT8 card)` This routine copies the codes required to send the card to the display buffer. If `card` is `BLANK`, the back of the card is displayed.

`UINT8 GetCardValue(UINT8 card)` This function returns the value of the card that is passed in the `card` parameter. An Ace always has a value of `11`, and a face card always has a value of `10`.

`UINT8 GetRemainingCards(void)` This function simply returns the number of cards remaining in the deck. It is used to determine when the deck needs to be reshuffled.

`shuffle.c` This module was changed to use events instead of activating a task when shuffling is complete.

6.5 Exercises

1. Modify the task you created in the last chapter that keeps track of the time the program has been running. Make this an extended task with an event that is set when the alarm expires.
2. Modify the previous task to reset the time when a key is pressed. Use the event mechanism to signal this event from the task `ProcessKeyPress`.

6.6 Summary

Events differentiate basic from extended tasks and are used primarily as a method of synchronization between tasks. An event is a combination of an event and an extended task. An event differs from an event mask, which is a specific bit value in a mask. Multiple tasks can use the event mask to create a series of unique events.

Any task and interrupt service routine and most hook routines can set and check the status of an event. However, only the extended task that owns the event can wait for it to occur or clear the event.

7

Chapter 7

Resources

Most multitasking/multiprocessing OSs provide a method for sharing a resource between tasks or processes. The typical methods are semaphores and mutexes (MUTual EXclusion). A drawback of these methods is possible priority inversion or deadlock. The OSEK/VDX OS also provides a method for managing resources that avoids these drawbacks. In this chapter, I discuss the issues of priority inversion and deadlock, then introduce the method used by OSEK/VDX to eliminate these issues — the priority ceiling protocol. I then discuss how resources are managed using the scheduler as a resource and the limitations to using resources in a system.

7.1 Priority Inversion and Deadlock

OSEK/VDX was designed to work within the critical environment of the automobile, in which a Ctrl-Alt-Del key does not exist to stop a task or restart the system, and a missed deadline may cause a failure of the system. Priority inversion and deadlock are two situations that are unacceptable in an automobile.

Priority inversion is a situation in which a lower priority task preempts a higher priority task while a resource is locked, as shown in Figure 7.1 for a general RTOS. In this example, Task A has priority 1, B priority 2, and C priority 3. All tasks are fully preemptive. Tasks A and C both use shared resource R. Task A is running at the beginning of the example. The sequence of events is as follows.

1. Task A is running and locks the shared resource R.
2. Task C is activated and preempts task A.

3. Task C attempts to lock resource R. Because the resource is already locked, Task C is placed in the WAITING state. This is similar to the WAITING state in OSEK/VDX. Task A resumes where it was preempted.
4. Task B is activated and preempts task A. At this point, priority inversion has occurred: Task C has to wait for task B to complete only because of the locked resource. Task B has effectively preempted task C.
5. Task B completes and task A resumes processing.
6. Task A releases resource R. Task C can then preempt task A again and complete processing.
7. Task C completes and terminates. Task A resumes running.
8. Task A completes and terminates.

Figure 7.1 Priority inversion.

	SUSPENDED	WAITING	READY	RUNNING	UNLOCKED	LOCKED
1	B C			A	R	
2	B C			A		R
3	B		A	C		R
4	B	C		A		R
5		C	A	B		R
6	B	C		A		R
7	B		A	C	R	
8	B C			A	R	

PriorityInversion

Because of priority inversion, the amount of time that C can be delayed is nondeterministic. Without priority inversion, the maximum amount of time that C can be delayed can be calculated by taking the set of all lower priority tasks that share resource R. For each task, you can calculate the amount of time that resource R is locked by the task. The longest time that C can be delayed is the maximum time that any lower priority task has locked the resource.

Deadlock is a much more serious situation, where the locking of resources causes a conflict between two tasks, where each task has locked a resource that the other needs and neither task is allowed to complete. In an automotive or other critical embedded system, the possibility of killing the tasks that are deadlocked is not possible. Figure 7.2 illustrates deadlock in a general RTOS system.

Figure 7.2 Deadlock.

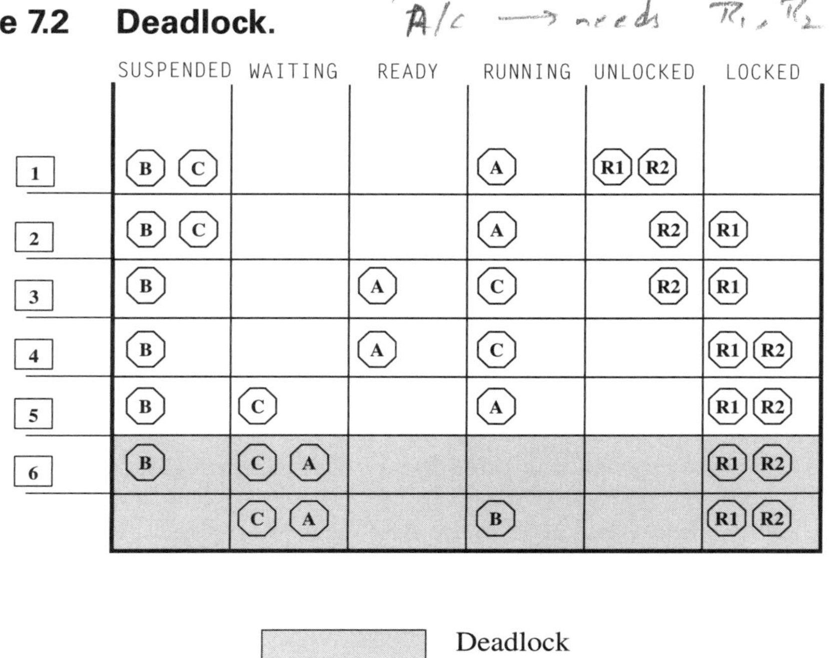

SUSPENDED
WAITING
READY
RUNNING
UNLOCKED
LOCKED
1
B C
A
R1 R2
2
B C
A
R2
R1
3
B
A
C
R2
R1
4
B
A
C
R1 R2
5
B
C
A
R1 R2
6
B
C A
R1 R2
C A
B
R1 R2
Deadlock

These are the same tasks discussed in the priority inversion example, except task A and task C share two resources — R1 and R2. The sequence of events that illustrate deadlock are as follows.

1. Task A locks resource R1.
2. Task C preempts task A.
3. Task C locks resource R2.
4. Task C attempts to lock resource R1. Because task A has already locked the resource, task C is placed in the `WAITING` state and task A resumes.
5. Task A attempts to lock resource R2. Because task C has already locked the resource, task A is placed in the `WAITING` state. At this point, both tasks A and C are `WAITING` and will never leave `WAITING` because neither resource can be released.
6. Task B is activated and runs normally.

Because of its nature, deadlock might not be discovered during normal testing and might occur only after the product has been released. Even worse, deadlock could be misdiagnosed as a partial failure of the system and could create large warranty costs before the actual failure is determined. This typically occurs when a technician replaces the "malfunctioning" component with a new component, which "fixes" the problem. When the original component is returned to the manufacturer for diagnosis, no problem is found because the act of removing power from the component resets the software and eliminates the deadlock.

Many manual methods can eliminate priority inversion and deadlock from a system. These usually entail strict programming standards that must be followed by the application programmer. As with any manual system, these methods are ripe for human error. The only surefire way of eliminating priority inversion and deadlock is to use an automatic method that is inherent to the OS. The priority ceiling protocol of OSEK/VDX is one such automatic method.

7.2 Priority Ceiling Protocol

In Chapter 4, I mentioned that tasks have a static priority defined at compile time that cannot be changed. One exception to this rule is the priority ceiling protocol. When a task locks a resource, it assumes the priority of the resource while that resource is locked. The functioning of the priority ceiling protocol is as follows.

1. A resource is defined in the OIL configuration file. This resource is then defined for a set of tasks in the application.
2. When the system is generated using this configuration file, the ceiling priority for the resource is set.
   (a) The ceiling priority will be greater than or equal to the highest priority of all the tasks that access this resource.
   (b) The ceiling priority will be less than the lowest priority of all tasks that do not access the resource and have a priority greater than the highest priority found in item (a) above.
3. When the task locks a resource, its priority is temporarily set to the ceiling priority of the resource.
4. When the task releases the resource, its priority is returned to the statically defined priority for the task.

With a priority ceiling protocol, priority inversion is eliminated because only one task is capable of locking a resource. In OSEK/VDX, it is not possible for a task to enter a `WAITING` state because of a resource locked by another task when it requests that resource. In the previous example, the priority of task A is set to the ceiling priority of the resource when it locks the resource. The ceiling priority will be at least `3` — the priority of task C. Consequently, tasks B or C will never preempt task A, and priority inversion cannot occur. The revised sequence of events is shown in Figure 7.3.

The sequence of events in this figure is as follows.

1. Task A locks resource R and has its priority raised to the ceiling priority of the resource.
2. Task C is activated. Because of the priority ceiling protocol, this task remains in the `READY` state.
3. Task B is activated. Again, because of the priority ceiling protocol, this task remains in the `READY` state.
4. Task A releases resource R and has its priority reverted to the static priority. Task C enters the `RUNNING` state.
5. Task C terminates and task B enters the `RUNNING` state.
6. Task B terminates and task A resumes running.
7. Task A terminates.

Figure 7.3 Priority ceiling and priority inversion.

	SUSPENDED	WAITING	READY	RUNNING	UNLOCKED	LOCKED
1	B C			A	R	
2	B C			A		R
3	B		C	A		R
4			C B	A		R
5			A B	C	R	
6	C		A	B	R	
7	B C			A	R	

As illustrated in Figure 7.3, the priority ceiling protocol allows tasks to be scheduled as expected. Because task C is activated before task B, it is proper for task B to remain in the READY state and not preempt task A. However, if task B is activated before task C but after task A locks the resource, it would be expected that task B preempts task A. With the priority ceiling protocol active, this preemption would not occur. This is one drawback of the priority ceiling protocol, where a lower priority task can inhibit a higher priority task that is lower than the ceiling priority. However, the time that a resource is locked should be minimized by good application design. When a task releases a resource, the scheduler runs immediately and the preemption will occur at that point. Because the time that a resource is locked can be calculated for all tasks, the maximum latency until preemption occurs can be addressed. This drawback of the priority ceiling protocol is less severe than the effect of priority inversion or deadlock and can be addressed in the application design.

Deadlock is eliminated in much the same way. Task A is set to the ceiling priority of resource R1 when it locks this resource. Again, the ceiling priority will be at least 3, the priority of task C. Task C will never preempt task A and will not lock resource R2. Task A can lock resource R2 successfully because task C is not allowed to preempt task A. The priority of Task A may be raised if the ceiling priority of R2 is greater than R1. The revised sequence of events from the previous example of deadlock is shown in Figure 7.4.

The sequence of events in Figure 7.4 is as follows.

1. Task A locks resource R1 and has its priority raised to the ceiling priority of the resource.
2. Task C is activated. Because of the priority ceiling protocol, this task remains in the READY state.
3. Task A locks resource R2 and has its priority set to the maximum ceiling priority of R1 and R2.

Figure 7.4 Priority ceiling and deadlock.

	SUSPENDED	WAITING	READY	RUNNING	UNLOCKED	LOCKED
1	B C			A	R1 R2	
2	B C			A	R2	R1
3	B		C	A	R2	R1
4	B		C	A		R1 R2
5	B		C	A	R2	R1
6	B		A	C	R1 R2	
7	B C			A	R1 R2	

4. Task A releases resource R2 and has its priority set to the ceiling priority of R1.
5. Task A releases resource R1 and has its priority reset to the statically defined priority of the task. At this point, scheduling occurs and task C preempts and begins running.
6. Task C terminates and task A resumes running.
7. Task A terminates.

Notice in steps 4 and 5 above that the resources were released in a last in, first out (LIFO) order. This is a requirement of the OSEK/VDX standard that must be followed by the application. In the extended status mode, a violation of the release order is identified by the OS.

The previous examples have focused on the required priority ceiling protocol for all tasks. The OSEK/VDX standard allows the optional extension of the priority ceiling protocol to interrupt levels. Because interrupt handling is processor dependent, the standard leaves a description of how software priorities and hardware interrupt levels are handled to the implementation. For example, one processor might be able to mask an interrupt in hardware, and another processor might be required to handle the interrupts in software. When a task is raised to an interrupt level priority, the implementation must mask all interrupts of lower priority.

The extension of the priority ceiling protocol for interrupts is handled as follows.

1. The set of all possible priorities is divided into two sections: the lower section is reserved for tasks and the upper section is reserved for Interrupt Service Routines (ISR). The upper section of priorities is referred to as virtual priorities because they function differently from the normal task priorities.
2. Each ISR is assigned a virtual priority in the configuration file.

3. The priority ceiling protocol, as seen from the application, appears to function exactly the same. However, because the ceiling priority for a resource could be a virtual priority, the effect to the implementation could be extensive. Interrupt masking is hidden from the application, but it will affect the time to lock resources and activate tasks.

As can be seen in these revised examples, the priority ceiling protocol effectively eliminates the problems of priority inversion and deadlock.

7.3 Managing Resources

To use a resource, define it in the OIL configuration file using the `RESOURCE` object. The `RESOURCE` object in the OIL definition does not have any attributes defined. However, in a specific implementation, optional attributes may be available. It is not recommended to use these optional attributes, since they limit portability. After the resource name has been defined, it must be assigned to every task that uses it. For the example program, I define the resource as the deck of cards with the name `CARDDECK`. Whenever an action is taken on the card deck, this resource is locked in three tasks — `ShuffleCards`, `DealCards`, and `ProcessKeyPress`. This resource must be locked before `DealCard()` is called to pull the next card off of the deck. The modified task definitions and the resource definition from the OIL configuration file are shown in Listing 7.1.

Listing 7.1 Resource definitions in the OIL file.

```
TASK DealCards {
        TYPE = EXTENDED;
        SCHEDULE = FULL;
        PRIORITY = 10;
        ACTIVATION = 1;
        AUTOSTART = FALSE;
        STACKSIZE = 64;
        SCHEDULE_CALL = FALSE;
        EVENT = { ABORT_SHUFFLE, SHUFFLED };
        RESOURCE = { CARDDECK };
  };
  TASK ShuffleCards {
        TYPE = BASIC;
        SCHEDULE = FULL;
        PRIORITY = 4;
        ACTIVATION = 1;
        AUTOSTART = FALSE;
        STACKSIZE = 64;
        SCHEDULE_CALL = FALSE;
        RESOURCE = { CARDDECK };
```

```
};
/***************************************************/
/*              Resources                          */
/***************************************************/

RESOURCE CARDDECK {
        /* No attributes defined */
};
```

In the definition of a task, an additional attribute, `RESOURCE`, is required. Like the `EVENT` attribute defined in the last chapter, `RESOURCE` is a multiple-reference attribute and can include multiple resources within the attribute. Once the resource has been defined, the tasks that use the resource must be modified. The modified `ShuffleCards` task in `carddeck.c` is shown in Listing 7.2.

Listing 7.2 `ShuffleCards` modified to use a resource.

```
TASK(ShuffleCards)
{
UINT8 count = (UINT8)(((UINT32)rand() * 100u) / RAND_MAX) + 1;
UINT8 location1, location2,tempcard;

   deckStart = cardDeck;
   remainingCards = 52;
   GetResource(CARDDECK);
   while((count--)>0){
      location1 = ((UINT32)rand() * 52u) / RAND_MAX;
      if(location1==52) location1 = 51;
      location2 = ((UINT32)rand() * 52u) / RAND_MAX;
      if(location2==52) location2 = 51;
      tempcard = cardDeck[location1];
      cardDeck[location1] = cardDeck[location2];
      cardDeck[location2] = tempcard;
   }
   ReleaseResource(CARDDECK);
   strcpy(displayBuffer,busyDisplay[busyLocation++]);
   if(busyLocation == 4) busyLocation = 0;
   ActivateTask(OutputDisplay);
   TerminateTask();
}
```

The CARDDECK resource was defined to guarantee that the deck of cards is not corrupted by dealing a card while the deck is being shuffled. This could occur under the following scenario.

1. The shuffle switch toggles from low to high and SHUFFLE_COUNTER increments to the point where ShuffleAlarm is triggered. This activates the ShuffleCards task.
2. The shuffle switch is immediately released by the player.
3. Because of preemption, ShuffleCards does not run immediately, but IOSampleShuffleSwitch continues to execute.
4. ShuffleCards finally begins and shuffles the cards. The point in the shuffle when a card has been moved from one location to another and now exists temporarily in two locations is reached when the task is preempted by IOSampleShuffleSwitch.

   ```
   tempcard = cardDeck[location1];
          cardDeck[location1] = cardDeck[location2];
             <<Preemption occurs here>>
          cardDeck[location2] = tempcard;
   ```

   The two locations of the duplicated card will be referred to as the original and the new locations.
5. IOSampleShuffleSwitch identifies that the switch has been released and sets the SHUFFLED event. This releases the DealCards task from the WAITING state.
6. In the example program, DealCards has a higher priority than ShuffleCards. It executes next and deals the cards to start the game. Among the cards that have been dealt is the card that exists in two places. The original location is dealt.
7. ShuffleCards resumes and replaces the card at the original location with the shuffled card. However, because the original location has already been dealt to a player, the shuffled card is not used.
8. Later in the game, the new location of the card is used and appears again in the game, causing a failure.

This situation has a low probability of occurring, but as the program is expanded (i.e., to add sound, animation, etc.), the probability increases. If the deck of cards is defined as the CARDDECK resource, the priority ceiling protocol eliminates the possibility of a corrupted deck because DealCards is never allowed to preempt ShuffleCards. However, IOSampleShuffleSwitch will still preempt ShuffleCards because it has a higher priority.

The astute reader will notice that another method to eliminate this situation is possible. If the priorities are changed such that ShuffleCards has a higher priority than DealCards, the corruption will not occur. Although this could be a short-term solution, it might not be possible in the long run as the application matures and grows. Only resource management guarantees that the deck of cards will not be corrupted by multiple tasks.

Resource management is accomplished with the use of two API services: GetResource() and ReleaseResource(). In the ShuffleCards task, these two services surround the section of the task in which the card deck is shuffled. The GetResource() service locks the resource.

```
StatusType GetResource(ResourceType resource);
```

It compares the priority of the calling task with the ceiling priority of the resource. If the ceiling priority is greater than the priority of the calling task, the calling task is raised to the higher priority. The possible return values from the service are

- `E_OK` if no error occurs,
- `E_OS_ID` in extended status mode if the resource parameter is invalid,
- `E_OS_ACCESS` in extended status mode if the resource is already occupied by another task or ISR, or
- `E_OS_ACCESS` in extended status mode if the priority statically assigned to the calling task is greater than the calculated ceiling priority.

`GetResource()` can be invoked from the task or the interrupt level; it cannot be invoked from any of the hook routines.

`ReleaseResource()` is recommended to appear in the same function as `GetResource()` and exits the critical section that was entered using `GetResource()`.

```
StatusType ReleaseResource(ResourceType resource);
```

The return values in this service are

- `E_OK` if no error occurs,
- `E_OS_ID` in extended status mode if the resource parameter is invalid,
- `E_OS_NOFUNC` in extended status mode if the resource is not occupied by another task or ISR,
- `E_OS_NOFUNC` in extended status mode if another resource must be released prior to the requested resource, or
- `E_OS_ACCESS` in extended status mode if the priority statically assigned to the calling task is greater than the calculated ceiling priority.

`ReleaseResource()` can be invoked from the task or the interrupt level; it cannot be invoked from any of the hook routines.

7.3.1 Standard Resource

In any OSEK/VDX implementation, there is one resource that is required to be provided by default. This is the OS scheduler, which appears as a resource to the application. The predefined resource RES_SCHEDULER is available to any application that requires the critical section of code to not be preempted by another task. While the scheduler is locked, interrupts are still received and processed. The interrupted task, however, is temporarily considered to be a non-preemptive task and will not be preempted when the ISR completes.

7.3.2 Resource Limitations

The use of resources has a number of limitations, some of these limitations have been discussed earlier, but I will cover them here again.

1. Nested access to a resource is strictly forbidden.
2. The application cannot call `TerminateTask()`, `ChainTask()`, or `WaitEvent()` while a resource is locked. If the resource is still locked in standard status mode, the behavior is undefined.

3. If a task locks multiple resources, the resources must be released in a LIFO order.
4. Critical sections in the application should be kept as short as possible to limit the amount of time that the priority ceiling protocol is in effect. This limits the latency of tasks with priorities between the priority of the task that locks the resource and the ceiling priority of the resource.

7.3.3 Other Resource Services

Similar to task, alarm, and event functions, `DeclareResource()` declares a resource external to a module.

```
DeclareResource(ResourceIdentifier);
```

The entry for `ResourceIdentifier` is the name of the resource as it appears in the OIL configuration file.

7.4 Example Program

7.4.1 Modules

The only modules that have been changed in this chapter are `cardgame.c` and `carddeck.c`.

`cardgame.c` Whenever `DealCard()` is called in the `ProcessKeyPress` and `DealCards` tasks, the function call is surrounded by the locking and unlocking functions `GetResource()` and `ReleaseResource()`. The resource is locked here instead of in the function because the priority ceiling protocol requires a task to use a resource, not a function. If locking and releasing were to occur in the function, it would be very difficult to identify which tasks used the resource. It is also a good practice to lock and release a resource at the task level.

`carddeck.c` As with the previous module, the only change here is in the `ShuffledCards` task, where the `CARDDECK` resource is locked.

7.5 Exercises

1. Create a new task called `DealerCheat` that resides in `carddeck.c` and has a priority higher than `DealCards`. In this task, pull a card from the deck into a static variable that the dealer can use later. It also should lock the `CARDDECK` resource when it is adjusting the deck. Activate this task after the dealer has dealt the first card in the `DealCards` task. Run the program and observe the action of the tasks.
2. Define the display as a resource and lock the resource everywhere the `displayBuffer` global variable is updated. This includes the `OutputDisplay` task. In tasks where the `displayBuffer` variable is modified, make sure that the task activation for `OutputDisplay` is contained within the resource locking.

7.6 Summary

In this chapter, I discussed the resource management method in the OSEK/VDX OS, and I defined the priority ceiling protocol and explained how it eliminates priority inversion and deadlock. Resource management is usually critical in any real-time control system where multiple tasks can access the same resource. This resource could be a piece of hardware, such as an I2C or SPI serial communication port that is connected to multiple high-speed devices and requires handshaking (when the time to transmit a message is short, defining a port as a resource works well), or a software entity, such as the deck of cards in the example program.

The OSEK/VDX method works well where a shared resource needs to be locked for a short period of time. If a resource must be locked for an extended period of time, such as during an EEPROM erase or write, the application developer must devise another method.

Chapter 8

Interrupts

The next major object in the OSEK/VDX OS is the interrupt. In many embedded applications, interrupts are critical interfaces with external asynchronous events. Examples of interrupts that can be found in embedded systems are real-time clocks, sensors that send a stream of pulses, and interrupts based on an action by the user. In this chapter, I discuss the interrupt types identified in the OSEK/VDX OS standard and the services that manage the interrupts.

8.1 Types of Interrupts

OSEK/VDX defines three types of interrupts by ISR category: 1, 2, and 3. ISR categories 1 and 2 are required in all implementations, whereas category 3 is optional in the latest version of the OS (v2.1 revision 1).

The fastest ISR is a category 1 interrupt, which does not require OS API calls. ISRs in this category typically generate an output signal, such as a frequency signal or a pulse width-modulated signal in a microcontroller that does not have an advanced timer management unit. Because these ISRs do not interact with the OS, they have the least overhead of any ISR category.

ISR category 2 interrupts call API services. These interrupts typically require a counter to be incremented, a task to be activated, an event to be set, or a message to be sent. Examples of these interrupts include receiving and counting a series of pulses, receiving a serial communication message, or identifying an external user event.

The final ISR is a category 3 interrupt, which is a combination of the first two. Most often, this interrupt does not have to call an API service, although occasionally it does. Access to the API service is allowed within a block encompassed by two additional API services: `EnterISR()` and `LeaveISR()`. An example of an ISR category 3 interrupt is the transmission of a message over a serial link. The serial communication driver interrupts software after the transmission of every byte of data. If there is still data to be transmitted, the ISR simply transmits the next byte of data and returns. However, after the last byte is transmitted, you might need to set an event indicating that it has occurred, in which case, the only time an API service is called is after the last byte has been transmitted. Therefore, it is more efficient to incur the overhead required for an API service access only when needed.

8.2 Interrupt Services

The OSEK/VDX OS provides multiple services to manage interrupts, most of which control masking responses to interrupts. The first two services — `EnterISR()` and `LeaveISR()` — were discussed in the previous section. Neither service can be used at task level or in a hook routine.

```
void EnterISR(void);
```

`EnterISR()` can be invoked only from within a category 3 ISR. This service tells the OS that an interrupt has been entered that will request an API service at some point. The OS sets up the necessary conditions to handle API calls from an interrupt. How this situation is handled is highly specific to the CPU architecture, which is a complication to the developer of the implementation but is transparent to the application.

```
void LeaveISR(void);
```

`LeaveISR()` also can be invoked only within a category 3 ISR. It is the counterpart to `EnterISR()` and must be the last instruction executed in the ISR after `EnterISR()` has been invoked. If `EnterISR()` has not been invoked, as in the previous example where the ISR dumps a buffer to a serial port and the buffer is not empty, `LeaveISR()` must not be invoked because the OS might or might not return from `LeaveISR()`, depending on the status of the system, which can change in response to the API functions invoked in the ISR.

Neither of these functions returns a `StatusType` because in many microcontrollers, it is impossible to determine from whence the service was invoked. Consequently, there is no way to know that the service was called from a task or hook routine and return `E_OS_CALLEVEL`, which is the expected return for a call from the wrong level.

In the example program, the `IOSampleShuffleSwitch` task has been eliminated and replaced with the ISR category 3 routine `IOShuffleSwitchISR` shown in Listing 8.1.

This routine is triggered on any rising edge of the shuffle switch input. Because this is a valid input only when the system is in the shuffling state, the ISR first checks for this state after resetting the interrupt. This switch is on the MDASM12 port of the MPC555, and the status register that is reset is defined in `register.h`. If the game state is `GAME_SHUFFLING`, the edge is processed and the counter is incremented. If the game state is any other state, the ISR immediately returns to the calling routine.

Listing 8.1 Shuffle switch ISR.

```
INTERRUPT void IOShuffleSwitchISR(void)
{
TickType tick;
UINT32 temp;
```

```
    temp = mios1Int.mios1sr0;
    mios1Int.mios1sr0 = ~(0x1000);
    if(GetGameState() == GAME_SHUFFLING){
        EnterISR();
        if(GetAlarm(ShuffleAlarm,(TickRefType)tick) == E_OS_NOFUNC){
            SetAbsAlarm(ShuffleAlarm,5,3);
            strcpy(displayBuffer,"\fSHUFFLING -");
            ActivateTask(OutputDisplay);
        }
        CancelAlarm(ShufflingCompleteAlarm);
        SetRelAlarm(ShufflingCompleteAlarm,1000,0);
        IncrCounter(SHUFFLE_COUNTER);
        LeaveISR();
    }
}
```

I also have added an alarm — ShufflingCompleteAlarm — that replaces SampleShuffleSwitchAlarm. This alarm is reset each time an edge is received. When it expires, the shuffling switch is considered released and the ShufflingComplete task (Listing 8.2) is activated. It manually sets the two events set previously in IOSampleShuffleSwitch because an alarm can only activate one task or set one event.

Listing 8.2 ShufflingComplete task.

```
TASK(ShufflingComplete)
{
    SetEvent(DealCards,SHUFFLED);
    SetEvent(ProcessKeyPress,SHUFFLED);
    TerminateTask();
}
```

One important difference between the example here and the code on the accompanying CD is that the MPC555 processor has only one interrupt vector for all seven external and 24 internal interrupts. The OSEKWorks BSP has created a very efficient interrupt dispatch routine, but to optimize it, interrupt category 3 is not supported. Because this category is optional, this is not a problem; however, in the sample code, I commented the calls to EnterISR() and LeaveISR() because calling the services twice in the same ISR does very nasty things to the program.

In a category 3 interrupt, the routine is a normal ISR with the addition of the EnterISR() and LeaveISR() API services. To define a category 2 ISR, the application must use the following method.

```
ISR (ISRname)
{
}
```

The hardware used with the example program has a keyboard decoding chip that provides an interrupt when a key is pressed. I used this capability to eliminate the `IOSampleKeypad` task, and I replaced it with the category 2 ISR `IOReadKeypadISR` (Listing 8.3) because the interrupt always activates the `ProcessKeyPress` task. The ISRs also must be defined in the OIL configuration file prior to use (Listing 8.4).

Listing 8.3 Keypad ISR.

```
ISR(IOReadKeypadISR)
{
char tempKey;

   usiuReg.sipend = 0x00800000;  /* Clear Interrupt Bit */
   tempKey = HWGetValue(&KEYPAD);
   if(tempKey != 0){
      *keyBufferEnd = tempKey;
      if((++keyBufferEnd) == keyBuffer + KEY_BUFFER_SIZE){
         keyBufferEnd = keyBuffer;
      }
      SetEvent(ProcessKeyPress,KEYPRESS);
   }
}
```

The ISR object in the OIL configuration file has three possible attributes. The first, `CATEGORY`, is required and has the value `1`, `2`, or `3`. The second attribute, `RESOURCE`, is optional and has exactly the same format as the `RESOURCE` attribute for the `TASK` object definition discussed in Chapter 7. The final attribute, `ACCESSOR`, is also optional and is discussed in Chapter 9, "Interprocess Communication." For the example ISR, I am not concerned with resources or interprocess messages.

The remaining API services associated with interrupts are concerned with masking interrupts and defining critical sections in application code. The services are divided into four categories.

Listing 8.4 ISR OIL definition.

```
/*****************************************************/
/*              ISRs                                 */
/*****************************************************/

ISR IOReadKeypadISR {
        CATEGORY = 2;
};
```

```
ISR IOShuffleSwitchISR {
        CATEGORY = 3;
};
```

The first category of API services is a query category in which the application can check which interrupts are enabled or disabled. This category has one service, `GetInterruptDescriptor()`.

```
StatusType GetInterruptDescriptor(IntDescriptorRefType descriptor);
```

For most implementations, this service sets the bits in the variable pointed to by the `descriptor` reference to correspond to the current state of the interrupts. If an interrupt is enabled, the bit corresponding to that interrupt is set to `1`; otherwise, it is set to `0`. The mapping of the interrupt sources to the bits in the descriptor variable is dependent on both processor and implementation. For example, a powerful 32-bit processor with more interrupt sources than there are bits in a machine word would result in a completely different definition and interpretation of `IntDescriptorRefType` and would include an implementation-specific service to control the interrupts individually. Use of `GetInterruptDescriptor()` should be limited to modules in an application that are specific to the microcontroller used, such as hardware device drivers.

This service always returns an `E_OK` status in both standard and extended modes. This service can be invoked from the task or interrupt level and from `ErrorHook()`, `PreTaskHook()`, and `PostTaskHook()`.

To debug the system, I modified `ErrorHook()` (Listing 8.5), where errors are logged. In the modified routine, I now obtain the current interrupt descriptor and save it in the error log array. Because this routine is only used to debug a specific application on a given microcontroller and a specific OSEK/VDX implementation, portability of the code is not a concern. In this hook routine, I have explicitly checked if the routine is called recursively, using the flag recursive. This is recommended if the OS version is 2.0 or earlier. In version 2.1, the OS is not allowed to call `ErrorHook()` recursively.

Listing 8.5 Modified `ErrorHook()` routine.

```
void ErrorHook(StatusType error)
{
static UINT8 recursive=0;

   if(recursive==0){
      recursive=1;
      nextErrorLog->error = error;
      GetTaskID(&nextErrorLog->task);
      GetInterruptDescriptor(&nextErrorLog->descriptor);
      ++nextErrorLog;
```

```
        if(nextErrorLog > errorLog + sizeof(errorLog))
        {
            nextErrorLog = errorLog;
        }
    }
    recursive=0;
}
```

The second category of interrupt API services is a pair of interrupt masking services that are similar to the services provided in most OSs — `EnableInterrupt()` and `DisableInterrupt()`.

```
StatusType DisableInterrupt(IntDescriptorType descriptor);
StatusType EnableInterrupt(IntDescriptorType descriptor);
```

These services take the information passed in the `descriptor` parameter and either enable or disable the corresponding interrupt sources. If the bit in `descriptor` is set to 1, that interrupt source is either enabled or disabled. If the bit is set to 0, then the interrupt source is not affected. As with the service `GetInterruptDescriptor()`, `DisableInterrupt()` and `EnableInterrupt()` are specific to the particular microcontroller hardware and the OSEK/VDX implementation chosen. Their use should also be limited in the application.

The return value from these services is

- `E_OK` if no error occurs or
- `E_OS_NOFUNC` in extended status mode if at least one interrupt source is not enabled or disabled, depending on the service.

These services can be invoked from the task or the interrupt level, but they cannot be invoked from any hook routines.

If the current state of the interrupts has to be restored after the critical section, it must be stored temporarily in a local variable using `GetInterruptDescriptor()` before disabling the interrupts.

The third category of interrupt masking services allows you to mask all interrupt sources for a critical section and then restore all interrupts to the prior status automatically. The two functions provided, new to the version 2.1 OS specification, are `EnableAllInterrupts()` and `DisableAllInterrupts()`.

```
void DisableAllInterrupts( void );
void EnableAllInterrupts( void );
```

When `DisableAllInterrupts()` is invoked, the OS automatically saves the states of all interrupts. These states are restored when `EnableAllInterrupts()` is invoked. At this point, the application has entered a critical section. The OS standard requires you to observe the following limitations within the application.

- Your application must not invoke any API services from within the critical section.
- You cannot nest critical sections using these two services. If a nesting could occur (as is possible in a library function), the implementation should ignore it by using the next category of interrupt masking services that disables all ISR 2 or 3 interrupts.

These services may be called from the task or the interrupt level, but cannot be called from any hook routines.

In the example program, I modified one of the functions to enter a critical section while the display is updated; the `OutputDisplay` task calls `OutputNewDisplay()` (Listing 8.6).

Listing 8.6 `OutputNewDisplay()` with critical section.

```
void OutputNewDisplay(void)
{
   UINT8 *displayControl = DISPLAY_CONTROL_LOCATION;
   UINT8 *display = DISPLAY_BUFFER_LOCATION;
   UINT8 i,outputRow;
   UINT8 translateRow = 0;

   *displayControl = 0x01;
   wait(30000);
   DisableAllInterrupts();
   while(translateRow < MAX_DISPLAY_ROWS)
   {
      outputRow = RowTranslation[translateRow++];
      for(i=0;i<MAX_DISPLAY_LINE_LENGTH;i++)
      {
         *display = displayMessage[outputRow][i];
         wait(1000);
      }
   }
   i=((cursorPosition.row&0x01)*0x40) +
     ((cursorPosition.row&0x02)/2*MAX_DISPLAY_LINE_LENGTH) +
         cursorPosition.column;
   *displayControl = 0x80+i;
   wait(1000);
   EnableAllInterrupts();
}
```

In the task, I added `DisableAllInterrupts()` and `EnableAllInterrupts()` to create a critical section while the routine writes the current display value to the display. This critical section was added to ensure that the display is completely updated and not preempted in the middle of an update. If an interrupt occurs and the task is preempted, one-half of the display can be modified before a noticeable pause occurs and the rest of the display is updated. This interruption appears as a flicker and can be annoying to the user, so the critical section eliminates that possibility.

The fourth category of interrupt masking services disables all interrupts of category 2 or 3. This pair of services, SuspendOSInterrupts() and ResumeOSInterrupts(), have the following function prototypes.

```
void SuspendOSInterrupts(void);
void ResumeOSInterrupts(void);
```

When SuspendOSInterrupts() is invoked, it saves the current state of all interrupts. This state is restored when ResumeOSInterrupts() is invoked. Unlike the previous category of interrupt masking services, these two services can be nested. The original states of all interrupts that were saved when SuspendOSInterrupts() was first invoked will be restored when the final call to ResumeOSInterrupts() is performed. How this is actually performed in an implementation is dependent on the characteristics of the microprocessor.

As with the previous category of interrupt masking services, the application is not allowed to invoke any API service while in this critical section. These services can be called from the task or the interrupt level but cannot be called from any hook routines.

One point made in the OSEK/VDX OS standard is that these two services are only intended to disable category 2 and 3 interrupts. However, if the implementation cannot disable these interrupts in a limited and efficient manner, other interrupts could be disabled, which indicates that there might be no differences between these final two categories of interrupt masking services in some implementations.

In the OutputDisplay task described with the previous category of services, the critical section also can be realized using this category of interrupt masking services. Because ISR category 1 interrupts are typically very short, this category of interrupts should not affect the user's perception of the display update.

8.3 Startup Operation

When the OS first starts, it performs a series of functions as described in Chapters 1 through 3. Prior to executing the first user task, the final function performed enables the user interrupts. This is accomplished with the use of an application-specific constant defined by the developer to enable the interrupts. This constant, INITIAL_INTERRUPT_DESCRIPTOR, is specific to both the application and the implementation. In this constant, any bit set to 1 enables the corresponding interrupt source. Essentially, the OS uses this constant as a parameter that is passed to EnableInterrupt().

8.4 Example Program

The example program now is optimized to use the power of interrupts to eliminate sampling of the shuffling switch and keypad. If I were to apply a profiler to the software at this point, I would observe that almost all of the time the software is running, it is in the background task. The only time the application runs is after the player presses a key and a calculation is made. In an application running in a battery-operated device, the background task would perform power management duties during these idle times to conserve the batteries.

8.4.1 Modules

The modules startup.s, initspr.s, cinit.s, init.c, hw.c, and carddeck.c were not modified.

main.c This module was modified to add a specific initialization function required by the board support package provided by Wind River. Init_ExtISRs() initializes the Wind River external ISR routines to a dummy ISR routine that traps spurious interrupts.

debug.c This module was modified to allow the ErrorHook() hook routine to log the current status of the interrupt mask to the error log. In addition, a special flag was added to avoid recursive calls of ErrorHook() because the current version (as of the writing of this book) of OSEKWorks only meets the OSEK/VDX OS v2.0 requirements. In the version 2.1 specification, recursive calls to this hook routine are prevented — the OS will not call ErrorHook() if an error occurs while it is running. The application must check service return values to trap an OS error in a service called from within ErrorHook().

cardgame.c This module was modified to eliminate the alarm SampleShuffleSwitchAlarm, which is not needed when using interrupts. In addition, one function was added to support the ISR.

```
GameState GetGameState(void)
```

This function simply returns the current state of the blackjack game, which is used in the ISR.

dispdrv.c OutputNewDisplay() now disables all interrupts while writing to the display, as discussed in this chapter.

keypad.c This module was extensively modified to support an interrupt-based keypad versus a sampled keypad. The IOSampleKeypad task was replaced by the ISR IOReadKeypadISR and was significantly shortened. In addition, one new function was added.

```
void InitKeypad(InitType type)
```

This initialization function is invoked by InitSystem() and registers the ISR in the OSEKWorks-specific board support package. The initialization of the registers required to handle an interrupt is performed during startup within InitReg16() and InitReg32() using the tables defined in init.cfg with the names InitHardwareRegs16 and InitHardwareRegs32.

os.c This module was modified to add DisableAllInterrupts() and EnableAllInterrupts(), which are new to version 2.1 of the OS. In order to test the application code using these services, I had to simulate the function because OSEKWorks v4.0 only supports OSEK/VDX OS v2.0. When the new version of OSEKWorks is released, these two services will have to be removed or the build will fail at the link stage.

shuffle.c This module was also modified extensively to support the interrupts generated by the shuffle switch.

```
void InitShuffleSwitch(InitType type)
```

This initialization routine was modified to remove the initial state of the input and to register the ISR to the OSEKWorks board support package.

`IOShuffleSwitchISR` This ISR, which was discussed in this chapter, replaces the prior task, `IOSampleShuffleSwitch`, and extensively shortens the code. The `INTERRUPT` modifier is not defined because the board support package does not support ISR category 3 interrupts. However, if this routine is used on a different processor, the `INTERRUPT` macro should be defined as the modifier for an interrupt routine for the specific compiler. The definition for `INTERRUPT` is found in `os.h`.

`ShufflingComplete` **task** This task is activated when `ShufflingCompleteAlarm` times out, indicating that the switch is released.

8.4.2 Exercises

1. In an exercise in Chapter 5, a switch was added and the number of times that it was depressed was counted. Make sure that the switch is connected to an input that can generate an interrupt when the switch is depressed and modify the routine to be an ISR.
2. Set a breakpoint in `OutputNewDisplay()` after the interrupts are disabled. Also set a breakpoint at the entrance to the keypad ISR. Press a key on the keypad and then step through the rest of the routine. Verify that the interrupt does not occur until after `EnableAllInterrupts()` is invoked.
3. Review the source code and determine if there are other critical sections that need to be added.

8.5 Summary

In this chapter, I discussed how interrupts are handled in the OSEK/VDX OS. The categories of ISRs were introduced and the requirements for each category, with respect to the OS, was described. In addition, the many different methods of enabling and disabling interrupts and determining current interrupt status were discussed.

Interrupts are the most powerful method of optimizing throughput in the application. However, when interrupts are introduced into an application, the possibility of problems increases because it is very difficult to debug interrupt-driven software. The example program uses interrupts for all user inputs because the application will probably be installed in a battery-driven system, so it is very important to conserve battery power. The developer of the application will have to make the trade-off decision about using interrupts — complexity versus efficiency.

9

Chapter 9

Interprocess Communication

The final OS objects are interprocess communication, or messaging, objects that are actually part of the communication (COM) standard. In version 2.1 of the OS standard, any OS that is OSEK/VDX-compliant must support, at a minimum, conformance class A from the COM standard. Some implementations could include communication conformance class B, but this chapter describes the attributes of conformance class A only and the services available to support this level of interprocess communication.

The OSEK/VDX COM standard is very complex and is covered in detail in Part 2. However, some of the features, as they apply to the minimal requirements of the OS, are introduced here.

9.1 Communication Model

The OSEK/VDX COM standard supports both interprocess and interprocessor communication. Many different features are required to support this wide range of communication. The communication model for the limited requirements of a conformance class A implementation is as follows.

Unqueued messages Messages are not queued under a conformance class A implementation. This means that a message can be read by an application any number of times and the data received last is returned every time; that is, it is not consumed by being read.

With- and without-copy In a with-copy scenario, messages are sent and received using a copy of the message object that is available to the application. This allows the application to access the message data without concern to corrupting the data or creating inconsistent data. In the without-copy scenario, the application accesses the message object directly, and a concern arises about corruption of the data. Conformance class B provides mechanisms to address this concern, and will be discussed in Part 2.

Asynchronous communication All communication is performed asynchronously. When a task sends a message, the API service returns immediately to the invoking task and does not wait until the message is successfully transferred to the receiving task. The application determines when the message has been sent successfully through the notification method of the OSEK/VDX COM standard.

1:1 and 1:many messaging Messages are sent by one task, but they can be received by one or a multitude of tasks. Inputs sampled and filtered by one task but used by many tasks use 1:many messaging, often referred to as 1:*n*.

9.2 Notification

The OSEK/VDX COM standard has five notification classes through which the communication system notifies an application of a message status. Only notification class 1 is available for conformance class A. Class 1 notification is also referred to as message reception notification. For internal communication, which is the only kind of communication supported by the OS, notification occurs as soon as the message is transmitted.

Four types of mechanisms are available for notification: Task, Event, Callback Routine, and Flag. Task and Event notification require an OS that supports these mechanisms. Task refers to the mechanism that activates the task when the notification occurs. Event refers to the mechanism that sets an event when the notification occurs.

The OSEK/VDX COM standard was intended as a stand-alone specification and does not require an OSEK/VDX-compatible OS to support its lower conformance classes. Consequently, the communication component can be used in an application that does not support activating tasks or setting events. To handle this eventuality, the Callback Routine and Flag notification mechanisms were added to support more general RTOSs or applications without an RTOS, such as a cyclic executive. Because this chapter discusses the use of messages within the OSEK/VDX OS, I do not discuss these mechanisms until Part 2, which covers the Communication Specification.

To demonstrate the use of messages and notifications, I will modify the example program and create a simple message that is sent to the display. This replaces the `displayBuffer` global variable, which was used as a temporary location for the message. I will use the messaging capability of the OS to perform most of the work. First, I create the definition of the message in the OIL configuration file (Listing 9.1) and modify whichever task uses the message.

The `MESSAGE` object defines a message structure to the application. The first attribute is `TYPE`. For conformance class A, the only type available is `UNQUEUED`. For other conformance classes, `QUEUED` is also available and is discussed in Part 2.

Listing 9.1 Message and task OIL definitions.

```
TASK OutputDisplay {
        TYPE = BASIC;
        SCHEDULE = FULL;
        PRIORITY = 12;
        ACTIVATION = 1;
        AUTOSTART = FALSE;
        ACCESSOR=SENT {
            MESSAGE = DisplayMessage;
            WITHOUTCOPY = TRUE;
            ACCESSNAME = displayMirror;
            };
        STACKSIZE = 128;
        SCHEDULE_CALL = FALSE;
  };

  TASK OutputDisplayBuffer {
        TYPE = EXTENDED;
        SCHEDULE = NON;
        PRIORITY = 14;
        ACTIVATION = 1;
        AUTOSTART = TRUE;
        ACCESSOR=RECEIVED {
            MESSAGE = DisplayMessage;
            WITHOUTCOPY = FALSE;
            ACCESSNAME = displayMirrorTemp;
            };
        STACKSIZE = 128;
        SCHEDULE_CALL = FALSE;
        EVENT = { BUFFER_CHANGED, DISPLAY_READY };
  };
/*************************************************************************/
/*          Messages                                                     */
/*************************************************************************/

  MESSAGE DisplayMessage {
        TYPE = UNQUEUED;
        CDATATYPE= "DISPLAY_MESSAGE_TYPE"
        ACTION=SETEVENT {
```

```
                TASK = OutputDisplayBuffer;
                EVENT = BUFFER_CHANGED;
                };
            LENGTH = 80;
            ALIGNMENT = 1;
            USAGE = SEND_RECEIVE;
            ACCESSNAMES = { displayMirrorTemp, displayMirror };
    };
```

The second attribute in the MESSAGE object definition is CDATATYPE, a string that describes the data type of the message. This can be either a standard C data type such as int or char, or it can be a user-defined type such as DISPLAY_MESSAGE_TYPE, as in this example, which is defined in dispdrv.h. It defines a local copy of the message that appears on the display. This type definition defines a structure of one character array of 80 characters, as shown in Listing 9.2. The constants MAX_DISPLAY_ROWS and MAX_DISPLAY_LINE_LENGTH define the number of rows and lines on the display.

Listing 9.2 DISPLAY_BUFFER_TYPE type definition.

```
typedef struct DISPLAY_MESSAGE_TYPEtag {
   char message[MAX_DISPLAY_ROWS*MAX_DISPLAY_LINE_LENGTH];
   }DISPLAY_MESSAGE_TYPE;
```

The final attribute in the MESSAGE object definition can appear multiple times in each object definition. The ACTION attribute defines the action or actions that are taken when the message is transmitted according to notification class 1. Under conformance class A, this attribute can take on one of four values: NONE, ACTIVATETASK, SETEVENT, or CALLBACK. The fifth notification mechanism, FLAG, is not available in conformance class A.

The NONE attribute value typically is used when a message is buffered by the OS and the current value will be polled by other tasks. The ACTIVATETASK attribute value indicates that the message will use the notification method of activating a task when the message is sent. This action has one parameter, TASK, which is set to the name of the task to be activated. This task must be defined within the current OIL configuration file.

SETEVENT indicates that an OS event is set when the message is transmitted. This action requires two parameters: TASK and EVENT. TASK is set to the name of the task that owns the event, and EVENT is set to the name of the event. Both the task and the event must be defined elsewhere in the OIL configuration file.

CALLBACK, as mentioned previously, is used primarily with applications that do not have an OSEK/VDX-compliant OS. I cover this attribute in Part 2.

Within the TASK object definition, one additional attribute is required whenever a message is sent or received by the task. The ACCESSOR attribute defines how the task accesses the message. Figure 9.1 shows the relationship between the message object and the task object.

Figure 9.1 Message, task, and ACCESSOR relationship.

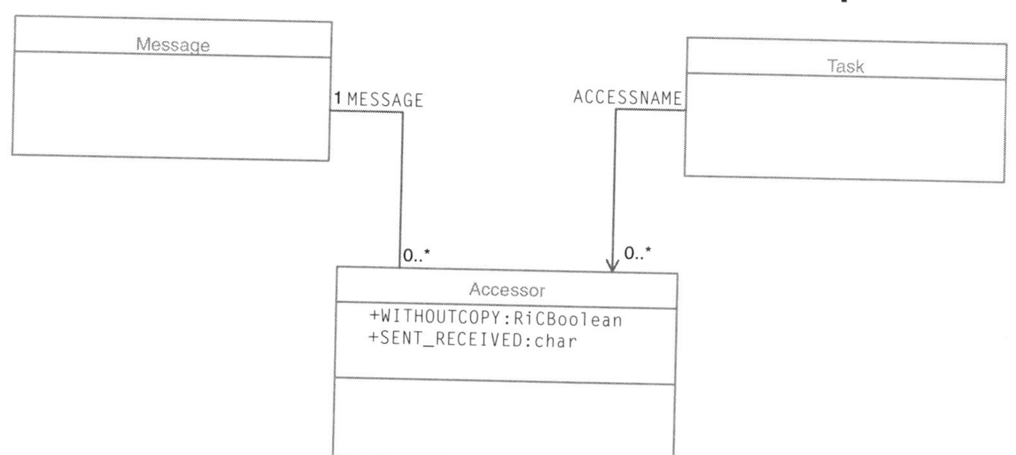

Because the relationship between the task class and the message class is a many:many relationship, ACCESSOR is a container object that maps this relationship. For each task, zero to many accessors could be defined. Each accessor maps to only one message, but multiple accessors can and will map to one message.

The ACCESSOR attribute has a value of SENT or RECEIVED and sets three parameters: MESSAGE, WITHOUTCOPY, and ACCESSNAME. The MESSAGE parameter is the name of the message to which the relationship is mapped. This message must be defined elsewhere in the OIL configuration file. The WITHOUTCOPY parameter is a Boolean TRUE or FALSE. Finally, the ACCESSNAME parameter is the name of the accessor that is typically created by the OIL configuration utility and referenced by the task.

The message accessor concept within the OSEK/VDX COM specification appears confusing at first. In the COM v2.0 specification, the implementation of an accessor was left to the developer. However, since COM v2.2, it simply defines the name of the variable that is visible to the application and is used by the task to send or receive data. This global variable is created by the OIL configuration utility.

When the OIL configuration file is processed, an implementation typically creates the message object in the OIL output source file. It then selects all of the message accessors defined within the TASK object definitions that have the WITHOUTCOPY parameter set to FALSE and creates a duplicate copy in the output file. For all tasks with the ACCESSOR parameter WITHOUTCOPY set to TRUE, the configuration utility will create an alias name that allows the application to access the message object using the accessor name. Use of these access names is discussed in the examples.

One drawback of accessors is the way they are used in some of the implementations on the market. When a message is defined, the message object is created as a RAM variable. For every accessor that is defined with the WITHOUTCOPY parameter set to FALSE, a variable of the same type as the message is created and is available globally. It is the responsibility of the application to ensure that the only task that accesses this variable is the one to which the accessor name is defined. This also limits the ability of an application to create a locally defined variable into which the message is copied and which is destroyed when the task terminates. From the implementation standpoint, however, these multiple copies make the implementation much more efficient and robust.

In an application that has limited RAM memory, this drawback can be addressed by accessing all message objects using `ACCESSOR` objects with the `WITHOUTCOPY` parameter set to `TRUE`. This limits the creation of only one message object in RAM. If the application requires a local copy of the message object when received, then the application can use the C library function `memcpy()` to do a byte-wise copy of the global message object into a local message object. However, the application must ensure that the local object has the exact same `CDATATYPE` as the global object. Because of some quirks of C , this is not guaranteed to work.

A message is now defined that will be used by the `OutputDisplay` task to send a message to the `OutputDisplayBuffer` task, which then outputs the message to the display.

9.3 Communication Services

Now that the message is defined and the use of the message has been explained, the next step is to modify the program to use the services of the communication API with respect to the limited case of OS interprocess communication. First, the COM component must be initialized, started, stopped, and closed. Initializing and closing of the COM component can be accomplished either outside the OS (i.e., before the call to `StartOS()` and after the return from `StartOS()`), within the application at task level, or within the hook routines `StartupHook()` and `ShutdownHook()`. If performed within the application at task level, interrupts must be disabled when the service is called. I have chosen to initialize and close the COM component within the hook routines (Listing 9.3).

Listing 9.3 `StartupHook()` with COM initialization.

```
void StartupHook(void)
{
    InitSystem(INIT_STARTUP);
    InitCOM();
}
```

In `StartupHook()`, the COM component starts with a call to `InitCOM()`.

```
StatusType InitCOM(void);
```

The purpose of `InitCOM()` is to initialize any hardware and low-level resources of the COM component. When used in the OS for interprocess communication only, this service performs little or no processing; in a normal COM application, it initializes the networking hardware.

Listing 9.4 `ShutdownHook()` **with COM closure.**

```
void ShutdownHook(StatusType error)
{
    if(error!=E_OK)
    {
        LastError = error;
    }
    CloseCOM();
    InitSystem(INIT_SHUTDOWN);
}
```

The `InitCOM()` return value, which is the same whether the system is in standard or extended status mode, is

- `E_OK` if the initialization completes successfully or
- specific to the implementation if the initialization does not complete successfully.

An OSEK/VDX task can invoke `InitCOM()`; however, all interrupts must be masked prior to calling it, and if it is called while the COM component is active, its behavior is not defined by the OSEK/VDX specification.

Within the `ShutdownHook()` hook routine, `CloseCOM()` closes the COM component.

```
StatusType CloseCOM(void);
```

This API service is the complement of `InitCOM()`. `CloseCOM()` releases the low-level hardware resources that were initialized in `InitCOM()`. When `CloseCOM()` is invoked, all COM operations are halted, and any messages queued for transmission or partially received are lost. Typically, this service is not invoked while the COM component is active.

Once the communication component is initialized and the OS is started, the communication component can be started and stopped using `StartCOM()` and `StopCOM()`. `StartCOM()`, unlike `StopCOM()`, must be called from the task level within the OS. The specification indicates that `StopCOM()` can use any OS service; consequently, it will most likely be called from the task level because many OS API services are not allowed at interrupt level or during hook routines.

To use these two API services, I renamed the `InitAlarms` task `InitOS` and created a second task, `CloseOS`. The first task to execute is `InitOS` (Listing 9.5). The OIL configuration definition of this task is shown in Listing 9.6. Notice that `InitOS` has the same attributes defined in the OIL configuration file as the prior task `InitAlarms` and will remain the highest priority task in the system. These tasks are found in `init.c` because they only use OSEK/VDX standard interfaces. If they used implementation-specific interfaces, they would be moved to `os.c`.

First I start the communication component with `StartCOM()`, and then I autostart the alarms as described in Chapter 5.

```
StatusType StartCOM(void);
```

`StartCOM()` starts the OSEK/VDX communication component and initializes internal states and variables. It also initializes OS resources, such as counters, alarms, and tasks, used by the communication component.

Listing 9.5 `InitOS` task.

```
TASK(InitOS)
{

    InitAlarmType const *list = AlarmAutostartList;
    UINT32 currentAppModeMask = ConvertAppMode(APP_MODE_MASK);

    StartCOM();
    while(list->appmodemask != 0x00000000){
        if((list->appmodemask & currentAppModeMask)!= 0){
            if(list->alarmtype == ALARM_REL){
                SetRelAlarm(list->alarm,list->start,list->cycle);
            }
            else{
                SetAbsAlarm(list->alarm,list->start,list->cycle);
            }
        }
        list++;
    }
    TerminateTask();
}
```

Listing 9.6 `InitOS` OIL task definition.

```
TASK InitOS {
        /*@*****************************************************************/
        /* Must be highest priority in the system.                          */
        /*@*****************************************************************/

        TYPE = BASIC;
        SCHEDULE = FULL;
        PRIORITY = 16;
        ACTIVATION = 1;
        AUTOSTART = TRUE;
        STACKSIZE = 128;
        SCHEDULE_CALL = FALSE;
};
```

For example, if the communication component needs an extended task to perform a certain function, `StartCOM()` will activate that task. It gets tricky here because the OSEK/VDX COM specification was written to be independent of the OS. If the communication component uses counters, alarms, or tasks as defined in the OSEK/VDX OS, it might not be portable. I discuss this relationship between the OS and the communication component in more detail in Part 2. At this time, I am not concerned with the issue since I only use the OS portion of the OSEK/VDX COM specification.

The return value, which is the same whether the system is in standard or extended status mode, is

- `E_OK` if the startup completes successfully or
- specific to the implementation if the startup does not complete successfully.

`StartCOM()` must be called from within a task and must be called after `InitCOM()` and before `CloseCOM()` or else the behavior is undefined.

`InitCOM()` and `CloseCOM()` were added in the latest COM specification to allow the initialization of communication hardware before the OS starts. In earlier COM implementations, these services were not present, and in most current implementations, they exist but do nothing, especially where the OS and COM modules are integrated.

As mentioned earlier, messages can be sent and received with- or without-copy. If the message is handled without-copy, the variable that holds the copy needs to be initialized prior to use. Many times, this variable will be global and needs to be set to a default value by the application. This is accomplished from within `StartCOM()` by optionally using the user-defined callback routine `MessageInit()`.

```
StatusType MessageInit(void);
```

This routine allows the application to initialize all application-specific message objects. Although provided by the specification, the application is not required to provide this callback routine and could use another method of initializing message objects.

Message object initialization can be accomplished a number of ways. The two most common methods is either to set the global variable to a constant for without-copy messages or to send a message initially using `SendMessage()`, which is described later in this chapter. `SendMessage()` cannot be invoked from within `MessageInit()`.

Because COM only allows messages to be sent from one location within the system, the initial value of any message sent with-copy theoretically can only be set by that task or function. Consequently, if an internal message is received before the application sends the message, the value of the data is indeterminate. In the COM specification v2.2.2 released in early 2001, the return status for an unqueued message that indicates a message was never sent or received was removed from the standard. The COM specification requires that the value returned to the application be the value set at initialization. However, there is no description of how the message is initialized. To resolve this, the application has a number of options to initialize messages sent by the application.

1. If the COM implementation does not enforce sending messages from only one task or function, the application can send the message from one task or function during initialization and from the regular location during normal operation. This option can affect portability of the application and could require changes if a different COM implementation is used. However, if the initialization of the message data for all messages in the system is

kept within one task or function, porting to a new implementation would be minimized. This option typically would be performed immediately after the return from the function `StartCOM()`. You should take care during normal operation of the application that the message is sent only from one location. This option is only available for internal and internal–external messages.

2. Activate all tasks and execute all functions that send messages immediately after the communication component starts. This would occur in the same location as option 1 mentioned previously. The drawback of this method is that there is no guarantee the tasks will be performed in the proper order to ensure data consistency.
3. Send all internal messages without-copy and receive them either with- or without-copy. In this manner, the application can initialize the global variable either within the `MessageInit()` callback function or within the task that executes `StartCOM()`. This requires that a coding standard is enforced globally within an application.
4. Create a flag for every unqueued message using the COM notification mechanism. These flags can be reset in the routine that calls `StartCOM()` and then checked whenever a message is needed. If the flag is set to `TRUE`, the message has been sent or received at least once by the COM component. If the flag is set to `FALSE`, the message has never been sent or received since the COM component was started. The drawbacks of this method are the added overhead every time a message is received by an application task and the unavailability of flags in conformance class A.

Because of the extensive effort required to initialize unqueued messages, the COM specification still needs some work. A revised COM specification or the next release of the OIL specification could address how message data is initialized. Until that time, I recommend that you select a COM implementation that does not enforce sending messages from a single point as in option 1. When the initialization issue is addressed, only a single routine in an application will have to be changed.

The other task to be created is `CloseOS`, which has exactly the same attributes in the OIL configuration file as the previous task, `InitOS`, does not start automatically, and has a priority of one less than `InitOS`. A priority of one less than `InitOS` maintains a level 1 (BCC1/ECC1) system that results in a more optimal implementation. To move to a level 2 (BCC2/ECC2) system, the priority of `CloseOS` if you could be the same as that of `InitOS`.

The `CloseOS` task performs application-specific housekeeping procedures prior to shutting down the OS. It is activated by `ChangeMode()`, which was created in Chapter 1. `ChangeMode()` activates the task `CloseOS` instead of calling `ShutdownOS()`. I do not discuss `ChangeMode()` here because the changes are minimal. You can refer to `main.c` on the accompanying CD to view the modified service. I have also added one small application service called `GetRequestedMode()`, which simply returns the requested `APPMODE`. Listing 9.7 shows the `CloseOS` task and Listing 9.8 shows the OIL configuration for this task.

In `CloseOS`, `StopCOM()` stops the communication component and `ShutdownOS()` shuts down the OS and sets the status type parameter to `E_OK`.

```
StatusType StopCOM(Scalar mode);
```

Listing 9.7 `CloseOS` **task.**

```
TASK(CloseOS)
{
    StopCOM();
    ShutdownOS(E_OK);
    TerminateTask();
}
```

Listing 9.8 `CloseOS` **OIL task definition.**

```
TASK CloseOS {
            TYPE = BASIC;
            SCHEDULE = FULL;
            PRIORITY = 15;
            ACTIVATION = 1;
            AUTOSTART = FALSE;
            STACKSIZE = 64;
            SCHEDULE_CALL = FALSE;
    };
```

`StopCOM()` immediately stops all OSEK/VDX communication activity, frees all OS resources used or puts the resources in an inactive state, and prepares the communication component for the next invocation of `StartCOM()`. Because the level of support for OSEK/VDX COM in an OS environment only allows internal messages, `StopCOM()` does not have to worry about initializing hardware or waiting for messages in the process of transmission to complete. The function of the communication component with respect to external communication is discussed in Part 2.

The `mode` parameter passed to `StopCOM()` tells the service how to shut down the communication component. The OSEK/VDX COM specification only defines one possible value for this parameter, `COM_SHUTDOWN_IMMEDIATE`. If this value is passed to the service, the service shuts down the communication component immediately without waiting for pending operations, such as transmissions in progress, to complete. This behavior directly contradicts the `StopCOM()` definition, which says the system should complete sending messages before it shuts down. The original proposal for `StopCOM()` included the `COM_SHUTDOWN_GRACEFUL` parameter, which allowed operations to complete, if necessary, or would cause the service to return `E_COM_BUSY` if the application locked one of COM's resources, such as a message buffer, preventing its release. This feature was removed from the published standard. Specific implementations could define additional modes, but to ensure portability, they should not be used.

In the listing, `StopCOM()` is shown without a parameter. This is due to the fact that the example was written for an implementation that was compliant to the OSEK/VDX COM standard version 2.1, which did not have this service explicitly defined.

The return value from StopCOM(), which is the same whether the system is in standard or extended status mode, is

- E_OK if the communication component stops successfully or
- E_COM_BUSY if the communication component cannot shut down because a resource owned by the component is in use by the application.

With these changes to the initialization of the communication component, an application can now use interprocess communication. The first task is to modify how messages are output to the display. In Chapter 4, I created the OutputDisplay task, which uses a global variable to obtain the information to be displayed. The simplest way to modify this task would be to create a message that contains the information to be displayed. The application sends this message to this task, so it has to be able to send it from multiple locations (many:1 communication). However, the OSEK/VDX COM standard only allows 1:1 and 1:many communication.

To get around this limitation of the system, I made extensive modifications to how the application handles the display. In prior examples, the application wrote the data to a global variable. This created all of the problems associated with global variables; namely, multiple tasks can update the single variable. To address this, I created two display services that encapsulate the output buffer: WriteDisplay() and WriteDisplayAt(). WriteDisplayAt() includes two additional parameters, the row and the column from which to begin displaying the value, whereas WriteDisplay() is implemented as a call to WriteDisplayAt(), with the row and column set to 0xFF, indicating that output should occur at the current cursor position. WriteDisplayAt() (Listing 9.9) buffers the information and the desired cursor position.

Listing 9.9 WriteDisplayAt().

```
BOOLEAN WriteDisplayAt(UINT8 row, UINT8 column, const char * text)
{
BOOLEAN result=TRUE;

   if(displayBufferError == FALSE){
      SuspendOSInterrupts();
      displayBuffer[displayBufferEnd].row = row;
      displayBuffer[displayBufferEnd].column = column;
      strcpy(&displayBuffer[displayBufferEnd].buffer,text);
      if(++displayBufferEnd == DISPLAY_BUFFER_SIZE){
         displayBufferEnd = 0;
      }
      if(displayBufferEnd == displayBufferStart){
         displayBufferError = TRUE;
      }
      ResumeOSInterrupts();
      ActivateTask(OutputDisplay);
   }
```

```
    else{
        result = FALSE;
    }
    return result;
}
```

Listing 9.10 OutputDisplay **task.**

```
TASK(OutputDisplay)
{
    while((displayBufferError == TRUE) ||
        (displayBufferStart != displayBufferEnd)){
        if(displayBuffer[displayBufferStart].row != 0xff){
            SetDisplayPosition(displayBuffer[displayBufferStart].row,
                displayBuffer[displayBufferStart].column);
        }
        PackDisplay(displayBuffer[displayBufferStart].buffer);
        if((++displayBufferStart) == DISPLAY_BUFFER_SIZE){
            displayBufferStart = 0;
        }
        Schedule();
    }
    SendMessage(DisplayMessage,displayMirror);
    TerminateTask();
}
```

The `WriteDisplayAt()` service first ensures that sufficient space exists in the display buffer before transmitting the information into `displayBuffer`, which is now static to this module and which allows multiple tasks to send messages to the display without worrying about overwriting someone else's message. `WriteDisplayAt()` guarantees that a message cannot be preempted by another task while writing to the buffer by creating a critical section using `SuspendOSInterrupts()` and `ResumeOSInterrupts()`. If the information is buffered successfully, `WriteDisplayAt()` activates the `OutputDisplay` task and returns `TRUE`. If an error occurs, such as insufficient buffer space, and the information cannot be buffered, the service returns `FALSE`. The `OutputDisplay` task (Listing 9.10) must now be modified to take advantage of the new format of the display buffer.

`OutputDisplay` first checks the information in the display buffer. If the cursor needs to move, it invokes `SetCursorPosition()` then formats the internal copy of the display using `PackDisplay()` (Listing 9.11), which is specific to the display.

`PackDisplay()` performs multiple actions, but I have only shown the section where the message object is accessed. In Listing 9.1, an `ACCESSOR` named `displayMirror` was defined for the `OutputDisplay` task and had `WITHOUTCOPY` set to `TRUE`. The configurator created the message object and defined the `displayMirror` `ACCESSOR` as a reference to the message object.

Because displayMirror is a structure, the message object is accessed inside PackDisplay() using display->membername, where membername is replaced with the structure member name (i.e. message).

Because the display buffer can hold information from multiple tasks, OutputDisplay uses a while loop to pull multiple messages from the buffer if they exist. The while loop is required because OutputDisplay is a single-activation task by definition. If this task were allowed to have multiple activations, the while loop would not be required because each activation would process one package of information from the application.

Listing 9.11 PackDisplay().

```
void PackDisplay(char *string)
{
UINT8 i,j;

   while(*string != 0)
   {
      switch(*string)
      {
...
         default:
            if(*string >= 240)
            {
             displayMirror->message[cursorPosition.row*MAX_DISPLAY_LINE_LENGTH
                   + cursorPosition.column++] = *string - (char)240;
            }
            else
            {
             displayMirror->message[cursorPosition.row*MAX_DISPLAY_LINE_LENGTH
                   + cursorPosition.column++] = *string;
            }
            if(cursorPosition.column == MAX_DISPLAY_LINE_LENGTH)
            {
               OutputNewLine();
            }
      }
      ++string;
   }
}
```

My decision to limit the example application to a level 1 conformance class and to limit the number of extended tasks illustrates the problems inherent in determining the conformance class to use. If a task with a higher priority than `OutputDisplay` attempts to display information between the end of the `while` loop and the termination of the task (preemption), information would be locked into the buffer and would not be output until the next time a task attempted to send information to the display. The sequence of events that can cause this to occur is shown in Figure 9.2, in which Task A is priority `13`, Task B is priority `14`, Task C is priority `15`, and `OutputDisplay` is priority `12`.

Figure 9.2 Information lost by preemption.

	SUSPENDED	WAITING	READY	RUNNING	BUFFER DEPTH
1	B C			A	0
2	C		A	B	1
3	C		A	B	0
4			A B	C	0
5			A B	C	1
6	C		A	B	1
	B C			A	1

The sequence of events shown in Figure 9.2 proceed as follows.

1. Task A is `RUNNING` and adds information to the buffer. It then activates Task B, which preempts Task A.
2. Task B pulls the information from the buffer.
3. An alarm expires and Task C is activated. It preempts Task B.
4. Task C adds information to the buffer and attempts to activate Task B. Because Task B is already in the Ready state, activation does not occur. If operating in the standard status mode, no error is returned.
5. Task C completes and terminates. Task B resumes processing. However, it thinks that the buffer is empty and does not attempt to pull another item from the buffer.
6. Task B terminates with information still in the buffer. This information will not be obtained until the next time something is written to the buffer.

One method of resolving this issue is to make the task that extracts information from the buffer an extended task and to clear the event that signals that the information has been added to the buffer prior to flushing the buffer. When an item is added to the buffer, an event must be set. This will need to be added to tasks A and C above. If the situation in number 4 above occurs, the event remains set, and as soon as the task attempts to wait on the event again, it immediately resumes and flushes the remaining item from the buffer. The drawback to this method is that it requires an extended task, which increases the size of the kernel and the resources used.

A method that would work with basic tasks is to make the task that extracts information from the buffer non-preemptive and use `Schedule()` to multitask cooperatively. In the example program, I made `OutputDisplay` a non-preemptive task. However, I allow preemption to occur after one piece of information has been processed from the buffer and prior to the check for an empty buffer. In this manner, preemption is allowed under the control of the application and addresses the issue described in Figure 9.2.

After all pieces of information have been removed from the information buffer, the mirror buffer with the copy of the display is transmitted to the output display driver using `SendMessage()`.

```
StatusType SendMessage(SymbolicName message, AccessNameRef data);
```

When invoked, the function that is performed by `SendMessage()` is dependent on the value of the `WITHOUTCOPY` parameter in the `ACCESSOR` attribute of the `TASK` object definition in the OIL configuration file. If set to `FALSE`, the message object created within the communication component will be updated with the values contained in the variable referenced by the `data` parameter. If `WITHOUTCOPY` is `TRUE`, the message object, if it exists, is not updated. `SendMessage()` then performs the notification defined for the message referenced in the `message` parameter. Notification is not dependent on the value of the `WITHOUTCOPY` parameter.

The status that is returned from `SendMessage()` can be one of the following.

- If the service cannot guarantee that access to the message is safe, it returns `E_COM_LOCKED`. Determining when access cannot be granted to the message object is specific to the implementation.
- If the `WITHOUTCOPY` parameter is `FALSE` for this accessor and the communication component identifies that the message is set to `BUSY`, the service returns `E_COM_LOCKED`. This situation only occurs in an implementation with conformance class CCCB or higher (discussed in Part 2).
- If the service executes successfully, it returns `E_OK`.
- In extended status mode only, the service returns `E_COM_ID` if the message referenced in the `message` parameter is not valid.

The transmitted message, `OutputDisplayMessage`, was shown in Listing 9.1 with the task definition for `OutputDisplay`. This message is sent without-copy; therefore, the message object is available to all tasks within the application. When this message is sent, the notification mechanism sets the `BUFFER_CHANGED` event for the `OutputDisplayBuffer` task, which will communicate with the display and take care of the handshaking (Listing 9.12).

Listing 9.12 `OutputDisplayBuffer` **task.**

```
TASK(OutputDisplayBuffer)
{
   UINT8 *displayControl = DISPLAY_CONTROL_LOCATION;
   UINT8 *display = DISPLAY_BUFFER_LOCATION;
   UINT8 i,outputRow;
   UINT8 translateRow;

   WriteDisplay(InitMessage);
   while(1){
      translateRow = 0;
      WaitEvent(BUFFER_CHANGED);
      ClearEvent(BUFFER_CHANGED);
      ReceiveMessage(DisplayMessage,displayMirrorTemp);
      *displayControl = 0x01;
      SetRelAlarm(DisplayWaitAlarm,10,0);
      WaitEvent(DISPLAY_READY);
      ClearEvent(DISPLAY_READY);
      DisableAllInterrupts();
      while(translateRow < MAX_DISPLAY_ROWS){
         outputRow = RowTranslation[translateRow++];
         for(i=0;i<MAX_DISPLAY_LINE_LENGTH;i++){
            *display = displayMirrorTemp->message
               [outputRow*MAX_DISPLAY_LINE_LENGTH + i];
            wait(1000);
         }
      }
      i=((cursorPosition.row&0x01)*0x40) +
          ((cursorPosition.row&0x02)/2*MAX_DISPLAY_LINE_LENGTH) +
            cursorPosition.column;
      *displayControl = 0x80+i;
      wait(1000);
      EnableAllInterrupts();
   }
}
```

`OutputDisplayBuffer` is an extended task that starts automatically when the OS starts. It waits for the `BUFFER_CHANGED` event to be set and enters the `WAITING` state. Because the display is relatively slow compared to the speed of the application, the local copy of the display can be modified and thereby corrupted during the write operation. Consequently, OutputDisplayBuffer accesses the message with-copy using the access name displayMirrorTemp prior to writing the information to the display. I also added a delay early in the task after I clear the display and return the cursor to the home position. An alarm moves this task out of the WAITING state while the display clears, which can take up to 10 milliseconds.

ReceiveMessage() copies the message object to the copy object.

```
StatusType ReceiveMessage(SymbolicName message, AccessNameRef data);
```

When invoked, the function performed by ReceiveMessage() is dependent on the value of the WITHOUTCOPY parameter in the ACCESSOR attribute of the TASK object definition in the OIL configuration file. If this parameter is FALSE, the message object created within the communication component updates the values contained in the variable referenced by the data parameter. If the WITHOUTCOPY parameter is TRUE, only the status of the message is returned. In a conformance class A communication system, the notification mechanism is only invoked when the message is sent, not when the message is received.

The status returned from ReceiveMessage() can be one of the following.

- If the service cannot guarantee that access to the message is safe, it returns E_COM_LOCKED. Determining when access cannot be granted to the message object is specific to the implementation.
- If the WITHOUTCOPY parameter is FALSE for this accessor and the communication component identifies that the message is set to BUSY, the service returns E_COM_LOCKED. This situation only occurs in an implementation with conformance class CCCB or higher.
- If the service executes successfully, it returns E_OK.
- Other return values will only be effective if the message is queued (discussed in Part 2).
- In extended status mode only, the service returns E_COM_ID if the message referenced in the message parameter is not a valid message.

The temporary copy of the buffer, which cannot be corrupted, is output to the display using an alarm, based on the real-time clock, that handles the delays necessary between commands and characters written to the display. As with the displayMirror ACCESSOR, the displayMirrorTemp ACCESSOR is a reference to the copy of the message object that can be accessed by the application using displayMirrorTemp->membername.

9.4 Example Program

The example program now allows interprocess communication using the OSEK/VDX messaging system. At this time, I have created only one message, OutputDisplayMessage, which illustrates the interprocess communication capabilities of an OS. In Part 2, I add more messages to the example program and expand the COM specification.

9.4.1 Modules

The modules startup.s, initspr.s, cinit.s, debug.c, hw.c, os.c, and keypad.c were not changed in this chapter. The following modules were changed.

`init.c` The `InitAlarms` task was renamed `InitOS` and the `CloseOS` task was added. In addition, the `MessageInit()` callback routine was provided, but at this point, it does not perform any actions.

`main.c` `ChangeMode()` was modified to activate a task instead of shutting down the system. The hook routines `StartupHook()` and `ShutdownHook()` were modified to initialize a communication component. Finally, `GetRequestedMode()` was added.

`AppModeType GetRequestedMode(void)` This function simply returns the requested mode that is stored in the `SelectedMode` static variable.

`cardgame.c` A number of tasks and functions within this module were modified to use the new interfaces `WriteDisplay()` and `WriteDisplayAt()` instead of the `displayBuffer` global variable.

`dispdrv.c` Many changes were made to the tasks and functions found in this module.

`void InitDisplay(InitType type)` This function no longer automatically writes to the display. Instead, the initialization message is written in the `OutputDisplayBuffer` task.

`void PackDisplay(char *string)` This function now updates the message object referenced by the `displayMirror` accessor instead of the `displayMessage` static variable.

`void OutputNewLine(void)` Similar to `PackDisplay()`, this function manipulates `displayMirror` instead of `displayMessage`.

```
BOOLEAN WriteDisplay(const char * text)
BOOLEAN WriteDisplayAt(UINT8 row, UINT8 column, const char * text)
```

`WriteDisplay()` and `WriteDisplayAt()` were described in detail in this chapter and will not be repeated here.

`OutputDisplayBuffer` **task** This task first writes the initialization message to the display and then waits for a message to be sent. `OutputDisplayBuffer`, which was discussed in detail in this chapter, replaces `OutputNewDisplay()` from Chapters 4 and 8.

`OutputDisplay` **task** This task was modified extensively from the versions in Chapters 4 and 8.

`carddeck.c` This module was modified to support the new interfaces `WriteDisplay()` and `WriteDisplayAt()`. The following function was modified.

`void DisplayCard(UINT8 card, char * displayBuffer)` Because the `displayBuffer` global variable is no longer available, this routine now has to be told where to put the display information, which is passed as a reference to a string, before placing the information into that string.

`shuffle.c` This module also was modified to support the new interfaces `WriteDisplay()` and `WriteDisplayAt()`.

9.4.2 Configuration Files

The `cardgame.oil` file in the `cfg` directory on the CD is different from the OIL listings in this chapter because, as of the writing of this book, Wind River had not yet released the new version of OSEKWorks that was compatible with the OS standard v2.1, the COM standard v2.2, and the OIL standard v2.2. When the new version is released, I will update all the files on the CD, which you can download from the Web site http://www.osekbook.com.

9.5 Exercises

1. Create a message that contains a single character. Whenever a key is pressed on the keypad that is not required for the game, send a message with this character. Create a task in the `debug.c` module to receive this message, and activate the task whenever the message is sent. Log the last 20 illegal characters pressed. Send and receive messages with-copy.
2. Create a message that contains a structure that has the current game time from the task that was created in Chapter 5, Exercise 3. Whenever the deck is shuffled, send a message with the current running time. Create a new task in the `cardgame.c` module that receives this message and calculates the average time it takes to play a hand. Remember to ignore the first shuffle. Send and receive messages without-copy; however, perform a manual copy to a local variable within the task. This manual copy was discussed in Section 9.2, "Notification," which discusses RAM.

9.6 Summary

In this chapter, I discussed the interprocess communication support required in an OSEK/VDX-compliant OS. These services are a subset of the OSEK/VDX COM specification and implements, at a minimum, communication conformance class A. Most OSEK/VDX implementations probably will implement conformance class B. A description of conformance class B is provided in Part 2.

To provide interprocess communication, the system must be initialized and started before messages are sent and received. Because the COM specification is intended to operate independently of the OS, you can start and stop communication and initialize and close the communication component without leaving the OS.

This concludes the coverage of the OSEK/VDX OS specification. I recommend that you take some time now to play with a stand-alone application, if you have an implementation available, and really learn the intricacies of the system and your particular implementation.

PART 2

Communication

The second specification in the OSEK/VDX system, communication (also referred to as COM), defines the interfaces and the protocols for both intertask and interprocessor communication within an application and across applications. The OSEK/VDX COM specification is similar to the OS specification in that it provides a standard API with services. Because each OSEK/VDX standard is capable of operating on its own, you might have skipped the OS portion of this book and moved directly to this section. Consequently, items of overlap between the OS and COM systems that were covered in Chapter 9, "Interprocess Communication," and brief definitions of tasks, alarms, and events are repeated throughout Part 2.

10

Chapter 10

Communication

10.1 Communication Model

The OSEK/VDX communication standard supports both intertask communication and interprocessor communication. It is intended to be independent of protocol and flexible enough to use in any environment. To reach these goals, a five-layer system was developed that has some parallels to the International Organization for Standardization open systems interconnection (ISO/OSI) seven-layer model. This chapter describes the attributes of the communication model and builds the foundation on which the rest of Part 2 rests. I've included very few examples in this chapter, but each chapter builds on a part of the model introduced here.

The communication model is complex and not easily understood. This chapter introduces all of the attributes of messages at one time in a summary format and could appear confusing on first read. If something is not clear in this chapter, read on into the next chapters, for more detailed discussions.

10.1.1 Communication Model Overview

The OSEK/VDX COM specification describes a method of exchanging data between different tasks on a single processor and between multiple processors over a network. The most common network hardware used with COM is the controller area network (CAN), an industry-standard networking protocol used in automotive and industrial applications. However, the specification does not eliminate other networks such as TCP/IP over Ethernet, point-to-point protocol, or proprietary protocols, and several hardware networking standards can be mixed in a single COM environment.

The COM specification defines an asynchronous communication model in which the application is not required to wait for a message before it resumes processing and it is not blocked if a message is not available when it is requested. To implement this model, COM defines a number of notification mechanisms that assist the application in understanding when a message has been sent or received.

Each message defined for an application can have only one sender within the system, but it can be received by one or many receivers. These receivers can be tasks that are internal, external, or both.

10.1.2 OIL for COM

Unlike the OS, for which the OIL configuration file defines a very detailed configuration mechanism, no common method of defining COM messages is available at this time. The exception is intertask-only messages, which is a requirement of the OS specification. The latest COM specification defines the generation requirements for the system that are intended to be guidelines for the development of the COM OIL configuration file. When I refer to the specification requirements within this chapter, I refer to the terminology that appears in the communication specification, which can change in the final OIL specification. The OSEK/VDX OIL working group is in the process of defining these requirements in the OIL definition. The release version should be out in 2002.

Throughout this part of the book, the examples for message configuration use Wind River OSEKWorks terminology, which might or might not be equivalent to that in the final OIL specification; however, it is sufficient to illustrate the concepts presented. I note in the discussions any difference between the name used by Wind River and the recommended name in the specification. If you use a different implementation of OSEK/VDX COM, you will have to refer to your documentation for the specific terminology required to configure the COM implementation.

10.1.3 OSEK/VDX versus ISO/OSI

The OSEK/VDX five-layer communication model and the ISO/OSI seven-layer model are shown in Figure 10.1.

The layer model in Figure 10.1 is a conceptual model; the COM implementation does not have to use a layered approach. The intention is to utilize a layered approach to develop a concise description of the specification, but allow the implementation the flexibility to optimize the communication component for the particular processor.

The first layer, the physical layer, consists of the physical hardware that performs the communication. The amount of message processing performed by this layer is dependent on the hardware used. This layer will not be discussed in this book.

The second layer, the data link layer, consists of the software required to interface with the hardware and is dependent on both protocol and hardware. One implementation can have multiple, simultaneous data link layers, one for each protocol used. The data link layer is usually invisible to the application and provides extensive services to the next layer, the network layer, and to a network management component if it exists. Because the focus of this book is primarily on the use of the system from the application programmer's viewpoint, I do not discuss these services in detail; rather, they are covered in the specification included on the CD.

Figure 10.1 OSEK/VDX communication model.

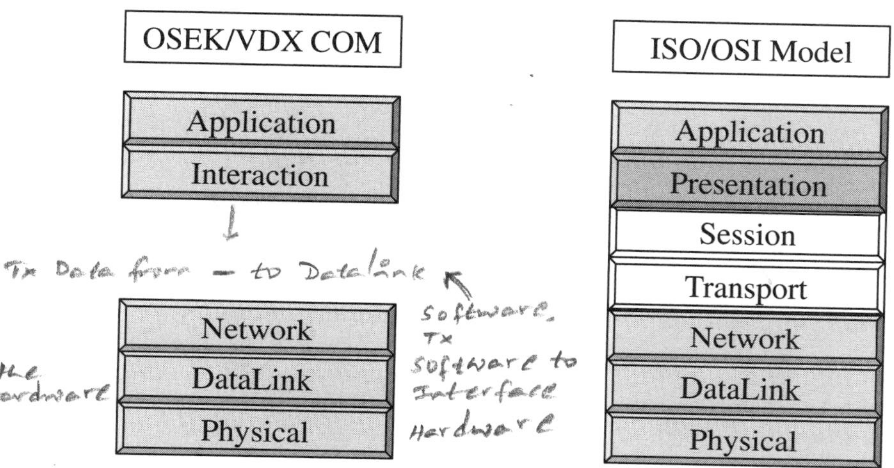

The third layer, the network layer, consists of the software that transfers messages from the interaction layer to the data link layer. Like the data link layer, there can be multiple network layers, one for each protocol used in the system. The network layer provides services to the interaction layer and uses the services of the data link layer to provide two types of data transfer: unacknowledged unsegmented data transfer (UUDT) and unacknowledged segmented data transfer (USDT). This layer is described in more detail in Chapters 12 and 13. The network layer knows to which data link layer to send the message and the maximum size of the message allowed over the network. One network layer can interface with multiple data link layers.

The fourth layer, the interaction layer, interacts directly with the application. This layer understands two types of messages (internal and external), provides all of the API services to the application, and uses the network layer to transfer external messages over the network. If the message is internal, it is completely processed in this layer. This layer is described in more detail in Chapter 11. Figure 10.2 shows an example application in which an electronic control unit (ECU) is attached to four separate networks. An ECU, as defined within the OSEK/VDX standard, is an electronic device that consists of at least one microcontroller. This particular example has a single microcontroller. CAN typically operates at 125 kbits/sec to 1 mbit/sec. J1850 also is an automotive industry–standard communication protocol, but it runs at a much slower rate. Both protocols allow the use of different physical layers. Figure 10.2 shows both a single-wire and a differential dual-wire physical layer, each requiring a different data link component because of hardware differences. When hardware differences are not an issue, a single data link layer can support both physical layers.

10.2 Message Attributes

Each message has a number of different attributes that can be defined and will affect how the message is handled when it is sent and received. Each attribute is discussed in more detail in the following sections. Throughout this section and the following sections, I refer to a number of messages as examples. The OIL configuration for these messages is shown in Listing 10.1 and is referred to throughout this chapter. This configuration uses the implementation-specific attributes found in the OSEKWorks implementation.

Figure 10.2 Example application with four networks.

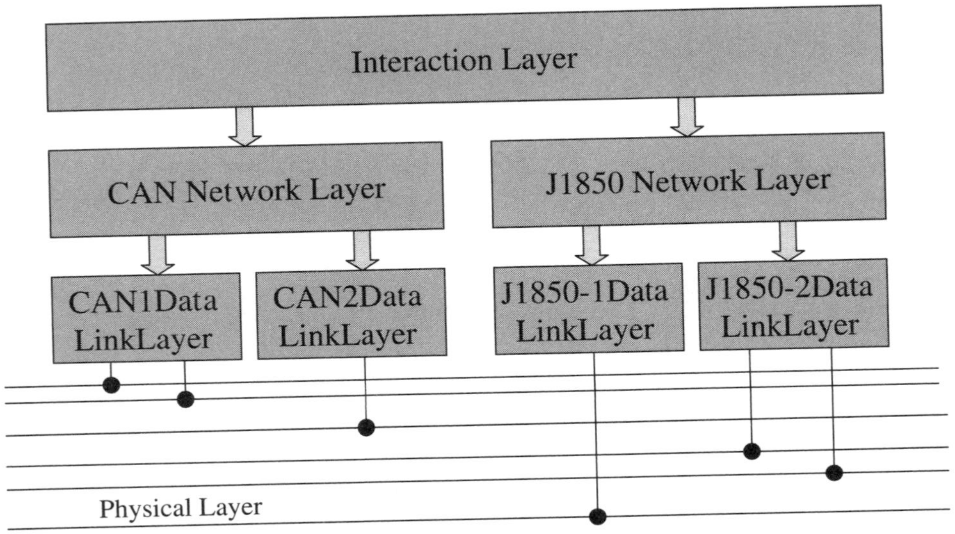

Interaction Layer

CAN Network Layer

J1850 Network Layer

CAN1Data LinkLayer

CAN2Data LinkLayer

J1850-1Data LinkLayer

J1850-2Data LinkLayer

Physical Layer

10.2.1 Internal versus External

Messages can be defined as either internal, external, or internal–external. Internal messages are sent and received by the application running on the local processor. External messages are either sent by or received by the application over an external network, although they can be internal to a multiprocessor ECU. Internal–external messages are sent by the application but are received by the local application and by an application running on a different processor over a network.

In the example listing from OSEKWorks, the `TYPE` and `USAGE` attributes of the `MESSAGE` object define the routing of a message. In the COM specification, the attribute name is `SCOPE`, and in the OIL specification, this attribute is not yet defined. The OSEKWorks `TYPE` attribute, however, conflicts with the OIL attribute that defines internal queued or unqueued messages, and it will probably change in the next release. The example application at this point has defined four messages: `CardMessage`, `DisplayMessage`, `KeyPressMessage`, and `OpponentMessage`. `CardMessage` transmits the values of the cards as they are dealt when two players are playing head to head. `DisplayMessage` is sent from the application to the display driver to define the contents of the LCD display and is intended for internal communication only. `KeyPressMessage`, also an internal message, holds a queue of key presses and buffers the keys as they are pressed and before they are processed by the application. `OpponentMessage` is an external message that sends a message to a player's opponent and flashes on the opponent's display.

Listing 10.1 Message configuration definitions.

```
MESSAGE CardMessage {
        TYPE = EXTERNAL;
        LENGTH = 4;
        ALIGNMENT = 1;
        USAGE = SEND;
        QUEUED = FALSE;
        TX_NOTIFICATION = ON_DEADLINE;
        RX_NOTIFICATION = NONE;
        TRANSMISSION = DIRECT;
        ACCESSNAMES = { cardData };
        TX_DEADLINE_ALARM = CardMessageAlarm;
        TX_DEADLINE_TIME = 10;
        CAN_ADDRESSES = { CardMessageAddress };
  };
  MESSAGE DisplayMessage {
        TYPE = INTERNAL;
        LENGTH = 80;
        ALIGNMENT = 1;
        USAGE = SEND_RECEIVE;
        QUEUED = FALSE;
        TX_NOTIFICATION = NONE;
        RX_NOTIFICATION = ON_SUCCESS;
        TRANSMISSION = DIRECT;
        ACCESSNAMES = { displayMirrorTemp, displayMirror };
        RX_SUCCESS_TASK = OutputDisplayBuffer;
        RX_SUCCESS_EVENT = BUFFER_CHANGED;
  };
  MESSAGE KeyPressMessage {
        TYPE = INTERNAL;
        LENGTH = 1;
        ALIGNMENT = 1;
        USAGE = SEND_RECEIVE;
        QUEUED = TRUE;
        QUEUE_SIZE = 9;
        TX_NOTIFICATION = NONE;
```

```
            RX_NOTIFICATION = ON_SUCCESS;
            TRANSMISSION = DIRECT;
            RX_SUCCESS_TASK = ProcessKeyPress;
            ACCESSNAMES = { keyValue };
    };
    MESSAGE OpponentMessage {
            TYPE = EXTERNAL;
            LENGTH = 80;
            ALIGNMENT = 1;
            USAGE = RECEIVE;
            QUEUED = FALSE;
            TX_NOTIFICATION = NONE;
            RX_NOTIFICATION = ON_SUCCESS;
            TRANSMISSION = DIRECT;
            RX_SUCCESS_TASK = ProcessOpponentMessage;
            ACCESSNAMES = { opponentMessageString };
            CAN_ADDRESSES = { OpponentMessageAddress };
    };
```

10.2.2 Message Length

The length of a message is defined in the above examples with the LENGTH attribute, which is the length in bytes. In addition, the alignment with respect to the memory is set using the ALIGNMENT attribute, which aligns the data in memory on a word or double word boundary if necessary for the particular processor used. The OIL specification defines an additional attribute, CDATATYPE, from which the size of the message can be gleaned, along with the alignment, if the C language type is described by this attribute is used to create the message objects.

10.2.3 Queued versus Unqueued

The QUEUED attribute for each message defines whether the message is queued or unqueued. Again, the OIL specification uses the TYPE attribute to define queued and unqueued messages. Queued messages use a FIFO buffer to store the messages as they are received. The size of this FIFO buffer is set statically in the OIL configuration file using the QUEUE_SIZE attribute. In the OIL specification, the queue size is defined using the QUEUEDEPTH parameter of the TYPE attribute. As messages are read from the buffer, the message is flushed from the buffer. Consequently, when a queued message is read, it is consumed from the message queue belonging to the task that is reading it. In addition, the standard explicitly limits queued messages to being received only in one place in the application. Although the standard allows a message to be transmitted to many receivers under a 1:many transmission model (see below), queued messages are limited to one internal receiver. However, multiple external receivers are allowed. If multiple internal receivers were allowed, each receiver would have to have its own message reception queue, which would be very costly in scarce RAM resources. Queued messages typically are used for a sequence of events that must be processed in a particular order.

Unqueued messages only contain one copy of the message, which is destroyed whenever the message is sent by the application or received from the network. This message, however, remains valid, no matter how many times the application reads the data. Unqueued messages are used more frequently than queued messages, typically when the most recent value of the data contained in the message is necessary. `DisplayMessage` is an example of an unqueued message and is defined by setting the `QUEUED` attribute to `FALSE`.

The other three messages are queued messages and are defined by setting the `QUEUED` attribute to `TRUE`. In addition, the `QUEUE_SIZE` attribute has been added, which defines the size of the queue that must be reserved within the communication component when the system is generated. This value is the number of messages in the queue, not the size in bytes.

10.2.4 Segmented versus Unsegmented

A message is transmitted across a network in one of two forms: segmented or unsegmented. This segmentation attribute is only applicable to external messages and applies to how the message is sent over the external network. Segmented messages are broken into pieces by the network layer and sent in sequential frames over the network. The receiving processor reassembles the frames into the message for the receiving application. Unsegmented messages are sent in their entirety in one frame over the network.

Whether a message is segmented or unsegmented is unknown to the application for fixed-length messages; instead, it is a function of a combination of the network and the data link layers and the maximum transmission unit of a frame on the network. For example, in an automotive or industrial application that is hooked to a CAN network, the maximum size of a frame is limited to eight bytes. Ethernet connections, however, can send messages up to 1,500 bytes in a single frame. One important difference between segmented and unsegmented messages is that a segmented message can have a variable length determined at run time; however, segmented messages can never be queued.

All internal messages are, by definition, unsegmented, and a message only becomes segmented when it is passed from the interaction layer to the network layer. Consequently, segmented messages are either internal–external or external messages. Although some implementations might allow API services intended for segmented messages to be performed on internal messages, I would not recommend taking advantage of this feature because it would probably result in nonportable code. I discuss how segmentation is accomplished in Chapter 14.

10.2.5 1:1 and 1:Many

Messages can have only one sender within the system but many receivers, which defines the message as a 1:1 or a 1:many (also called 1:*n*) message. This limitation does not allow messages to be sent from more than one location within the application. The intention is to prevent obscure application errors when the same message is sent accidentally on the same system; however, it is practically impossible to enforce without a system-wide configuration tool and time-consuming run-time checking. If you implement the single-sender rule, you will always be able to track down the source of a stray message.

10.2.6 With-Copy and Without-Copy

The final attribute of a message object discussed here is whether the data for a message is accessed by copying the message or is obtained directly from the message object. Messages are accessed either with a copy (with-copy) or without a copy (without-copy) with respect to the task that is accessing the message object. This attribute is the parameter `WITHOUTCOPY` of the `ACCESSOR` attribute of a task when used within the OSEK/VDX OS. If an application uses the communication component but not the OSEK/VDX OS, the COM specification recommends a new object also called `ACCESSOR`, which defines whether the message is accessed with-copy or without-copy. Because it is an attribute of the `ACCESSOR` and not of the message itself, one accessor can access the message without-copy and other accessors can access the message with-copy. To better describe what is occurring in an application, refer to Figure 10.3. This example describes how with-copy and without-copy are usually implemented. The OSEK/VDX COM specification does not define a particular implementation. Some implementations can function differently.

Figure 10.3 Message copy example.

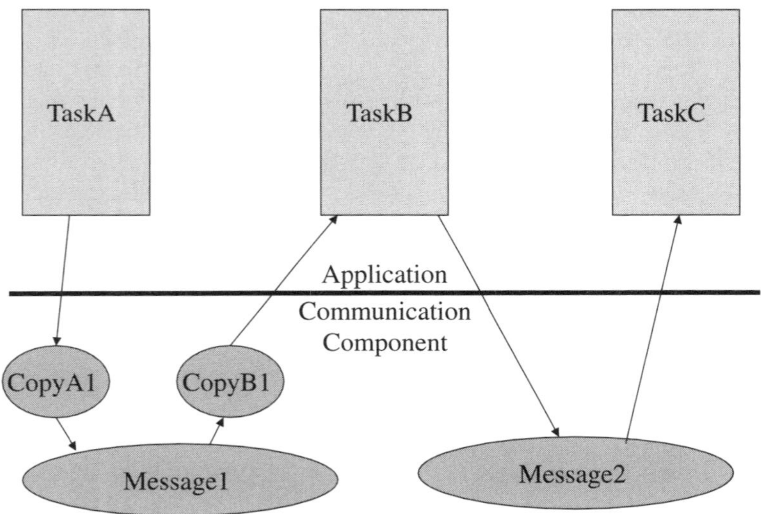

In Figure 10.3, two messages —Message1 and Message2 — and three application tasks —TaskA, TaskB, and TaskC — exist. When a message is sent with-copy, the communication component maintains a copy of the message internally and copies the data from it into the message object when sent. When received with-copy, it puts the data into this internal copy from the message object. The internal copy is visible to the application through the accessor. In the example, when TaskA updates Message1, it updates the data in CopyA1, which is accessed using the access name defined in the OIL configuration file for the accessor. When the message is sent, the communication component copies the data from CopyA1 into the data section of Message1. When TaskB receives Message1 that was sent by TaskA, the communication component copies the data out of the data section of Message1 into CopyB1. TaskB can then access the copy of the data using the access name defined in the OIL configuration file for the accessor.

When a message is sent without-copy, the communication component exposes the message object as a global variable. In the example in Figure 10.3, when TaskB accesses the data in Message2, it updates the message object. When the message is sent, the communication component does not copy any data; instead, it updates the status of the message. When TaskC receives Message2, the communication component only returns the status of the message and takes no action on the message data itself. TaskC, if the return status indicates that the message is valid, will access the message object directly because it must be visible to both TaskB and TaskC.

In the case where a message is accessed both with- and without-copy, the communication component creates a copy for the with-copy accessor and allows the task that has defined a without-copy accessor to access the message object directly. In the example, if TaskB sends Message2 without-copy and TaskC receives the message with-copy, the implementation creates CopyC2 into which the message object is copied, when received, and is accessible to TaskC.

One obvious drawback is that with-copy access requires that additional copies of the message object be created for every task. In some implementations, these copies are defined statically and use scarce RAM resources, even when the sending or receiving task is suspended. This drawback was addressed by creating the without-copy access method. However, the message object now becomes a global variable, which can be corrupted by the sender before the receiver has completed processing the last message, so this also is not a good practice. To address the access issue with global variables, the OSEK/VDX COM specification has created a method of locking a COM resource.

In some cases, an application might need to conserve scarce RAM resources, but it still requires a local copy of a message object that is destroyed when the function or task terminates. To accomplish this, perform the following.

- Create the message and access it without copy.
- Lock the message resource.
- Copy the global message object to the local object. This might require the use of `memcpy()`, so make sure that the message object and the local object are identical.
- Release the resource.

The task now has a local copy of the message object, and the sending task is now free to update the message object without affecting the data used by the receiving task. This particular scenario is discussed in more detail in an example in Chapter 11.

All queued messages must be accessed with-copy because, by definition, the communication component must create the queue internally. Unqueued messages, however, can use the global variable created by the communication component to hold the message data and can be accessed without-copy.

With-copy messages guarantee data consistency to the application at the expense of a message buffer for each receiving task and the time required to make the copy. Without-copy messages are faster and use less RAM, but the application programmer is responsible for ensuring data consistency (i.e., preventing the sender and receiver from using the buffer at the same time).

The message attributes introduced throughout Section 10.2 are defined in more detail in the chapters that follow, along with examples showing how each affects the messages.

10.3 Transmission Modes

Another characteristic of messages is the mode in which the message is transmitted when the application sends the message. Three modes are available in the OSEK/VDX communication specification: direct, periodic (referred to as periodical in the specification), and mixed. Mixed transmission mode is not really a third mode; instead, it describes a message that is transmitted using both the direct and periodic modes. The transmission mode for a given message is set in the OIL configuration file using the `TRANSMISSION` attribute of the `MESSAGE` object and cannot be changed dynamically by the application. The COM specification defines three mutually exclusive attributes: `DIRECT_TRANSMISSION_MODE`, `PERIODICAL_TRANSMISSION_MODE`, and `MIXED_TRANSMISSION_MODE`. Each message can have its own mode that will be a reference to a specific transmission mode object defined elsewhere in the configuration file. Figure 10.4 is an example of an application sending three messages simultaneously, each using a different transmission mode.

10.3.1 Direct

Direct transmission describes a mode in which the message is sent only when the application requests it. By definition, internal messages can only be direct messages because as soon as they are sent, they are available to be read by another task in the application. External messages that are defined as direct messages are transmitted on the external bus as soon as possible after the application sends the message. This message is delayed based only on the priority within the protocol chosen for the external network and the depth of the queue of messages in the data link layer.

10.3.2 Periodic

Periodic transmission mode, referred to as periodical transmission mode in the specification, describes a message that is sent periodically with the period defined statically by the system. Periodic messages must also be defined as external messages. The application can start and stop transmission of all periodic messages as a group, but not individual periodic messages.

If an application sends a periodic message without-copy, the application must lock the message resource while it is being updated. If the COM component transmits the message data while the message is being updated, inconsistent data will be transmitted on the network bus. Locking is not required for messages that are sent with-copy because the COM component insures consistency of data.

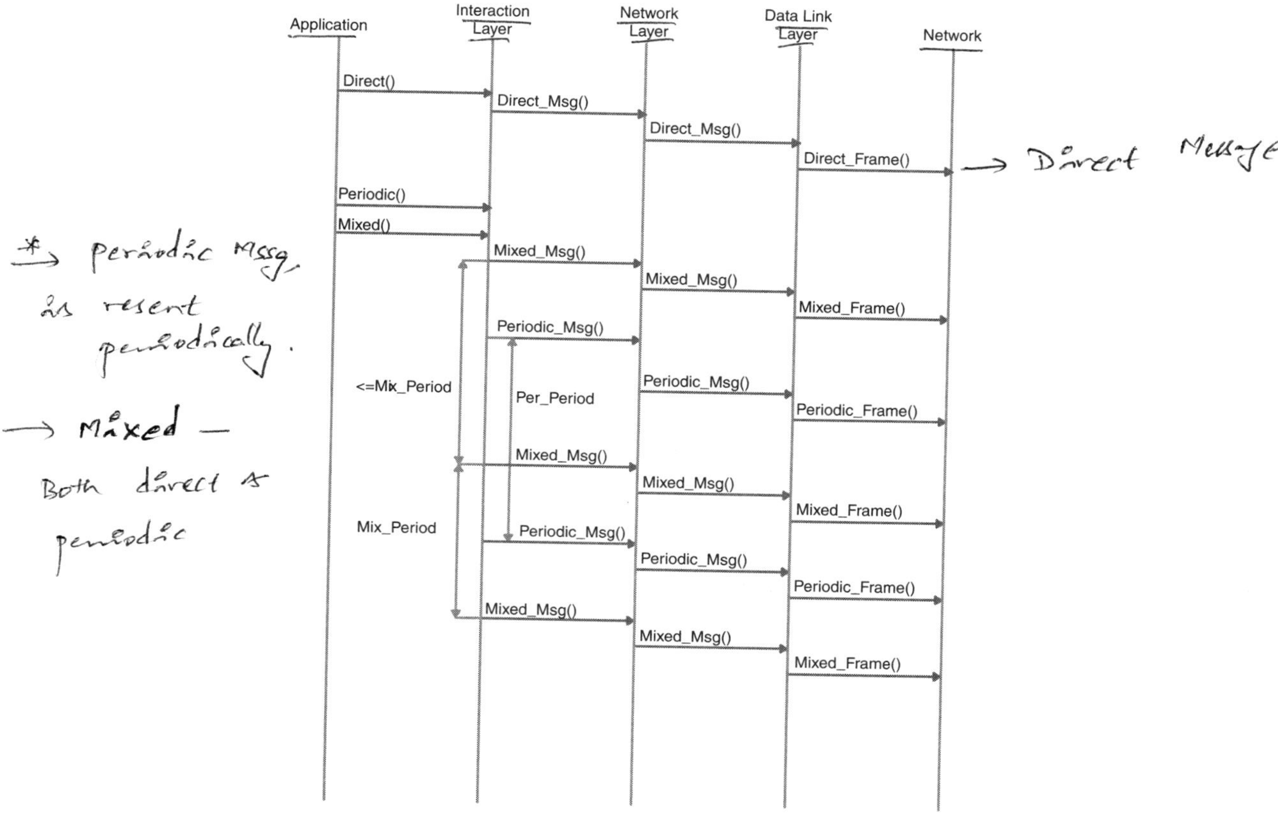

Figure 10.4 Transmission mode.

10.3.3 Mixed

The final transmission mode is mixed mode, in which an external or internal–external message is sent both directly and periodically. In Figure 10.4, the mixed message is sent at a fixed period. Whenever the application sends the message, it is sent out on the network based on a set of conditions that are defined statically. The possible conditions under which the message is sent are shown in Table 10.1. Keep this table in mind because the conditions used here are used later when I discuss conditional notification of message reception.

Conditional transmission assumes that a comparison can be made between two message objects that would require that a value in the message could be compared using the normal C logical functions, although it would be specific to the implementation. If this is the case, then messages that consist of a structure, strings, or arrays cannot be compared and, therefore, will always be transmitted. However, if the implementation provides a mechanism to compare more complex messages, such as a callback function, it might not be portable and should be avoided (i.e., the callback function should emulate the situation described above and always send the message.)

Table 10.1 Conditional mixed-mode message transmission.

Change	Description
Less than	The value of the message object is less than a constant value
Greater than	The value of the message object is greater than a constant value
Equal	The value of the message object is equal to a constant value
Delta less than	The difference (current – previous) in the values of the message object is less than a constant
Delta greater than	The difference (current – previous) in the values of the message object is greater than a constant
Delta equal	The difference (current – previous) in the values of the message object is equal to a constant
Always	A relevant change is always detected
User defined	The user defines a relevant change (implementation specific)

In mixed message transmission mode, the message is transmitted on the network without regard to when the periodic message is scheduled to be sent next. Sending the direct message does not restart the timer that determines when the next periodic message is sent. Consequently, a message could be transmitted twice in a row over the network if the application sends the message just prior to or just after the periodic message is transmitted.

10.4 Message Addressing and Length

If the underlying data link network supports message addressing, the target address of transmitted messages can be defined in the configuration file. For UUDT messages, which are always transmitted to the same location, this address is always defined statically in the configuration file. For USDT messages, which can be transmitted to the same address or selectively to different addresses, the address can be defined statically or set dynamically by the application at run time. Transmission and reception of dynamically addressed messages use different API services and are discussed in more detail in Chapter 13. The definition of the address is specific to the network protocol and is probably defined in a protocol-specific object. This object might or might not be defined in a future OIL standard.

The length of the message is defined statically in the configuration file. In the case of a UUDT message, the length of the message is always the value in the configuration file. In the case of a USDT message, the length of the message is less than or equal to the length in the configuration file. The length of the message is defined by the `LENGTH` attribute in the message object. If the message will always be the same size, then the length in the configuration file is the length of the message and the message is defined as a static length message. However, if the message can be of variable size, then the length in the configuration file is the maximum length for the message and the message is referred to as a dynamic length message. Like dynamically address messages, dynamic length messages also use different API services. Note that a variable length message is limited to a maximum of 4,095 bytes by the COM specification.

10.5 Deadline Monitoring

The next characteristic, which refers to how an individual message is handled, is a characteristic of the COM specification rather than the message itself. OSEK/VDX COM defines a method of monitoring a deadline within which a message must be received or transmitted successfully over the network. Because the communication model is asynchronous, this method ensures that the application can be noticed if and when the message appears on the physical layer bus.

The deadline monitoring mechanism determines whether a message is actually transmitted over the network when sent, is successfully transmitted periodically, or is received within a predefined period of time. The mechanism functions differently depending on whether the message is sent (transmitted) by the application or received by the application. It also depends on whether a message is transmitted using the direct, periodic, or mixed transmission mode.

Definition of deadline monitoring is in the `MESSAGE` object in the OIL configuration file. In the OSEKWorks implementation, deadline monitoring is set using the `TX_NOTIFICATION` attribute, which is set to the value `ON_DEADLINE`, and two additional attributes: `TX_DEADLINE_ALARM` and `TX_DEADLINE_TIME`. OSEKWorks assumes that an OSEK-compliant OS is available, and utilizes the `ALARM` object to monitor the deadline. This `ALARM` object must be defined separately. The task that is activated or the event that is set when the deadline is reached is defined in the `ALARM` object when it expires. In the COM specification, it is suggested that a separate deadline monitoring object called `TRANSMISSION_DEADLINE_MONITOR` should be created and referenced by the message object. Likewise for reception, OSEKWorks includes an `RX_NOTIFICATION` attribute, and the specification suggests an object called `RECEPTION_DEADLINE_MONITOR`.

10.5.1 Direct Mode Transmission Monitoring

The sequence of events that occur when monitoring the transmission of a message in direct transmission mode is shown in Figure 10.5 for both a successful and a failed transmission. In this example, the application sends a message to the interaction layer, which then forwards the message to the network and data link layers. The interaction layer then starts the deadline monitor timer and returns to the application. According to the COM specification, the time-out value of the monitor timer can be unique for every message or can be shared by two or more messages. However, a separate timer is required for each message that is monitored.

At some future point in time, the message is transmitted successfully on the network. How this is determined is specific to the network. Once successfully transmitted, the data link layer notifies the network layer, which in turn notifies the interaction layer. The interaction layer then cancels the timer and the transaction is complete. Later, the application sends the message again, it is forwarded to the network and data link layers, and the timer is restarted. This time, however, the timer expires before the message is transmitted successfully on the network. The timer notifies the interaction layer that this has occurred, and the interaction layer then notifies the application. How the interaction layer notifies the application is discussed in Section 10.6, "Notification Mechanisms."

10.5.2 Periodic Mode Transmission Monitoring

The sequence of events that occur when monitoring the periodic transmission of a message is shown in Figure 10.6 for a successful and a failed transmission. In this example, when the interaction layer determines that a periodic message is to be sent, it notifies the network layer and starts a deadline monitor timer that is twice the period. The value of this timer must be an integer multiple of the period of the message and is determined statically during system configuration. When the network layer notifies the interaction layer that the message has been transmitted successfully over the physical network, the interaction layer stops the timer.

Figure 10.5 Direct transmission mode deadline monitoring.

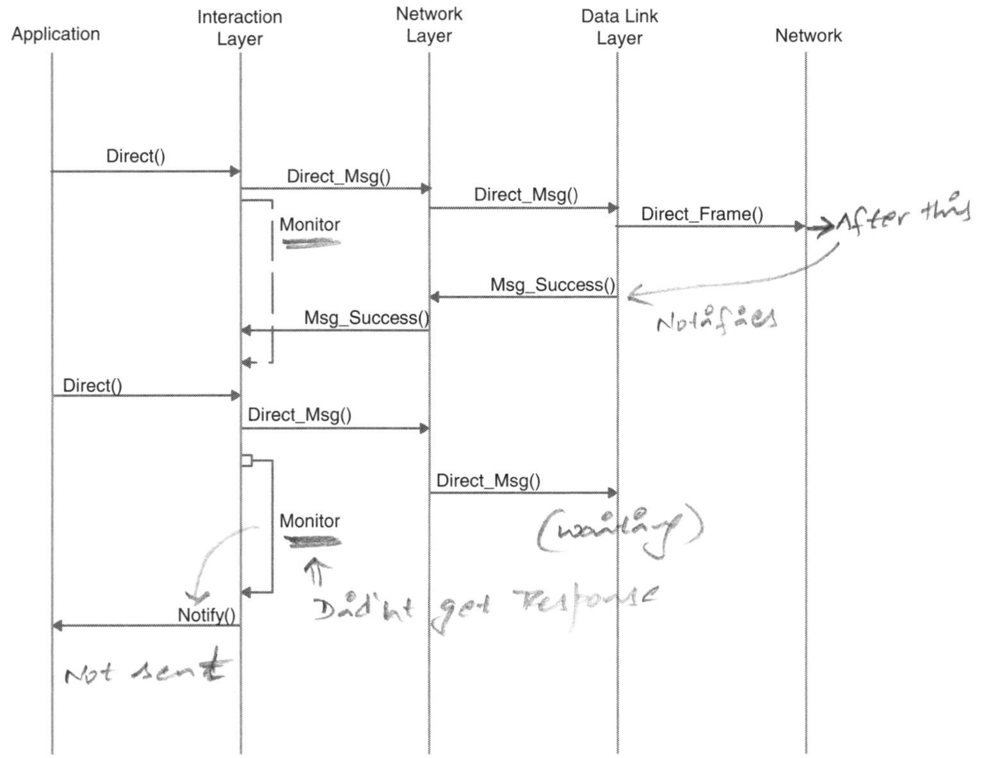

In the second part of the example, the timer expires prior to notification by the network layer that the message has been transmitted successfully. This will coincide roughly with the time to transmit the third message. If this occurs, the timer function notifies the interaction layer that time has expired, and the interaction layer then notifies the application by invoking one of the notification mechanisms. The interaction layer, however, will continue to attempt to send the periodic message. If the timer is not running or has expired, the interaction layer restarts the timer when the message is sent; however, if the timer is still running, it is not restarted. This addresses the instance where the integer multiple of the period is greater than one, as in the final part of the example.

Figure 10.6 Periodic transmission mode deadline monitoring.

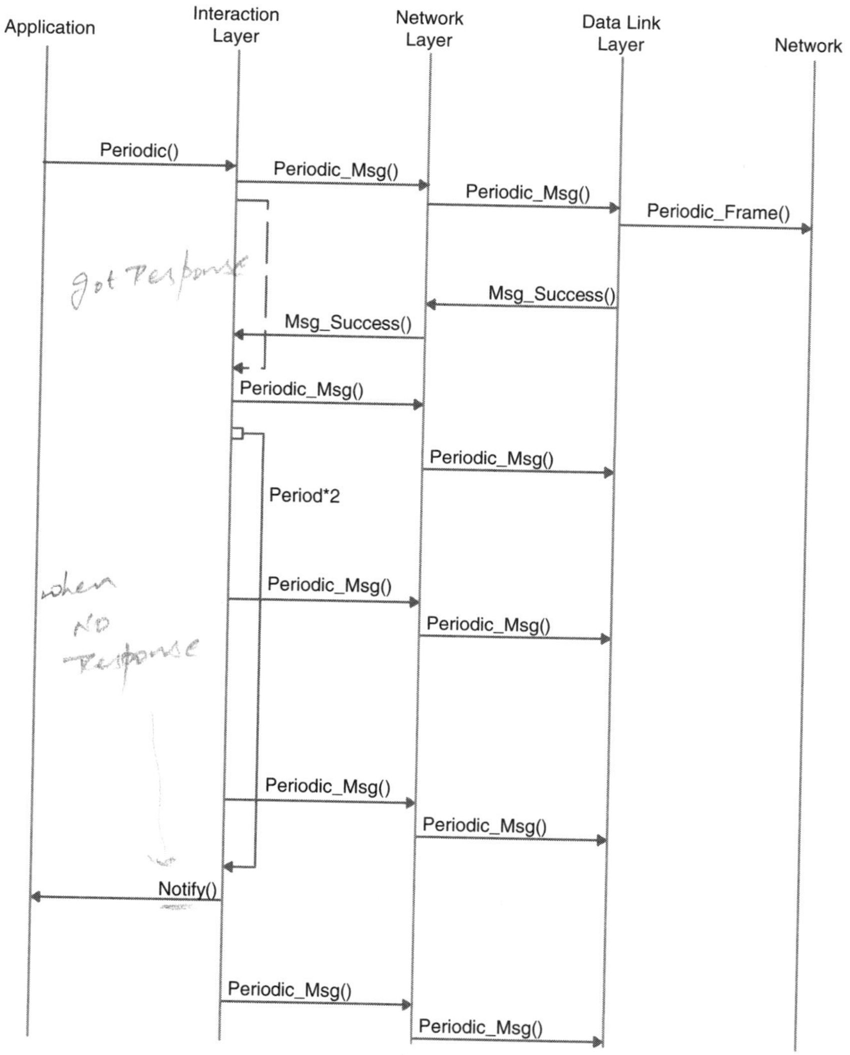

When the periodic timeout is greater than one, the timer is allowed to run until it expires or one of the messages is sent successfully on the network. If the timer expires before one message is sent successfully, then the notification mechanism is activated again.

10.5.3 Mixed-Mode Transmission Monitoring

The final method for transmission deadline monitoring is the case of mixed-mode transmission of a message (Figure 10.7). In this mode, the timer is started whenever it is not running and a message is sent from the interaction layer to the network/data link layer. This can occur when the interaction layer determines that a message should be transmitted under the periodic portion of mixed transmission mode, or when the application requests a direct transmission, in which case, the message is transmitted conditionally. The conditions under which a direct transmission can occur were discussed in Table 10.1. The value of the timer used for mixed-mode deadline monitoring is the same as that calculated for monitoring the transmission of periodic messages. Cancellation of the timer occurs if the network layer notifies the interaction layer of successful transmission of the message over the physical network.

In the first part of Figure 10.7, the timer is restarted when the periodic message is sent by the application with a value that meets the conditions for direct transmission and canceled on receipt of confirmation that the message was sent. In the second part of the figure, the timer is started after the periodic message is sent to the network layer and expires before a confirmation of successful transmission is received. In this case, the interaction layer notifies the application of the transmission failure.

10.5.4 Periodic Message Reception Monitoring

The final OSEK/VDX COM deadline monitoring mechanism is of periodic messages received over the physical network, which only applies to external messages (Figure 10.8). When the application initializes and starts the COM system, a timer is started for each message to be monitored. The first timeout period can be set optionally to a different value than subsequent timeouts. In Figure 10.8, the message is received successfully twice before a message is missed. When the message is received successfully, the interaction layer immediately restarts the timer. If the timer expires, the interaction layer immediately invokes the proper notification mechanism for the missed deadline.

10.6 Notification Mechanisms

OSEK/VDX COM notifies an application of the state of a message using one of four notification mechanisms: activate a task, set an event, call back a function, and set a flag. Activate a task and set an event require an OS that provides specific services for the mechanism. An OSEK/VDX OS provides these services but is not required for COM to operate. The last two mechanisms are intended for use in an application with either no OS or with an OS that does not support the first two mechanisms. Even if an OS that supports the first two mechanisms is used, the last two mechanisms can still be used.

The actions taken by the OS when a task is activated are specific to the OS. However, a task typically is moved into a state where it is ready to be executed. Based on the priority of the task, the task can execute immediately or some time in the future. Similarly, setting an event behaves differently in different OSs, but typically, the OS releases a task that is waiting for the event to occur and allows the task to execute in the future.

Figure 10.7 Mixed transmission mode deadline monitoring.

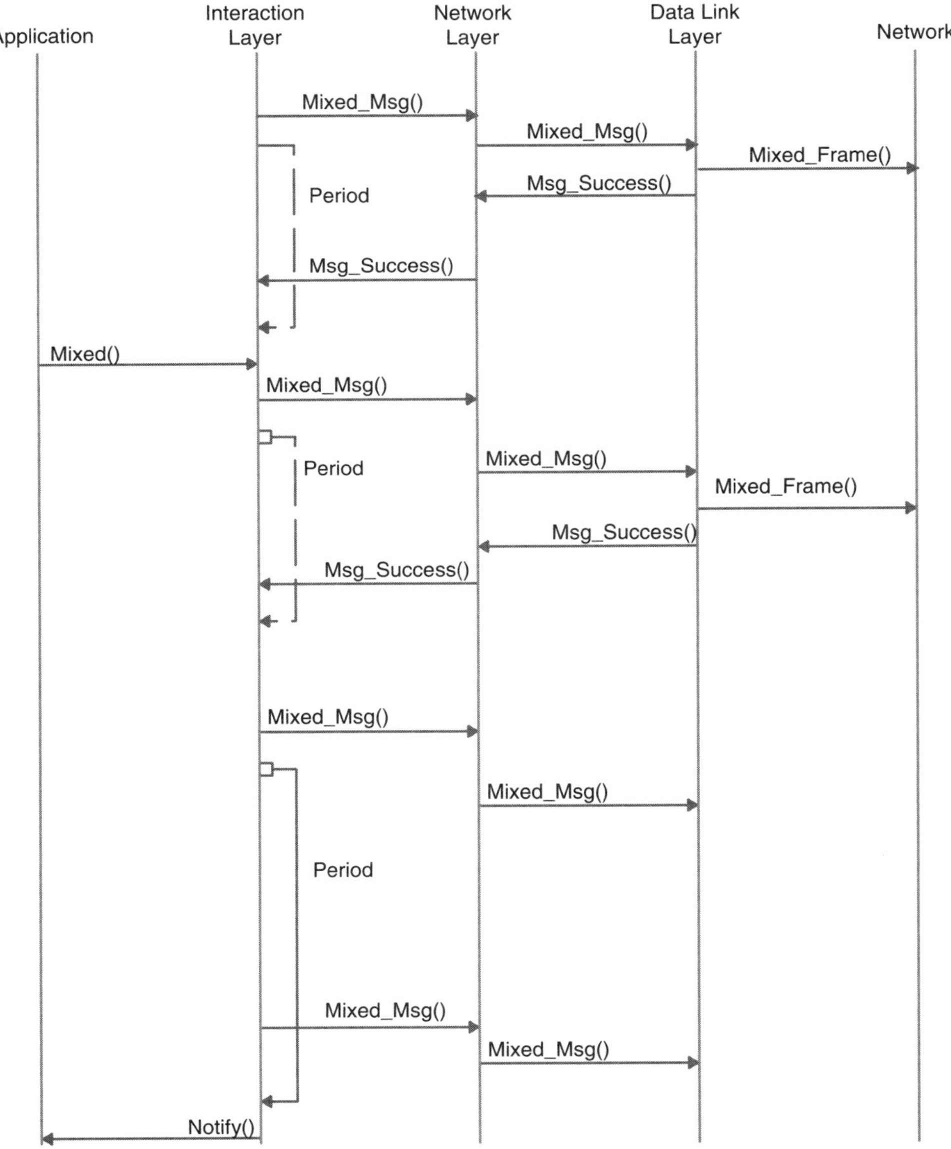

Figure 10.8 Periodic message reception deadline monitoring.

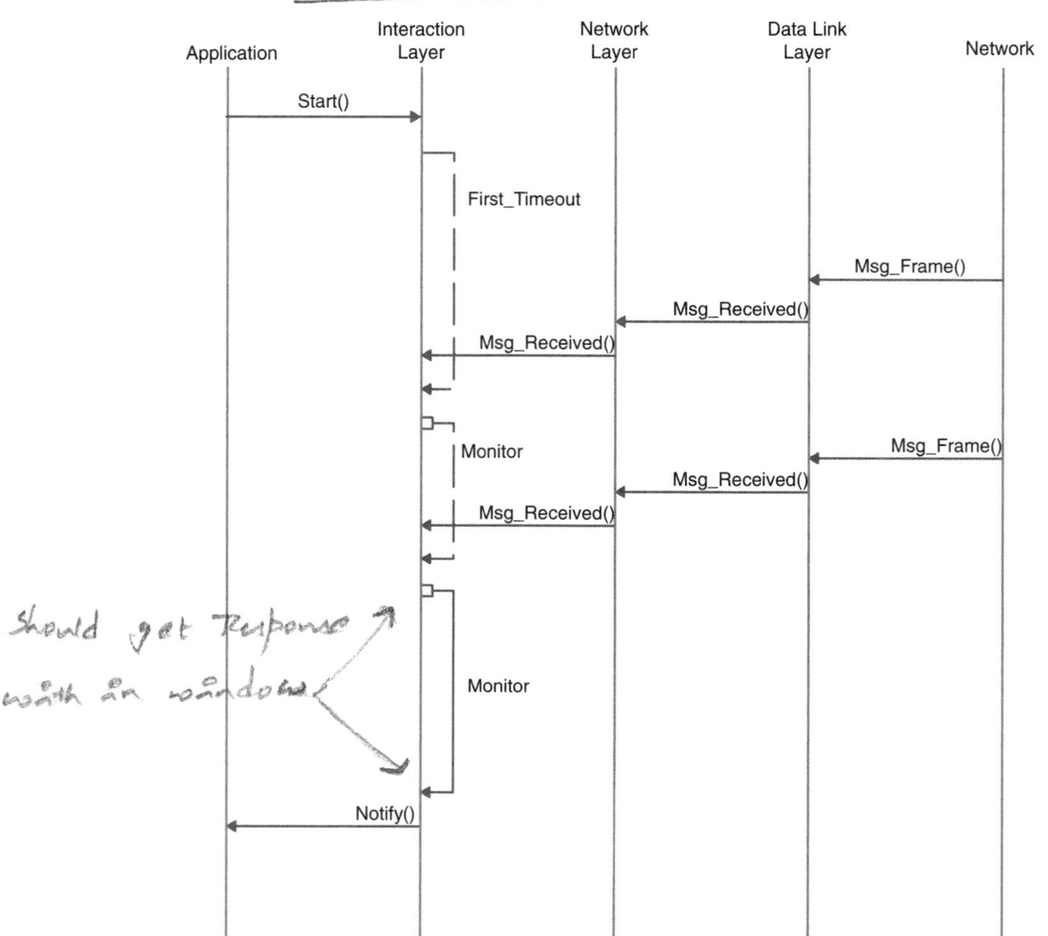

The mechanisms of callback and flag were added in the COM v2.2 specification. Because the goal of COM was to create a specification that could stand on its own, a method to notify an application not using an OS was required. Under the callback mechanism, the COM component executes a function when a notification is to occur. This function must have the following C prototype.

```
void CallbackFunc(void);
```

Because `CallbackFunc()` is executed immediately when notification is required, it could be evoked at the interrupt level if the COM component determines that notification is required from within an ISR, which could affect interrupt latency.

The flag mechanism works in an OS that polls the status of messages from within tasks that are executed either in a round-robin or a time-sliced executive. API services that check the status of the flag and reset the flag were added.

The COM specification also defines five classes of notification (Table 10.2). Within each of these classes, all notification mechanisms are available. A conditional version of the first class that limits execution of a notification, based on the condition of the data in the message, could be considered a sixth class. The available conditions are exactly the same as the conditions under which a direct message is transmitted in the mixed mode of transmission. The use of these notification classes is discussed in more detail in the following chapters.

Table 10.2 Classes of notification.

Class	Class Name	Description
1	Message reception	Notification occurs when the message is received (can be conditional based on the value). For internal and internal–external messages, notification occurs when the message is sent.
2	Message transmission	Notification occurs when the message is successfully transmitted over the physical layer.
3	Message reception error	Notification occurs when deadline monitoring of periodic received messages indicates that the message has not been received.
4	Message transmission error	Notification occurs when deadline monitoring of transmitted messages indicates that the message was not successfully transmitted.
5	USDT first frame indication	Notification occurs when the first frame of a USDT message is received. USDT messages are discussed later.

In the COM specification, it is possible to notify an application when a deadline monitor expires and also when a reception or transmission fails. The difference between these two notification methods is the time lag. A deadline error is not recognized until the timer expires, whereas an unsuccessful transmission is noted immediately from the data link layer. In earlier versions of the standard, only one notification mechanism was allowed per message, and only one action could be taken. For an unqueued message in the present version, multiple actions of the same type (e.g., activate task, set event) are allowed for each type of notification mechanism employed. The implementation can optionally allow multiple types of action to be taken.

10.7 Conformance Classes

All of the message attributes discussed in this chapter lead to the concept of conformance classes, which is unique to OSEK/VDX. In Part 1, the conformance class was discussed as it relates to the OS. A COM conformance class is defined as a specific realization of the COM requirements that contain a defined set of services available for all messages in the application. Five conformance classes are available: CCCA and CCCB only support internal messages, CCC0 and CCC1 support internal and external UUDT messages, and CCC2 supports all types of messages. The attributes that define the conformance class are shown in Table 10.3.

Table 10.3 Communication conformance class determination.

Feature	CCCA	CCCB	CCC0	CCC1	CCC2
UUDT			X	X	X
USDT					X
Internal messages	X	X	X	X	X
External messages			X	X	X
Unqueued messages	X	X	X	X	X
Queued messages		X	O	O	X
Direct transmission mode			X	X	X
Periodic transmission mode				X	X
Mixed transmission mode				X	X
Message reception notification (1)	X	X	X	X	X
Message transmission notification (2)			X	X	X
Message reception error notification (3)				X	X
Message transmission error notification (4)				X	X
USDT first frame indication notification (5)					X
Message resource supported		X	X	X	X
Dynamic addressing					X
Dynamic size					X

An X indicates mandatory support of the attribute, and an O indicates optional support. Each conformance class is discussed in more detail in the following chapters.

Note that queued messages are optional in CCC0 and CCC1. The consequence is that some implementations require you to use all of the features of CCC2 to obtain the queued message capability. Be careful of this fact when you search for an implementation.

10.8 Example Program

The example program that was created in Part 1 was not modified in this chapter because I only provide an overview of the COM specification. Changes are made in the following chapters as messages are covered in depth.

10.9 Summary

In this chapter, I covered a lot of information concerning the attributes of messages. If your head is not spinning, then you are one of the few in the world who understand this subject the first time! Don't worry, each area is discussed in more detail in the following chapters as I consider each type of message and use the attributes in examples.

11

Chapter 11

Internal Communication

As seen in the last chapter, the OSEK/VDX COM specification describes a complex system with many levels of capability. To better understand how a COM implementation works, I dive deeper in this chapter into different types of communication, starting with internal communication. Internal communication is supported in all conformance classes, with CCCA and CCCB offering internal intertask communication only.

As with all of the OSEK/VDX specifications, COM is never complete. In the chapters of Part 2, I identify issues that could cause concern in the use of COM, and as I develop the chapters, I discuss ways to work around these concerns.

Throughout this and the succeeding chapters, the examples I develop use OSEK/VDX OS tasks to illustrate how communication works. If your application does not use an OSEK/VDX OS, these tasks can be replaced with functions or tasks for the OS being used, and you can ignore the task OIL configuration file listings.

11.1 Internal Communication Overview

Internal communication describes the function of a system when tasks communicate exclusively with each other within a single microcontroller. By definition, a physical network does not exist in the application. COM conformance classes CCCA and CCCB allow only internal communication. A COM component that operates in CCCA or CCCB implements only the interaction layer and not the network or data link layers. This is the smallest implementation available.

The first part of this book, which covered the OS standard, introduced conformance class A (CCCA). This level of communication is required in any OSEK/VDX OS. The question then is whether the interaction layer is part of COM or part of the OS. The answer is that it is a part of COM, but any OS must implement this portion of COM with CCCA conformance.

The concept of internal communication is shown Figure 11.1, which shows a simple application with four tasks that communicate using two internal messages.

Figure 11.1 Internal communication.

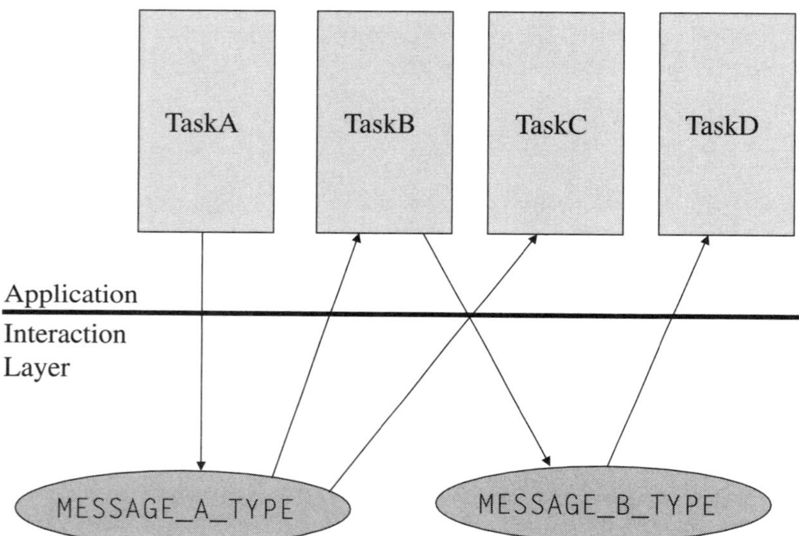

TaskA sends a message using the interaction layer. The content of this message is a `MESSAGE_A_TYPE` data type, which could be an integer type (`char`, `short`, `long`) or a user-defined type such as a structure. The interaction layer processes the message and returns to the application. I discuss the details of how the message is processed throughout this chapter. At some point in the future, TaskB and TaskC execute and request the data from the interaction layer. These tasks know the type of data that was sent and can therefore properly access it and process it. Based on this data, a second message is sent by TaskB, which is later received by TaskD. The data is accessed by the tasks using message accessors. How these accessors are defined and used is discussed throughout this chapter. This is a high-level description of the functioning of intertask communication but should work as a good overview for the sections to follow.

11.2 COM Startup and Shutdown

OSEK/VDX COM provides services that initialize, start, stop, and close the COM component. Startup and shutdown of the COM component was discussed in Chapter 9. I duplicate that information here for readers who do not use an OSEK/VDX OS and have jumped directly to this part of the book. Although this section is very similar to the information presented previously, additional issues with the full COM implementation are discussed that were not discussed as part of the OS. I recommend that you at least review this section to pick up the additional items that were not discussed earlier.

The COM component can be initialized and closed either outside the OSEK/VDX OS (i.e., before the call to `StartOS()` and after the return from `StartOS()`) or within the hook routines `StartupHook()` and `ShutdownHook()`. In a non-OSEK/VDX OS, call the initialization service before starting the OS and the closing service after the OS completes (if applicable). I have chosen to initialize and close the COM component within the hook routines (Listings 11.1 and 11.2).

Listing 11.1 `StartupHook()` with COM initialization.

```
void StartupHook(void)
{
   InitSystem(INIT_STARTUP);
   InitCOM();
}
```

Listing 11.2 `ShutdownHook()` with COM closure.

```
void ShutdownHook(StatusType error)
{
   if(error!=E_OK)
   {
      LastError = error;
   }
   CloseCOM();
   InitSystem(INIT_SHUTDOWN);
}
```

In `StartupHook()`, the COM component is initialized with a call to `InitCOM()`. The other services in this routine are application specific and are described in more detail in the example program section at the end of the chapter.

```
StatusType InitCOM(void);
```

The purpose of `InitCOM()` is to initialize any hardware and low-level resources of the COM component. When used for interprocess communication only, this service performs little or no processing. If the communication component is capable of sending or receiving external messages, then the service can initialize the hardware for each individual physical connection to a network. Hardware initialization could include such items as baud rate, data frame format, and interrupt handling.

The return value from this service, which is the same whether the system is in standard or extended status mode, is

- E_OK if the initialization completes successfully or
- specific to the implementation if the initialization does not complete successfully.

An OSEK/VDX task can invoke InitCOM(); however, all interrupts must be masked prior to calling it, and if it is called while the COM component is active, its behavior is not defined by the OSEK/VDX specification.

Within ShutdownHook(), CloseCOM() closes the COM component.

```
StatusType CloseCOM(void);
```

This API service is the complement of InitCOM(). CloseCOM() releases the low-level hardware resources that were initialized in InitCOM(). When CloseCOM() is invoked, all COM operations are halted, and any messages queued for transmission or partially received are lost. Typically, this service is not invoked while the COM component is active.

Once the communication component is initialized and the OS is started, StartCOM() and StopCOM() can start and stop the communication component. StartCOM(), unlike StopCOM(), must be called from the task level within the OS. The specification indicates that StopCOM() can use any OS service; consequently, it will most likely be called from the task level because many OS API services are not allowed at interrupt level or during hook routines.

StartCOM() and StopCOM() allow an application to use COM only when necessary because COM can consume resources that might be needed for other purposes. This is not an issue in the example here, so to demonstrate these two API services, I use two tasks: InitOS and CloseOS. If the application does not use an OS, these tasks will be functions. InitOS (Listing 11.3) executes first. The OIL configuration definition of this task is shown in Listing 11.4. InitOS will be the highest priority task in the system to ensure that it executes first after the OS starts.

First, I start the communication component with StartCOM(), and then I perform specific OS initializations. Because the example was developed using an OSEK/VDX OS, this task automatically starts the alarms that the system requires.

```
StatusType StartCOM(void);
```

StartCOM() starts the OSEK/VDX communication component and initializes internal states and variables. It also initializes OS resources used by the communication component. For example, if the communication component needs a task to perform a certain function on starting, StartCOM() will activate that task. It gets tricky here because the OSEK/VDX COM specification was written to be independent of the OS. If the communication component requires the OS or application to provide resources — resources required for the component to run, not the notification mechanisms of COM — the component might not be portable. In particular, if a COM component expects an OSEK/VDX OS to be available, the component will not function in another OS unless the application provides the required services.

Listing 11.3 `InitOS` **task.**

```
TASK(InitOS)
{

   InitAlarmType const *list = AlarmAutostartList;
   UINT32 currentAppModeMask = ConvertAppMode(APP_MODE_MASK);

   StartCOM();
   while(list->appmodemask != 0x00000000){
      if((list->appmodemask & currentAppModeMask)!= 0){
         if(list->alarmtype == ALARM_REL){
            SetRelAlarm(list->alarm,list->start,list->cycle);
         }
         else{
            SetAbsAlarm(list->alarm,list->start,list->cycle);
         }
      }
      list++;
   }
   TerminateTask();
}
```

Listing 11.4 `InitOS` **OIL task definition.**

```
TASK InitOS {
        /*@**************************************************************/
        /* Must be highest priority in the system.                      */
        /*@**************************************************************/

        TYPE = BASIC;
        SCHEDULE = FULL;
        PRIORITY = 16;
        ACTIVATION = 1;
        AUTOSTART = TRUE;
        STACKSIZE = 128;
        SCHEDULE_CALL = FALSE;
};
```

The typical services required by a COM component include task scheduling, some form of timer, the handling of interrupts, and possibly memory allocation. Some COM implementations might provide these services at the cost of additional overhead. When determining which COM implementation to use, unless you are purchasing an entire OSEK/VDX solution from one supplier, make sure that you fully understand the requirements to integrate the implementation into your system. This is very much a concern in the automotive industry, where automobile manufacturers typically supply or specify a particular implementation for the communication component but do not supply or specify the OS. This might change as OSEK/VDX matures and obtains ISO standardization.

The return value, which is the same whether the system is in standard or extended status mode, is

- `E_OK` if the startup completes successfully or
- specific to the implementation if the startup does not complete successfully.

`StartCOM()` must be called from within a task and must be called after `InitCOM()` and before `CloseCOM()` or else the behavior is undefined.

As mentioned earlier, messages can be sent and received with or without a copy being made. If the message is handled without a copy, the variable that holds the copy needs to be initialized prior to use. Many times, this variable will be global and needs to be set to a default value by the application. This is accomplished from within `StartCOM()` by optionally using the user-defined callback routine `MessageInit()`.

```
StatusType MessageInit(void);
```

This routine allows the application to initialize all application-specific message objects. Although defined in the specification, the application is not required to provide this callback routine and could use another method of initializing message objects.

Message object initialization can be accomplished a number of ways. The two most common methods is either to set the global variable to a constant for without-copy messages or to send a message initially using `SendMessage()`, which is described later in this chapter. However, `SendMessage()` cannot be invoked from within `MessageInit()` because it requires `StartCom()` to be complete before it can be invoked. It must be invoked from the task level after `StartCom()` returns.

Because COM only allows messages to be sent from one location within the system, the initial value of any message sent with-copy theoretically can only be set by that task or function. Consequently, if an internal message is received before the application sends the message, the value of the data is indeterminate. For a queued message, the returned status for a received message indicates that the queue is empty and can be handled by the application. In the COM specification v2.2.2 released in early 2001, the return status for an unqueued message that indicates a message was never sent or received was removed from the standard. The COM specification requires that the value returned to the application be the value set at initialization. However, there is no description of how the message is initialized. To resolve this, the application has a number of options.

1. If the COM implementation does not enforce sending messages from only one task or function, the application can send the message from one task or function during initialization and from the regular location during normal operation. This option can affect portability of the application and could require changes if a different COM implementation is

used. The single-sender rule is normally considered a global system design concept rather than something to be enforced at the source code level. However, if the initialization of the message data for all messages in the system is kept within one task or function, porting to a new implementation would be minimized. This option typically would be performed immediately after the return from `StartCOM()`. You should take care during normal operation of the application that the message is sent only from one location. This option is only available for internal and internal–external messages.

2. Activate all tasks and execute all functions that send messages immediately after the communication component starts. This would occur in the same location as option 1 mentioned previously. The drawback of this method is that there is no guarantee the tasks will be performed in the proper order to ensure data consistency.
3. Send all internal messages without-copy and receive them either with- or without-copy. In this manner, the application can initialize the global variable either within the `MessageInit()` callback function or within the task that executes `StartCOM()`. This requires that a coding standard is enforced globally within an application.
4. Create a flag for every unqueued message using the COM notification mechanism. These flags can be reset in the routine that calls `StartCOM()` and then checked whenever a message is needed. If the flag is set to `TRUE`, the message has been sent or received at least once by the COM component. If the flag is set to `FALSE`, the message has never been sent or received since the COM component was started. The drawback of this method is added overhead every time the message is received by an application task.

Because of the extensive effort required to initialize unqueued messages, the COM specification still needs some work. A revised COM specification or the next release of the OIL specification could address how message data is initialized. Until that time, I recommend that you select a COM implementation that does not enforce sending messages from a single point as in option 1. When the initialization issue is addressed, only a single routine in an application will have to be changed.

Initialization is problematic for external unqueued messages received by the local application. Because an application has no way to initialize a message received from an external source, the application must rely on a combination of system design and network management. Network management is discussed in more detail in Part 3, when I discuss the OSEK/VDX Network Management specification. From the system design angle, the network system designer needs to implement a method that sends all external messages at least once immediately after communication begins. One hopes that the OSEK/VDX COM working group will address this issue soon. Until then, the reader should look for a COM implementation that provides a mechanism to initialize external messages within `StartCOM()`.

The other task to be created is `CloseOS`, which has exactly the same attributes in the OIL configuration file as the previous task, `InitOS`, does not start automatically, and has a priority of one less than `InitOS`. A priority of one less than `InitOS` maintains a level 1 (BCC1/ECC1) system that results in a more optimal implementation. If you move to a level 2 (BCC2/ECC2) system, the priority of `CloseOS` could be the same as that of `InitOS`.

The `CloseOS` task performs application-specific housekeeping procedures prior to shutting down the OS. It is activated by the application service `ChangeMode()`, which was created in Chapter 1 and modified in Chapter 9. `ChangeMode()` is specific to an OSEK/VDX OS and enables `APPMODE` switching. No changes have been made to this service since Chapter 9. Listing 11.5 shows the `CloseOS` task and Listing 11.6 shows its OIL configuration listing.

Listing 11.5 `CloseOS` task.

```
TASK(CloseOS)
{
   StopCOM(COM_SHUTDOWN_IMMEDIATE);
   ShutdownOS(E_OK);
   TerminateTask();
}
```

Listing 11.6 `CloseOS` OIL task definition.

```
TASK CloseOS {
           TYPE = BASIC;
           SCHEDULE = FULL;
           PRIORITY = 15;
           ACTIVATION = 1;
           AUTOSTART = FALSE;
           STACKSIZE = 64;
           SCHEDULE_CALL = FALSE;
   };
```

In `CloseOS`, `StopCOM()` stops the communication component and `ShutdownOS()` shuts down the OS.

```
StatusType StopCOM(Scalar mode);
```

`StopCOM()` immediately stops all OSEK/VDX communication activity, frees all OS resources used or puts the resources in an inactive state, and prepares the communication component for the next invocation of `StartCOM()`. `StopCOM()` also deinitializes the microcontroller hardware after all messages in the process of transmission complete. Hardware deinitialization is minimal; it prepares the hardware to be started again. Complete hardware reconfiguration is performed by `CloseCOM()`.

The `mode` parameter passed to `StopCOM()` tells the service how to shut down the communication component. The OSEK/VDX COM specification only defines one possible value for this parameter, `COM_SHUTDOWN_IMMEDIATE`. If this value is passed to the service, the service shuts down the communication component immediately without waiting for pending operations, such as transmissions in progress, to complete. This behavior directly contradicts the `StopCOM()` definition, which says the system should complete sending messages before it shuts down. The original proposal for `StopCOM()` included the `COM_SHUTDOWN_GRACEFUL` parameter, which allowed operations to complete, if necessary, or would cause the service to return `E_COM_BUSY` if the application locked one of COM's resources, such as a message buffer, preventing its release. This feature was removed from the published standard. Specific implementations could define additional modes, but to ensure portability, they should not be used.

The return value from StopCOM(), which is the same whether the system is in standard or extended status mode, is

- E_OK if the communication component stops successfully or
- E_COM_BUSY if the communication component cannot shut down because a resource owned by the component is in use by the application.

Now that the communication component has been integrated into the application with the necessary functions to initialize, start, stop, and close the component, the application can now be modified to use intertask communication.

11.3 Unqueued Messages (CCCA)

The first type of message I add to the application is an unqueued internal message, which minimally requires conformance class A (CCCA) but is available in all conformance classes. CCCA is intended to allow a very lean implementation of a minimal communication component to be created. As such, only one notification mechanism for each message is allowed, and it can only notify one message consumer, which can be a task, a callback function, or an event. The mechanism that ensures data consistency by locking message resources is not available at this level.

First I create the DisplayMessage unqueued internal message. Ideally, it would send individual messages to the display, and the associated task would extract the data from the message and update only the areas of the display that are affected. This operation would require a message that could be sent to the task from multiple locations within the application (many:1 communication); however, the OSEK/VDX COM standard only allows 1:1 and 1:many communication.

To get around this limitation of the system, I created two display services that encapsulate the display message buffer: WriteDisplay() and WriteDisplayAt(). WriteDisplayAt() includes two additional parameters, the row and the column from which to begin displaying the value, whereas WriteDisplay() is implemented as a call to WriteDisplayAt(), with the row and column set to 0xFF, indicating that output should occur at the current cursor position. WriteDisplayAt() (Listing 11.7) buffers the information and the desired cursor position.

Listing 11.7 WriteDisplayAt().

```
BOOLEAN WriteDisplayAt(UINT8 row, UINT8 column, const char * text)
{
BOOLEAN result=TRUE;

   if(displayBufferError == FALSE){
      SuspendOSInterrupts();
      displayBuffer[displayBufferEnd].row = row;
      displayBuffer[displayBufferEnd].column = column;
      strcpy(&displayBuffer[displayBufferEnd].buffer,text);
      if(++displayBufferEnd == DISPLAY_BUFFER_SIZE){
```

```
            displayBufferEnd = 0;
        }
        if(displayBufferEnd == displayBufferStart){
            displayBufferError = TRUE;
        }
        ResumeOSInterrupts();
        ActivateTask(OutputDisplay);
    }
    else{
        result = FALSE;
    }
    return result;
}
```

The `WriteDisplayAt()` service first ensures that sufficient space exists in the display buffer before transmitting the information into `displayBuffer`, which is now static to this module and which allows multiple tasks to send messages to the display without worrying about overwriting someone else's message. `WriteDisplayAt()` guarantees that a message cannot be preempted by another task while writing to the buffer by creating a critical section using `SuspendOSInterrupts()` and `ResumeOSInterrupts()`. This critical section is implemented differently if a different operating environment is used. If the information is buffered successfully, `WriteDisplayAt()` activates the `OutputDisplay` task and returns `TRUE`. If an error occurs, such as insufficient buffer space, and the information cannot be buffered, the service returns `FALSE`. The `OutputDisplay` task (Listing 11.8) must now be modified to take advantage of the new format of the display buffer.

Listing 11.8 `OutputDisplay` task.

```
TASK(OutputDisplay)
{
    while((displayBufferError == TRUE) ||
        (displayBufferStart != displayBufferEnd)){
        if(displayBuffer[displayBufferStart].row != 0xff){
            SetDisplayPosition(displayBuffer[displayBufferStart].row,
                displayBuffer[displayBufferStart].column);
        }
        PackDisplay(displayBuffer[displayBufferStart].buffer);
        if((++displayBufferStart) == DISPLAY_BUFFER_SIZE){
            displayBufferStart = 0;
        }
        Schedule();
```

```
    }
    SendMessage(DisplayMessage,displayMirror);
    TerminateTask();
}
```

OutputDisplay first checks the information in the display buffer. If the cursor needs to move, it invokes SetCursorPosition() then formats the internal copy of the display using PackDisplay() (Listing 11.9), which is specific to the display.

Listing 11.9 PackDisplay().

```
void PackDisplay(char *string)
{
UINT8 i,j;

    while(*string != 0)
    {
        switch(*string)
        {
...
            default:
                if(*string >= 240)
                {
                  displayMirror->message[cursorPosition.row*MAX_DISPLAY_LINE_LENGTH
                        + cursorPosition.column++] = *string - (char)240;
                }
                else
                {
                  displayMirror->message[cursorPosition.row*MAX_DISPLAY_LINE_LENGTH
                        + cursorPosition.column++] = *string;
                }
                if(cursorPosition.column == MAX_DISPLAY_LINE_LENGTH)
                {
                   OutputNewLine();
                }
        }
        ++string;
    }
}
```

PackDisplay() performs multiple actions, but I have only shown the section where the message object is accessed. In order to access the message object, I have to define an ACCESSOR for the OutputDisplay task. Accessors, as discussed in Chapter 10, define how an application accesses the message data. Figure 11.2 shows the relationship between the message object and the task object. The task object can be replaced by an interrupt service routine or a function or callback routine when an OS is not used. For simplicity, only the task object is discussed here.

Figure 11.2 Message, task, and ACCESSOR relationship.

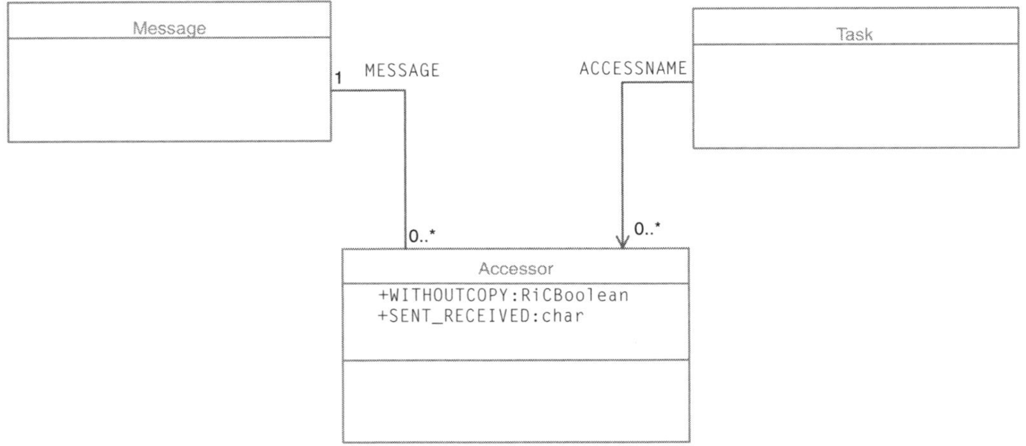

Because the relationship between the task class and the message class is a many:many relationship, ACCESSOR is a container object that maps this relationship. For each task, zero to many accessors could be defined. Each accessor maps to only one message, but multiple accessors can and will map to a message.

In the current OIL specification, the ACCESSOR object is an attribute of a task because only internal communication, as defined within an OS environment, is supported. The next version of the OIL specification will support the entire COM specification and expand the information available. Listing 11.10 shows the OIL configuration file entry for the OutputDisplay task.

The ACCESSOR attribute has a value of SENT or RECEIVED and sets three parameters: MESSAGE, WITHOUTCOPY, and ACCESSNAME. The MESSAGE parameter is the name of the message to which the relationship is mapped. This message must be defined elsewhere in the OIL configuration file. The WITHOUTCOPY parameter is a Boolean TRUE or FALSE. Finally, the ACCESSNAME parameter is the name of the accessor that is created by the OIL configuration utility and referenced by the task.

The message accessor concept within the OSEK/VDX COM specification appears confusing at first. However, it simply defines the name of the variable that is visible to the application and is used by the task to send or receive data. This global variable is created by the OIL configuration utility.

Listing 11.10 `OutputDisplay` **task definition.**

```
TASK OutputDisplay {
          TYPE = BASIC;
          SCHEDULE = NON;
          PRIORITY = 12;
          ACTIVATION = 1;
          AUTOSTART = FALSE;
          STACKSIZE = 128;
          SCHEDULE_CALL = TRUE;
          ACCESSOR = SENT {
             MESSAGE = DisplayMessage;
             WITHOUTCOPY = TRUE;
             ACCESSNAME = "displayMirror";
          }
   };
```

When the OIL configuration file is processed, an implementation typically creates the message object in the OIL output source file. It then selects all of the message accessors defined within the `TASK` object definitions that have the `WITHOUTCOPY` parameter set to `FALSE` and creates a duplicate copy of the message object in the output file. For all tasks with the `ACCESSOR` parameter `WITHOUTCOPY` set to `TRUE`, the configuration utility will create an alias name that allows the application to access the message object using the accessor name. Use of these access names is discussed in the examples.

One drawback of accessors is the way they are used in some of the implementations on the market. When a message is defined, the message object is created as a RAM variable. For every accessor that is defined with the `WITHOUTCOPY` parameter set to `FALSE`, a variable of the same type as the message is created and is available globally. It is the responsibility of the application to ensure that the only task that accesses this variable is the one to which the accessor name is defined. This also limits the ability of an application to create a locally defined variable into which the message is copied and which is destroyed when the task terminates. From the implementation standpoint, however, these multiple copies make the implementation much more efficient and robust.

In an application that has limited RAM memory, this drawback can be addressed by accessing all message objects using `ACCESSOR` objects with the `WITHOUTCOPY` parameter set to `TRUE`. This limits the creation of only one message object in RAM. If the application requires a local copy of the message object when received, then the application can use the C library function `memcpy()` to do a byte-wise copy of the global message object into a local message object. However, the application must ensure that the local object has the exact same `CDATATYPE` as the global object. Because of some quirks of C , this is not guaranteed to work.

The message constructed by the `OutputDisplay` task is called `DisplayMessage` (Listing 11.11).

Listing 11.11 `DisplayMessage` configuration.

```
MESSAGE DisplayMessage {
            TYPE = INTERNAL;
            LENGTH = 80;
            ALIGNMENT = 1;
            USAGE = SEND_RECEIVE;
            QUEUED = FALSE;
            TX_NOTIFICATION = NONE;
            RX_NOTIFICATION = ON_SUCCESS;
            TRANSMISSION = DIRECT;
            ACCESSNAMES = { displayMirrorTemp, displayMirror };
            RX_SUCCESS_TASK = OutputDisplayBuffer;
            RX_SUCCESS_EVENT = BUFFER_CHANGED;
    };
```

In this example and throughout this chapter, I use the OSEKWorks definition for messages because a standard COM OIL definition does not exist. `DisplayMessage` is configured as an internal unqueued message. The `RX_NOTIFICATION` attribute is set to `ON_SUCCESS`, which corresponds to notification class 1. The `RX_SUCCESS_EVENT` notification mechanism sets the `BUFFER_CHANGED` OS event that is associated with the `OutputDisplayBuffer` task defined by the `RX_SUCCESS_TASK` attribute. The example application uses an 80-character display; therefore, the message length is set to `80`. Because `DisplayMessage` is an internal message only, the segmented versus unsegmented, transmission mode, and deadline monitoring attributes are not applicable to this message and are set to default values. In addition, the `ACCESSNAMES` attribute defines the set of names that access this message. This setup is particular to versions of OSEKWorks that have not been updated to the new OIL specification and for which the accessor is defined as a separate object. In an implementation that uses the latest OIL specification, this information is available through the `ACCESSOR` attribute of the `TASK` object .

The current OSEK/VDX OIL specification defines additional attributes that should be a part of the `MESSAGE` object. The first attribute, `CDATATYPE`, defines the application-specific type of data to be used for the message object. `CDATATYPE` can be a standard C type or a user-specified data type, such as a structure. In OSEKWorks, which presently does not support the latest specification, this attribute is a part of the `ACCESSNAME` object. The other attribute, `ACTION`, defines the specific action taken for an internal message. Because only notification class 1 is allowed in conformance classes CCCA and CCCB, this attribute is limited to activating a task or setting an event in an OSEK/VDX OS. In the future, this will have to be expanded extensively to meet all of the actions possible.

I have now defined a message that the `OutputDisplay` task uses to send a message to the `OutputDisplayBuffer` task, which then outputs the message to the display. Additionally, I have an accessor, `displayMirror`, that accesses the message object without-copy.

Because the display buffer can hold information from multiple tasks, `OutputDisplay` uses a `while()` loop to pull multiple messages from the buffer if they exist. This `while()` loop is required because I defined the task to be a single-activation task. A task in a non-OSEK/VDX OS will probably also need this `while()` loop. A multiple-activation task would not need a `while()` loop because each activation of the task would process one package of information from the application.

After all pieces of information have been removed from the information buffer, the buffer with the copy of the display is transmitted to the output display driver using `SendMessage()`.

```
StatusType SendMessage(SymbolicName message, AccessNameRef data);
```

When invoked, `SendMessage()` performs a function that is dependent on the `COPY` value, which can be with-copy or without-copy, in the `ACCESSOR` object definition in the OIL configuration file. Presently, it is defined by the `WITHOUTCOPY` parameter of the `ACCESSOR` attribute in the `TASK` object. If this value is set to with-copy (`WITHOUTCOPY = FALSE`), then the message object created within the communication component is updated with the values contained in the accessor referenced by the `data` parameter. If the `COPY` value is set to without-copy (`WITHOUTCOPY = TRUE`), the message object is not updated. `SendMessage()` then performs the notification defined for the message referenced in the `message` parameter. Notification is not dependent on the value of `COPY`. In Listing 11.10, which defines the `ACCESSOR displayMirror` for the `OutputDisplay` task, the `WITHOUTCOPY` parameter is set to `TRUE`, which indicates that the application controls the data to be output to the display directly, instead of through a `COPY`.

The status returned from `SendMessage()` can be one of the following.

- If the service cannot guarantee that access to the message is safe, it returns `E_COM_LOCKED`. Determining when access cannot be granted to the message object is specific to the implementation.
- If the `WITHOUTCOPY` parameter is `FALSE` for this accessor and the communication component identifies that the message is set to `BUSY`, the service returns `E_COM_LOCKED`. This situation only occurs in an implementation with conformance class CCCB or higher
- If the service executes successfully, it returns `E_OK`.
- In extended status mode only, the service returns `E_COM_ID` if the message referenced in the `message` parameter is not valid.

The transmitted message, `DisplayMessage`, is shown in Listing 11.11. When this message is sent, the notification mechanism sets the `BUFFER_CHANGED` event for the `OutputDisplayBuffer` task (a high-priority task that dumps the buffer to the display), which will communicate with the display and take care of the handshaking. `OutputDisplayBuffer` is shown in Listing 11.12 and its definition in Listing 11.13. Only the portion of the task that demonstrates communication concepts is shown. The remainder (after the ellipses) writes to the display and is not discussed here.

Listing 11.12 `OutputDisplayBuffer` **task.**

```
TASK(OutputDisplayBuffer)
{
   UINT8 *displayControl = DISPLAY_CONTROL_LOCATION;
   UINT8 *display = DISPLAY_BUFFER_LOCATION;
   UINT8 i,outputRow;
   UINT8 translateRow;
   DISPLAY_MESSAGE_TYPE displayMirrorLocal;

   WriteDisplay(InitMessage);
   while(1){
      translateRow = 0;
      WaitEvent(BUFFER_CHANGED);
      ClearEvent(BUFFER_CHANGED);
      GetResource(RES_SCHEDULER);
      if(ReceiveMessage(DisplayMessage,displayMirrorTemp)==E_OK){
         memcpy(&displayMirrorLocal,displayMirrorTemp,
            sizeof(DISPLAY_MESSAGE_TYPE));
      }
      ReleaseResource(RES_SCHEDULER);
...
   }
}
```

`OutputDisplayBuffer` starts automatically when the OS starts. It waits for the `BUFFER_CHANGED` event to be set and enters the `WAITING` state. Because the display is relatively slow compared to the speed of the application and the message is received without-copy, the global copy of the display can be modified and thereby corrupted during the write operation. Consequently, `OutputDisplayBuffer` creates a local copy of the buffer prior to writing the information to the display. As mentioned in Chapter 10, creating a local copy of the message is typically not possible with most current implementations because with-copy access typically declares a static variable. Some implementations might function differently, but the ones I have worked with do not allow local copies of messages. You can make a copy using the without-copy capabilities of the system and `memcpy()`, but note the `memcpy()` argument names carefully. The `displayMessageTemp` argument is an accessor, which is defined as a reference to the message object. Consequently, it is already a pointer and is included directly. However, the local copy is a variable, so the address of the local copy must be sent. Copying occurs in a section in which the `RES_SCHEDULER` resource is locked to ensure that the buffer is not corrupted while it is copied. The event is cleared prior to locking the resource so that any changes to the buffer are processed on completion of the update.

Listing 11.13 `OutputDisplayBuffer` task definition.

```
TASK OutputDisplayBuffer {
            TYPE = EXTENDED;
            SCHEDULE = NON;
            PRIORITY = 14;
            ACTIVATION = 1;
            AUTOSTART = TRUE;
            STACKSIZE = 128;
            SCHEDULE_CALL = FALSE;
            EVENT = { BUFFER_CHANGED, DISPLAY_READY };
            RESOURCE = { RES_SCHEDULER };
            ACCESSOR = RECEIVED {
               MESSAGE = DisplayMessage;
               WITHOUTCOPY = TRUE;
               ACCESSNAME = "displayMirrorTemp";
            }
};
```

Before copying the buffer to the local data location, `ReceiveMessage()` is invoked to verify that the message is valid.

```
StatusType ReceiveMessage(SymbolicName message, AccessNameRef data);
```

The function performed by `ReceiveMessage()` is dependent on the `COPY` value in the `ACCESSOR` object definition in the OIL configuration file. This object is not defined in OIL, but is in the COM specification as a suggested object. The `COPY` value can be either with-copy or without-copy. If with-copy, the COM component updates the values in the accessor referenced by the `data` parameter. If without-copy, the `data` parameter is ignored. As with `SendMessage()`, the `TASK` object defines the `ACCESSOR` object in the current release of the OSEK/VDX OIL specification, as seen in Listing 11.13, which defines the `displayMirrorTemp` `ACCESSOR` for the `OutputDisplayBuffer` task. The `WITHOUTCOPY` parameter is set to `TRUE`, indicating that the COM component provides visibility to the task of the message object. If the `WITHOUTCOPY` parameter is `FALSE`, the message object is copied to a global accessor that is visible to the application.

The status returned from `ReceiveMessage()` can be one of the following.

- If the service cannot guarantee that access to the message is safe, it returns `E_COM_LOCKED`. Determining when access cannot be granted to the message object is specific to the implementation.
- If the `WITHOUTCOPY` parameter is `FALSE` for this accessor and the communication component identifies that the message is set to `BUSY`, the service returns `E_COM_LOCKED`. This only occurs in an implementation with conformance class CCCB or higher.
- If the service executes successfully, it returns `E_OK`.

- Other return values are effective only if the message is queued, which is discussed in "Queued Messages (CCCB)."
- In extended status mode only, the service returns `E_COM_ID` if the message referenced in the `message` parameter is not valid.

If the service returns `E_OK`, copy the message object to the local object. The original purpose of creating a local copy was to preserve memory by using a larger stack but less static memory; however, that is not the result in this example because `OutputDisplayBuffer` is an extended task and is always using resources. This example does show how a local copy of the message object can be created and used in a task that executes and then terminates, thereby preserving scarce RAM resources at the temporary cost of additional stack space.

Now that you have a local copy of the buffer that cannot be corrupted, you can send the output to the display with the use of a timer based on the real-time clock that creates the delays necessary between the commands and the characters written to the display.

11.4 Queued Messages (CCCB)

The queued message, which is the other available type of internal message, requires at least conformance class CCCB for implementation. In addition to providing the same level of support as CCCA, CCCB allows multiple notification mechanisms to multiple consumers and provides a mechanism that maintains data consistency by allowing the application to lock a message resource used in a without-copy format. The flag notification mechanism also requires conformance class CCCB at a minimum.

The queued message developed here is called `KeyPressMessage`. It contains a queue of key presses to be processed in the application in FIFO order. Because key processing is handled by a low-priority background task, the queue is needed to buffer multiple key presses. The configuration information for this message is shown in Listing 11.14.

Listing 11.14 `KeyPressMessage` configuration.

```
MESSAGE KeyPressMessage {
           TYPE = INTERNAL;
           LENGTH = 1;
           ALIGNMENT = 1;
           USAGE = SEND_RECEIVE;
           QUEUED = TRUE;
           QUEUE_SIZE = 10;
           TX_NOTIFICATION = NONE;
           RX_NOTIFICATION = ON_SUCCESS;
           TRANSMISSION = DIRECT;
           ACCESSNAMES = { keyPressed, keyValue };
           RX_SUCCESS_TASK = ProcessKeyPress;
           RX_SUCCESS_EVENT = KEYPRESS;
   };
```

KeyPressMessage is queued with a message size of one byte and a queue size of 10 messages. When sent, it sets the KEYPRESS OS event as a notification mechanism that is associated with the ProcessKeyPress task. Because KeyPressMessage is an internal message only, the segmented versus unsegmented, transmission mode, and deadline monitoring attributes are not applicable to this message.

The tasks that use KeyPressMessage are the next items to define. The OSEK/VDX COM specification limits internally the number of senders and receivers for a queued message to one each, because every queued message is consumed when it is received, so there must be a queue for every receiver of a message. This OSEK/VDX limitation is in response to the scarce memory resources in an application. However, each message can have multiple external receivers. I define OSEK/VDX OS tasks that sample the keypad and process the key presses (Listing 11.15). In Chapter 8, the keypad was handled by an ISR. I have to revert to sampling the keypad because of a limitation in the COM specification: Queued messages cannot be sent from an ISR. Originally, this was probably because of the overhead of processing queued messages in the kernel, which was considered too time consuming to allow. Consequently, to illustrate queued messages in this manner, I periodically sample the keypad.

Listing 11.15 IOSampleKeypad and ProcessKeyPress configuration.

```
TASK ProcessKeyPress {
        TYPE = EXTENDED;
        SCHEDULE = FULL;
        PRIORITY = 2;
        ACTIVATION = 1;
        AUTOSTART = TRUE;
        STACKSIZE = 192;
        SCHEDULE_CALL = FALSE;
        EVENT = { KEYPRESS, SHUFFLED };
        ACCESSOR = RECEIVED {
           MESSAGE = KeyPressMessage;
           WITHOUTCOPY = FALSE;
           ACCESSNAME = "keyValue";
        }
};

TASK IOSampleKeypad {
        TYPE = BASIC;
        SCHEDULE = FULL;
        PRIORITY = 13;
        ACTIVATION = 1;
        AUTOSTART = FALSE;
```

```
            STACKSIZE = 128;
            SCHEDULE_CALL = FALSE;
            ACCESSOR = SENT {
               MESSAGE = KeyPressMessage;
               WITHOUTCOPY = FALSE;
               ACCESSNAME = "keyPressed";
            }
    };
```

The task IOSampleKeypad is invoked periodically to determine if a key is pressed on the keypad (Listing 11.16). IOSampleKeypad reads the value of the keypad and debounces the key presses. When a key is pressed, the task sends the key value to the application using SendMessage(), which functions exactly as discussed in "Unqueued Messages (CCCA)" above. However you cannot send this message without-copy. The return status is also determined as for an unqueued message, but because the ACCESSOR parameter is defined for the task, any attempt to send an unqueued message without-copy should be caught by the system configuration tool when the OIL configuration file is processed. When the message is sent, the COM component sets the KEYPRESS event that is associated with the ProcessKeyPress task.

Listing 11.16 IOSampleKeypad task.

```
TASK(IOSampleKeypad)
{
static BOOLEAN keyState = FALSE;
char tempKey;
TaskStateType taskState;

   tempKey = HWGetValue(&KEYPAD);
   if(tempKey == lastKey){
      if(keyCount++ == KEY_DEBOUNCE_TIME){
         --keyCount;
         if(tempKey != 0){
            if(keyState ==  FALSE){
               *keyPressed = tempKey;
               SendMessage(KeyPressMessage,keyPressed);
               keyState = TRUE;
            }
         }
         else{
            keyState = FALSE;
         }
```

```
      }
    }
    else{
      keyCount = 0;
      lastKey = tempKey;
    }
    TerminateTask();
}
```

ProcessKeyPress (Listing 11.17) is a background task that is either always active or in the SUSPENDED state. It is a large task, so I show only the portions of the task that are applicable to the discussion here. The complete task is on the CD.

Listing 11.17 ProcessKeyPress routine.

```
TASK(ProcessKeyPress)
{
...
    while(1){
      WaitEvent(KEYPRESS);
      ClearEvent(KEYPRESS);
      while( ReceiveMessage(KeyPressMessage,keyValue) == E_OK){
        switch(CheckGameTransition(*keyValue)){
...
        }
      }
    }
}
```

When ProcessKeyPress is first activated, it immediately enters the SUSPENDED state and waits for a key to be pressed. When a key press occurs, the task is released from the SUSPENDED state and retrieves the value of the key press into the with-copy keyValue accessor using ReceiveMessage(). Again, the ACCESSOR for this task must be set up with-copy because the value is removed from the queue. The function of ReceiveMessage() is identical to the funtion described under unqueued messages above. However, the return status allows two additional status values for queued messages only, which are

- E_COM_NOMSG if the queue is empty or
- E_COM_LIMIT if the queue was full the last time the message was sent (internal or internal–external message) or was physically received (external message), indicating that at least one message was lost because the queue was full.

When an application operates in CCCB, the application can lock a message resource. This capability is typically used for unqueued messages accessed without-copy, where the message resource is a globally accessible variable. In the unqueued message example, the displayMirror accessor was created without-copy. To ensure that this data was not corrupted, the example application forces the OutputDisplay task to be non-preemptive. An alternative is to lock the message resource while the task updates the data and to allow preemption to occur normally. The updated OutputDisplay task is shown in Listing 11.18.

Listing 11.18 OutputDisplay task with message resource locking.

```
TASK(OutputDisplay)
{
   while((displayBufferError == TRUE) ||
      (displayBufferStart != displayBufferEnd)){
      if(displayBuffer[displayBufferStart].row != 0xff){
         SetDisplayPosition(displayBuffer[displayBufferStart].row,
            displayBuffer[displayBufferStart].column);
      }
      GetMessageResource(DisplayMessage);
      PackDisplay(displayBuffer[displayBufferStart].buffer);
      ReleaseMessageResource(DisplayMessage);
      if((++displayBufferStart) == DISPLAY_BUFFER_SIZE){
         displayBufferStart = 0;
      }
      Schedule();
   }
   SendMessage(DisplayMessage,displayMirror);
   TerminateTask();
}
```

In OutputDisplay, the resource is locked using GetMessageResource() just prior to calling PackDisplay().

```
StatusType GetMessageResource(SymbolicName message);
```

When GetMessageResource() is invoked, it attempts to set the message status to busy. Notice that this service works on the status of the message without regard to the ACCESSOR defined in the invoking task. However, GetMessageResource() can only lock a message with a without-copy configuration defined for the task. It is strongly recommended that the calls to this service and the corresponding ReleaseMessageResource() occur at the same function level. Also, the message must be released from the Busy state prior to completing the task or function or before entering the SUSPENDED state.

The return status of this API service is

- `E_COM_LOCKED` if the service cannot guarantee that access to the message is safe (determining when access cannot be granted to the message object is specific to the implementation),
- `E_OK` if the message status was successfully set to busy,
- `E_COM_BUSY` if the message status has already been set to busy, or
- `E_COM_ID` in extended status mode only if the message parameter is invalid.

After the task returns from `PackDisplay()`, it invokes `ReleaseMessageResource()`, which is the companion to `GetMessageResource()`.

```
StatusType ReleaseMessageResource(SymbolicName message);
```

`ReleaseMessageResource()` sets the status of the message in the argument to not busy. It does not check to see if the message previously has been set to busy or whether the message is locked. The OSEK/VDX COM specification also does not define whether nesting of message resource locking is allowed. Consequently, don't assume that nesting is available in all implementations, and refer to the implementation-specific documentation to determine support for nesting.

The return status from `ReleaseMessageResource()` is

- `E_OK` if the message is set to busy successfully or
- `E_COM_ID` in extended status mode only if the message parameter is invalid.

Now the `OutputDisplayBuffer` task must be modified to take advantage of the message locking capability of the COM component. The revised task is shown in Listing 11.19. As before, only the applicable portions of the task are shown.

Listing 11.19 `OutputDisplayBuffer` task with message resource locking.

```
TASK(OutputDisplayBuffer)
{
   UINT8 *displayControl = DISPLAY_CONTROL_LOCATION;
   UINT8 *display = DISPLAY_BUFFER_LOCATION;
   UINT8 i,outputRow;
   UINT8 translateRow;
   DISPLAY_MESSAGE_TYPE displayMirrorLocal;
   WriteDisplay(InitMessage);
   while(1){
      translateRow = 0;
      WaitEvent(BUFFER_CHANGED);
      ClearEvent(BUFFER_CHANGED);
      do{
         i=0;
```

```
        GetResource(RES_SCHEDULER);
        if(ReceiveMessage(DisplayMessage,displayMirrorTemp)==E_OK){
          memcpy(&displayMirrorLocal,displayMirrorTemp,
            sizeof(DISPLAY_MESSAGE_TYPE));
        }
        else{
          i=1;
        }
        ReleaseResource(RES_SCHEDULER);
        if(i==1){
          SetRelAlarm(DisplayWaitAlarm,10,0);
          WaitEvent(DISPLAY_READY);
          ClearEvent(DISPLAY_READY);
        }
      }while(i==1);
...
    }
}
```

In this revised task, the return value from `ReceiveMessage()` is checked to determine if the message was available. If the service returns anything other than `E_OK`, the task starts a timer and waits for the message to be unlocked.

Within an implementation operating under CCCB, one other API service, `GetMessageStatus()`, is available to the application. This service simply checks the message status without acting on the message itself.

```
StatusType GetMessageStatus(SymbolicName message);
```

This service returns the status as follows.

- If the service cannot guarantee that access to the message is safe, it returns `E_COM_LOCKED`. Determining when access cannot be granted to the message object is specific to the implementation.
- If the message is currently locked by the application and is considered busy, the service returns `E_COM_BUSY`.
- If the queue of a queued message is empty, the return value is `E_COM_NOMSG`.
- If the queue was full the last time the message was sent (internal or internal–external message) or physically received (external message), this service returns `E_COM_LIMIT`, indicating that at least one message was lost because the queue was full.
- If the service executes successfully, it returns `E_OK`.
- In extended status mode only, the service returns `E_COM_ID` if the message referenced in the `message` parameter is not valid.

11.5 Example Program

The functionality of the example program, a simple game of blackjack, has not changed based on the changes made in this chapter. From the player's point of view, the program still functions as it did at the end of Part 1. However, the program now uses more of the OSEK/VDX COM resources. If you skipped Part 1, you might want to skim Chapter 9 to gain a better understanding of the example program that I am developing throughout the book. In the next chapters, however, the example program changes greatly as I add external messages and allow one player to compete head-to-head against another player.

Because I duplicated a lot of information from Part 1 here for readers who jumped directly to this part of the book, I will discuss in this section just the differences between the example program in its current state and its state in Chapter 9.

11.5.1 Modules

`cardgame.c` The `ProcessKeyPress` task was modified as described in this chapter to use the intertask message capability to obtain the value of a key press.

`dispdrv.c` The `OutputDisplayBuffer` and `OutputDisplay` tasks were modified to use message resource locking to ensure that `OutputDisplay` does not try to write to the without-copy message object while the `OutputDisplayBuffer` task makes a copy of the message object. `OutputDisplayBuffer` also creates a local copy of the message object before writing to the display.

`keypad.c` The ISR `IOReadKeypadISR` was replaced by the `IOSampleKeypad` task to allow illustration of queued messages. Because queued messages are used now, the local queue is no longer required, and `GetKeyValue()` is not required and was removed.

11.5.2 Configuration Files

`hw.cfg` The keypad translation table was changed to sample the keypad instead of being handled by an ISR.

`init.cfg` The registers that had been initialized to allow interrupt driver sampling of the keypad were removed, and the alarm that periodically triggers the task was added to the autostart list of alarms.

11.6 Exercises

1. Create a new task that controls the display during a shuffle (displays the message "SHUFFLING –") and create an unqueued message that informs this task which direction to turn the "clock." The value of this message will be `0` for 12:00, `1` for 1:30, `2` for 3:00, and so on, up to `7` for 10:30. Whenever the clock needs to move, send the message to activate the task that calculates the output to the display.

2. Create a new task that outputs an error to the display, and create a queue of invalid key presses. First, the task should save the value of the display by receiving the `DisplayMessage` message and saving a copy. Whenever an invalid key is pressed (as indicated by the `NO_ACTION` action in the `ProcessKeyPress` task), send the key value using a new queued message. When the message is sent, the new task should display an error message, along with the invalid key that was pressed. Display for three seconds, then restore the display to the prior value if no other invalid key presses are in the queue.

11.7 Summary

In this chapter, I introduced the basis on which an application can use the OSEK/VDX COM standard. The services required by the application to initialize, start, stop, and close an OSEK/VDX COM component were discussed. I divided the chapter into two sections based on the two conformance classes that address internal, or intertask, communication: conformance classes A and B. The API services available in each of these conformance classes were described and examples were given. In addition, the function of locking a message resource in order to support without-copy configurations was discussed, and the API services were defined.

In Chapter 12, I dive into the topic that separates OSEK/VDX from other small real-time OSs — the support of distributed computing environments.

12

Chapter 12

Basic External Communication

Now that a basic communication component is up and running, I can discuss external communication over a network. As mentioned in Chapter 10, the OSEK/VDX communication specification does not limit the type of network allowed. In reality, most implementations today only support the controller area network (CAN) protocol. However, with the multitude of automotive-based networks that are presently in development, this definitely will change in the near future. Even networks that are typically PC or telecommunications based, such as IEEE1394, USB, and the myriad of cellular technologies, are finding their way into automobiles. For simplicity, I limit discussion in this book to the use of a CAN network.

12.1 CAN Overview

Before I discuss external communication, I want to provide a brief overview of CAN from the aspect of the application developer that will provide the definitions required to understand the rest of this chapter. Anyone developing drivers for CAN or designing a network would require greater knowledge.

CAN was designed to work in a noisy environment such as an automobile or a manufacturing facility. As such, extensive information in the serial data stream ensures that the data received is the data sent. The CAN bus is a broadcast type, where all devices on the bus can hear all messages that are sent. Four types of messages can be sent on the bus. From the application standpoint, I am only concerned with the data frame message. The remote, error, and overload frames should be invisible to the application and should only be used by the communication driver. The complete data frame for a CAN message is shown in Figure 12.1.

Figure 12.1 CAN data frame.

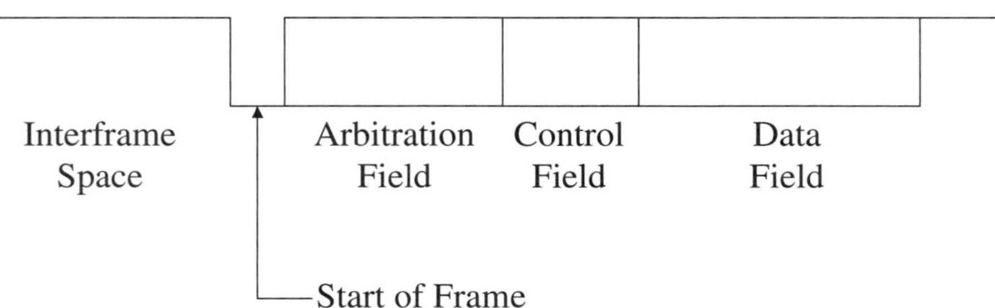

The arbitration and the data fields are the only portions of the CAN data frame of concern to an application. The two types of message defined in a CAN network, standard and extended, affect the number of bits in the arbitration field. Standard messages have an ID of 11 bits and extended messages of 29 bits; therefore, the arbitration field length is either 12 or 32 bits. The extra bit in the standard ID is called the remote transmission request bit and is not of concern to the application. This bit also resides in the arbitration field of an extended message, along with two additional bits that also are not of concern to the application. When defining the ID of the message in the configuration file, the application developer only defines the 11 or 29 bits of the identifier.

The arbitration field determines which device has control of the bus when two devices attempt to transmit at the same time through the concept of dominant and recessive states of the bus. Simply translated, this means that the transmission of a 0 bit will be dominant over the transmission of a 1 bit. Each device listens on a bit-by-bit basis to determine if its attempt to transmit a 1 on the bus is successful. If it was not successful, the device stops transmitting and waits until the current message is transmitted before it attempts to start again. Consequently, a message with an ID of 0 is the highest priority message on the bus.

Each CAN data frame can hold up to eight data bytes. The number of data bytes sent is defined in the message length of the external message in the OIL configuration file. At this time, the OSEK/VDX COM specification does not support sending multiple messages within one data frame, but this could change in the future. Messages that fit within these eight data bytes are sent within one data frame. If a message is larger than eight data bytes, the message is broken into multiple data frames. Transmission of multiple data frames is discussed in Chapter 13.

This has been a very brief overview of the function of the CAN network. More in-depth information can be obtained from a number of sources that can be found on the Internet.

12.2 Unacknowledged Unsegmented Data Transfer

Two methods of transferring data for external messages are defined in the OSEK/VDX COM specification: unacknowledged unsegmented data transfer (UUDT) and unacknowledged segmented data transfer (USDT). This chapter focuses on data transfer using UUDT, and Chapter 13 focuses on data transfer using USDT.

UUDT messages are unacknowledged by the receivers of the message, which does not mean that the transmission is not acknowledged, only that the application inside the device receiving the message does not acknowledge that it has successfully received and understood the message. Acknowledgment based in the network protocol still occurs and is identified by the OSEK/VDX COM component. For example in a CAN network, after the data frame has been sent, an acknowledgment sequence identifies that the message was successfully received by at least one other device on the network. This acknowledgment indicates that there was no corruption in the bitstream of data but does not indicate that anything was done with the data by the application on the receiving device. If any of the bits in the bitstream are corrupted because of noise, the acknowledgment sequence tells the low-level driver of the transmitting device to retransmit the data. When the acknowledgment is successful, this information can trigger a class 2 (message transmission) notification mechanism back to the application.

Unsegmented data transfer refers to messages that can be sent completely within one data frame on the network. For a CAN network, any message that is eight bytes or smaller is sent in one data frame. Messages larger than this are broken up into multiple data frames by the sender and reassembled into one message by the receiver. I discuss how this is performed in Chapter 13. This chapter focuses on UUDT messages only.

12.2.1 Direct Message Transmission (CCC0)

The first COM conformance class that supports external messages is CCC0. This conformance class provides the same level of support as CCCB, with the exception of queued messages. In CCC0, queued messages are optional and do not need to be supported for an implementation to claim conformance. Although unclear in the specification at this time, I would expect that an implementation that supports CCC0 would make queued messages optional for the conformance class and not for the implementation as a whole. In other words, the implementation will optimize itself if queued messages are not used but will not force the application to operate at a higher conformance class just to support queued messages. This issue should be discussed with the supplier of the COM implementation prior to purchase.

In an implementation operating in CCC0, only direct transmission mode and notification classes 1 and 2 are supported. The purpose of this conformance class is to provide a minimal communication component that still supports external communication. Consequently, it is the responsibility of the application to perform any deadline monitoring and periodic message transmission.

To illustrate external messages and direct message transmission, four messages have been created in the example application (Listing 12.1). The first two messages, `CardMessageOut` and `CardMessageIn`, transmit a card when it is dealt on the device that performs the dealer function and receive the card at the device in player mode. When received, the card is added to the hand on the display. The second two messages, `RequestModeMessageIn` and `RequestModeMessageOut`, request that the two devices enter into or leave, respectively, the head-to-head game mode and perform other program-related control operations. The first message is used to receive a request from the other player, and the second message is used to send a message to the other player.

Listing 12.1 Definition of direct messages.

```
MESSAGE CardMessageIn {
        TYPE = EXTERNAL;
        LENGTH = 3;
        ALIGNMENT = 1;
        USAGE = RECEIVE;
        QUEUED = TRUE;
        TX_NOTIFICATION = NONE;
        RX_NOTIFICATION = ON_SUCCESS;
        TRANSMISSION = DIRECT;
        ACCESSNAMES = { receivedCard };
        CAN_ADDRESSES = { CardMessageNode1 };
        QUEUE_SIZE = 5;
        RX_SUCCESS_TASK = CardReceived;
  };

  MESSAGE CardMessageOut {
        TYPE = EXTERNAL;
        LENGTH = 3;
        ALIGNMENT = 1;
        USAGE = SEND;
        QUEUED = TRUE;
        TX_NOTIFICATION = ON_SUCCESS;
        RX_NOTIFICATION = NONE;
        TRANSMISSION = DIRECT;
        ACCESSNAMES = { dealtCard };
        CAN_ADDRESSES = { CardMessageNode0 };
        QUEUE_SIZE = 12;
        TX_SUCCESS_TASK = ProcessKeyPress;
        TX_SUCCESS_EVENT = TRANSMIT_COMPLETE;
  };

  MESSAGE RequestModeMessageIn {
        TYPE = EXTERNAL;
        LENGTH = 1;
```

```
        ALIGNMENT = 1;
        USAGE = RECEIVE;
        QUEUED = FALSE;
        TX_NOTIFICATION = NONE;
        RX_NOTIFICATION = ON_SUCCESS;
        TRANSMISSION = DIRECT;
        RX_SUCCESS_TASK = ChangeGameMode;
        CAN_ADDRESSES = { RequestModeMessageNode1 };
        ACCESSNAMES = { requestedMode };
};

MESSAGE RequestModeMessageOut {
        TYPE = EXTERNAL;
        LENGTH = 1;
        ALIGNMENT = 1;
        USAGE = SEND;
        QUEUED = FALSE;
        TX_NOTIFICATION = NONE;
        RX_NOTIFICATION = NONE;
        TRANSMISSION = DIRECT;
        CAN_ADDRESSES = { RequestModeMessageNode0 };
        ACCESSNAMES = { requestMode };
};
```

`CardMessageOut` is accessed without-copy to conserve memory. Because it is an external message and will only be accessed from one location, corruption will not occur so without-copy can be used safely. If there is any possibility that the object can be accessed by multiple locations, then with-copy should be used.

The `CardMessage` messages are associated with two CAN addresses: `CardMessageNode0` and `CardMessageNode1`. Before continuing, I need to define some of the assumptions that must be understood when using an OSEK/VDX system. OSEK/VDX is a statically defined system; consequently, when it is defined, each device is statically defined to be at one location on the network. The CAN protocol is also defined such that only one node on the network can transmit a message with a given ID. Consequently, for a message to be sent by two nodes, the message IDs must be slightly different to indicate who is sending the message. In the example program, the distributed system was designed with the following system requirements.

- A maximum of two nodes are available on the network.
- If only one node is available on the network, that node operates as a single player, with both the dealer and the player on that node.
- When connected to a network, a node can request a head-to-head game against another node or can receive a request for a head-to-head game from another node. This request has to be granted before a head-to-head game begins.

- Every device is defined statically as either node 0 or node 1.

Obviously, these limitations for a game such as blackjack are not realistic. However, in a static system, such as inside an automobile, a manufacturing machine, or another type of embedded environment with multiple controllers, statically defining each controller with a unique ID is not unrealistic. To identify node 0 or node 1, I use the least significant bit in the CAN ID as the identifier. The examples in this book are from a node 0 application. The node 1 application is included on the accompanying CD. The definitions of the CAN addresses use a different object in the OIL configuration file. Again, a standard format has not been defined for creating these definitions. The OSEKWorks format for defining the CAN addresses is shown in Listing 12.2.

Listing 12.2 Definition of CAN addresses.

```
CANADDRESS CardMessageNode0 {
        NETWORK = Net1;
        TYPE = STANDARD;
        MESSAGE_ID = 2032;
};

CANADDRESS CardMessageNode1 {
        NETWORK = Net1;
        TYPE = STANDARD;
        MESSAGE_ID = 2033;
};

CANADDRESS RequestModeMessageNode0 {
        NETWORK = Net1;
        TYPE = STANDARD;
        MESSAGE_ID = 2034;
};

CANADDRESS RequestModeMessageNode1 {
        NETWORK = Net1;
        TYPE = STANDARD;
        MESSAGE_ID = 2035;
};
```

When defining the CAN address, the implementation needs to know on which network to transmit the data (NETWORK), whether the data is transmitted with standard or extended addressing (TYPE), and the address of the data frame (MESSAGE_ID). This configuration provides the information required by the network and data link layers to successfully transmit data over or receive data from the network. OSEK/VDX COM does not limit the number of networks to one; consequently the physical network on which a message is transmitted must be defined. The definition of the physical network or networks available is also performed in the OIL configuration file, but because this is specific to the implementation and target microcontroller, I do not include this definition here. The OIL configuration file on the accompanying CD includes this definition for the OSEKWorks implementation.

Now that I have defined a series of messages, I can modify the example program to use these messages to create a full-featured application that allows both stand-alone and head-to-head play. The first step is to modify the program to negotiate head-to-head play. The steps involved in head-to-head negotiation are shown in Figure 12.2.

Figure 12.2 Head-to-head negotiation.

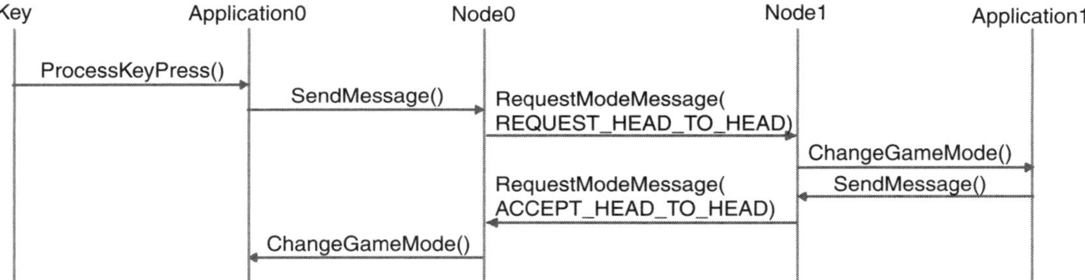

Initiation of head-to-head play occurs when one player presses the * key, and the key is processed in the `ProcessKeyPress` task (Listing 12.3). Because this task is very long, I only include that portion of the task necessary to demonstrate this message.

When the * key is pressed, the application sends the `RequestModeMessageOut` message with the `REQUEST_HEAD_TO_HEAD` data value in the ACCESSOR `RequestMode` using `SendMessage()`, which functions the same for external and internal messages. The COM implementation, however, performs a completely different series of functions for external messages, as illustrated in Figure 12.3.

Listing 12.3 `ProcessKeyPress` **task.**

```
TASK(ProcessKeyPress)
{
EventMaskType eventMask;
BOOLEAN shuffleComplete,dealComplete;
UINT8 i;
char tempBuffer[4];

   while(1){
      WaitEvent(KEYPRESS|SIM_KEY);
      GetEvent(ProcessKeyPress,(EventMaskRefType)&eventMask);
      ClearEvent(KEYPRESS|SIM_KEY);
      while((ReceiveMessage(KeyPressMessage,keyValue) == E_OK)||(
         (eventMask & SIM_KEY) != 0)){
         if((eventMask&SIM_KEY)!=0){
            i=simulatedKey;
            eventMask &= ~SIM_KEY;
         }
         else{
            i=*keyValue;
         }
         switch(CheckGameTransition(i)){
...
            case REQUEST_MULTIPLE:
               *requestMode = REQUEST_HEAD_TO_HEAD;
               SendMessage(RequestModeMessageOut,requestMode);
               requestHeadToHead = TRUE;
               SetRelAlarm(RequestModeAlarm,25000,0);
               WriteDisplay(RequestModeAwaitPrompt);
               gameState = GAME_AWAITING_RESPONSE;
               break;
...
            case NO_ACTION:
               break;
         }
      }
   }
}
```

Figure 12.3 Sending a direct message.

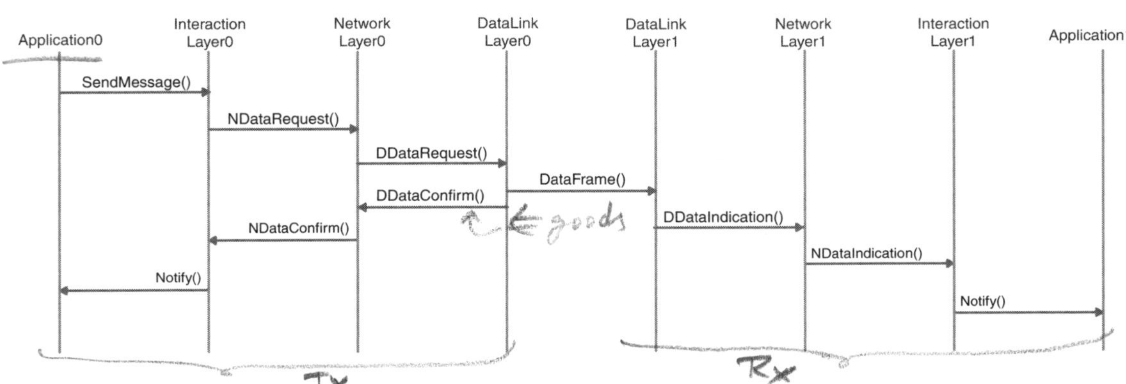

When the application sends the message, the interaction layer first determines whether the message is an internal or an external message. Internal messages are fully processed by the interaction layer, but an external message is forwarded to the network layer for further processing. Services that start with `NData` or `DData` are internal services and indicate the action that is taken. Because the layer model is a figurative model, these services might or might not actually exist as distinct functions. `Request` messages request message processing by the layer; `Confirm` messages indicate the result of the request; `Indication` messages indicate that a message has been received and needs to be processed.

If the message sent to the network layer is a UUDT message, then the network layer passes the message on to the data link layer. The data link layer formats the data frame and puts the data frame into the queue for transmission. The data link layer then returns to the network layer, which returns to the interaction layer, which returns to the application. If everything is successful, the return value to the application is `E_OK`. However, if the data link layer determines that it cannot safely transmit the data, it returns the status `E_COM_LOCKED`. The conditions under which the locked status is returned depends on the implementation.

Because OSEK/VDX COM is an asynchronous communication model, the application continues before the message is transmitted over the network. So that the application knows when a message is transmitted successfully, notification class 2 (as illustrated in Figure 12.3) provides confirmation from the data link layer through the network layer to the interaction layer that the message was transmitted successfully on the network. The interaction layer can then notify the application of the success. In the example application, this notification is not enabled for the `RequestModeMessageOut` message; however, it will be enabled for the `CardMessage` messages described in more detail later.

After the message has been sent, the application sets a local flag, `requestHeadToHead`, to `TRUE` and starts a 25-second timer. When the `RequestModeMessageIn` message is received or the timer expires, the `ChangeGameMode` task (Listing 12.4) is activated. Only the actions taken in `SINGLE_PLAYER` mode are shown for brevity.

Listing 12.4 ChangeGameMode task.

```
TASK(ChangeGameMode)
{
   TickType tick;
   if(GetActiveApplicationMode() == SINGLE_PLAYER){
      if(requestHeadToHead == TRUE){
         if(GetAlarm(RequestModeAlarm,&tick) == E_OK){
            CancelAlarm(RequestModeAlarm);
            ReceiveMessage(RequestModeMessageIn,requestedMode);
            if(*requestedMode == ACCEPT_HEAD_TO_HEAD){
               ChangeMode(HEAD_TO_HEAD);
            }
         }
         requestHeadToHead = FALSE;
         gameState = GAME_NORMAL;
         WriteDisplay(GameNormalPrompt);
      }
      else{
         ReceiveMessage(RequestModeMessageIn,requestedMode);
         if(*requestedMode == REQUEST_HEAD_TO_HEAD){
            WriteDisplay(RequestMultiPrompt);
            gameState = GAME_AWAITING_RESPONSE;
         }
      }
   }
   else{
...
   }
   TerminateTask();
}
```

The ChangeGameMode task determines which action is to be taken based on the status of the timer, the flag, and the message data as follows.

- If the requestHeadToHead flag is TRUE and the timer has expired, the request was not acknowledged in time. The task clears the flag, returns the task to a normal state, and terminates.
- If the requestHeadToHead flag is TRUE and the timer has not expired, the task receives the message data that was transmitted. If the request for a head-to-head game is granted by the other player, the task forces a mode switch from SINGLE_PLAYER to HEAD_TO_HEAD using

the ChangeMode() service. Because the ChangeMode service was designed for an OSEK/VDX OS, the system is forced to shut down and restart in a different mode.

- If the requestHeadToHead flag is FALSE, the task receives the message data that was transmitted. If this message requests a head-to-head game, the task asks the player to join the game, prompts the player for a response, and sets the state of the system to GAME_AWAITING_RESPONSE. When the player responds to the request, the ProcessKeyPress task sends the proper message. Listing 12.3 shows the execution as a result of this response.

Once the application is in the head-to-head mode, the program operates in a slightly different manner. An additional state allows the application to be either the dealer or the player. The dealer rules for a single player game are not applicable because the game is now a head-to-head competition. The dealer can hit or stay with any combination of cards. After the system is restarted and placed in the head-to-head mode, the dealer must press the "D" key to deal the first time. The display is the same on both devices, but an * is placed under the role played by each device and changes after each reshuffling of the deck. The display line opposite the local player shows the opponent's cards, with the first card down. An * appears after the name of the player whose turn it is to play.

Now when the player presses the letter "A" to hit or the letter "B" to stay, the actions taken by the ProcessKeyPress task are quite different. If the player is in the role of GAME_PLAYER, the REQUEST_CARD_DEALT action (Listing 12.5) is performed. I have only included the action taken when the player requests a card. The actions taken when the player and dealer stay (RELINQUISH_TURN) and when the dealer hits (DEAL_MULTI_CARD) are included in cardgame.c on the CD.

Listing 12.5 ProcessKeyPress task for REQUEST_CARD_DEALT.

```
TASK(ProcessKeyPress)
{
EventMaskType eventMask;
BOOLEAN shuffleComplete,dealComplete;
UINT8 i;
char tempBuffer[4];

   while(1){
...
         switch(CheckGameTransition(i)){
...
            case REQUEST_CARD_DEALT:
               dealComplete = FALSE;
               while(dealComplete == FALSE){
                  dealtCard->type = REQUEST_CARD;
                  SendMessage(CardMessageOut,dealtCard);
                  SetRelAlarm(CardMessageAlarm,5000,0);
```

```
                WaitEvent(TRANSMIT_COMPLETE|TRANSMIT_FAILED);
                GetEvent(ProcessKeyPress,(EventMaskRefType)&eventMask);
                if(eventMask&TRANSMIT_COMPLETE){
                   dealComplete = TRUE;
                   CancelAlarm(CardMessageAlarm);
                }
                ClearEvent(TRANSMIT_COMPLETE|TRANSMIT_FAILED);
             }
             break;
...
          case NO_ACTION:
             break;
       }
    }
 }
}
```

This action sends the CardMessageOut message, which requests a card, as a CARD_MESSAGE_TYPE structure (Listing 12.6).

Listing 12.6 CARD_MESSAGE_TYPE structure.

```
typedef struct CardMessageTypetag {
   UINT8 type;
   UINT8 position;
   UINT8 card;
   }CardMessageType;
```

The first member in the structure indicates the type of structure that is being sent and can be REQUEST_CARD, END_TURN, PLAYER_CARD, or DEALER_CARD. REQUEST_CARD is only used by the person who is not the dealer (Listing 12.5). END_TURN, when used by the person who is not the dealer, indicates that it is the dealer's turn; when used by the dealer, it indicates that the hand is over. The last two types are only used by the dealer to notify the other player of the cards that have been dealt. The second member is used when the type is either PLAYER_CARD or DEALER_CARD and indicates the position in the associated hand where the card belongs. The final member is the card that was dealt. When the dealer receives a REQUEST_CARD message, the dealer then responds with a card using the PLAYER_CARD type.

Because it is critical to the application that the CardMessageOut message is sent successfully, it uses notification class 2 when the message is transmitted successfully. The notification mechanism sets the TRANSMIT_COMPLETE event for the ProcessKeyPress task. Until this message has been transmitted successfully, no further messages are allowed by the application as follows.

- Once the message is sent, a timer of five seconds starts. This timer sets the TRANSMIT_FAILED event for the ProcessKeyPress task when it expires.
- The task enters the SUSPENDED state and waits for the transmission either to complete successfully or to fail.
- When either of these events occurs, the task exits the SUSPENDED state and determines which event occurred. If the transmission failed, the request is transmitted again. If the transmission completed successfully, the task completes and awaits the next key press.

This illustrates how, in a conformance class CCC0 implementation, the application must take into account deadline monitoring. The deadline timer is managed by the application, not by the COM component. If extensive deadline monitoring is required, it is better to use a higher conformance class implementation that provides these features. The application developer will have to analyze the cost–benefit analysis based on the individual implementation.

The counterpart of CardMessageOut is CardMessageIn. When CardMessageIn is received, the CardReceived task is activated and the message is processed. Because multiple messages can be sent, CardMessageIn is set up as a queued message to ensure that no message is lost.

The portion of the CardReceived task that responds to the REQUEST_CARD message is shown in Listing 12.7. ReceiveMessage() functions exactly the same as with internal messages. Because REQUEST_CARD has been set up as a queued message, the service returns an error when the queue is empty.

Listing 12.7 CardReceived task.

```
TASK(CardReceived)
{
BOOLEAN dealComplete;
char tempBuffer[4];
UINT8 i;
EventMaskType eventMask;

    while(ReceiveMessage(CardMessageIn,receivedCard) == E_OK){
        switch(receivedCard->type){
            case REQUEST_CARD:
```

```
            if(gameRole == GAME_DEALER){
               GetResource(CARDDECK);
               playerCards[playerPosition] =
                  DealCard(PLAYER,playerPosition,TRUE);
               ReleaseResource(CARDDECK);
               playerScore += GetCardValue(playerCards[playerPosition]);
               if(playerScore > 21){
                  for(i=0;i<=playerPosition;i++){
                     if(GetCardValue(playerCards[i])==11){
                        playerCards[i] = ACE_IS_ONE;
                        playerScore -= 10;
                        break;
                     }
                  }
               }
               simulatedKey = 'X';
               SetEvent(ProcessKeyPress,SIM_KEY);
            }
            break;
...
      }
   }
   TerminateTask();
}
```

At the end of the action taken when a card is requested, a static variable, `simulatedKey`, is set to `'X'`, and an event is set for the `ProcessKeyPress` task. Because the `ProcessKeyPress` task "owns" the `CardMessageOut` message, this mechanism triggers the task to send the message. These steps enforce the limitation that only one task can send a message.

12.2.2 Periodic Message Transmission (CCC1)

The next level of conformance class is CCC1, in which most of the functionality of a COM component is available. This level includes all of the functions available in CCC0 and adds the ability to transmit periodic messages and mixed-mode messages and to perform deadline monitoring of periodically transmitted and received messages. Like CCC0, queued messages in CCC1 are optional.

To illustrate periodic message transmission, I create special-status data frames, `Node0StatusMessage` and `Node1StatusMessage`, which are transmitted periodically once per second whenever the system is running. Depending on the node of the device, one message is received and the other is transmitted. The discussion in this section focuses on messages with respect to the device on node 0. These messages transmit a `NodeStatusType` data structure (Listing 12.8).

The first member in the structure is the role that is played by that node: `GAME_DEALER` or `GAME_PLAYER`. The default value when the system is operating in stand-alone mode is `GAME_DEALER`. The second member of the structure is the mode under which the node is operating: `SINGLE_PLAYER`, `HEAD-TO-HEAD`, or `TEST`. The complete message definition is found in the OIL configuration file (Listing 12.9).

Listing 12.8 `NodeStatusType` structure.

```
typedef struct NodeStatusTypetag{
   UINT8 role;
   AppModeType mode;
   }NodeStatusType;
```

Listing 12.9 Status message definition.

```
   MESSAGE NodeStatusMessageIn {
           TYPE = EXTERNAL;
           LENGTH = 2;
           ALIGNMENT = 1;
           USAGE = RECEIVE;
           QUEUED = FALSE;
           TX_NOTIFICATION = NONE;
           RX_NOTIFICATION = ON_SUCCESS;
           TRANSMISSION = DIRECT;
           RX_SUCCESS_TASK = SetNetworkFlag;
           CAN_ADDRESSES = { Node1StatusMessage };
           ACCESSNAMES = { externalNodeStatus };
   };

   MESSAGE NodeStatusMessageOut {
           TYPE = EXTERNAL;
           LENGTH = 2;
           ALIGNMENT = 1;
           USAGE = SEND;
           QUEUED = FALSE;
           TX_NOTIFICATION = ON_DEADLINE;
           RX_NOTIFICATION = NONE;
           TRANSMISSION = PERIODIC;
           TRANSMIT_INTERVAL = 100;
           TX_DEADLINE_ALARM = StatusMessageAlarm;
```

```
        TX_DEADLINE_TIME = 25;
        CAN_ADDRESSES = { Node0StatusMessage };
        ACCESSNAMES = { nodeStatus };
};
```

Because of the current COM specification limitations concerning initialization of message objects, I defined the transmitted message as being accessed from the ProcessKeyPress task without-copy. During initialization of the communication component, I check the current APPMODE in the callback function MessageInit() (Listing 12.10). Recall that MessageInit() is called at the end of StartCom() and was discussed in Chapters 9 and 11.

Listing 12.10 MessageInit() callback function.

```
StatusType MessageInit(void)
{
#ifdef NODE0
   nodeStatus->role = GAME_DEALER;
#else
   nodeStatus->role = GAME_PLAYER;
#endif
   nodeStatus->mode = GetActiveApplicationMode();
   return E_OK;
}
```

If the APPMODE is set head-to-head, I initialize the data and send it with the role of GAME_DEALER in head-to-head mode. In the node 1 device, the default role is GAME_PLAYER. The COM component does not automatically send periodic messages when it starts, so the next step is to send them. The application must determine when periodic messages should start appearing on the network bus with the use of StartPeriodical().

```
StatusType StartPeriodical(void);
```

When this service is invoked, the interaction layer of the COM component starts the timers that determine when the periodic messages are to be transmitted. The return status from this service is

- E_OK if the service executes successfully or
- specific to the implementation if the service fails (refer to the implementation documentation for a list of other possible return values).

I add a call to this function in the InitOS task immediately after a call to StartOS(). The sequence of functions that occur for a periodic message is shown in Figure 12.4.

The first step is to initialize the message object prior to transmission. As discussed earlier, the method of initialization is not standardized at this time. In the case of the status messages used here, the data is a global variable and the message is sent without-copy. Consequently, the application ensures that the data is valid prior to calling StartPeriodical(). When StartPeriodical() is invoked, the interaction layer starts the timer for the periodic message.

This first time interval is defined by the standard as the offset from initiation of sending the periodic message to the first transmission of the message. This time might or might not be the same as the period of the message.

Figure 12.4 Sending a periodic message.

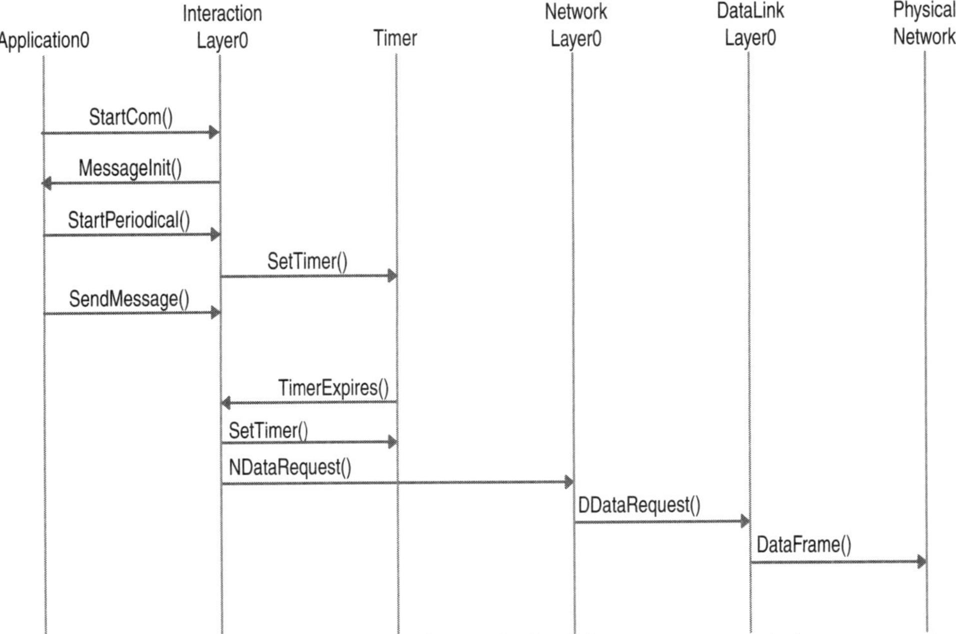

When the timer expires, it is reset to the period of the message, and the message is then sent with the same period until periodic transmission halts. The interaction layer then obtains the latest data from the message object and sends this to the network layer. Next, the network layer sends the message to the data link layer, which assembles the data frame and queues the message for transmission. This message uses notification class 4 to notify the application whether the message was successfully transmitted within 25 timer ticks (25 milliseconds) or not. If no one is connected on the network other than the device that sends a message, then no one is available to acknowledge that the message was sent. Consequently, the sending device will never be able to successfully transmit any message. The data link layer therefore never sends a confirmation to the interaction layer that the message was sent successfully. When the timer expires, notification class 4 informs the interaction layer. The notification mechanism used for this message is the callback function `SetDeviceLonely()` (Listing 12.11).

Listing 12.11 `SetDeviceLonely()` callback function.

```
void SetDeviceLonely(void)
{
   deviceLonely = TRUE;
}
```

`SetDeviceLonely()` is a `void` function with no parameters. The OSEK/VDX COM specification requires all callback functions to have this format. `SetDeviceLonely()` simply sets a flag so the application knows that it is the only device on the network. The application can use this flag to ignore a request to enter head-to-head mode or to show an error message to the player. I chose to use a callback function to demonstrate the callback capability of the COM component and because it executes very fast.

The reception of the status message uses notification class 1 to set the `StatusMessageReceived` flag, which is polled by the new `MonitorNetworkActivity` task (Listing 12.12), which periodically updates the outgoing status message and monitors the incoming status message.

Listing 12.12 `MonitorNetworkActivity` task.

```
TASK(MonitorNetworkActivity)
{
   if(ReadFlag(messageReceived)==TRUE){
      ClearLonelyFlag();
      ResetFlag(messageReceived);
   }
   else{
      SetLonelyFlag();
   }
   nodeStatus->role = gameRole;
   SendMessage(NodeStatusMessageOut,nodeStatus);
   *remainingCardsOut = GetRemainingCards();
   SendMessage(RemainingCardsMessageOut,remainingCardsOut);
   TerminateTask();
}
```

This task executes periodically at twice the period of the messages and checks the value of the flag using `ReadFlag()`.

```
FlagValue ReadFlag(FlagType flagname);
```

When invoked, `ReadFlag()` obtains the value of the flag and returns it to the application. The return value indicates the state of the flag and can take on one of the following values.

- If the conditions associated with a notification class to which the flag is attached have been met since the last time the flag was reset, the return value is `TRUE`.
- If the conditions have not been met, the return value is `FALSE`.

The interpretation of a flag set to `TRUE` is dependent on the notification class that set the flag. Table 12.1 shows an interpretation by class of a `TRUE` flag.

Table 12.1 Interpretation of a TRUE flag.

Notification Class	Interpretation
1	Message was received unconditionally or conditionally.
2	Message was transmitted successfully.
3	Message was not received successfully.
4	Message was not transmitted successfully.
5	USDT first frame was received.

In the example program, when the flag is set `TRUE`, it indicates that the message has been received at least once since the last time that the flag was reset. If the flag has been set, then the task clears the lonely status flag using `ClearLonelyFlag()`. If the flag has not been set and the return value is `FALSE`, the task sets the lonely flag using the previous callback routine `SetLonelyFlag()`. The task then resets the flag using `ResetFlag()`.

```
StatusType ResetFlag(FlagType flagname);
```

When invoked, `ResetFlag()` simply sets the value of the flag to `FALSE`. The possible return status values are

- `E_OK` if the flag is reset successfully or
- specific to the implementation if the reset fails (refer to the implementation documentation for a list of other possible return values).

The last two actions in the `MonitorNetworkActivity` task are discussed in the next section, "Mixed-Mode Message Transmission."

At some point when using periodic messages, the application might need to stop sending messages periodically but continue running the COM component, such as when an application is ready to enter a low-power mode but must delay for a short period of time to make sure that nobody else on the network requires information from the device. To stop periodic transmission, all periodic messages must stop at the same time. The API service that does this is `StopPeriodical()`.

```
StatusType StopPeriodical(void);
```

When this API service is invoked, the COM component cancels all timers that are running and disables the transmission of the periodic messages. The return status from this service is

- E_OK if the service executes successfully or
- specific to the implementation if the service fails (refer to the implementation documentation for a list of other possible return values).

12.2.3 Mixed-Mode Message Transmission

The final UUDT message that I discuss is a mixed-mode transmission message, which is a hybrid of the periodic and direct transmission modes. The message is transmitted periodically, but can be sent between periodic transmissions if a relevant change in the data of the message is detected. I will illustrate this transmission mode using an additional message that contains a single byte of data that includes the number of cards remaining in the deck. The node that acts as the dealer updates the value in this message in the MonitorNetworkActivity task, and the node that acts as the player echos the value received. The messages are RemainingCards-MessageOut and RemainingCardsMessageIn (Listing 12.13).

Listing 12.13 Message definition for remaining cards.

```
MESSAGE RemainingCardsMessageIn {
        TYPE = EXTERNAL;
        LENGTH = 1;
        ALIGNMENT = 1;
        USAGE = RECEIVE;
        QUEUED = FALSE;
        TX_NOTIFICATION = NONE;
        RX_NOTIFICATION = ON_DEADLINE;
        TRANSMISSION = DIRECT;
        ACCESSNAMES = { remainingCardsIn };
        CAN_ADDRESSES = { RemainingCardsNode1 };
        RX_DEADLINE_ALARM = RemainingCardsMissing;
        RX_DEADLINE_TIME = 700;
};

MESSAGE RemainingCardsMessageOut {
        TYPE = EXTERNAL;
        LENGTH = 1;
        ALIGNMENT = 1;
        USAGE = SEND;
        QUEUED = FALSE;
        TX_NOTIFICATION = NONE;
        RX_NOTIFICATION = NONE;
```

```
        TRANSMISSION = MIXED;
        TRANSMIT_INTERVAL = 500;
        VALUE_SIZE = ONE_BYTE;
        RELEVANT_CHANGE = NEQ;
        COMPARE_VALUE = 0;
        CAN_ADDRESSES = { RemainingCardsNode0 };
        ACCESSNAMES = { remainingCardsOut };
};
```

The message is transmitted every 500 milliseconds to indicate the number of cards remaining and for diagnostic purposes. In addition, whenever `SendMessage()` updates the message value and the new value is not equal to the old, a direct message is sent using the attributes `VALUE_SIZE`, `RELEVANT_CHANGE`, and `COMPARE_VALUE` in the OIL configuration file. Figure 12.5 shows the sequence of events with respect to this message.

Figure 12.5 Mixed-mode transmission sequence.

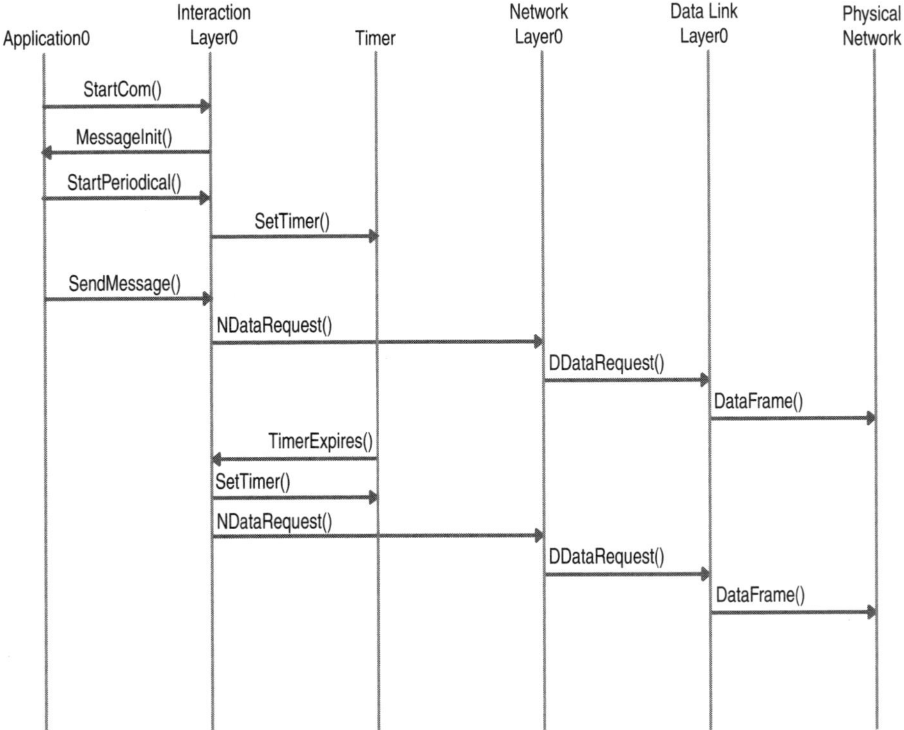

The sequence is as seen from the node 0 device when it is functioning as the dealer. Similar to a periodic message sequence, the message is initialized and then sent periodically after the call to `StartPeriodical()`. The difference occurs when the data is updated after a card is dealt or the deck is reshuffled. When this occurs, a message is transmitted immediately on the network with the new value.

At this point, the example program does not take any action if a discrepancy between message data and internally calculated data exists. However, it could be used as a method of handshaking to indicate that the `CardMessage` message was not received by the device operating in the role of player. For illustrative purposes, this message was added as an additional status message that also indicates that a device has left the network. When this message has not been received after 700 milliseconds, notification class 3 is invoked and the `LostOpponent` task is activated. This task simply notifies the person who is playing at that device that the opponent has shut down and then restarts the system in a single-player mode.

12.3 Example Program

The example application now becomes a truly connected program that can play head-to-head between two devices through the interchange of a number of external messages that use the different transmission modes available in the OSEK/VDX COM implementation. The different modes were chosen to illustrate how COM operates and is not necessarily the most efficient way to communicate. If the network is attached to a CAN network analysis tool, the messages can be seen in real time.

In this chapter, I used the callback and flag notification mechanisms. However, the current version of OSEKWorks supports COM specification v2.1, and these mechanisms were added in COM v2.2. I attempted to simulate these in the current example on the CD. When OSEKWorks is updated, I will update the software, and it will be available at http://www.osekbook.com.

The complete source code for the application, including the configuration files, is included in the accompanying CD. The function of the example program is as follows.

- When the system first starts, the startup message is displayed. The periodic messages are transmitted shortly afterwards.
- Pressing * requests head-to-head mode. A request is sent to the other device, which then asks whether the player wants to play head-to-head. If affirmative, the response is sent back and the system enters head-to-head mode with node 0 starting as the dealer. If the other player does not respond within 25 seconds, the system reverts to single-player mode.
- Pressing 'D' shuffles the cards for the first time and deals the first set of cards. In single-player mode, the computer acts as the dealer, and no messages are sent. In head-to-head mode, this key is only functional on the device set up as the dealer. When the cards are dealt, messages are sent so that the second device has knowledge of all the cards available. Each device shows that player's entire hand, plus all cards except the first dealt to the opposing player.
- The 'A' key hits and the 'B' key stays. Messages are transmitted from the player to the dealer to request the cards and from the dealer to the player to inform the player's device of the cards that have been dealt.
- The dealer must hit at 16 and stay at 17 in single-player mode. Aces count as 11 for the dealer unless it causes the dealer to bust, then it counts as one. In head-to-head mode, there is no limitation on the dealer: from a play standpoint, the dealer is capable of hitting and staying under the same rules as a normal player.

- At any time during a single-player game, pressing 'D' causes the system to reshuffle. In a head-to-head game, reshuffling only occurs as defined in the next item.
- When the hand is complete, pressing 'C' deals the next hand. In a head-to-head game, both players must press 'C' before the cards are dealt. If fewer than 10 cards remain in the deck, the deck is reshuffled. In a head-to-head game, the role of dealer changes at this time.
- Because this is an example program, I have not included betting, doubling down, or splitting as features. The reader can add this functionality if desired.

12.3.1 Modules

`makefile` The `makefiles` were changed to allow two types of builds: Node 0 and Node 1. This includes the `*.mk` files.

`carddeck.c` Definition of the `BLANK_CARD` macro has been moved from a local definition in `carddeck.c` to a global definition in `carddeck.h`.

`cardgame.c` Extensive changes to this module are as follows.

`ProcessKeyPress` was modified extensively to process key presses when the application is in `HEAD_TO_HEAD` mode.

`DealCards` was modified to recognize when a head-to-head game was in progress and to transmit the cards to the other player when the cards are dealt.

`ChangeGameMode` processes the `RequestModeMessageIn` message when it is received, switches between `SINGLE_PLAYER` and `HEAD_TO_HEAD`, and performs other control functions.

`CardReceived` processes the `CardMessageIn` message when a card is received from the other player or when a request for a card or end of turn is received.

`MonitorNetworkActivity` monitors the status messages periodically and updates the value to be sent in the `RemainingCardsMessageOut` message. It was added as a periodic task to demonstrate the capability of flags and of a mixed-mode transmission message. When operating under an OSEK/VDX OS, these functions will probably be activated by a task or by setting an event.

`LostOpponent` is called if `RemainingCardsMessageIn` is not received within the period set for the deadline monitor. If the application is in `HEAD_TO_HEAD` mode, the system switches back to `SINGLE_PLAYER` mode because the opponent has left.

`void InitGame(InitType type)` is called during system initialization to initialize a number of parameters based on the `APPMODE`.

`void SetDeviceLonely(void)` sets a flag when the status messages are no longer being received.

`void ClearDeviceLonely(void)` clears the flag when the status messages resume.

`dispdrv.c` This module was modified to display a different startup screen for `HEAD_TO_HEAD` versus `SINGLE_PLAYER` mode. The display is different on the `DEALER` node (node 0) than it is on the `PLAYER` node (node 1).

`init.c` This module was modified to initialize the periodic status message and to start and stop the transmission of periodic messages.

`main.c` This module now allows entry into the `HEAD_TO_HEAD` `APPMODE` in `ChangeMode()`.

`os.c` The `SetNetworkFlag` task simulates setting a flag when a message is received. This was required because OSEKWorks only supports COM v2.1. It will be removed when the examples are updated to the new version of OSEKWorks.

12.3.2 Configuration Files

`init.cfg` This configuration file now includes `InitGame()` in the list of initialization routines. It automatically starts a timer that activates the `MonitorNetworkActivity` periodic task.

12.4 Exercises

1. Create four new periodic or mixed-mode messages that contain five cards each for the dealer and player. Each node will transmit two messages that include the cards as each player should see them. If a given card was not yet dealt, then the value in the message should be zero. The node will also receive two other distinct messages for the cards as viewed by the opponent. If at any time there is a difference between the cards as dealt and as received, flash the message "Someone's Cheating," wait five seconds, then reset to single-player mode. To test this, you will have to write code in one device that corrupts the data of the message.
2. Create a direct message that is sent whenever the '0' (zero) key is pressed and include a small message of seven or fewer characters. When received by the other node, the message flashes for three seconds on the display. The contents of the direct message should always be constant, such as "Hello" or "I'm in."

12.5 Summary

In this chapter, I discussed basic external communication using an OSEK/VDX COM implementation. I provided examples of direct transmission mode, periodic transmission mode, and mixed-mode transmission, along with notification classes 2, 3, and 4. At this point, the portions of the OSEK/VDX COM specification that will be used in most embedded applications have been introduced and described. In Chapter 13, I introduce advanced external communication, which will probably appear in only a few applications.

13

Chapter 13

Advanced External Communication

The final topic to be covered in the OSEK/VDX COM standard is advanced external communication. The specification for COM is not divided into basic or advanced external communication — I have made this split because most embedded applications will not use the features available under the CCC2 COM conformance class.

The features available when the COM component is operating in CCC2 are

- transmission of messages segmented in multiple data frames on the network (USDT),
- dynamic message lengths,
- dynamic message addressing, and
- notification of the application when the first frame of the segmented message is received.

In this chapter, I discuss segmented messages and describe using these additional features.

13.1 Unacknowledged Segmented Data Transfer (CCC2)

Unacknowledged segmented data transfer (USDT) is used to transfer messages that are larger than the maximum transmission unit (MTU) of the network. For a CAN network, the maximum size that can be transmitted is eight bytes. Messages larger than eight bytes are segmented in the network layer of the COM implementation and is transparent to the application. Limitations to the type of message that can be sent as a segmented message are outlined in Table 13.1.

Table 13.1 USDT limitations.

Attribute	Limitation
Transmission type	Only direct transmission is allowed.
Size	Maximum size of the complete message is 4,095 bytes.
1:1/1:*n*	All messages are 1:1 only.
Queueing	All messages must be unqueued.

Although the USDT transmission mechanism is transparent to the application, understanding of the data frames that appear on the bus is critical when debugging the system; therefore, I discuss the mechanism used to transmit a segmented message across the bus first. The following terms will help you better understand the segmenting mechanism.

Network Protocol Data Unit (NPDU) The network protocol data unit is a unique data frame on the network used to transmit the segmented data. Four network protocol data units — single frame, first frame, flow control, and consecutive frame — are required and are defined later. Each NPDU has three fields: the address information, the protocol control information, and the data.

> **Network Address Information** (`N_AI`) This field contains information about the message that is to be transmitted and optionally includes the target address and source address. This identifier is the same for all frames transmitted on the network for a given message. For a CAN network, it is an 11- or a 29-bit identifier.

> **Network Protocol Control Information** (`NPCI`) This field of up to three bytes is embedded in the data frame of the network that defines information for the network protocol data unit that is being exchanged.

Single Frame NPDU This frame is used when the segmented message can be transmitted in a single frame. Because USDT is a segmented protocol, the size of the message that can be transmitted in a single frame is one less than the maximum size of a message that can be transmitted using the UUDT protocol because a single-byte NPCI is required in this frame. This NPDU exists because of support for dynamic message lengths. If a USDT message is transmitted with a length that fits within a single frame, then the message appears as a UUDT message on the network; that is, only one frame is transmitted.

First Frame NPDU This frame is transmitted first to initiate a segmented data transmission session. Included in this frame is the total length of the message. The first two bytes of the data frame constitute the first frame NPCI, followed by the first bytes of the message to be transmitted. In the case of a CAN network, six data bytes are transmitted in the first frame.

Flow Control NPDU This frame is transmitted by the device that receives the message and controls the flow of information from the transmitting device. This frame has three NPCI bytes and no data. Because USDT transmission only occurs in a 1:1 model, a unique receiving device for every message must be defined on the network.

Consecutive Frame NPDU This frame transmits the data in the message after the first frame has been transmitted. The flow control frames from the receiving device times and controls the frames.

Block Size (`BS`) This defines the number of consecutive frames that can be transmitted before the transmitting device stops and waits for a flow control message from the receiving device.

Separation Time (`ST`) This is the time between consecutive frames that the transmitting device must wait to allow the receiving device to process the message.

`N_As`, `N_Bs`, `N_Cs`, `N_Ar`, `N_Br`, `N_Cr` (Table 13.2) Timeout times for determining that the segmented message communication has been lost. The `s` stands for a time with respect to the sender of the message, and an `r` stands for a time with respect to the receiver of the message.

Table 13.2 USDT Timeouts

Time	Description
Sender	
`N_As`	From when the message was sent to when the message is transmitted successfully by the data link layer.
`N_Bs`	From confirmation that the message was transmitted successfully to when the flow control message is received by the sender.
`N_Cs`	From indication that the flow control message was received to when the next message is transmitted by the sender.
Receiver	
`N_Ar`	From confirmation that the message was received to when the message is transmitted by the data link layer.
`N_Br`	From when the message was sent to when the flow control message is transmitted successfully by the sender
`N_Cr`	From confirmation that the flow control message was transmitted to when the next message is received from the sender.

A good graphical depiction of these times can be found in section 3.2.4.7 of the standard, which is included in the file `COM2-2-2.PDF` on the CD. The standard values for `BS`, `ST`, and all the `N_` timeouts are defined in the OIL configuration files.

Two possible cases of segmented data transmission can appear on the network bus: single-frame and multiple-frame transmission. The maximum number of bytes that can be transmitted in the multiple-frame sequence is 4,095, whereas the maximum number of bytes allowed in a single-frame sequence is one less than the maximum transmission unit of the data link layer, or 15, whichever is less. Figure 13.1 shows a sequence diagram for a single-frame transmission.

Figure 13.1 Single-frame transmission sequence.

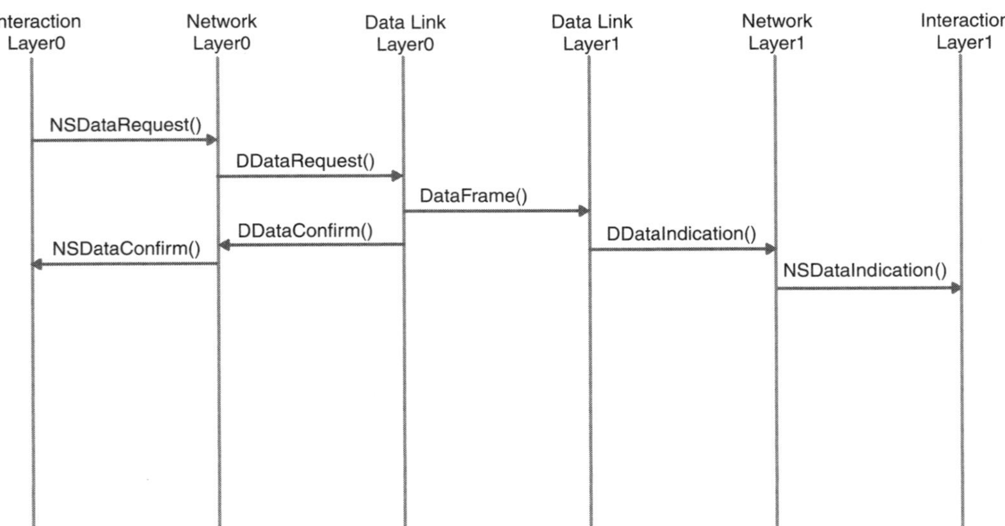

`NSDataRequest()` is similar to `NDataRequest()` introduced in Figures 12.4 and 12.5, except that the interaction layer recognizes that the message might have to be segmented and invokes a different routine in the network layer. When the interaction layer passes the message to the network layer, the network layer checks the length of the message and determines that the message is small enough to be sent in a single frame. The network layer then assembles the message that is to be transmitted on the network and sends this message to the data link layer. There is only one interface to the data link layer: `DDataRequest()`. From the data link layer perspective, and consequently on the bus, only one identifier is available for the complete sequence. From the data link layer viewpoint, all messages are UUDT. In the case of a CAN bus, a segmented message uses only one CAN identifier for transmission. Control of the individual NPDUs is performed by using information embedded in the data of the message. The data link layer has no knowledge of the segmentation of messages, it only passes the messages to the bus or retrieves the messages from the bus and sends them back to the network layer. All segmentation is performed in the network layer. The message includes the single-frame NPCI (Figure 13.2), which is the first byte to be transmitted in the single-frame NPDU.

Figure 13.2 Single-frame NPCI.

BitPosition	7	6	5	4	3:0
Value	0	0	0	0	DataLength

The single-frame NPCI informs the receiving device of the number of bytes in the only frame being transmitted. Because of the single-frame NPCI format, a maximum of 15 bytes can be transmitted in a single frame. This is not a problem with the CAN protocol, but it could be a limitation in other protocols.

The data link layer transmits the frame over the bus and provides confirmation back through the system that the frame was transmitted successfully. The receiving device also notifies its system that it has received the message. The network layer on the receiving device identifies that it is a single-frame message and processes the message completely.

The sequence diagram for multiple-frame segmented data transmission is shown in Figure 13.3 and shows the first part of the multiple-frame transmission sequence, where the session between the transmitting device and receiving device is created.

Figure 13.3 Multiple-frame transmission sequence negotiation.

Interaction Layer0
Network Layer0
Data Link Layer0
Data Link Layer1
Network Layer1
Interaction Layer1
NSDataRequest()
DDataRequest()
DataFrame(FirstFrame)
DDataConfirm()
DDataIndication()
NSDataIndication()
DDataRequest()
DataFrame(FlowControlCTS)
DDataIndication()
DDataConfirm()

When the interaction layer sends a message to the network layer, the network layer identifies that the message is segmented and will require more than one frame to transmit. The network layer then assembles the UUDT message that will be transmitted and sends it over the bus to the data link layer. The first two bytes of the data portion of this message is the first frame NPCI. The remaining bytes of the first frame are the first bytes of the message. For example in a CAN network, the first six bytes of the message are sent. The format of the two NPCI bytes is shown in Figure 13.4.

Figure 13.4 First frame NPCI.

	Byte1					Byte2
BitPosition	7	6	5	4	3:0	7:0
Value	0	0	0	1	DataLength	

As can be seen here, the maximum data length for a message is 4,095 bytes (2^{12}–1). Although it is theoretically possible to have data lengths of zero, the smallest number actually occurs in a first frame NPDU is the number of bytes in a single data frame of the data link layer, which is eight for a CAN network. Anything smaller is sent as a single frame.

When the data frame is received at the receiving device, the data link layer indicates to the network layer that it has received the message. The network layer then identifies it as the first frame of a segmented message and indicates to the interaction layer that the first frame was received. If notification class 5 is enabled, the interaction layer notifies the application.

The network layer then assembles the flow control message in response to the first frame and sends this message to the data link layer. This message consists of three bytes (Figure 13.5) that contain the flow control NPCI.

Figure 13.5 Flow control NPCI.

BitPosition	7	6	5	4	3:0
Value	0	0	1	1	FlowStatus

	Byte2
BitPosition	7:0
Value	BlockSize

	Byte3
BitPosition	7:0
Value	Minimum Separation Time

Two versions of the flow control NPCI exist: the Clear-to-Send and the Wait version. The response to a first frame message is always the Clear-to-Send version, and is identified by a value of `0x30` in byte 1 (`Flow Status = 0`). The second byte in this message is the block size parameter defined in the OIL file and defines the number of consecutive frames that can be transmitted by the sending device before waiting for another Clear-to-Send flow control NPDU. The third byte is the separation time between the transmission of consecutive frames, as defined in the OIL file, which is the time (in milliseconds) from the completion of transmission of one consecutive frame over the network to the initialization of transmission of the next consecutive frame. The sending device uses the information in the BS and ST bytes to coordinate data transmission. The sequence diagram in Figure 13.6 shows the sequence of events for the remainder of the segmented data transmission.

Figure 13.6 Multiframe data transmission sequence.

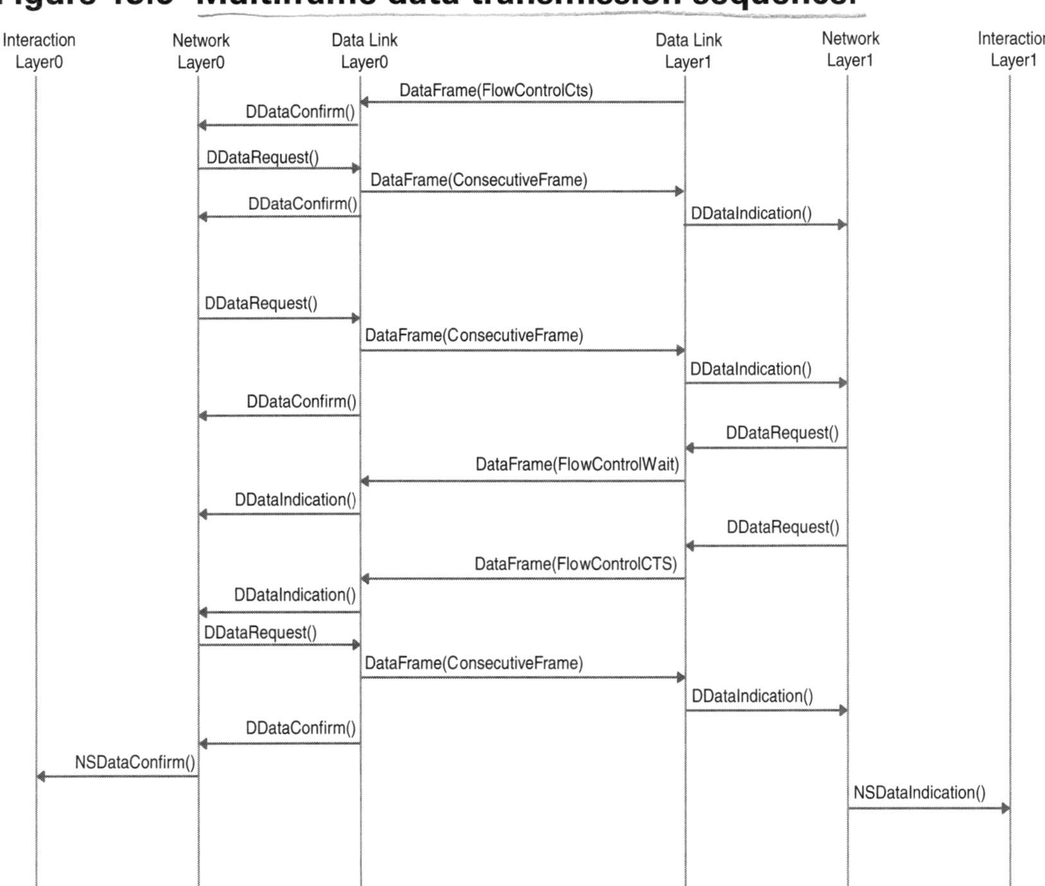

This example uses a block size of two to simplify the figure. After receiving the Clear-to-Send flow control NPDU, the sending device assembles the consecutive frame with the next bytes of data to be sent. The first byte of the consecutive frame is the consecutive frame NPCI, which is shown in Figure 13.7.

Figure 13.7 Consecutive frame NPCI.

BitPosition	7	6	5	4	3:0
Value	0	0	1	0	SequenceNo.

The four bits that define the sequence number define the sequence of messages that are transmitted by the sending device. By default, the first frame NPDU has a sequence number of 0, and the first consecutive frame that is transmitted has a sequence number of 1. Because the sequence number limit is 15, the consecutive frame immediately following a sequence number of 15 will wrap around to 0. The reception of flow control NPDUs does not affect the sequence number.

In Figure 13.6, two consecutive frames are transmitted and then the sending device waits for a flow control NPDU. The receiving device first sends a Wait flow control NPDU, because it is still busy processing the messages, and then sends a Clear-to-Send flow control NPDU. The sending device then sends the next consecutive frames. This process continues until all data has been transmitted. In this example, only one more consecutive frame is required. When the final frame has been transmitted, the receiving device notifies the interaction layer that the complete message has been received and reconstructed properly.

13.2 Dynamic Address Messages

Messages that are transmitted using the USDT protocol can be static messages, dynamic length and dynamically addressed messages, or dynamic length and statically addressed messages. From the application's viewpoint, sending and receiving a message that has a static length and address using USDT is exactly the same as sending a message under UUDT as discussed in Chapter 12. `SendMessage()` and `ReceiveMessage()` are used in exactly the same way and return the same values. In this section, I discuss messages that have both a dynamic address and length.

To illustrate dynamic address, dynamic length messages, the example program includes a message that allows the player at one device to send a text message of up to 60 characters to the player at the other device. The OIL configuration definition for the messages is shown in Listing 13.1. Both an outgoing and an incoming `OpponentMessage` must be defined. Because I have a maximum of two units on the network, the outgoing message only needs one CAN address. However, to demonstrate dynamic addressing, there must be at least two possible destinations. In the future, the program could be expanded to allow more players on the network simultaneously, in which case a unique CAN address will have to be defined for each node on the network. The outgoing message could then set the address to the proper destination so that other players cannot see the message.

Listing 13.1 `OpponentMessage` **definitions.**

```
MESSAGE OpponentMessageIn {
        TYPE = EXTERNAL;
        LENGTH = 60;
        ALIGNMENT = 1;
        USAGE = RECEIVE;
        QUEUED = FALSE;
        TX_NOTIFICATION = NONE;
        RX_NOTIFICATION = ON_SUCCESS;
        TRANSMISSION = DIRECT;
        ACCESSNAMES = { opponentMessageInBuffer };
        CAN_ADDRESSES = { OpponentMessageNode1, OpponentMessageNode2};
        RX_SUCCESS_TASK = OpponentMessageReceived;
  };

  MESSAGE OpponentMessageOut {
        TYPE = EXTERNAL;
        LENGTH = 60;
        ALIGNMENT = 1;
        USAGE = SEND;
        QUEUED = FALSE;
        TX_NOTIFICATION = NONE;
        RX_NOTIFICATION = NONE;
        TRANSMISSION = DIRECT;
        ACCESSNAMES = { opponentMessageOutBuffer };
        CAN_ADDRESSES = { OpponentMessageNode0, OpponentMessageNode2};
  };
```

Notice that there is no direct indication that this message will be sent via USDT. Because the message is not defined as being a USDT message until it is associated with a given network, the determination of this attribute is performed by the configuration utility that translates the OIL file into the proper code. At this time, it is the responsibility of the implementation to determine that it is a USDT message and to create the proper configurations that enable segmented versus unsegmented transmissions. Because only USDT messages can be dynamically addressed, the definition of two possible destinations indicates to the implementation that this will have to be a USDT message.

Initiation of the message is performed by pressing the # key on the keypad. A message then appears on the sender's display that prompts for the message. On the 16-key keypad used in the example program, words are entered using letters as found on a telephone keypad. The letter pressed selects the position of the letter that accompanies a telephone number as follows: Press 'A' for the first letter, 'B' for the second letter, and so on. For example, to send

"Hello," the player would press the keys 4-B, 3-B, 5-C, 5-C, and 6-C. The letter 'Q' is assumed to be in the second position of key number 7, and the letter 'Z' is in the fourth position of key number 9. A space is entered using the number 1, a period is entered using the number 0, and the backspace is the * key. When complete, the player presses the # key again, which sends the message to the other player. If no key is pressed for 10 seconds, the display returns to the prior display and the message is aborted.

To implement this messaging system, extensive changes have to be made to the `ProcessKeyPress` task. Some of these changes are shown in Listing 13.2, which only shows the areas concerned with sending the message.

Listing 13.2 `ProcessKeyPress` modified task.

```
TASK(ProcessKeyPress)
{
EventMaskType eventMask;
BOOLEAN shuffleComplete,dealComplete;
UINT8 i,pressedKey;
char tempBuffer[4];

   while(1){
...
         switch(CheckGameTransition(pressedKey)){
...
            case CREATE_OPPONENT_MESSAGE:
               messageSize = 0;
               messageNumber = '2';
               gameState = GAME_CONSTRUCT_OPPONENT_MESSAGE;
               WriteDisplay(OpponentMessagePrompt);
               break;
...
            case SEND_OPPONENT_MESSAGE:
               opponentMessageOutBuffer[messageSize++] = 0;
               SendMessageTo(OpponentMessageOut,opponentMessageOutBuffer,
                  messageSize,messageOpponent);
               gameState = GAME_NORMAL;
               WriteDisplay(GameNormalPrompt);
               break;
            case CLEAR_OPPONENT_MESSAGE:
               WriteDisplay(GameNormalPrompt);
               gameState = GAME_NORMAL;
               break;
```

```
                case NO_ACTION:
                    break;
            }
        }
    }
}
```

Pressing the # key presents two possibilities: starting a message and sending a message. The rest of the task, in which the message buffer is constructed in preparation for transmission, is pretty self-explanatory. I have not included it in this listing to conserve space, but it can be viewed on the CD in `cardgame.c`.

When the # key is pressed the first time, `CREATE_OPPONENT_MESSAGE` executes. During this action, the buffer is cleared, the state is set to `GAME_CONSTRUCT_OPPONENT_MESSAGE`, local variables are initialized, and the display is updated. If the # key is pressed a second time while the state is `GAME_CONSTRUCT_OPPONENT_MESSAGE`, then `SEND_OPPONENT_MESSAGE` executes and the message is sent to the opponent defined by the `messageOpponent` variable. Although this limited example has only one opponent, the code allows a message to be sent to one of a number of opponents. The size of the message was calculated by the `messageSize` variable as the message was constructed. The message is transmitted using the COM API service `SendMessageTo()`.

```
StatusType SendMessageTo(SymbolicName message, AccessNameRef data,
                         LengthRef length, AddressRef target);
```

The `message` and `data` parameters have the exact same definition as the similar parameters in `SendMessage()`, which was discussed in Chapters 9 and 11. The `length` parameter defines the length of the message that is to be sent. This value must be less than or equal to the length of the message as defined in the OIL configuration file. Finally, the `target` parameter is the address of the target that receives the message. The interpretation of this parameter is very specific to the network protocol being used. In the case of a CAN network, `target` is typically the complete identifier for the data frame, either 11 or 29 bits, or a reference to a CAN address with a unique identifier.

When invoked, `SendMessageTo()` functions exactly as `SendMessage()`. The return status values are also the same. The only difference is that the interaction layer passes additional information to the network layer. For a message sent with `SendMessage()`, the interaction layer can use the network layer service defined in the specification as `N_UUData.req` (`NDataRequest`) in the sequence diagram Figure 12.3 or it can use `N_USData.req` (`NSDataRequest`) in the sequence diagram Figures 13.1 and 13.3, depending on the length of the message defined in the OIL configuration file. Because only USDT messages can use `SendMessageTo()`, the interaction layer always uses `N_USData.req` (`NSDataRequest`).

At this point, how the application handles a USDT message can get confusing. If a message is defined with only one CAN address in the OIL configuration file, it must be sent with `SendMessage()` or `SendDynamicMessage()` (defined later). However, if a message is defined with more than one CAN address, it must be sent with `SendMessageTo()`. This is true for the OSEK Works implementation. However, other implementations may function differently. Until the OIL standard is updated to address the requirements of the COM standard, each implementation is free to realize dynamically addressed messages in their own way.

When the system is up and running and a network analysis tool is monitoring the network when the message is sent, two different sequences of messages will be seen depending on the length of the message that the one player sends. If the length of the message is less than the maximum number of bytes per data frame, a single-frame message is sent. In the example application with a CAN network, sending the message "Hello" would result in a single-frame message. Longer messages would result in multiple data frames, as described earlier.

At the other end of the network, the receiving device has two notification classes for receiving USDT messages: Notification class 1 is triggered when the entire message is received, and notification class 5, available only for USDT messages, is triggered on receipt of the first frame. In the example application, I defined two tasks that are activated based on these notification classes. The first task is `IncomingMessage` (Listing 13.3), which is activated when the first frame is received over the network. It puts the message "Incoming Message" on the display, sets the state of the card game to `GAME_RECEIVING_OPPONENT_MESSAGE`, and starts a timer that requires that the message is received within 10 seconds. If the timer expires, the `AbortMessage` task is activated, returning the program to normal operation. I do not discuss `AbortMessage` here, but it is included on the accompanying CD.

Listing 13.3 `IncomingMessage` task.

```
TASK(IncomingMessage)
{
   WriteDisplay(IncomingMessageNotice);
   SetRelAlarm(IncomingMessageAlarm,10000,0);
   gameStateOld = gameState;
   gameState = GAME_RECEIVING_OPPONENT_MESSAGE;
   TerminateTask();
}
```

When the entire message has been received and reassembled, the COM component notifies the application by activating the `OpponentMessageReceived` task (Listing 13.4), which first obtains a copy of the message that was received using `ReceiveMessageFrom()`.

```
StatusType ReceiveMessageFrom(SymbolicName message, AccessNameRef data,
                              LengthRef length, AddressRef sender);
```

`ReceiveMessageFrom()` functions identically to `ReceiveMessage()`, discussed in Chapters 9 and 11, with the following exceptions.

- The length of the message is copied into the variable referenced by the `length` parameter.
- The address of the device that sent the message is copied into the variable referenced by the `sender` parameter. In the case of a CAN network, which has no concept of the sender or receiver address, the value used for this variable is specific to the implementation and can be as simple as the CAN message ID.

After receiving the message, the task sends it to the local display and waits for the local player to press the # key to clear the display and return to normal operation. The # keypress is handled by the `ProcessKeyPress` task using the `CLEAR_OPPONENT_MESSAGE` action shown in Listing 13.2.

Listing 13.4 `OpponentMessageReceived` **task.**

```
TASK(OpponentMessageReceived)
{
DataLength messageSize;
AddressType messageSource;

   ReceiveMessageFrom(OpponentMessageIn,opponentMessageInBuffer,
      &messageSize,&messageSource);
   ReceiveMessage(OpponentMessageIn,opponentMessageInBuffer);
   WriteDisplay("\f");
   WriteDisplay(opponentMessageInBuffer);
   gameState = GAME_RECEIVED_OPPONENT_MESSAGE;
   WriteDisplayAt(3,0,OpponentMessageReceivedPrompt);
   CancelAlarm(IncomingMessageAlarm);
   TerminateTask();
}
```

13.3 Dynamic Length Messages

Messages that have a static address and static length and messages that have a dynamic address and dynamic length have both been covered in this and previous chapters. One other type of message defined by the OSEK/VDX COM specification has a static address and a dynamic length. These messages must be USDT messages and are handled in the same manner as other USDT messages, except that the API services that access these messages differ slightly from the services that access USDT messages.

```
StatusType SendDynamicMessage(SymbolicName message,
                              AccessNameRef data, LengthRef length);

StatusType ReceiveDynamicMessage(SymbolicName message,
                                 AccessNameRef data, LengthRef length);
```

These two API services work identically to `SendMessageTo()` and `ReceiveMessageFrom()` but do not have the address parameter passed to them. The interaction layer of the COM component knows what the address is supposed to be and attaches that value automatically to the message when it is sent to the network layer. Because messages that are dynamic in length only are almost identical to messages that are dynamic in both address and length, I have not provided an example here.

13.4 Example Program

In this chapter, I added one small feature to the example blackjack game — the ability of one player to send a text message to the other player during the game. This is possible whenever the game is in the "normal" mode, which is whenever a hand is not in play or the cards are not being shuffled. The message is initiated by pressing the # key and sent in the same way after the message is typed on the keypad using a combination of numbers and letters, as described in "Dynamic Address Messages."

13.5 Modules

`cardgame.c` This module was modified extensively to support the added feature of sending messages. The following tasks were created or changed.

`ProcessKeyPress` This task was modified to process the request to send a message, construct the message as keys are pressed, send the message, and clear a message sent by an opponent.

`OpponentMessageReceived` This task is activated whenever a complete opponent message has been received successfully. It clears the display and outputs the message. The player must hit the # key to clear the screen.

`IncomingMessage` This task is activated after the first frame is received. It indicates on the display that a message is incoming and starts a timer. Because the network often is very fast, the message on the display usually flashes for less than a second unless the message is lost, in which case, the timer elapses and the display is cleared.

`AbortMessage` This task aborts the incoming message when the timer mentioned under `IncomingMessage` expires.

`UINT8 ConvertKeyCombo(UINT8 messageNumber,UINT8 pressedKey)` This function converts a number and letter combination on the keypad into a distinct letter from A to Z (caps only).

13.6 Exercises

1. A set of messages was created in Chapter 12 that transmitted the dealer and player hands periodically. Because the maximum CAN message has eight bytes, and transmitting all possible cards in one message requires 10 bytes, four messages of five bytes each were used. Modify the program you wrote to use two segmented 10-byte messages.

13.7 Summary

In this chapter, I discussed the advanced external communication capabilities of an OSEK/VDX COM implementation. Segmenting a large message across multiple data frames on a network is very complex; however, the OSEK/VDX COM specification encapsulates this complexity so that the application no longer has to be concerned with the size of the messages it transmits. I describe this capability as advanced because most small embedded controllers work with data that is, at most, four bytes long and will fit in one data frame on all currently used networks. However, with the advent of multiple new networks and the addition of Internet TCP/IP capabilities into embedded devices, it is no longer science fiction to conceive of an embedded device that has to communicate with both CAN and TCP/IP networks. In this scenario, it is possible that a TCP/IP message 1,500 bytes long would need to be transmitted over a CAN network. OSEK/VDX COM will perform this function, and it will be transparent to the application.

Now that the complete OSEK/VDX COM specification has been introduced and described, a number of issues that have been identified throughout Part 2 need to be resolved. How does an application differentiate between signals that are received via an external network and signals that are measured from internal ports on the controller? At first glance, it would appear that a separate API is required for local signals and an additional API — the OSEK/VDX COM API — for signals received over a network. In addition, how do you handle the case where multiple signals are packed into one message? I would recommend an additional I/O layer that provides signal information to the application and encapsulates the source of or destination for a particular signal. This is typically referred to as a presentation layer, which presents the application with the data in the expected format. One drawback of another layer is the additional time expended in accessing the signal; however, a properly designed system should be able to save time somewhere else. The discussion of a presentation layer, and the methods of accessing signals or data, is an entirely different subject and is not covered in this book. At this time, I am unaware of any other book that would describe this topic.

PART 3

Network Management

This final specification to be discussed is the OSEK/VDX Network Management (NM) specification. The NM specification defines a methodology and API services used to monitor the nodes on a network. Similar to the communication specification, the network management specification is intended to function with any physical network protocol. In this part of the book, I provide an overview and discuss the two types of network management: direct and indirect.

As with the OSEK/VDX OS and COM specifications, the NM specification was written to stand alone. It does not require either of the OSEK/VDX OS or COM components to function. In reality, most NM implementations are tightly integrated with an existing COM implementation.

14

Chapter 14

Network Management Overview

The OSEK/VDX Network Management (NM) specification defines the algorithms that monitor the status of nodes on a static network, provides an API for control of the NM component, and develops information that reports network status and configuration to the application. Because NM was originally developed for an automotive environment, the network is assumed to be static, which means that the total set of possible nodes on the network is fixed and known by every node on the network, although every node does not have to be available in an application. Optional nodes, such as navigation systems, entertainment devices, and security devices, can be defined that might not reside in a particular automobile but can be added later. However, each of these nodes has a unique identifier that is known to all possible nodes in the network. The diagram of network management with respect to other portions of an application is shown in Figure 14.1.

14.1 Network Management Components

A network management implementation consists of a number of components, numbered 1 through 7 in Figure 14.1. Each of these components are described in this section.

Station Management (1) The station management component resides within the user's application and provides system-dependent algorithms to coordinate the network. Based on the requirements of the application, this component queries the NM component to determine the status of the nodes on the network and either takes action or provides the information back to the application in an application-specific format. This particular component is not defined by the NM specification.

As an example of how station management might work, consider an application in which the station management component monitors message data and the network status. If a node on the network is identified by NM as not being available, the station management component could provide a default value for the message back to the application so that the application could continue in a reduced functionality mode. This would be accomplished by creating an additional layer that is responsible for presenting the data in the proper format between the functional application and the COM and NM components. The application would then request the data, which would be dependent on the status of the network and the values within the messages that are received, from this additional layer. The component described here would be the presentation layer mentioned briefly at the end of Chapter 13.

Another function that station management could perform is changing the overall functioning of the application based on the status of nodes within the network. If the application is operating within an OSEK/VDX OS, the station management component could identify when the APPMODE must be changed because critical data is not available from an external node.

Figure 14.1 Network management environment.

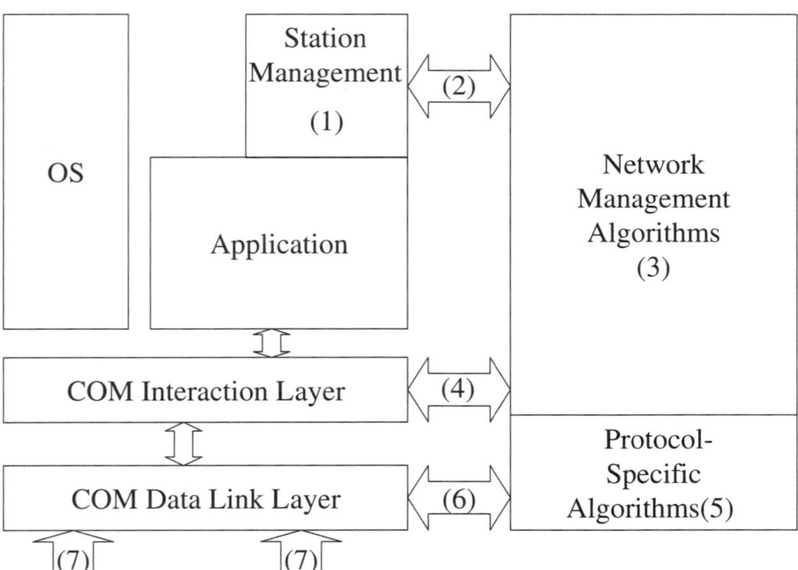

Network Management APIs (2) The NM component provides a number of API services that can be used by the station management component to initialize, control, and query the status of the NM component. These API services are categorized into three types of services:

common, direct NM, and indirect NM. Each of these services will be described in more detail in the following chapters.

Network Management Algorithms (3) This section of the NM component contains the specific algorithms for both direct and indirect NM. These algorithms determine the current configuration of the network and identify the status of each node. They will be discussed in more detail in the following sections.

Interaction Layer Interface (4) This interface is provided by the interaction layer of the COM component for use by the indirect NM portion of the NM component. It was not discussed in Part 2 because it is not visible to the application. The services provided by this interface are discussed in Chapter 16, "Indirect Network Management."

Network Management Protocol-Specific Algorithms (5) The network management algorithms discussed previously are divided into two parts: general algorithms and protocol-specific algorithms, which are based on the type of physical network connected to the node. There is one set of protocol-specific algorithms for each type of physical network that is connected. These are discussed in the following chapters.

Data Link Layer Interface (6) Similar to the interaction layer interface discussed previously, the data link layer of the COM component must provide an API for the NM component. These services also were not discussed in Part 2 but are discussed in the following chapters.

Multiple Network Interfaces (7) The model of network management comprehends the possibility of multiple networks attached to a particular device. These might be multiple similar networks or completely unique networks. Each network must be supported by a protocol-specific algorithm, as mentioned earlier.

14.2 Summary

In this chapter, I looked at the basic architecture of network management and how it interacts with an application and other components. The OSEK/VDX NM specification defines two algorithms that have minimal overlap: direct NM, which is covered in Chapter 15, and indirect NM, which is covered in Chapter 16.

15

Chapter 15

Direct Network Management

Various forms of direct network management (NM) are used extensively in the European automotive industry that require an extensive, robust NM component and can identify changes to the configuration of the network rapidly. In this chapter, I introduce the concept of direct NM and describe how network management is configured and used by an application. The station management component is developed as an example throughout this chapter.

15.1 Direct Network Management Concept

Direct NM uses a logical ring concept to identify the status of the network. Figure 15.1 illustrates a system of two physical networks — network 1 and network 2 — that interconnect seven electronic control units (ECUs). Each node on the network has a unique number from 1 to 4. The NM specification does not define a maximum number of nodes allowed on a network; however, there is seldom a need for more than 255. Although the physical network might not support message addressing, direct NM requires that it be supported. I discuss how this is accomplished later in this chapter. In Figure 15.1, ECU G functions as a gateway. Although only one microcontroller is internal to this unit, two physical networks are connected to it, requiring two nodes. The number of each node will probably be different. A network management implementation must identify multiple nodes on the device and keep track of information for each node separately.

Figure 15.1 Example system for direct NM.

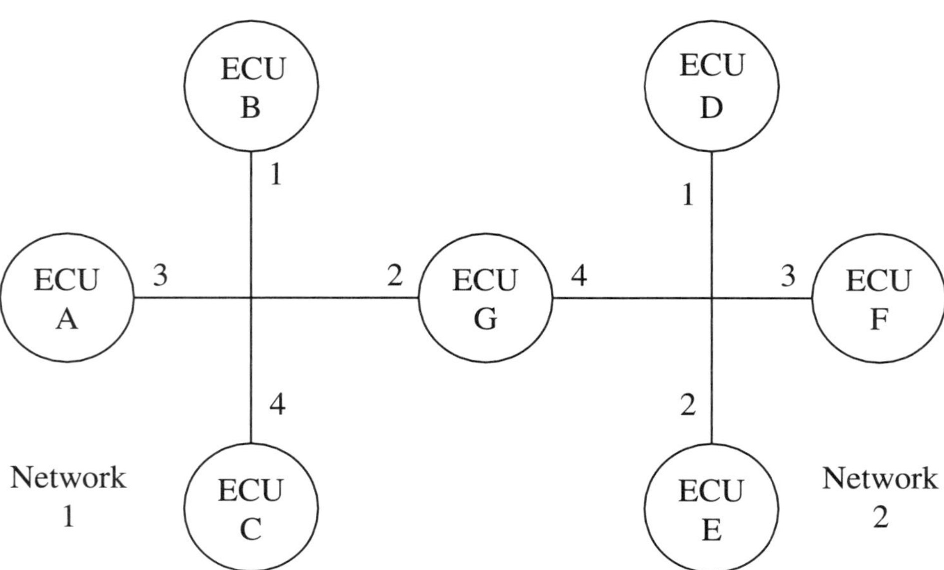

The logical ring is implemented by passing a "Ring" message sequentially from the smallest to the largest numbered node, which then passes the Ring message back to the smallest numbered node. Direct NM also requires a broadcast type of network implementation so that every node can hear the messages that are being sent. Two additional types of messages are broadcast asynchronously on the network: an "Alive" message and a "Limp Home" message. The Alive message identifies a new node on the network and puts the system into a transient state. When the new node has identified all nodes on the network, the system transitions into a stable state. In the stable state, the NM component is fully aware of the status of all nodes on the network. A node that is not functioning properly transmits the Limp Home message. Each of these messages are discussed in more detail later in this chapter.

The NM component uses information from the transmission of these messages to determine the status and configuration of the network. The status of the network provides information on the state in which network management is presently operating. The three main states for network management are shown in Figure 15.2.

When the system is reset, network management enters the `NMOff` state. When the application invokes `StartNM()`, the NM component enters the `NMOn` state.

```
StatusType StartNM(NetId net);
```

Figure 15.2 Network management state chart.

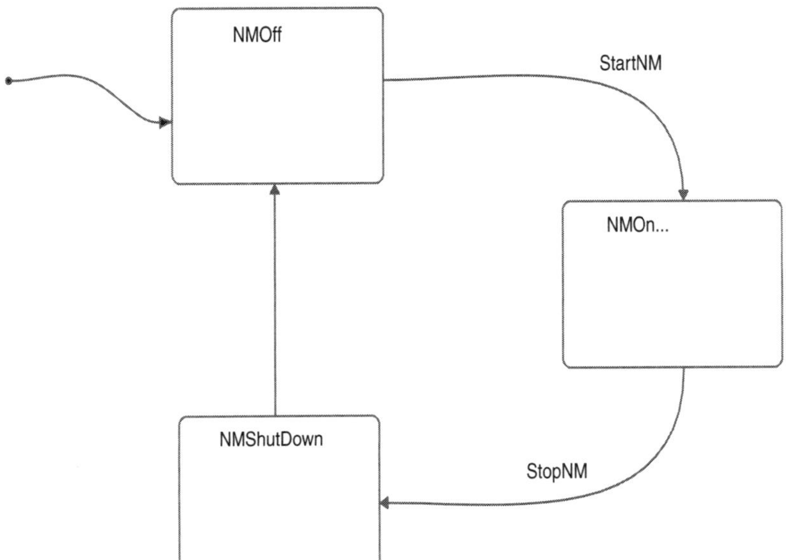

Core versus Optional Services Within the OSEK/VDX NM specification, all API services are defined as either core or optional. In version 2.51 of the specification, the only core services are `StartNM()` and `StopNM()`; consequently, a minimal implementation of a NM component could participate in the logical ring yet provide little or no information to the application. As an example, the network management version included in the WindRiver OSEKWorks implementation provides three levels of network management — Full Master, Master, and Slave — which corresponds with the suggested implementation that is included in the OSEK/VDX NM specification. The Full Master level includes most of the services defined in the NM specification but also requires the most system resources. The Master level provides status information only and requires fewer resources. Finally, the Slave level provides only the services defined as core to the NM specification that will allow participation in the ring. Although no conformance classes are defined in the NM specification, the three suggested levels of services are similar to conformance classes. The next version of the NM specification could include a set of conformance classes for direct NM.

When choosing a network management implementation, you must determine which services are supported before deciding which to use. As I mentioned, only `StartNM()` and `StopNM()` are required. Consequently, an implementation can claim OSEK/VDX NM conformance, yet not provide any status or configuration information to the application. This might be acceptable in some applications, but not in others.

StartNM() initiates participation in the network management ring on the network defined by the net parameter without affecting other networks that might be connected to this device. Consequently, if multiple networks are connected to the same device, as in ECU G in Figure 15.1, each network functions separately and has to be started individually. The NM component for the network that is being started transitions from the NMOff to the NMOn state. E_OK is the only return value defined for StartNM(). One restriction for this API service is that the communication component must already be running. For an OSEK/VDX COM component, this means that StartCOM() has completed. In the example program, I added this network management API service in the InitOS task (Listing 15.1).

Listing 15.1 InitOS with network management initialization.

```
TASK(InitOS)
{
   InitAlarmType const *list = AlarmAutostartList;
   UINT32 currentAppModeMask = ConvertAppMode(APP_MODE_MASK);

   StartCOM();
   StartPeriodical();
   StartNM(NM1);
   while(list->appmodemask != 0x00000000){
      if((list->appmodemask & currentAppModeMask)!= 0){
         if(list->alarmtype == ALARM_REL){
            SetRelAlarm(list->alarm,list->start,list->cycle);
         }
         else{
            SetAbsAlarm(list->alarm,list->start,list->cycle);
         }
      }
      list++;
   }
   TerminateTask();
}
```

The NMShutDown state is entered when the application invokes StopNM().

```
StatusType StopNM(NetId net);
```

The only action taken by StopNM() is to move the NM component for the network identified by the net parameter into the NMShutDown state. Once this state is entered, the NM component performs all the housecleaning required, such as stopping timers and clearing flags, and then immediately enters the NMOff state. As with StartNM(), the only status returned is E_OK.

It is possible for only one network to be in the NMOff state while the other networks are operating in the NMOn state. In the example program, the NM component is shut down just before the communication component is stopped in the CloseOS task (Listing 15.2).

Listing 15.2 CloseOS with network management shutdown.

```
TASK(CloseOS)
{
    StopNM(NM1);
    StopPeriodical();
    StopCOM();
    ShutdownOS(E_OK);
    TerminateTask();
}
```

15.1.1 NMOn State

The NMOn state is shown as parallel substate diagrams in Figure 15.3. The NMInit and NMActive states are entered by default when the NMOn state is entered. NMInit is a transient state in which the NM component is initialized internally. Actions taken in this state are implementation dependent and are not observed on the network. After completion of the initiation tasks, the state immediately transitions to the NMAwake state. It remains in this state until all the conditions have been met to place the network in a bus sleep state, at which point it transitions to the NMBusSleep state. The details of how the system determines that the bus is ready to sleep are defined later in this chapter. Whenever a network management message is received while in the NMBusSleep state, the system transitions to the NMInit state.

In the parallel state diagram, when in the NMActive state, network management communication occurs normally. When the optional API service SilentNM() is invoked, the local node enters the NMPassive state and ceases to participate in the logical ring.

```
StatusType SilentNM(NetIDType net);
```

E_OK is the only return value for this service. To return to the NMActive state, the application invokes TalkNM().

```
StatusType TalkNM(NetIDType net);
```

TalkNM() also returns only E_OK. When the NM component is in the NMPassive state, it still monitors the activity on the network, and state changes can still occur based on the other messages being transmitted on the network (e.g., when the application is operating in a mode that limits resource utilization by shutting down most communication on the network). This can occur when the device attempts to reprogram memory and is receiving the new program data at a high rate over the network.

Figure 15.3 NMOn **state chart.**

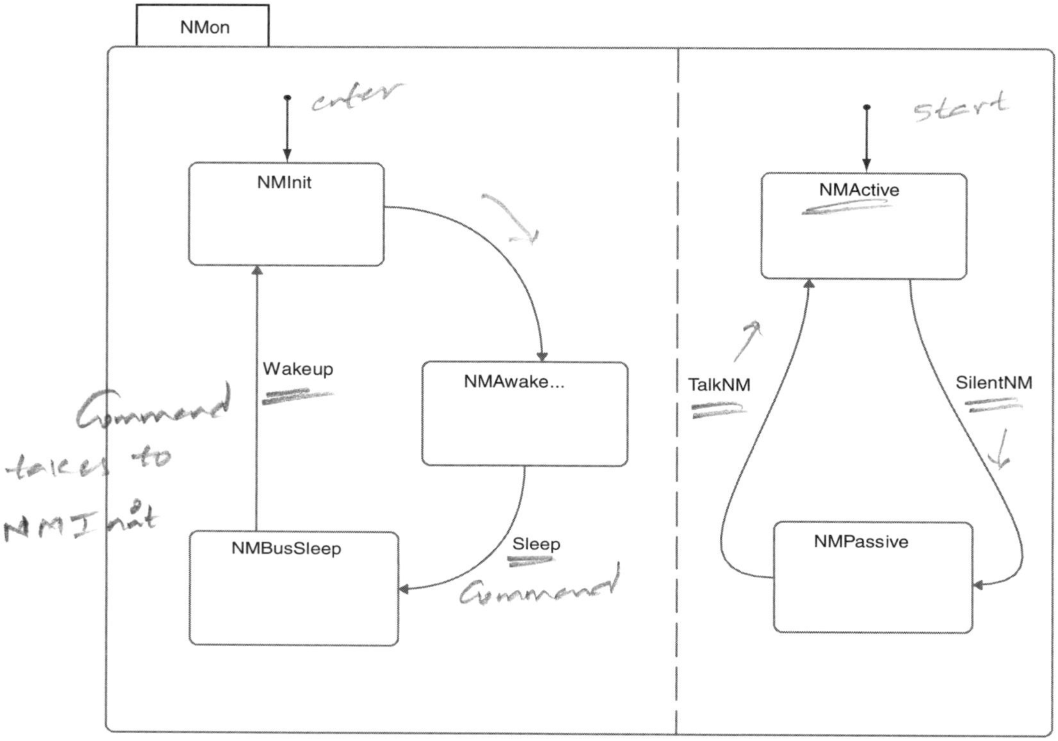

15.1.2 NMAwake State

After the system has performed all the activities required on entering the NMInit state, it automatically transitions to the NMAwake state, which has three substates (Figure 15.4).

The NMReset substate is entered by default on entering the NMAwake state. In this state, the NM component initializes Normal operation. As mentioned earlier, the data link layer of the communication component provides a number of services to network management. The two services that are invoked in this state are D_Init and D_Online. How the services are invoked is specific to the implementation and is not covered here. From an application viewpoint, it is sufficient to understand that the NM component uses the services to initialize the data link layer and to put it online so that messages can be transmitted. Once complete, the NM component checks to make sure that transmission and reception of network management messages is occurring properly and then transitions into the NMNormal state. However, if the NM component determines that a transmission of the Alive message is not possible, it will transition into the NMLimpHome state. The NMNormal state transitions to the NMLimpHome state directly whenever it determines that transmission of NM messages is no longer possible and transitions back to the NMReset state whenever an error occurs during message reception. This reception error can occur when a node goes offline and the timer expires, as I discuss later.

Figure 15.4 `NMAwake` **state chart.**

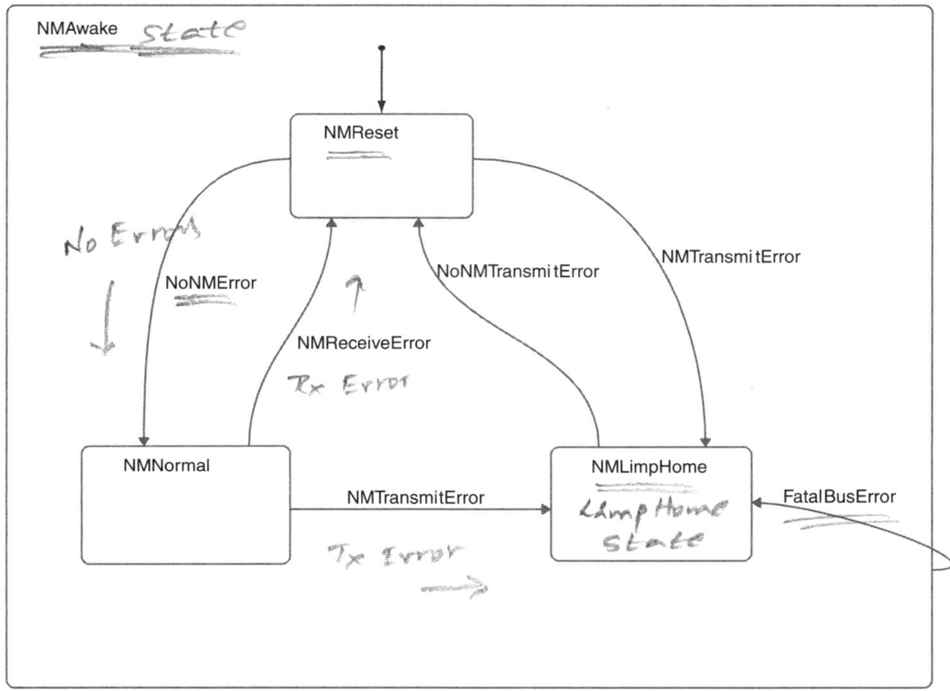

In the `NMLimpHome` state, the NM component continues to monitor the network to determine if message transmission has been restored, which could indicate an intermittent connection somewhere in the system. While the system is in this state, a periodic Limp Home message is transmitted. If transmission is restored, the system transitions back into the `NMReset` state and reinitializes.

15.1.3 `NMNormal` State

The `NMNormal` state is where most of the work is performed. In this state, the network management Ring messages are transmitted and received periodically, and the configuration of the network is managed. When either the status of network management or the configuration changes, the NM component can optionally notify the application. Again, as with many API services, indicating changes to status or configuration does not have to be supported in the NM component. When researching network management software, make sure you understand all of the features that it does and does not support. In the OSEKWorks implementation, notification of the application is not supported at this time; consequently, the status and configuration have to be polled to determine when a change occurs. The OIL configuration file for the `NM` object, as output by OSEKWorks, is shown in Listing 15.3.

Listing 15.3 NM OIL configuration.

```
/*************************************************************************/
/*              Network Management                                       */
/*************************************************************************/

    NM NM1 {
            TYPE = FULL_MASTER;
            IDBASE = 1792;
            WINDOW_MASK = 469762048;
            NODE_ID = 1;
            RX_LIMIT = 10;
            TX_LIMIT = 10;
            MAX_NODES = 4;
            NM_TASK = NMProcessing;
            NM_NETWORK = Net1;
            RING_DELAY = 250;
            RX_TIMEOUT = 2000;
            LIMPHOME_TIMEOUT = 5000;
            BUSSLEEP_TIMEOUT = 6000;
            RETRANSMIT_TIMEOUT = 150;
            CAN_MSGTYPE = STANDARD;
    };
```

Many attributes of the NM object are discussed throughout this chapter, so don't worry if it is a little confusing at this point. Like the OSEK/VDX COM specification, the NM specification does not have a standard OIL configuration format. Your specific implementation could be slightly different from this listing; however, the concepts defined in the NM specification will be the same. The first attribute in this configuration object is TYPE, which describes the specific types of FULL_MASTER, MASTER, or SLAVE. The next attribute of concern is NM_TASK, which defines the task activated when activity related to network management occurs on the network. In this case, instead of processing the messages at the driver level, a task is activated that processes the received messages. This task is created by the OIL configuration utility automatically and is not a task that needs to be created by the application developer. It is unique to OSEKWorks. The NM_NETWORK attribute defines the physical network on which this particular network management object participates. This network is defined as part of the COM component. With this configuration, a different task is activated for changes in each of the networks attached to the device. To accomplish this, each NM object requires a unique name for the NM_TASK attribute.

The OSEK/VDX NM specification defines a number of support items to generate system configurations. These items are optional and not implemented by OSEKWorks; however, they affect operation in the `NMNormal` state and need to be discussed because they could be encountered in an implementation that realizes these configuration items in the OIL configuration file or as macros included in the application source.

`InitDirectNMParams` sets the direct NM timer values.

`InitCMaskTable` initializes the mask of configuration items that signals a changed configuration. This mask resides in a table of masks and has two types: Normal and Limp Home. Each mask is given a handle that can be used later.

`InitTargetConfigTable` defines a target configuration and also resides in a table. Each target is given a mask.

`InitIndDeltaConfig` defines the way the application is notified when the configuration changes. The notification mechanism either activates a task or sets an event.

`InitSMaskTable, InitTargetStatusTable, InitIndDeltaStatus` function identically to the same configuration items but are based on a change in the network status.

`InitIndRingConfig` defines the way the application is notified when the Ring message is received. The notification mechanism either activates a task or sets an event.

15.2 Status Monitoring

Because application task signaling is optional, I added the `StationManagement` task, which executes periodically (Listing 15.4), to the example program.

Listing 15.4 `StationManagement` task.

```
TASK(StationManagement)
{
ConfigType networkConfigurationNormalNew;
ConfigType networkConfigurationMask= OTHER_NODE_MASK;

   GetStatus(NM1,&networkManagementStatus);
   GetConfig(NM1,&networkConfigurationNormalNew,NMCFG_NORMAL);
   if(CmpConfig(NM1,&networkConfigurationNormalNew,
                &networkConfigurationNormal,
                &networkConfigurationMask)!= TRUE){
      if((networkConfigurationNormalNew & OTHER_NODE_MASK)==0){
         if(GetActiveApplicationMode() == HEAD_TO_HEAD){
            ChangeMode(SINGLE_PLAYER);
         }
      }
```

```
    }
    memcpy(&networkConfigurationNormal,&networkConfigurationNormalNew,
          sizeof(ConfigType));
    TerminateTask();
}
```

When run, the StationManagement task obtains the current status of the network using GetStatus().

```
StatusType GetStatus(NetIdType net, NetworkStatusType status);
```

When GetStatus() is invoked, the NM component obtains the current status of the network identified by the net parameter and places it in the variable referenced by the status parameter. The definition of this API service in the NM specification indicates that the status parameter is a variable. However, the definition identifies it as an output parameter, which indicates that it is a reference to a variable in the application. Under the naming conventions used in both the OS and COM specifications, this parameter would be a NetworkStatusTypeRef type. In OSEKWorks, GetStatus() expects a pointer to a variable of type NetworkStatusType, and I would expect most other implementations to behave in the same manner.

Two types of status are available: standard and extended. Standard status provides information about the state of the NM component for that network. Extended status also provides information on the configuration of the external network, including the amount of time the network has been in a given state and, perhaps, additional implementation-dependent data.

The interpretation of the NetworkStatusType variable type is implementation dependent; however, the specification recommends that it be implemented as a bit-encoded flag for standard status. The recommended format given in the OSEK/VDX specification is shown in Table 15.1.

Table 15.1 Standard status bit encoding.

Bit	Description	Interpretation of a 0	Interpretation of a 1
0	Present network configuration stable	Not stable	Stable
1	Operating mode of network physical interface	No error	Error, bus blocked
2	NM mode active/passive	NMPassive	NMActive
3	NM mode on/off	NMOn	NMOff
4	Limp Home mode	Not in NMLimpHome	NMLimpHome
5	Bus sleep mode	Not in NMBusSleep	NMBusSleep
6	Waiting for bus sleep	Not waiting for Twbs to expire	Waiting for Twbs to expire
7	Ring data valid	Ring data access allowed	Ring data access not allowed
8	GoToMode() last call	Awake called	BusSleep called

The extended status format recommended by the specification is less clear. It extends the second bit of the standard status into two bits to indicate one of three possible states. In addition, it defines four additional fields that can be implemented in any manner by the user. An interpretation of how this might be implemented is shown in Table 15.2. This information would probably be in addition to the standard status format. The `StationManagement` task simply saves the current status into the `networkManagementStatus` static variable.

Table 15.2 Extended status bit encoding.

Description	Definition
Operating mode of the network interface	Expands the standard status bit to two bits, which are interpreted as follows: `00` — No error `01` — Error but communication is possible `10` — Error and communication is not possible `11` — Reserved
Number of nodes identified on the logical ring	The number of nodes actively participating in the logical ring.
Number of nodes on the logical ring in Limp Home mode	The number of nodes sending a Limp Home message.
Time elapsed in the stable state	The amount of time that the network has been operating in the stable state. The units are not defined by the standard and are implementation specific.
Time elapsed in the dynamic state	The amount of time that the network has been operating in the dynamic state. The units are not defined by the standard and are implementation specific.

Two additional API services are defined as optional and have not been included in the example application. `SelectDeltaStatus()` is the first service.

```
StatusType SelectDeltaStatus(NetIdType net, StatusHandleType status,
                             StatusHandleType mask);
```

`SelectDeltaStatus()` notifies the application of the network status changes of its choosing. The values passed to the NM component are handles to a network status and the status mask defined by the `Init` configuration items discussed earlier in this section. The handle refers to the particular mask and target from the table. How this is implemented is not defined in the specification. Whenever the status changes, the NM component checks to see whether the mask bit that corresponds to the status change is set and whether the new value of that bit is equal to the value in the corresponding bit in the `status` parameter before notification occurs. The task or event that is triggered is configured using `InitIndDeltaStatus`, discussed earlier. The status returned from this API service is always assumed to be `E_OK`; however, the status in the specification indicates that no status is returned, which directly contradicts many of the standards created in the OSEK/VDX specifications and is probably in error.

The next optional API service is CmpStatus(), which compares two status values with respect to a mask and determines if the required status values have changed. Although optional, it is a simple test to perform if the status is implemented as a bit field–encoded integer, as recommended, and can be implemented as a macro.

```
StatusType CmpStatus(NetIdType net, StatusRefType test,
                     StatusRefType ref, StatusRefType mask);
```

The values passed in the test, ref, and mask parameters are references to variables within the application. The parameters are passed by reference because, in the extended status case, these variables can be very large structures and should not be passed by value to any API service. The logic performed by the service for each status item is

```
(test XOR ref) AND mask.
```

If all of the tests for all of the status values return 0, then none of the desired status values have changed and the service returns TRUE. If any of the tests return a value of 1, then at least one status parameter has changed and the service returns FALSE. As with SelectDeltaStatus(), there appears to be an error in the specification. The StatusType return type is typically defined with the prefix E_, and the values TRUE and FALSE do not fit within this convention. The return type should more correctly be defined as BOOLEAN. If the status being tested is fully implemented as an integer, with bit fields representing the status, then this function can be defined using the following macro.

```
#define CmpStatus(net, test, ref, mask) (((test^ref)&mask)==0?TRUE:FALSE)
```

Note that the net parameter is not used in this macro. The assumptions are that the status type is integer. Because one application can be connected to multiple networks through multiple nodes and because each node can use a different type of network management with a different reporting status, if CmpStatus() is implemented in the NM component, the network that is referenced must be transmitted to the network management routine. For example, StatusRefType can be a void pointer, and CmpStatus() will cast the pointer based on the characteristics of the network. This simplified macro is not capable of performing that task.

15.3 Configuration Management

The NM component maintains the current configuration of the network and can provide this information to the application on request. Because the API services that maintain and report the network configuration are optional, the application might not be able to obtain the status of other nodes on the network.

As mentioned earlier, the two levels of configuration stored by the NM component are Normal and Limp Home. The Limp Home configuration indicates which nodes are presently in the Limp Home mode, which is discussed later. The Normal configuration indicates the presence or absence of individual nodes on the network. The result is the following possible configurations of each node on the network.

1. For external nodes, the NM component can determine whether that node is Present, Absent, or in Limp Home mode.

2. For its own node, the NM component can determine whether the node is Mute, Not Mute, or in Limp Home mode. This information is obtained in GetStatus(), discussed in Section 15.1.3.

In the StationManagement task, after the status of the system has been obtained and stored, GetConfig() obtains the system configuration.

```
StatusType GetConfig(NetIdType net, ConfigRefType config,
                     ConfigKindType kind);
```

When GetConfig() is invoked, it places the current configuration for the network defined by the net parameter into the variable referenced by the config parameter. The kind parameter defines the configuration type and can be either Normal or Limp Home when the network is operating under direct NM. The config variable must be provided by the application. The status returned from GetConfig() is always E_OK.

The format of the ConfigRefType data type is implementation dependent. For example in OSEKWorks, this is an array of bytes such that the least significant bit of the first byte in the array corresponds to node 0. The number of bytes in the array (n) is calculated using the following equation.

$$n = (\text{total number of nodes modulo } 8) + 1$$

This creates a very compact configuration structure; however, it assumes that the nodes are sequentially numbered beginning at zero for all possible nodes on the network. If another numbering scheme is used, then a different method of storing the configuration is required.

After I obtain the current configuration for the example application, I compare it to the previous configuration to determine whether one of the nodes on the network has changed. This comparison uses CmpConfig(), which is similar to the previously discussed CmpStatus().

```
StatusType CmpConfig(NetIdType net, ConfigRefType test,
                     ConfigRefType ref, ConfigRefType mask);
```

CmpConfig() performs exactly the same calculation as CmpStatus() and returns TRUE if no bits have changed.

The only action taken in the example application is when the opposite node in a head-to-head game disappears. In this case, the mode of the system changes to SINGLE_PLAYER. CmpConfig() replaces RemainingCardsMessage from Chapter 12 in which case, the application reverted to SINGLE_PLAYER when the periodic message went missing. Direct NM now identifies when the node is missing and performs this same function.

The StationManagement task shows how an application module is required to intermediate between the NM component and the application to handle differences in the way the NM component functions. Many times, the details of the NM component, such as supported API services and the size and format of the different network management data types, are defined by the implementation as a result of the requirements of the organization responsible for the entire system, which will be different from organization to organization. The abstraction provided by the StationManagement task is critical to the portability of the application. In an implementation where notification of the application through task activation is allowed, this task will be activated whenever the status or configuration changes. However, if task activation is not supported, this task will be executed periodically to check the current status.

Two additional API services are optional. The first, `SelectDeltaConfig()`, functions identically to `SelectDeltaStatus()` but is based on changes to the network configuration, not the network status.

```
StatusType SelectDeltaConfig(NetIdType net, ConfigKindName kind,
                             ConfigHandleType handle,
                             ConfigHandleType mask);
```

`SelectDeltaConfig()` includes one more parameter than `SelectDeltaStatus()`. The `kind` parameter determines whether this `Delta` configuration applies to the Normal or Limp Home configurations.

The other optional API service is `InitConfig()`, which forces the NM component to move from the `NMNormal` state to the `NMReset` state and to restart network configuration monitoring.

```
StatusType InitConfig(NetIdType net);
```

When `InitConfig()` is invoked, the configuration of the node in the application is considered Mute, and all other nodes are considered Absent. Nodes are then added based on an algorithm defined later in this chapter, and the local node is Not Mute as soon as a network management message is sent successfully. The status returned from this service is always `E_OK`.

Now that I have described the basic concept of direct NM, I will now describe in more detail the mechanics of the method, although in most applications, the implementation is transparent. However when debugging the system, it is imperative to know about the messages that are running around on the network and how they function.

15.4 Network Management Protocol Data Unit

The first item to understand in network management is the network management protocol data unit, or NMPDU (Figure 15.5). This data structure is specific to network management. It contains all the information required for the network management message, plus optional data, and it is used to create the message that is transferred from one node to the next.

Figure 15.5 Network management protocol data unit.

AddressField		**ControlField**	**DataField**
SourceI D	Destination ID	Opcode	Data
Mandatory			*Optional*

The first field in the NMPDU is the source node identifier. This is typically the number of the node from which the NMPDU has been received or the node that is about to transmit the NMPDU. The second field in the NMPDU is a destination node identifier, which is the opposite of the source node identifier, and identifies either the receiving node (i.e., local node) or the external node to which the NMPDU is to be transmitted. In an implementation, the size and format of this identifier will be identical to the size and format of the source identifier.

The third field is the operation code (opcode), which identifies the type of NMPDU that is being referenced. The NM specification does not define the size or the format of the identifiers for the source or destination; however, the specification does suggest a CAN message implementation, which I discuss shortly.

The NM specification defines three message classes that correspond to eight different messages. As with the identifiers mentioned previously, the specification does not define this opcode format. It does, however, require that any unused bits in the opcode be transferred verbatim from the received message to the sent message in the case of Ring messages, which I discuss later. The three classes of message and eight types of messages are shown in Table 15.3.

Table 15.3 Direct NM opcode types.

Opcode	Type	`sleep.ind`	`sleep.ack`	Description
`XXXX0000`	Ring	`FALSE`	`FALSE`	Normal Ring message
`XXXX0001`	Ring	`TRUE`	`FALSE`	Ring message requesting bus sleep
`XXXX0010`	Ring	`FALSE`	`TRUE`	Ring mode acknowledging bus sleep
`XXXX0011`	Ring	`TRUE`	`TRUE`	Same as above; `sleep.ind` is ignored whenever `sleep.ack` is `TRUE`.
`XXXX0100`	Alive	`FALSE`	`FALSE`	Normal Alive message
`XXXX0101`	Alive	`TRUE`	`FALSE`	Alive message requesting bus sleep
`XXXX1000`	Limp Home	`FALSE`	`FALSE`	Normal Limp Home message
`XXXX1001`	Limp Home	`TRUE`	`FALSE`	Limp Home message requesting bus sleep

Table 15.3 also includes an opcode example for each type of message. These opcodes are only suggestions, and probably will be different in an actual implementation. The three classes of messages — Ring, Alive, and Limp Home — are discussed in more detail in the following sections.

The final field of the NMPDU is optional and contains data that is specific to the application. It is typically transmitted in the Ring message. The API services that access this data are discussed in more detail in Section 15.4.2, "Ring Message."

As with the NPDU described in Chapter 13, "Advanced External Communication," the OSEK/VDX NM specification does not define how the NMPDU is mapped into the data frame of the particular network. In Figure 15.6, I show the suggested method, mapped into both 11- and 29-bit identifier messages, from the NM specification using the CAN network protocol.

Figure 15.6 NMPDU to CAN mapping.

CANIdentifier		DLC	CANData Field		
IDBase	SourceID	=8	Dest.ID	Opcode	Data
3(21)	8		8	8	48

The source ID is a straight 8-bit field with values from 0 to 255. In order to identify the difference between a network management message and any other message, an IDBASE and a WINDOW_MASK is also recommended. For example, if four nodes, numbered 0 to 3, are possible in a given configuration, an 11-bit WINDOW_MASK would be 0x7FC and a 29-bit window mask would be 0x1FFFFFFC. A message is considered to be a network management message if the result of the ID of the message ANDed with the WINDOW_MASK equals the IDBASE. If the IDBASE is 0x700, any message with an ID from the set {0x700, 0x701, 0x702, 0x703} would be considered a network management message. The destination ID is held in the first byte of the CAN data field, and the opcode, which is discussed later, is in the second byte. The remaining six bytes might or might not be used. In various implementations of the NM specification, these fields can be smaller, larger, or encoded differently. The format of this field is typically defined by the organization that is responsible for defining the system. The local node number is defined in the NODE_ID attribute at the OIL confiuration file, and the maximum number of nodes is defined in the MAX_NODES attribute. The size of the identifier for the CAN message, either 11 or 29 bits, is defined by the attribute CAN_MSGTYPE.

The OSEK/VDX COM component must provide a number of services to the NM component to allow the transmission of the particular network data frame. The first set of services is identified in the COM specification as D_WindowData and includes a request, confirm, and indication service. The request service is responsible for mapping the NMPDU to the transmitted data frame, and the indication service is responsible for extracting the NMPDU from a received data frame. The confirmation service confirms to the NM component that a previously requested message has been sent. The COM specification only defines the functioning of the service, not the function prototype, because these services are not available to the application and are specific to the implementation.

15.4.1 Alive Message

The sequence of events that are performed at the beginning of network startup are shown in Figure 15.7. These particular events are descriptive and might or might not represent actual functions. They illustrate an application where all nodes start at essentially the same time, such as a switch that applies power to all the nodes simultaneously when turned on. When network management first starts with StartNM(), the NM component performs a series of initializations and then sends the first network management message, the Alive message. The default version of the Alive message transmitted is the version that does not request sleep mode. Requesting sleep mode is discussed later in the section.

The Alive message is intended to inform the other nodes on the network that the current node has entered the ring. At this point, the first of five timers that are applicable to network management is started. The TTyp timer defines the typical time between the reception of a

Ring message at a given node and the transmission of the Ring message to the logical successor. In the OIL file from Listing 15.3, this is defined by the RING_DELAY attribute. This timer is discussed in more detail in the next section. The Normal and Limp Home configurations are initialized such that no nodes are identified in the Limp Home mode, and the only node Present on the network is the local node. In addition, the logical successor is also set to the local node ID.

Figure 15.7 Startup of direct NM.

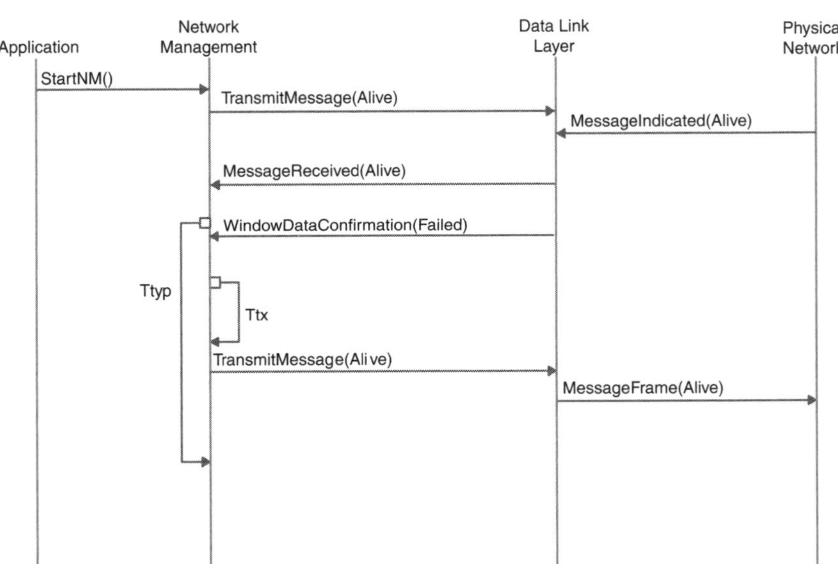

When an Alive message is received by an active node, the following steps are performed.

1. The sending node is added to the configuration of the network as being Present.
2. The local node determines whether the new node is the new logical successor on the ring. (Definition of logical successors is discussed in more detail in the next section.)

If the communication component indicates to the NM component through service D_WindowData.confirmation (WindowDataConfirmation(Failed) message in Figure 15.7) that the Alive message could not be transmitted, a second timer, TTx, starts and a counter increments. This timer is defined by the RETRANSMIT_TIMEOUT attribute in the OIL file. If the counter exceeds a certain threshold, then the NM component enters the Limp Home mode. This threshold is defined by the TX_LIMIT attribute; otherwise, when TTx expires, the Alive message is retransmitted by the NM component. This timer is used for the transmission of either Alive or Ring messages.

15.4.2 Ring Message

The main message that performs direct NM is called the Ring message. It is similar to a token ring, in which only one node controls the Ring message. The message is passed on after TTyp time has expired from the point that the Ring message was received. Because direct NM requirements dictate that messages be communicated on a broadcast bus, each node monitors the Ring messages to assist in building the configuration and identifying when a node has disappeared from the network. In this section, I describe the movement of Ring messages around the logical ring.

Network Startup When network management first starts and after the Alive message is transmitted, the network is considered to be in the dynamic state. During this state, the NM component monitors the bus for both Alive and Ring messages. A number of different scenarios can occur during this state.

1. If an Alive message is received, the configuration and successor are updated. This was discussed in the previous section.
2. If at any point before the `TTyp` timer expires a Ring message is received, then the timer is canceled and the Ring message is processed. Processing of Ring messages is discussed shortly.
3. When the `TTyp` timer expires, the local node transmits the Ring message.
4. If a Ring message is received between the time that the local node sends it to the data link layer and the time that the data link layer confirms back to the NM component that the message has been sent, it is ignored.

Figures 15.8 and 15.9 show the sequence of events during network startup for two scenarios: `TTyp` expires before a Ring message is received and a Ring message is received before `TTyp` expires.

Figure 15.8 Startup of direct NM with received Ring message.

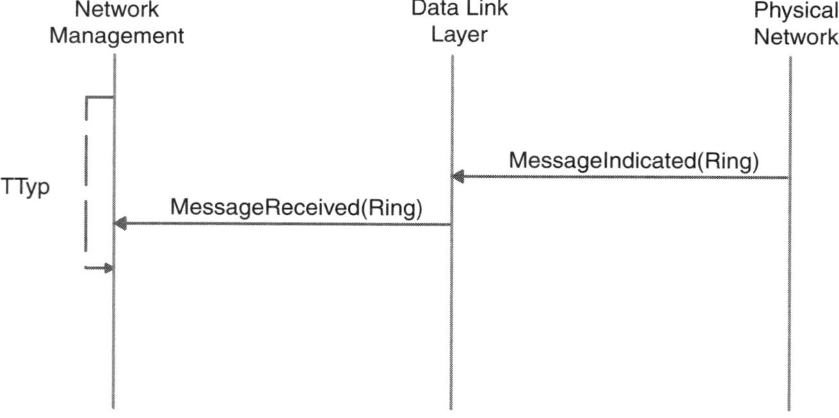

Figure 15.9 Startup of direct NM with Ring message.

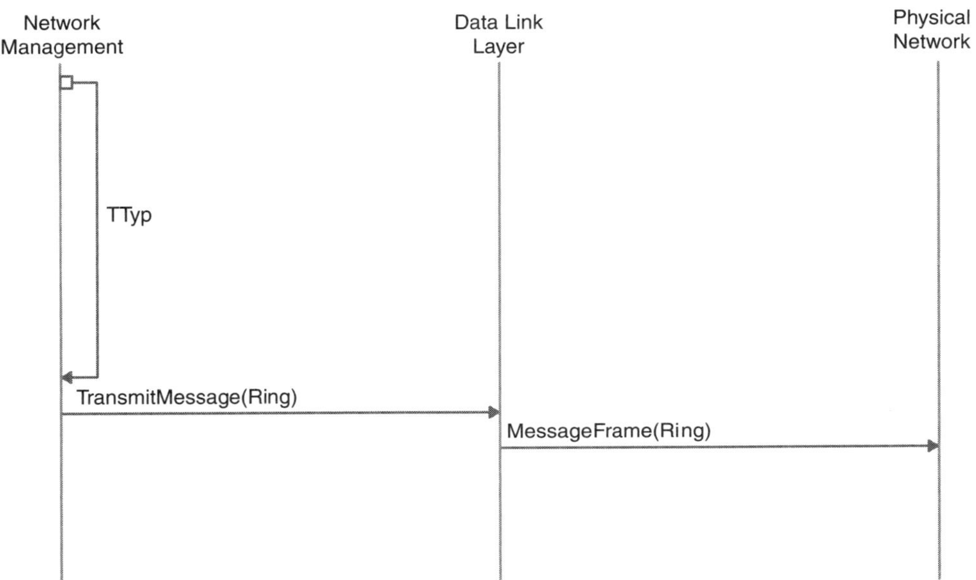

During the time that the network is in the dynamic state, multiple Ring messages can be traveling at the same time. However, based on the actions that are taken when a Ring message is received, these multiple Ring messages disappear rapidly.

Processing Ring Messages When a Ring message is received, the local node checks the destination ID of the NMPDU. The following actions are taken based on the value of this field.

1. If the Ring message is not destined for the local node, the `TTyp` timer is canceled, then the `TMax` timer is started if it is not running or restarted if it is running. `TMax` is defined by the `RX_TIMEOUT` attribute. The NM component checks the nodes in the source and destination identifiers and updates the network configuration based on these identifiers.
2. If the Ring message is destined for the local node, the `TMax` timer is canceled, then the `TTyp` timer is started if it is not running or restarted if it is running. If the source ID is indicated as Absent in the configuration management information, the state of the source node is changed to Present.
3. If the NM component has sent the ring NMPDU to the data link layer and is awaiting confirmation, the Ring message that was received is ignored.

The sequence of events in Figure 15.10 clearly shows how multiple Ring messages that exist at startup could disappear quickly. If a Ring message is received by a node while it is waiting to transmit a Ring message, the pending Ring message is canceled, thereby eliminating one of the extra messages. This occurs whether or not the new Ring message is destined for the local node. If a Ring message is received during the time frame between sending the NMPDU to the data link layer and the confirmation of the transmission, the new Ring message is discarded, thereby eliminating the extra message.

Figure 15.10 Processing Ring messages.

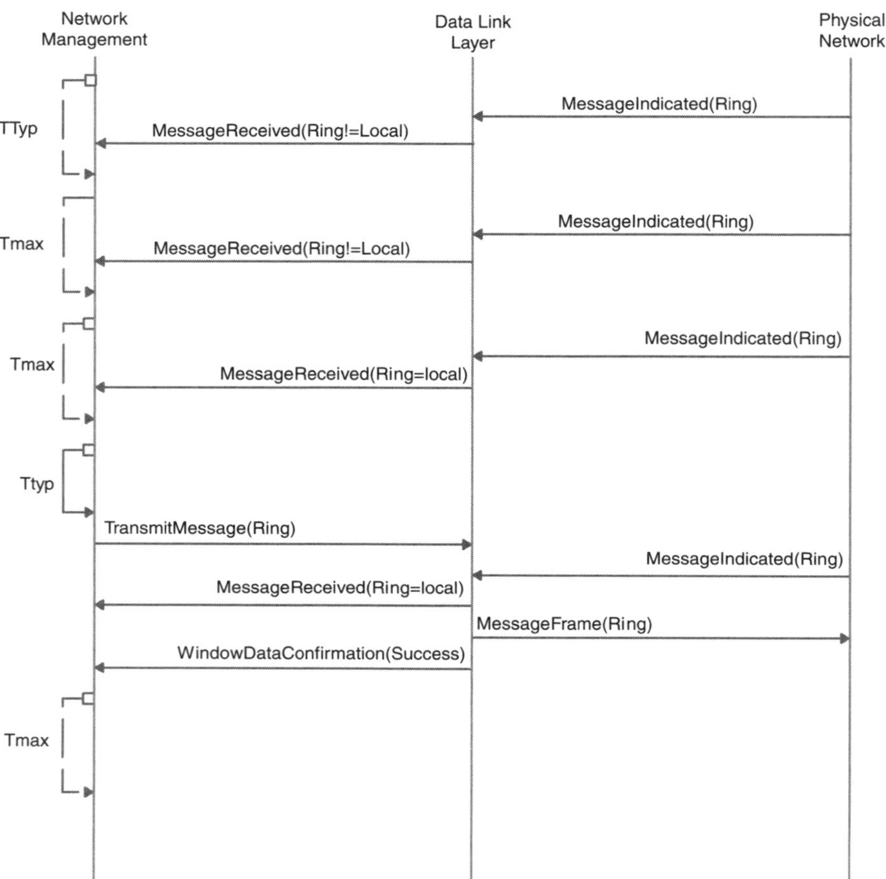

When superfluous Ring messages are canceled and one Ring message completely circles the logical ring without an Alive message transmission, the state of the network transitions from dynamic to stable. It is only during the stable state that optional data can be added to a network message. During the dynamic state of the network, data in these fields is ignored.

When a Ring message is received and the network is in the stable state, the NM component can notify the application that a Ring message has been received. The optional configuration item that defines the task or event to be triggered is `InitIndRingData`. If this functionality is implemented, the NM component would be able to activate a task or set an event in the same manner as notification of status and configuration management changes. The `StationManagement` task in the example application would have two additional API services to manipulate this data. These functions would be called only if the status indicates that the ring data could be updated.

```
StatusType ReadRingData(NetIdType net, RingDataType data);

StatusType TransmitRingData(NetIdType net, RingDataType data);
```

When ReadRingData() is invoked, it obtains the data received from the last Ring message or written by the last TransmitRingData(), depending on which occurred last. This data is then written to the variable referenced by the data parameter. TransmitRingData() places data into the Ring message prior to transmission on the network. These API services can be invoked only while the local node has control of the Ring message, which corresponds to the time that the TTyp timer is running. These services return a status of E_OK if no error occurs and a status of E_NotOK if the local node does not have control of the Ring message when the service is invoked or if the logical ring is not running in the stable state.

Because the time between Ring messages is typically much longer than most of the periodic messages on the network, the Ring message should not be used for critical data that is required for the operation of other nodes. The following are examples of data that can be transmitted safely in a Ring message.

1. Key operating parameters that are also transmitted with a normal periodic message for comparison and diagnostic purposes. Inconsistent data could indicate a malfunctioning node.
2. A time base and message counter for the transmitting node.
3. The present operating state of the node. You could use this information for diagnostic purposes and eliminate it in production.

Detection of an Absent Node The NM component detects when a node is no longer participating in the logical ring if the TMax timer expires. When this occurs, the following steps are taken.

1. The NM component enters the NMReset state.
2. A receive counter is incremented. If this counter exceeds the threshold, Limp Home mode is entered.
3. An Alive message is transmitted.
4. The state of the network is set to dynamic.
5. The configuration management is reset such that the local node is the only node on the network and the logical successor is set to local node.
6. The TTyp timer is started.
7. The NM component moves back into the NMNormal state.

Operation continues from this point in the same manner as it did during the startup of network management.

Skipped Nodes As Ring messages are transmitted around the logical ring, each node checks to ensure that it has not been skipped. Because a Ring message is transmitted from the logically lower to the next logically higher ID number, wrapping around from the highest to the lowest number, it is very easy for a node to determine whether a Ring message was addressed properly or not. If a node is skipped, it immediately sends an Alive message to notify everyone that it is still on the network. Figure 15.11 shows an example of how a node can be skipped.

Figure 15.11 Skipped node.

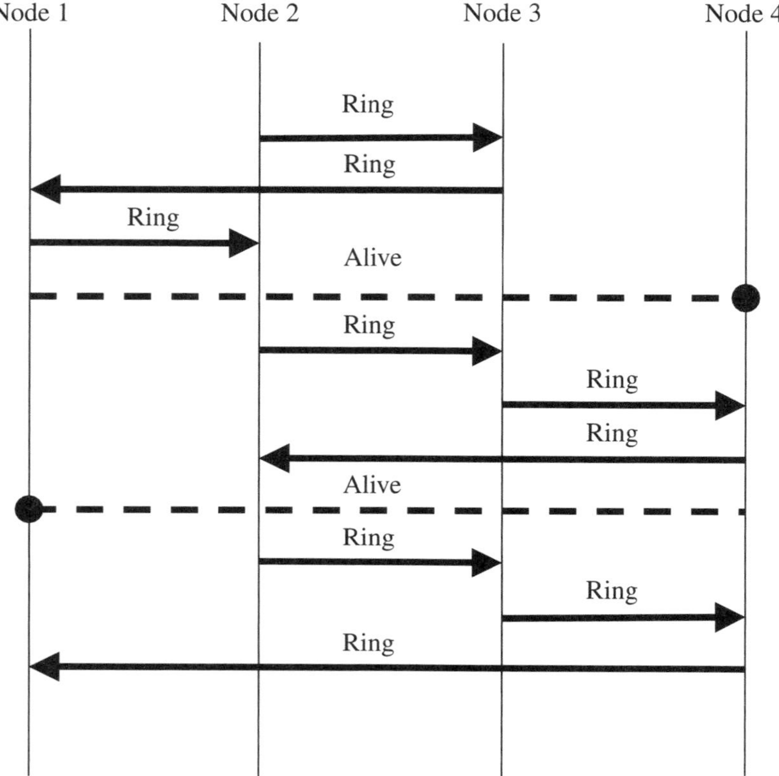

In this scenario, nodes 1, 2, and 3 are actively transmitting Ring messages around the stable network. Immediately after the Ring message is transmitted to node 2, node 4 comes alive and sends out its Alive message. It then monitors the Ring messages, identifies those from 2 and 3, and updates its configuration. When node 4 receives the Ring message from node 3, it only knows about the existence of nodes 2, 3, and itself, so it transmits the Ring message to node 2. Node 1 detects that it has been skipped and sends the "I'm here" Alive message.

15.4.3 Limp Home Mode

Under certain conditions, the NM component might indicate that messages are no longer being transmitted or received on the network. When this occurs, it enters the Limp Home mode. Entry into Limp Home mode can occur under conditions that I discussed before and summarize here.

1. The data link layer indicates that the transmission of the previously requested NMPDU was not successful. When this has occurred a preset number of times, the NM component enters Limp Home mode.

2. The NM component fails to receive a valid Ring message within the TMax time period. When this has occurred a preset number of times, the NM component enters Limp Home mode.

When the node is in the Limp Home mode, it periodically transmits a Limp Home message, just in case someone on the external network can still hear it. The time period between Limp Home messages is defined by TError time, which is defined by the LIMPHOME_TIMEOUT OIL attribute. The Limp Home mode continues until the NM component is stopped, the bus goes to sleep, or a valid message is received from the network. At this point, the node enters the NMReset state and performs the initialization functions already defined in this chapter.

When a node receives a Limp Home message from another node, it updates the Limp Home configuration to identify the malfunctioning node. The Normal configuration is also updated to indicate that that node is Absent (i.e., it is not participating in the logical ring).

15.5 Sleep

The final item I discuss in direct NM is the ability to put the bus to sleep. Two types of nodes can exist on the network, particularly in an automobile. The first type is a switched node, in which power to the node is switched on and off directly. When switched off, the node stops participating in the logical ring, and a timeout error occurs. The other type is a constantly powered node (e.g., powered by a battery), which must decide when to turn off in order to preserve battery power. The OSEK/VDX NM specification provides a negotiation method to ensure that all nodes attached to the network go to sleep at the same time. The application initiates the transition into NMBusSleep using GotoMode(), which is an optional service having the following function prototype.

```
StatusType GotoMode(NetIdType net, NMModeName mode);
```

When GotoMode() is invoked, it indicates to the network identified by the net parameter that it wants to transition into the mode defined by the mode parameter. The mode parameter can be either BusSleep, to transition to the NMBusSleep state, or Awake, to transition to the NMAwake state.

Negotiation of the transition into the sleep mode is accomplished using the sleep.ind and sleep.ack opcodes as follows.

1. The application calls GotoMode(BusSleep) requesting that the bus go to sleep. The next time the node receives the Ring message, the NM component sets the opcode to the Ring message with the sleep.ind option set to TRUE.
2. If the node is operating in the Limp Home mode, the next Limp Home message sent has the sleep indication field set to TRUE. This message is sent after TMax, instead of TError, has elapsed.
3. While sleep negotiation is ongoing and if it is necessary to send an Alive message, then the Alive message is transmitted with the sleep indication field set to TRUE.
4. When the Ring message has completely traveled around the logical ring with the sleep indication field of all received network management messages set to TRUE, the first node to pass the Ring message sets sleep.ack to TRUE.
5. All nodes that receive a Ring message with the sleep acknowledge field set to TRUE stop transmitting Ring messages, start the TWaitBusSleep timer, and enter the NMTwbsNormal

state. The timer is defined in the OIL file with the `BUSSLEEP_TIMEOUT` attribute. Because it is a change in status, the NM component notifies the application that bus sleep is about to occur so the application can enter a state in which messages are no longer sent.

6. When the `TWaitBusSleep` timer expires, the NM component stops all transmissions on the bus and transitions into the `NMBusSleep` state. It is a change of status, so the application is notified through the indication mechanism.

Figure 15.12 shows a typical sequence of Ring messages around the network during sleep negotiation. The time delay from the point where the sleep acknowledge Ring message is received and bus sleep occurs allows all nodes to complete transmission of messages that are presently in the queue.

Figure 15.12 Sleep negotiation scenario.

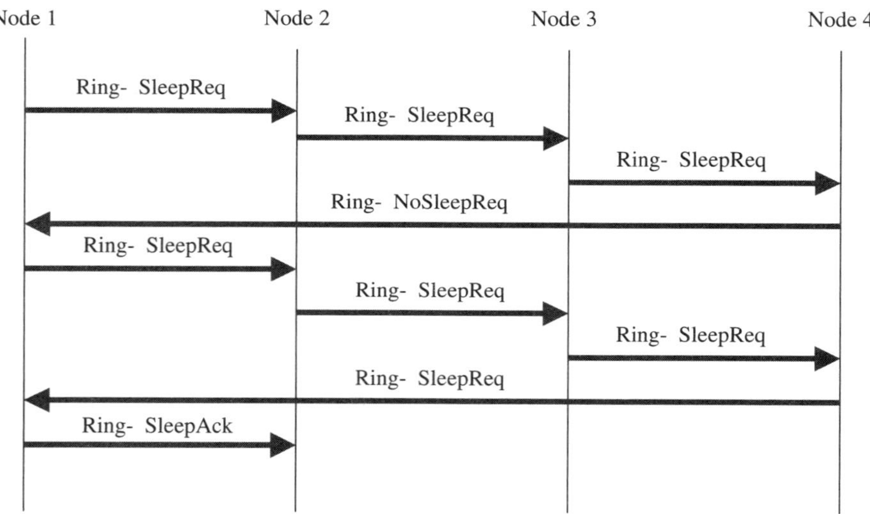

While the node is in the `NMTwbsNormal` state, it continues to monitor messages on the network. If any network management message (Alive, Ring, or Limp Home) is received with the sleep indication bit set to `FALSE`, the node restarts by entering the `NMReset` state. This also occurs if the application invokes `GotoMode(Awake)`. After the node transitions into the `NMBusSleep` state, it remains asleep until one of the following occurs.

1. The application invokes `GotoMode(Awake)`.
2. The data link layer of the COM component notifies the NM component that the bus has awoken. This uses the `D_Status.ind` service defined in the COM specification. How a bus is awoken is a function of the network.
3. The data link layer notifies the NM component that a network management message has been received.

15.6 Example Program

After this chapter, you would think that I would have made extensive changes to the example program to support direct NM. In reality, there are very few changes to the application. Previously, the application was notified that an opponent in the `HEAD_TO_HEAD` mode disappeared whenever a periodic message disappeared. When network management is added, the NM component performs this function, and it is transparent to the application.

The major change to the example program was the addition of the `StationManagement` task, which creates the interface between the application and the NM component. It is responsible for controlling the function of the application based on the status and configuration of the network.

15.6.1 Modules

`nm.c` This is a new module that contains the `StationManagement` task.

`init.c` The `InitOS` and `CloseOS` tasks were modified to start and stop network management.

`cardgame.c` The `LostOpponent` task was removed because it is now performed by the `StationManagement` task.

15.6.2 Configuration Files

`init.cfg` `StationManagementAlarm` was added. This alarm starts automatically and triggers the `StationManagement` task to check for status and configuration changes.

15.7 Exercises

1. When a node is added to the network, detect the configuration change and display a prompt that allows the player to immediately change to `HEAD_TO_HEAD` mode.
2. After five minutes has expired, put the bus to sleep.

15.8 Summary

Direct NM does very little in an application, but it is very complex to understand. I attempted to explain how direct NM functions from the viewpoint of messages transmitted across the bus. The NM specification, which is included on the accompanying CD, includes extensive state transition diagrams and flow charts that describe in gory detail how network management works under the covers. One warning: many of the state transition diagrams are inconsistent in their format and terminology. Hopefully, after reading this chapter these inconsistencies will become apparent.

Throughout this chapter, I have discussed a number of timers. Table 15.4 summarizes these timers and provides typical values for each. In addition, I have shown the scope of each timer — either global for all nodes or local to a specific node. When a timer is global to all nodes, it must be the same on all of the nodes. Local timers can differ from node to node.

Table 15.4 Summary of timers.

Timer	Description	Typical Value (ms)	Scope
TTyp	Typical time from receipt of a Ring message to retransmission of the message.	100	Global
TTx	Time to wait before retransmitting a Ring message.	25	Local
TMax	Maximum time to wait after a Ring message is transmitted before determining that the destination node is missing.	250	Global
TError	Time between transmissions of Limp Home message.	1000	Local
TWaitBusSleep	Time after bus sleep has been acknowledged before entering NMBusSleep	1500	Global

Direct NM provides a critical service to an application that is operating in a distributed environment. It is imperative for the application to know as soon as possible if information that it requires is no longer available from an external node. Direct NM performs this function with minimal overhead to the application and a high level of portability across multiple functions and applications.

16

Chapter 16

Indirect Network Management

Indirect network management is much simpler to implement but is less robust than direct NM. It is implemented by passively monitoring network messages that are sent periodically by the individual nodes on the network. If a periodic message is not received within a certain time frame, the node is considered Absent. Because some periodic messages can transmit at a very low rate, such as once per second, indirect NM might not be able to identify when a node is no longer available within the required period of time.

In this chapter, I discuss the concept of indirect NM and identify the differences between direct and indirect NM. I assume you have read the chapter on direct NM. Indirect NM is not supported in the current release of OSEKWorks; therefore, an example program using this form of network management was not developed. However, the API services between the two forms of network management are almost identical, and the effect on the application would be minimal. I will describe any differences that occur in the API services.

16.1 Indirect NM Concept

To a network, the difference between direct and indirect NM is logical instead of physical. Figure 15.1 is repeated here as Figure 16.1 with some modifications, illustrating two physical networks.

Figure 16.1 Example system illustrating direct and indirect network management.

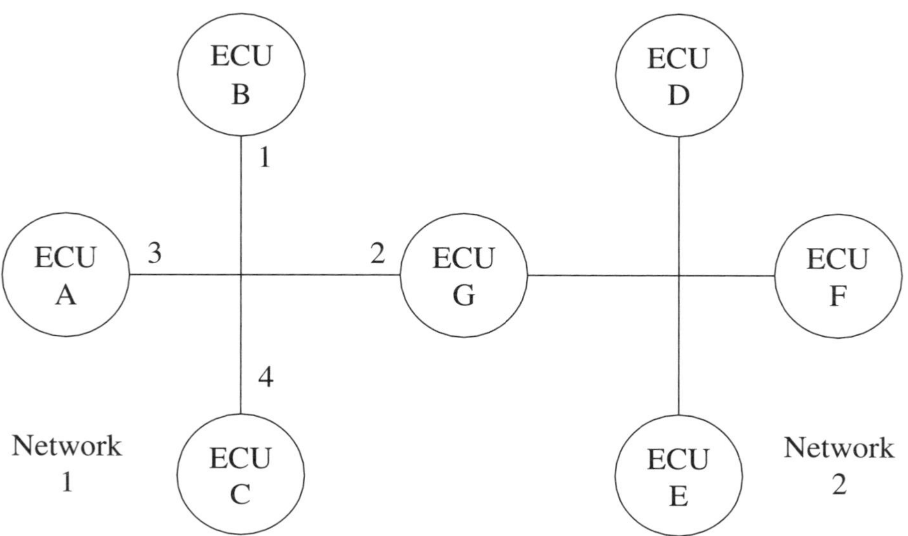

Network 1 continues to operate under the direct NM protocol, but network 2 will now operate under the indirect NM protocol. The node identification numbers in network 2 have been removed in this figure. Indirect NM has no concept of a node address or identifier. Although all nodes on a given network must use the same form of network management, an individual ECU can use different forms for the different nodes. This is illustrated in gateway unit ECU G.

Under indirect NM, the system can operate in one of two states: `NMOff` or `NMOn` (Figure 16.2).

In this state chart, the `NMShutdown` state that existed under direct NM no longer exists. It is no longer required because indirect NM passively monitors the network and nothing needs to be shut down. `StartNM()` and `StopNM()` are invoked in exactly the same manner as under direct NM; consequently, the example program does not have to change to handle these services. `StopNM()` performs a slightly different function under indirect NM by transitioning the system directly from `NMOn` to `NMOff`.

The OSEK/VDX network management specification recommends that an indirect NM implementation be scalable to address different requirements of different applications. This would indicate that an implementation might have multiple configurations, similar to the Full Master, Master, and Slave configurations discussed under direct NM.

Figure 16.2 Indirect NM state chart.

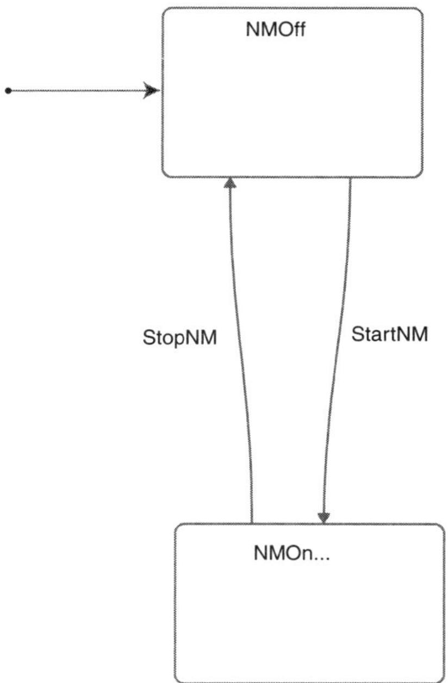

16.1.1 NMOn State

The NMOn state consists of two states (Figure 16.3): NMBusSleep and NMAwake. The NMInit state that existed under direct NM is not required for indirect NM because of the passive nature of network monitoring. In addition, the parallel state chart that included the NMActive and NMPassive states does not exist. As a result, TalkNM() and SilentNM() are not available under indirect NM. The conditions under which NMAwake transitions to NMBusSleep are discussed in Section 16.7, "Sleep." The communication bus wakes up when either the application calls GoToMode() with the argument Awake or a wake-up signal that is specific to the network protocol is received from the bus.

Figure 16.3 NMOn state chart under indirect NM.

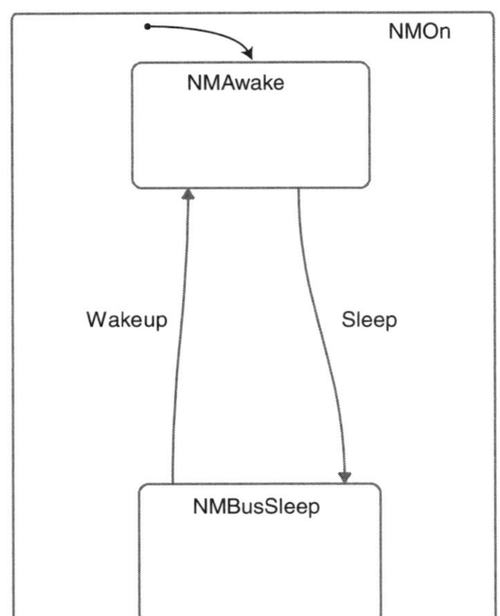

16.1.2 NMAwake State

The default substate within the NMOn state is NMAwake (Figure 16.4). When the NMAwake state is first entered, it immediately enters the NMNormal state (discussed in Section 16.1.3, "NMNormal State"). The NMReset direct NM state does not exist under indirect NM. The NMLimpHome state, which has the same name as the similar state from direct NM, works quite differently. Under indirect NM, this state is only entered when the data link layer identifies that a fatal bus error has occurred. While in this state, the NM component continues to monitor the bus, and as soon as message transmission or reception is once again possible, it reenters the NMNormal state. NMWaitBusSleep is a transient state that exists between the call to GoToMode() and the point where the system enters the NMBusSleep state. It is discussed in Section 16.7, "Sleep."

Figure 16.4 `NMAwake` **state chart under indirect NM.**

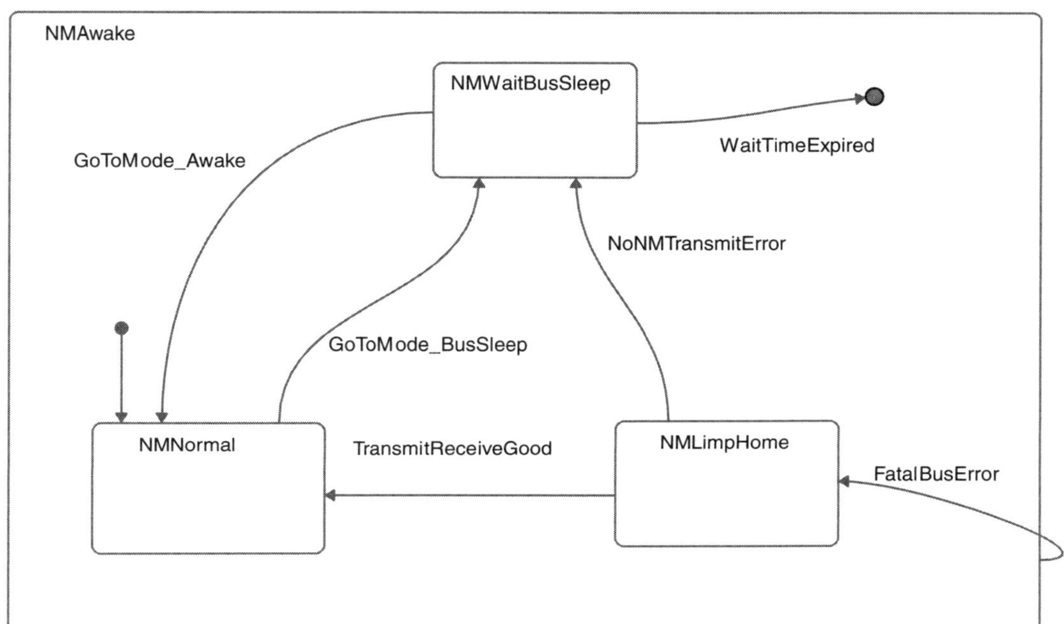

16.1.3 `NMNormal` State

Indirect NM functions mostly in the `NMNormal` state. However, the actions that occur when the system is in this state are entirely different from the actions that occur under direct NM. The algorithm that determines the current status and configuration of the network is discussed in Section 16.3, "Message Monitoring." The system generation support items defined under direct NM are also supported under indirect NM, with the exception of `InitDirectNMParams`, which is replaced by `InitIndirectNMParams`, and `InitIndRingConfig`, which is not supported. `InitIndirectNMParams` initializes the indirect NM timer values, which are described in the following section. The `InitCMaskTable` configuration item configures Normal and Normal Extended masks. Limp Home masks are not supported under indirect NM.

The status of the network is obtained using the same API service, `GetStatus()`, that was used for direct NM. However, status encoding is different under indirect NM. The suggested standard status encoding is shown in Table 16.1, and extended status encoding is shown in Table 16.2.

Table 16.1 Indirect NM standard status bit encoding.

Bit	Description	Interpretation of a 0	Interpretation of a 1
0	Operating mode of network physical interface	`No Error`	Error, bus blocked
1	NM mode on/off	`NMOn`	`NMOff`
2	Limp Home mode	Not in `NMLimpHome`	`NMLimpHome`
3	Bus sleep mode	Not in `NMBusSleep`	`NMBusSleep`
4	Waiting for bus sleep	Not waiting for `Twbs` to expire	Waiting for `Twbs` to expire

Table 16.2 Indirect NM extended status bit encoding.

Description	Definition
Operating mode of the network interface	Expands the standard status bit to two bits, which are interpreted as follows: 00 — No error 01 — Error but communication is possible 10 — Error and communication is not possible 11 — Reserved

The bit positions are my additions and are not defined in the specification. The selected bit positions can be the same or different bit positions as in direct NM. `SelectDeltaStatus()` and `CmpStatus()` are also supported under indirect NM and function in the same manner as they do under direct NM. However, because the masks can be different between the two implementations, code written for a direct NM implementation will probably have to be modified to function under indirect NM.

16.2 Configuration Management

Under indirect NM, the network has two different levels of configuration: Normal and Normal Extended. The Normal configuration is interpreted in a similar manner to direct NM. If the network management message from a given node is no longer received, it is considered to be Absent from the network. Once the message is received again, the node is considered to be Present on the network. The Normal Extended configuration works differently. For each node on the network, a counter is incremented every time the message is not received within its deadline and is decremented every time the message is received. When the counter reaches a threshold, the node is considered Absent statically, and when the counter is below the threshold, the node is considered Present statically. This algorithm is defined in more detail in Section 16.3, "Message Monitoring." Also within the configuration is information concerning the local node, which is considered Mute if it determines that nobody can hear its messages and is considered Not Mute when it determines that the messages can be heard again. How it determines that the messages are heard on the network is dependent on the physical network protocol. The Normal Extended configuration works in a similar manner for the local node and determines whether the node is Mute statically or Not Mute statically.

The API services that support configuration management — `GetConfig()`, `CmpConfig()`, `SelectDeltaConfig()`, and `InitConfig()` — function identically under indirect NM. However, the `kind` parameter used in `GetConfig()` and `SelectDeltaConfig()` has the possible values of Normal and Normal Extended. Limp Home is no longer valid.

16.3 Message Monitoring

As mentioned in the introduction, indirect NM passively monitors periodic messages. To accomplish this, each node must send a periodic message, which could require creating a state-of-health message from a given node in order for the system to recognize that the node is still active.

Two methods are defined to monitor periodic messages: one timeout for all messages and one timeout per message. The individual timeout per message leverages the capability of the OSEK/VDX COM component to monitor periodically received messages. The following sections describe system configuration, startup, and operation in more detail.

16.3.1 Configuration

System configuration requires additional objects in the OIL configuration file. The current version of the OSEK/VDX OIL specification does not define the objects for network management. First, the periodic messages have to be defined for the COM component. Next, the network management objects need to be defined. The following classes of objects are typical of objects that need to be defined for network management. Because the current OIL specification does not define naming standards for network management objects, refer to the implementation-specific documentation to determine those names.

Monitored node is monitored on the network and has to be linked to a monitored message. If node monitoring is performed with one timeout per message, the timeout period must be included. In addition, the increment and decrement counter values for extended network configuration are set for each node. From the set of monitored nodes, the default configuration of the network can be developed.

Timeout for observation is the time of one global timeout, also known as TOB. It is part of the `InitIndirectNMParams` configuration item.

Time for error recovery is the time after entering the `NMLimpHome` state before network management attempts to restart communications. It also is part of the `InitIndirectNMParams` configuration item.

Wait for sleep timeout is the time to wait before going to sleep and is included in `InitIndirectNMParams`.

Extended configuration threshold is the extended network configuration counter value that determines whether a node is either statically Absent or Mute. Only one threshold value is recommended for the entire network.

16.4 Network Startup

When the system starts using StartNM(), the node immediately assumes that all nodes defined in the configuration file are available under indirect NM. The NM component then begins to monitor periodic messages. No specific network management messages are sent on startup. Unlike direct NM, the system does not identify a static and dynamic state.

16.4.1 Single Timeout Network Monitoring

If a single timeout is used, the operation is as shown in Figure 16.5, which shows a simple system with two nodes available. When the system starts, a local copy of the configuration is created with all nodes Absent and the local node Mute. As monitored messages are received, the local configuration is updated to show the node as Present. When the local node successfully sends its own monitored message, the local configuration is updated to show the local node as Not Mute. In the top half of the diagram, the periodic messages are received from both nodes prior to expiration of the timer. In addition, the local node successfully transmits its own message. When the timer expires, the Normal configuration is updated with the values in the local configuration, showing that all nodes are Present or Not Mute.

In the bottom half of the diagram, one periodic message is not received and the local node is not able to transmit it own message. Consequently, when the timer expires, the Normal configuration of the network is updated with the local configuration, which includes the Present and Absent nodes and the local node as Mute. I discuss how the Normal extended configuration is updated later in this chapter. The normal configuration is the configuration returned from the API service GetConfig().

16.4.2 Individual Timeouts Network Monitoring

If each monitored network message has its own timeout, then the system operates as shown in Figure 16.6 and uses the periodic reception capabilities of the COM component to monitor the message timeouts. When the COM component determines that a periodic message has not been received, it uses the I_MsgTimeout.ind service defined in the specification (MessageTimeout in Figure 16.6) to signal the NM component that a message was missed. This service is provided by the NM component for use by the COM component. When a message is missed, the NM component updates the configuration to indicate that the node is Absent. A similar service exists to indicate that a message transmitted by the local node was not transmitted over the network successfully. I do not discuss in detail how the COM component identifies that a message is missing because I discussed this in Chapter 12.

Figure 16.5 Single timeout monitoring of periodic messages.

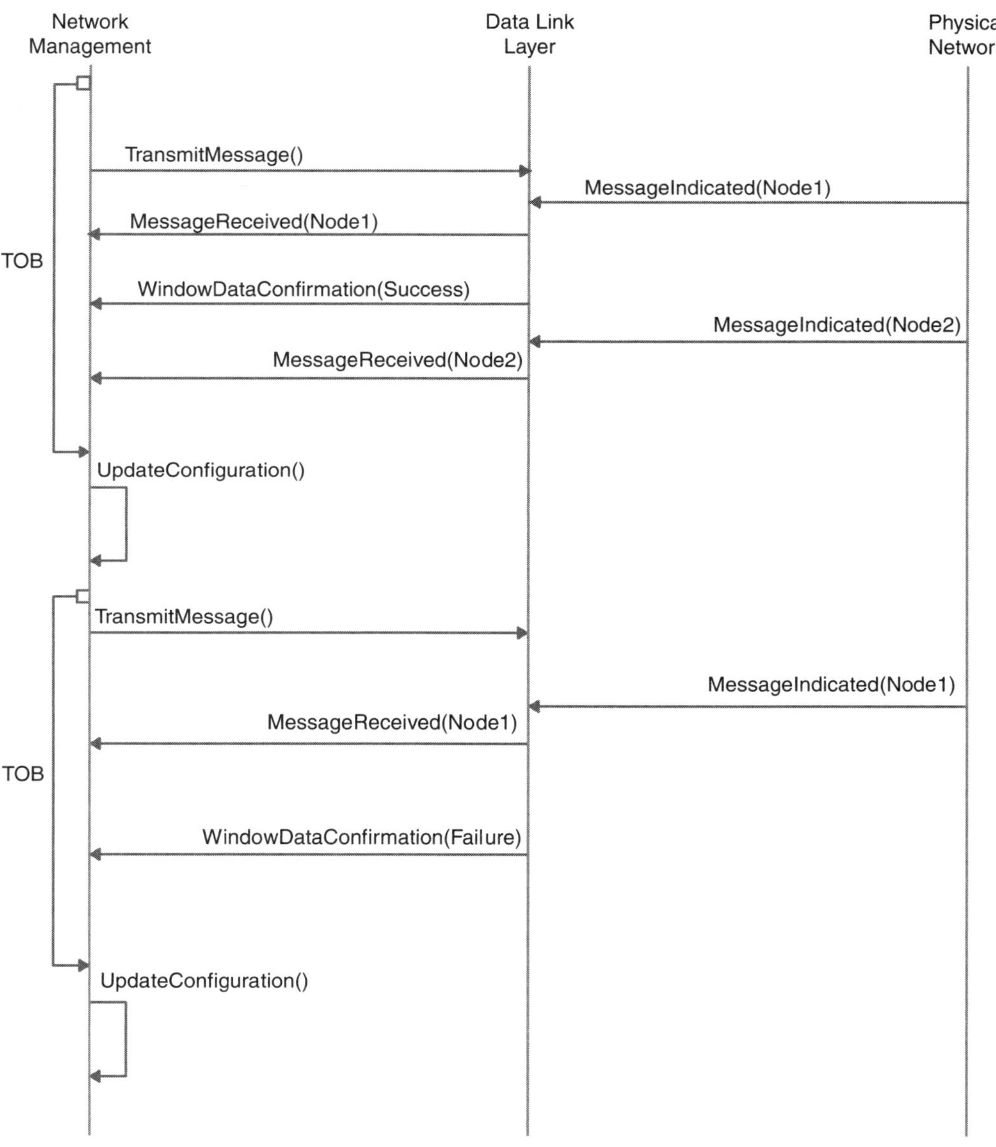

Figure 16.6 Individual timeout monitoring of periodic messages.

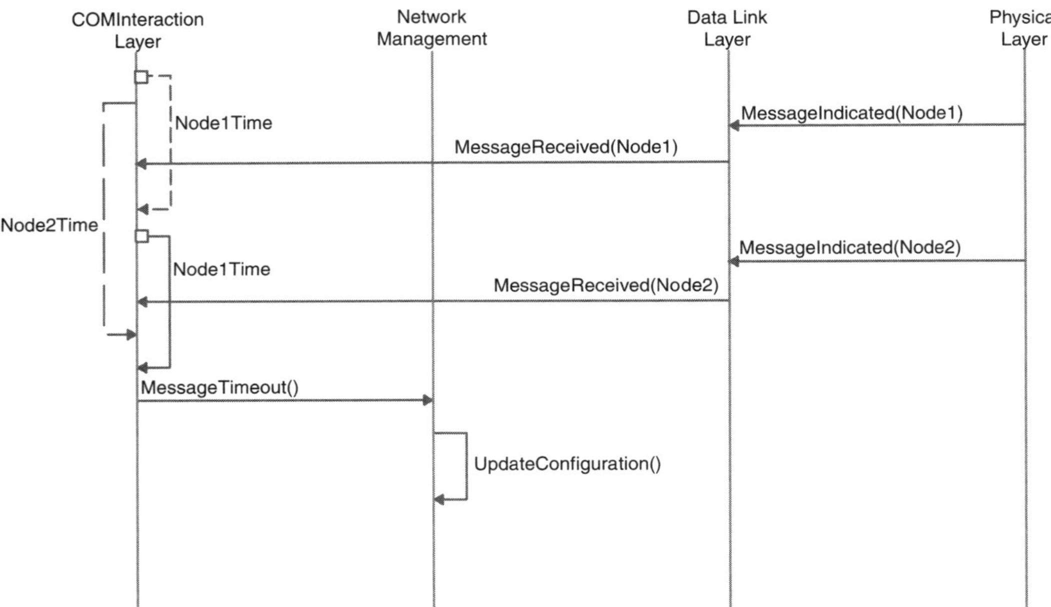

The decision to use a single timeout or individual timeouts usually depends on the period of the messages that are to be monitored. If all messages are approximately the same period (i.e., every 80–120 ms), then one timeout is probably best. However, if the periodic messages vary extensively (i.e., 80–1,000 ms) and responding to missed messages is critical, then individual timeouts are necessary. Individual timeouts have the added overhead of one additional timer per message.

16.5 Extended Configuration

Indirect NM provides an additional network configuration: Normal Extended. In this configuration, nodes are defined statically as Present or Absent or Mute or Not Mute. The extended configuration is determined by assigning a counter to each monitored node. Whenever the NM component determines that a node is Absent or Mute, the counter related to that node is incremented by the amount defined in the OIL configuration file for that node. Whether the node is Absent or Mute is determined using one of the two previously defined methods of network monitoring. When the counter reaches the value of the threshold defined globally in the configuration file, the particular node is defined statically as Absent or Mute. Whenever the node is identified as Present or Not Mute, the individual counter is decremented by the amount defined for that node in the OIL configuration file. The counter is bounded between zero and the threshold value; an example of the counter value over time is shown in Figure 16.7 for an external node. The counter for the self node is identical, except the counter is updated based on Mute and Not Mute status.

Figure 16.7 Extended configuration counter example.

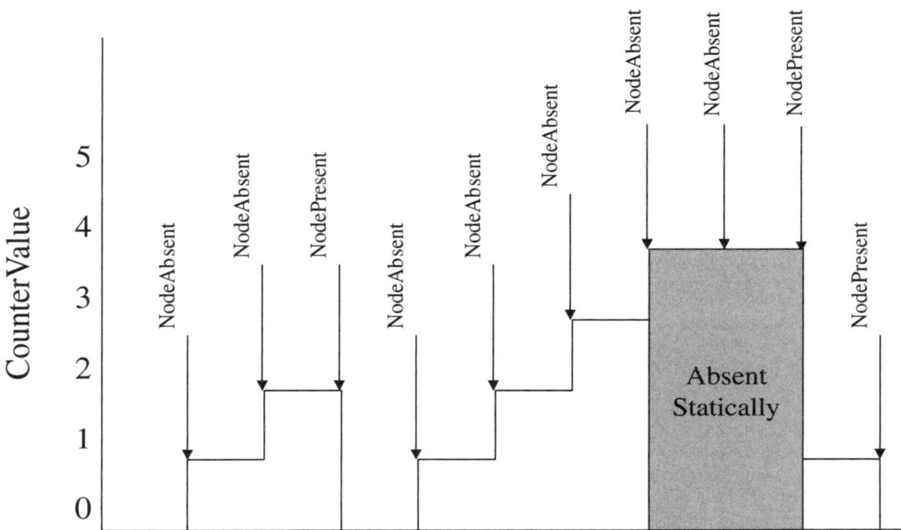

In Figure 16.7, extensive noise in the system causes the periodic message to be missed randomly. Whenever the timers expire and the periodic message is missing, the counter is incremented by one. Whenever the message is received, the counter is decremented by three. The threshold value is four. Extended configuration management allows some level of noise tolerance in the system, whereas the Normal configuration management does not tolerate any noise.

16.6 Limp Home

Indirect NM defines a Limp Home state, which is entered whenever the system identifies that a fatal bus error has occurred, either because a physical error has occurred or because of the inability to detect a successful transmission. In a CAN network, a Bus Off condition or the lack of receipt of an acknowledge frame could incur a failure. The only function performed by the NM component when it is in the Limp Home mode is network monitoring. When messages can again be transmitted and received, the NM component immediately returns to the `NMNormal` state.

16.7 Sleep

`GoToMode()` with the `BusSleep` argument initiates the transition into the `NMBusSleep` state under indirect NM. When this occurs, the `TWaitBusSleep` timer is started and the `NMWaitBusSleep` state is entered. When this timer expires, the `NMBusSleep` state is entered immediately. Unlike direct NM, negotiation of transition into the Sleep state does not occur.

The OSEK/VDX NM specification describes a methodology called Master–Slave that allows sleep negotiation. It is implemented by defining one node on the network as the Master node; it reserves one bit as the sleep bit in a normal application message. All remaining nodes on the network are Slave nodes and monitor the sleep bit. When the Master has determined that it is time for the bus to go to sleep, it sets this bit. Each Slave node then executes `GoToMode()` to put its bus to sleep. This methodology is not supported by an indirect NM component, so you will have to develop it for each application.

16.8 Example Program

As I mentioned at the beginning of this chapter, I have not modified the example program to function under indirect NM because it is not supported by OSEKWorks. However, most of its features can be included manually in an application. The following exercises allow an application to determine the network configuration using the indirect NM methodology.

16.9 Exercises

1. Create an indirect NM module that uses the capabilities of the COM and OS components to monitor periodic messages from multiple nodes and to construct a network configuration. This module can use either one timeout per node or one global timeout to perform the monitoring. Determine both Normal and Normal Extended configuration.
2. Implement a Master–Slave sleep module that provides the `GoToMode()` service and monitors the network sleep message. For simplicity, create a new message that is used exclusively to trigger bus sleep. Because the application is not capable of controlling the COM data link layer, it will not be possible to shut down the network, but the new module should stop all periodic messages when it is time to put the bus to sleep.

16.10 Summary

Indirect NM is the last topic in the OSEK/VDX set of standards to be covered in this book. This form of network management is much simpler to implement than direct NM, but it is also less robust. For systems that do not require the rapid response of direct NM or that have limited resources, this form of network management is an ideal alternative.

The OSEK/VDX standards are constantly evolving. Shortly, the OSEK/VDX implementation language (OIL) will be updated to include standard objects and attributes that define COM messages. A set of OSEK/VDX standards for time-critical applications, referred to as OSEKTime, also is in the process of being developed. Finally, an OSEK run-time interface (ORTI) is being developed that will assist application development by providing a standard interface to development tools. As I complete this book, the first version of ORTI has been released for comments. To keep up-to-date on the standards, visit the OSEK/VDX organization's Web site at http://www.osek-vdx.org. The OSEK/VDX steering committee has submitted a set of standards (ISO-17356) to the International Standards Organization (ISO), making it a candidate for standardization.

A

Appendix A

Choosing an Implementation

This appendix provides information that could be helpful when searching for an OSEK/VDX implementation. It is arranged as a series of questions that should be answered by the vendor prior to evaluating the implementation. A discussion is also included to describe more about the question, why it should be asked, and what else might be required.

A.1 Certification

Is the implementation certified OSEK/VDX compliant?

Although OSEK/VDX is an open standard, the name is still a trademark and can only be used with the approval of the OSEK/VDX Steering Committee. The process is simple, and no licensing fees are required. However, there is a cost to have the test suite analyzed by an outside company. See the licensing process on the Web site at http://www.osek-vdx.org if you want to license the trademark name. This site also lists the names of the products that are currently certified to be compliant and are authorized to use the trademark. When looking for an OSEK/VDX implementation, check for certification both with the vendor and with the site. In many cases, the vendor will be in the process of certification and will not yet appear on the site. Make sure that the certification has been completed before finalizing an agreement with the vendor.

A.2 Conformance

Which conformance classes or API services are supported?

As mentioned throughout this book, each of the three standards have different levels of conformance. The OS standard has BCC1, BCC2, ECC1, and ECC2, along with CCCA and possibly CCCB borrowed from the COM standard for intertask communication. The COM standard has CCCA, CCCB, CCC0, CCC1, and CCC2 conformance classes. Finally, the NM standard does not define conformance classes, but does define many optional API services. This makes it difficult to determine what level of conformance a particular NM implementation meets. Make sure that the NM implementation provides the necessary services. (Is the current configuration of the network available to the application? Can the Ring message data be read and modified? And so on.).

It is important to know the level of conformance because the OSEK/VDX standard does not require a particular implementation to support all conformance classes. Many smaller implementations support only the simpler conformance classes but are very compact and fast. If your application is growing or will be scaled across many products with different RTOS requirements, an implementation that supports more features would be required.

A.3 GUI Configuration

Is there a graphical configuration utility available for generating the `.oil` file?

If an implementation does not provide a GUI configuration utility, then the OIL configuration file will have to be edited manually. This is not a pretty job. I strongly recommend that you bypass any implementation that requires manual editing of the configuration file. At this time, I am not aware of any implementations like this.

A.4 Processor and Driver Support

Which processors are or will be supported?

Which device drivers are available?

This question is critical when considering the purchase of any RTOS, but it is not as critical for an OSEK/VDX system. However, because applications written for an OSEK/VDX environment are not 100% portable, the more processor support by the vendor, the better. The second question is more concerned with the COM specification, where drivers might be required for external communication chips.

A.5 Network Protocols

Which networking protocols are or will be supported by data link layers?

This is specific to the OSEK/VDX COM specification, where messages can be sent out over multiple networks from one application.

A.6 Development Environment

Is the implementation integrated with a complete development environment?

If a stand-alone implementation, which compilers and debuggers are supported?

There are many OSEK/VDX implementations on the market today. Some are part of a complete development environment, such as the Wind River OSEKWorks system, used in this book, whereas others, such as the systems from Vector Informatik and Realogy, are developed independently and work with different development environments. If your organization has an established compiler/debugger infrastructure, a stand-alone OSEK/VDX RTOS might be an option. However, check the other questions in this appendix first; sometimes the costs saved in sticking with a given compiler can be offset by the additional labor required to support a nonintegrated approach.

A.7 Benchmarks

What are the benchmarks of the implementation?

Benchmarks include the ROM and RAM size based on the options used, the context switch time, and the additional overhead in ROM and RAM per object the application uses.

A.8 Object Limitations

What is the maximum number of objects allowed by the implementation?

This includes the maximum number of tasks, alarms, resources, events, messages, and so on. Depending on how an implementation is realized, these limitations could affect the application.

A.9 Priority Limitations

How many task priorities are allowed?

How many tasks can be in a state other than SUSPENDED?

These values vary greatly from implementation to implementation. For example, the OSEK-Works implementation allows 256 distinct priorities, which should be more than enough for most small embedded applications, to which the OSEK/VDX standard is targeted. The OSEK/VDX OS specification requires that the minimum number of task priorities for an implementation is eight.

The number of tasks that are not in the SUSPENDED state at any one time will affect the amount of resources used. The specification requires that an implementation allow a minimum of eight nonsuspended tasks for basic conformance classes and 16 tasks for extended conformance classes.

A.10 Network Management

How is the NMPDU mapped into the network message?

How are the opcodes defined?

Can these values be modified?

Are the requirements of the system integrator met?

In Chapter 15, "Direct Network Management," the NMPDU-to-network data frame mapping is not specified in the standards, but a recommended implementation is discussed. It is critical for this type of network management to use a common mapping of the NMPDU into the network frames for all ECUs on the network. Some implementations might allow some crafting of the data frame or provide the ability to modify the code to create unique mappings. If you need to integrate into multiple systems, this flexibility might be necessary.

B

Appendix B

Example Program Build Structure

This appendix describes the format of the sample code and documentation on the accompanying CD. The directory tree is as shown in Figure B.1.

B.1 Directory Structure

The entire structure should be copied into a new directory on your hard disk, such as `c:\OSEKBook` or `/home/name/OSEKBook`. The `doc` subdirectory includes all of the OSEK/VDX specifications that were current as of the publishing date and are included here with permission. The latest versions can be obtained at http://www.osek-vdx.org. The files in this directory are

- `os21r1.pdf` The operating system (OS) specification.
- `com2-2-2.pdf` The communication (COM) specification,
- `osek_nm251.pdf` The network management (NM) specification, and
- `oil2-2.pdf` The OSEK/VDX implementation language specification.

Figure B.1 Directory structure of CD.

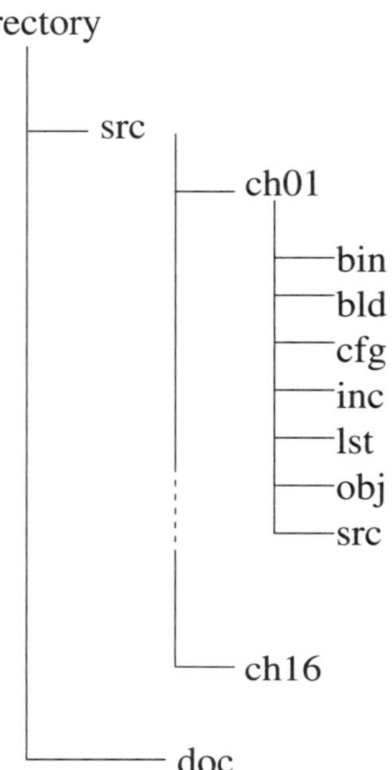

The src subdirectory contains all of the source code discussed in the book, including the source files, header files, configuration files, and all files required to rebuild the application. Because of licensing requirements, object files are not included; however, empty directories for the object files, listings files, and map files are included in the directory tree. Within the src subdirectory is a unique subdirectory for each chapter in the book. The layout of the chapter subdirectories follows.

`bin` This subdirectory is empty on the CD but will contain the binary outputs of the complete application, the map file, and the hexadecimal file encoded in Motorola S19 format.

`bld` This subdirectory contains the files required to build the application.

`Makefile` **and** `*.mk` These are the makefiles used to build the application and are written for GNU make. `Makefile` is the main makefile; the other files are included as necessary. All `make` references are relative to the start directory, which is required to be `chXX\bld`. The following dummy targets are available and can be passed using `make`.

- `clean` Cleans the directory structure.
- `build_ram` Builds the application with a RAM memory target for the application.
- `build_flash` Builds the application with a FLASH memory target for the application.

- `rebuild_ram` **and** `rebuild_flash` Performs a `clean` then a `build_ram` or `build_flash`.

The `NODE` variable must be defined as `NODE0` or `NODE1`. When Node 1 is being created, the `TARGET_NODE` variable is set to `1`. Depending on the values of the command line parameters, the proper `make` and link files are used to build the application.

To build the application for Node 0 in RAM, execute the following command from the `chXX\bld` directory.

```
make build_ram NODE="NODE0"
```

Some changes might be needed in these files based on your specific host configuration. Although I hate to do this, please refer to the files for a discussion of what needs to be changed. Documentation separate from the actual files should be provided, but because the changes are minimal and linked directly with the files, I am breaking my own rule in this case. Search on the characters `CHANGE_ME` for the comments on what needs to be changed.

`*.lk` These files are used by the program linker to place the files in the proper location in memory. The `program.lk` file maps the program into RAM on the Axiom board, and the file `progflsh.lk` maps the program into the FLASH memory.

B.2 Porting to Different Implementations

As mentioned in the introduction, this example was developed using the WindRiver OSEK-Works implementation with the Diab development environment and was run on an Axiom manufacturing MPC555 board. If a different implementation or a different target is used, you will have to modify these files. Please check my web site (http://www.osekbook.com) first for ports to different implementations. If you port the example program to a different implementation, please forward the files that you change in each directory to me at author@osekbook.com so that I can share them with others.

`cfg` This directory contains the OIL configuration file, along with the application-specific configuration files that are discussed in each chapter.

`inc` This directory contains all of the include files used by the application.

`lst` This empty directory will receive all of the listings from the build of the application. The `make` file creates a listing with the assembly code interleaved with the source code.

`obj` The individual module object files will be placed in this directory after build. The linker will look in this directory for all nonlibrary files to build.

`src` This directory contains the source files for the application in both C and assembly.

B.3 Axiom CME 555 Setup

To set up the Axiom boards for the example program, do the following.

Mode switches All switches are in the OFF position except SW1 number 2 and SW2 number 6.

Jumpers The jumpers are as follows.

- JP1 — On 1-2
- JP2 — On
- JP3 — On 1-2
- JP4 — On
- JP5–JP7 — Off
- JP8 — On
- JP9 — Off
- JP10 — Both vertical
- JP11 — On
- JP12 — On
- JP13 — N/A
- FPROG_EN — Off
- VPP_EN — Off
- EXT_CFG — On
- EXT_EN — On
- MEM_OPT — 5, 7 On
- M-SEL — 2
- FLSH_SEL — 3
- RAM_SEL — 1
- MEM-VOLT — 5V

CAN interconnect Connect pin J1-1 on one board to pin J1-1 on the second board. Do the same for J1-2 pins. Terminate at each end with a 150-ohm resistor.

C

Appendix C

OSEK/VDX API Reference

This appendix provides a description of all API components provided in each of the OSEK/VDX specifications. Included in this section are the API services, defined as C functions, plus the configuration and declaration items, which are usually defined as macros. Each description in this section is a brief reference to the component. Refer to the details in the text of the book more information. In the Return section, the S column is the return under STANDARD status and the E is returned under EXTENDED status.

Because most of the current OSEK/VDX implementations include a GUI configuration utility to create the OIL file, I have not included the OIL objects and attributes in this section. If necessary, the OIL specification on the CD is very clear about how the objects are defined and can be referenced. All components are listed in alphabetical order.

ActivateTask()

Prototype

```
StatusType ActivateTask(TaskType taskID);
```

Inputs

`taskID` Name of the task that is to be activated. This is the task name exactly as it appears in the OIL configuration file.

Outputs

None.

Return

Status	Description	S	E
E_OS_ID	Input `taskID` is not a valid task.		X
E_OS_LIMIT	Too many activations of `taskID` task. Only applicable in XCC2 conformance classes. Activation is ignored.		X
E_OK	Service executed without error.	X	X

Function

This API service moves the task identified by the input `taskID` from the `SUSPENDED` state to the `READY` state. If the service is invoked from a preemptive task when the `RES_SCHEDULER` resource is not locked, the scheduler is entered and preemption occurs if the activated task is a higher priority than the invoking task. If the service is invoked from a non-preemptive task from the ISR level or from within a critical section in which `RES_SCHEDULER` is locked, the scheduler will not be invoked and preemption will not occur.

Specification/Conformance Class Usage

OS Conformance Classes/Call Levels

BCC1	BCC2	ECC1	ECC2	TASK	ISR
X	X	X	X	X	X

Hook Routines Allowed

Error	Startup	Shutdown	PreTask	PostTask
	X			

CancelAlarm()

Prototype

```
StatusType CancelAlarm(AlarmType alarmID);
```

Inputs

`alarmID` Name of the alarm that is to be canceled. This is the alarm name exactly as it appears in the OIL configuration file.

Outputs

None.

Return

Status	Description	S	E
E_OS_ID	Input `alarmID` is not a valid alarm.		X
E_OS_NOFUNC	Alarm defined by `alarmID` is not in use.	X	X
E_OK	Service executed without error.	X	X

Function

This service cancels an alarm that has been set but has not yet been triggered. If the application wants to restart an alarm that is currently running, it must first invoke this service before it can reset the value of the alarm.

Specification/Conformance Class Usage

OS Conformance Classes/Call Levels

BCC1	BCC2	ECC1	ECC2	TASK	ISR
X	X	X	X	X	X

Hook Routines Allowed

Error	Startup	Shutdown	PreTask	PostTask

ChainTask()

Prototype

```
StatusType ChainTask(TaskType taskID);
```

Inputs

`taskID` Name of the task that is to be activated. This is the task name exactly as it appears in the OIL configuration file.

Outputs

None.

Return

Status	Description	S	E
E_OS_ID	Input taskID is not a valid task.		X
E_OS_LIMIT	Too many activations of taskID task. Only applicable in XCC2 conformance classes. Activation is ignored.		X
E_OS_RESOURCE	Invoking task still occupies resources and termination is not safe.		X
E_OS_CALLEVEL	Service was invoked from the interrupt level.		X
E_OK	This status is never returned because service does not return if successful.	X	X

Function

This service terminates the invoking task, moves the task identified by the input `taskID` from the `SUSPENDED` state to the `READY` state, and reschedules the application. Because the invoking task terminates first, invoking this service with `taskID` set to the same ID as the invoking task does not cause multiple activations. All resources locked by the invoking task must be released using `ReleaseResource()` prior to invoking this service. This service only returns in the extended status state when an error occurs. All tasks must end with either `ChainTask()` or `TerminateTask()`.

Specification/Conformance Class Usage

OS Conformance Classes/Call Levels

BCC1	BCC2	ECC1	ECC2	TASK	ISR
X	X	X	X	X	

Hook Routines Allowed

Error	Startup	Shutdown	PreTask	PostTask

ChangeProtocolParameters()

ChangeProtocolParameters()

Prototype

```
StatusType ChangeProtocolParameters (SymbolicName message, ParamValue bsValue,
                                     ParamValue stValue);
```

Inputs

`message` Symbolic name of the USDT message that is targeted. This is the name of the message as it appears in the OIL configuration file.

`bsValue` Value to be used for the block size (`BS`) of the USDT message. This value is the number of frames transmitted before waiting for a flow control frame from the receiving controller.

`stValue` Value used for the minimum separation time (`STmin`) of the USDT message. This is the minimum time required in milliseconds between transmission of consecutive frames.

Outputs

None.

Return

Status	Description	S	E
`E_COM_ID`	The input `message` is not a valid message.		X
`E_COM_RX_ON`	The parameters were not changed because there is a message reception in progress.	X	X
`E_OK`	Service executed without error.	X	X

Function

This service changes the block size (`BS`) and separation time (`STmin`) parameters for the USDT message defined by the input `message`. These parameters override the default values for this message and are not required to set the original values.

Specification/Conformance Class Usage

COM Conformance Classes

CCCA	CCCB	CCC0	CCC1	CCC2
				X

ClearEvent()

Prototype

```
StatusType ClearEvent(EventMaskType mask);
```

Inputs

`mask` Event mask of the events that are to be cleared. This is a logical `OR` of the event names as they appear in the OIL configuration file.

Outputs

None.

Return

Status	Description	S	E
E_OS_ACCESS	Service was not invoked from an extended task.		X
E_OS_CALLEVEL	Service was invoked on the interrupt level.		X
E_OK	Service executed without error.	X	X

Function

This service clears all of the events based on the events that are included in the input `mask`. This service can only be invoked from the extended task that owns the events. Typically, this service will be invoked after the task returns from the `WAITING` state and has processed a particular event or set of events.

Specification/Conformance Class Usage

OS Conformance Classes/Call Levels

BCC1	BCC2	ECC1	ECC2	TASK	ISR
		X	X	X	

Hook Routines Allowed

Error	Startup	Shutdown	PreTask	PostTask

CloseCOM()

Prototype

```
StatusType CloseCOM(void);
```

Inputs

None.

Outputs

None.

Return

Status	Description	S	E
E_OK	Service executed without error.	X	X
Other	Other implementation-specific return values are returned if the service does not complete successfully.		

Function

This service releases all hardware and low-level resources that were used by the communication component. It will not release any OS resources, which are only released by `StopCOM()`. This service is typically called prior to `StopCOM()` if a critical error occurs to reinitialize the complete system; otherwise, `StopCOM()` is typically called first. `CloseCOM()` is typically called during or immediately after shutting down the OS. It might be possible to invoke this service from within an OS task; however, all interrupts must be masked prior to invoking the service. During processing, all communications that are in process will be aborted and data will be lost.

Specification/Conformance Class Usage

OS/COM Conformance Classes/Call Levels

BCC1	BCC2	ECC1	ECC2	TASK	ISR
X	X	X	X	X*	
CCCA	CCCB	CCC0	CCC1	CCC2	
X	X	X	X	X	

Hook Routines Allowed

Error	Startup	Shutdown	PreTask	PostTask
	X			

CmpConfig()

Prototype

```
StatusType CmpConfig(NetIdType netID, ConfigRefType testRef,
                     ConfigRefType baseRef, ConfigRefType maskRef);
```

Inputs

`netID` Identifier of the communication network on which the configuration will be compared. This is the network name exactly as it appears in the OIL configuration file.

`testRef` Reference to a variable of type `ConfigType` that is being checked for changes.

`baseRef` Reference to a variable of type `ConfigType` that is being checked against for changes.

`maskRef` List of relevant nodes that are being tested for changes.

Outputs

None.

Return

Status	Description	S	E
TRUE	Returned if all of the relevant nodes in the test configuration have the same state as those in the base configuration.	X	X
FALSE	Returned if any of the relevant nodes in the test configuration have a different state from those in the base configuration.	X	X

Function

This service compares a test configuration to a base configuration to determine if any of the nodes have changed state. Only the nodes that are defined by the list of relevant nodes will be checked. If all of the relevant nodes have the same state between the test and base configurations, the service returns `TRUE`; otherwise, the service returns `FALSE`. These return values do not fit the format of the type `StatusType` but are valid values.

Specification/Conformance Class Usage

NM type (X = Required, O = Optional)

Direct	Indirect
O	O

CmpStatus()

Prototype

```
StatusType CmpStatus(NetIdType netID, StatusRefType testRef,
                     StatusRefType baseRef, StatusRefType maskRef);
```

Inputs

`netID` Identifier of the communication network on which the status will be compared. This is the network name exactly as it appears in the OIL configuration file.

`testRef` Reference to a variable of type `StatusType` that is being checked for changes.

`baseRef` Reference to a variable of type `StatusType` that is being checked against for changes.

`maskRef` List of relevant status values that are being tested for changes.

Outputs

None.

Return

Status	Description	S	E
TRUE	Returned if the test status and the base status are the same.	X	X
FALSE	Returned if the test status is different from the base status, and the new status is defined in the mask.	X	X

Function

This service compares a test status to a base status to determine if the network has changed state. A difference is only indicated if the new status is included in the mask. Note that the status type variable that is being referenced is different than the return value and will probably have a different name in the actual implementation.

Specification/Conformance Class Usage

NM type (X = Required, O = Optional)

Direct	Indirect
O	O

DeclareAlarm()

Syntax

```
DeclareAlarm(alarmId)
```

Inputs

`alarmId` Name of the alarm that is being declared. This is the alarm name exactly as it appears in the OIL configuration file.

Outputs

None.

Function

This declaration provides an external declaration of an alarm. It could be used by an implementation to declare an alarm that is referenced by the application code in a given module. In many OSEK/VDX implementations, the utility that translates the OIL file into a header file will typically include the declaration in the global include file, and this macro will be defined as a blank macro.

Specification/Conformance Class Usage

OS Conformance Classes/Call Levels

BCC1	BCC2	ECC1	ECC2	TASK	ISR
X	X	X	X		

Hook Routines Allowed

Error	Startup	Shutdown	PreTask	PostTask

DeclareEvent()

Syntax

`DeclareEvent(eventId)`

Inputs

`eventId` Name of the event that is being declared. This is the event name exactly as it appears in the OIL configuration file.

Outputs

None.

Function

This declaration provides an external declaration of an event. It can be used by an implementation to declare an event that is referenced by the application code in a given module. In many OSEK/VDX implementations, the utility that translates the OIL file into a header file typically includes the declaration in the global include file, and this macro will be defined as a blank macro.

Specification/Conformance Class Usage

OS Conformance Classes/Call Levels

BCC1	BCC2	ECC1	ECC2	TASK	ISR
		X	X		

Hook Routines Allowed

Error	Startup	Shutdown	PreTask	PostTask

DeclareResource( )

Syntax

```
DeclareResource(resId)
```

Inputs

`resId` Name of the resource that is being declared. This is the resource name exactly as it appears in the OIL configuration file.

Outputs

None.

Function

This declaration provides an external declaration of a resource. It can be used by an implementation to declare a resource that is referenced by the application code in a given module. In many OSEK/VDX implementations, the utility that translates the OIL file into a header file typically includes the declaration in the global include file, and this macro will be defined as a blank macro.

Specification/Conformance Class Usage

OS Conformance Classes/Call Levels

BCC1	BCC2	ECC1	ECC2	TASK	ISR
X	X	X	X		

Hook Routines Allowed

Error	Startup	Shutdown	PreTask	PostTask

DeclareTask()

Syntax

```
DeclareTask(taskId)
```

Inputs

`taskId` Name of the task that is being declared. This is the task name exactly as it appears in the OIL configuration file.

Outputs

None.

Function

This declaration provides an external declaration of a task. It can be used by an implementation to declare a task that is referenced by the application code in a given module. In many OSEK/VDX implementations, the utility that translates the OIL file into a header file typically includes the declaration in the global include file, and this macro will be defined as a blank macro.

Specification/Conformance Class Usage

OS Conformance Classes/Call Levels

BCC1	BCC2	ECC1	ECC2	TASK	ISR
X	X	X	X		

Hook Routines Allowed

Error	Startup	Shutdown	PreTask	PostTask

DisableAllInterrupts()

Prototype

```
void DisableAllInterrupts(void);
```

Inputs

None.

Outputs

None.

Return

Status	Description	S	E
None		X	X

Function

This API service saves the current state of all interrupts, disables all interrupts that are enabled, and identifies the beginning of a critical section. Within the critical section, no API service calls are allowed. How the system interrupts are disabled will differ between implementations and between microcontrollers. However, the effect on the application will be the same. This service does not allow nesting of critical sections. Library routines and hardware API routines should use `SuspendOSInterrupts()` and `ResumeOSInterrupts()` instead, which may be nested.

Specification/Conformance Class Usage

OS Conformance Classes/Call Levels

BCC1	BCC2	ECC1	ECC2	TASK	ISR
X	X	X	X	X	X

Hook Routines Allowed

Error	Startup	Shutdown	PreTask	PostTask

DisableInterrupt()

Prototype

```
StatusType DisableInterrupt(IntDescriptorType descriptor);
```

Inputs

`descriptor` Bit mask hardware-dependent descriptor of interrupts that are to be disabled. A `1` means to disable the interrupt.

Outputs

None.

Return

Status	Description	S	E
E_OS_NOFUNC	At least one of the interrupt sources could not be disabled.		X
E_OK	Service executed without error.	X	X

Function

This service disables the interrupts indicated by a `1` in the input parameter. The interpretation of the descriptor is hardware dependent. If all interrupts requested cannot be disabled, an error is returned, but the other interrupts will be disabled. This service should only be used in hardware-dependent routines, such as hardware device drivers. Application modules should use the more abstract `DisableAllInterrupts()` and `SuspendOSInterrupts()`.

Specification/Conformance Class Usage

OS Conformance Classes/Call Levels

BCC1	BCC2	ECC1	ECC2	TASK	ISR
X	X	X	X	X	X

Hook Routines Allowed

Error	Startup	Shutdown	PreTask	PostTask

EnableAllInterrupts()

Prototype

```
void EnableAllInterrupts(void);
```

Inputs

None.

Outputs

None.

Return

Status	Description	S	E
None.		X	X

Function

This API service enables all interrupts that were enabled prior to the previous call to `DisableAllInterrupts()` and identifies the end of a critical section. Within the critical section, no API service calls are allowed. If `DisableAllInterrupts()` was not previously called, the action taken is undefined by the specification. How the system interrupts are re-enabled will differ between implementations and between microcontrollers; however, the effect to the application will be the same.

Specification/Conformance Class Usage

OS Conformance Classes/Call Levels

BCC1	BCC2	ECC1	ECC2	TASK	ISR
X	X	X	X	X	X

Hook Routines Allowed

Error	Startup	Shutdown	PreTask	PostTask

EnableInterrupt()

Prototype

```
StatusType EnableInterrupt(IntDescriptorType descriptor);
```

Inputs

`descriptor` Bit mask hardware-dependent descriptor of interrupts that are to be enabled. A `1` means to enable the interrupt.

Outputs

None.

Return

Status	Description	S	E
E_OS_NOFUNC	At least one of the interrupt sources could not be enabled.		X
E_OK	Service executed without error.	X	X

Function

This service enables the interrupts indicated by a `1` in the input parameter. The interpretation of the descriptor is hardware dependent. If all interrupts requested cannot be enabled, an error is returned, but the other interrupts will be enabled. This service should only be used in hardware-dependent routines, such as hardware device drivers. Application modules should use the more abstract `EnableAllInterrupts()` and `ResumeOSInterrupts()`.

Specification/Conformance Class Usage

OS Conformance Classes/Call Levels

BCC1	BCC2	ECC1	ECC2	TASK	ISR
X	X	X	X	X	X

Hook Routines Allowed

Error	Startup	Shutdown	PreTask	PostTask

EnterISR()

Prototype

```
void EnterISR(void);
```

Inputs

None.

Outputs

None.

Return

Status	Description	S	E
None		X	X

Function

This API service is only used in a category 3 ISR to notify the implementation that the ISR intends to invoke an OS service. The actions taken when this service is invoked are specific to the implementation and to the microcontroller targeted. Although this service should only be called from a category 3 ISR, invoking the service from the task level or from a different ISR level might or might not result in an error.

Specification/Conformance Class Usage

OS Conformance Classes/Call Levels

BCC1	BCC2	ECC1	ECC2	TASK	ISR
X	X	X	X		3

Hook Routines Allowed

Error	Startup	Shutdown	PreTask	PostTask

ErrorHook( )

Prototype

```
void ErrorHook(StatusType error);
```

Inputs

`error` Error that caused the hook routine to be invoked.

Outputs

None.

Return

Status	Description	S	E
None.			

Function

This hook routine, if used, must be provided by the application and defined as available in the OIL configuration file. The prototype for the routine in the application must be identical to the prototype here. This hook routine is called by the OS whenever an API service is about to return a status value other than `E_OK` to the application or an error occurs when an alarm expires and a task is activated or an event is set. It is not called recursively if an error occurs within an API service invoked from the hook routine. It is typically used in Extended Status mode and is not included in the final release code.

Specification/Conformance Class Usage

OS Conformance Classes

BCC1	BCC2	ECC1	ECC2
X	X	X	X

GetActiveApplicationMode()

Prototype

```
AppModeType GetActiveApplicationMode(void);
```

Inputs

None.

Outputs

None.

Return

This service returns the current `APPMODE` that was defined when the OS was started. This value will be the exact value defined in the OIL configuration file.

Function

This service is typically used in applications that take different actions based on the current `APPMODE`.

Specification/Conformance Class Usage

OS Conformance Classes/Call Levels

BCC1	BCC2	ECC1	ECC2	TASK	ISR
X	X	X	X	X	X

Hook Routines Allowed

Error	Startup	Shutdown	PreTask	PostTask
X	X	X	X	X

GetAlarm()

Prototype

```
StatusType GetAlarm(AlarmType alarmID, TickRefType tickRef);
```

Inputs

`alarmID` Name of the alarm that is to be checked. This is the alarm name exactly as it appears in the OIL configuration file.

Outputs

`tickRef` Reference to a variable of type `TickType` into which the service places the remaining counter ticks before the alarm expires. If this service returns the value `E_OS_NOFUNC`, then the variable is undefined.

Return

Status	Description	S	E
E_OS_ID	The alarm is not a valid alarm.		X
E_OS_NOFUNC	The alarm is not presently used. This typically indicates that the alarm has not been set or has already expired.	X	X
E_OK	Service executed without error.	X	X

Function

This service checks the requested alarm to determine if it has been set and has not yet expired. If this is true, it then sets the variable referred to by the parameter `tickRef` to the number of counter ticks remaining before the alarm expires.

Specification/Conformance Class Usage

OS Conformance Classes/Call Levels

BCC1	BCC2	ECC1	ECC2	TASK	ISR
X	X	X	X	X	X

Hook Routines Allowed

Error	Startup	Shutdown	PreTask	PostTask
X			X	X

GetAlarmBase()

Prototype

```
StatusType GetAlarmBase(AlarmType alarmID, AlarmBaseRefType baseRef);
```

Inputs

`alarmID` Name of the alarm that is to be checked. This is the alarm name exactly as it appears in the OIL configuration file.

Outputs

`baseRef` Reference to a structure of type `AlarmBaseType` into which the service places the current characteristics of the alarm identified by the input `alarmID`.

Return

Status	Description	S	E
E_OS_ID	The alarm is not a valid alarm.		X
E_OK	Service executed without error.	X	X

Function

This service sets the values in the structure defined by `baseRef` to the current characteristics of the alarm. The members of the structure follow.

`maxallowedvalue` The maximum allowed value of the alarm counter in ticks.

`ticksperbase` The number of counter ticks required to reach a counter-specific unit. This value is vaguely defined in the specification and is typically not used.

`mincycle` The smallest allowed value for the cycle parameter when setting the alarm.

Specification/Conformance Class Usage

OS Conformance Classes/Call Levels

BCC1	BCC2	ECC1	ECC2	TASK	ISR
X	X	X	X	X	X

Hook Routines Allowed

Error	Startup	Shutdown	PreTask	PostTask
X			X	X

GetConfig()

Prototype

```
StatusType GetConfig(NetIdType netID, ConfigRefType configRef,
                     ConfigKindName kind);
```

Inputs

`netID` Identifier of the communication network about which the configuration is to be reported. This is the network name exactly as it appears in the OIL configuration file.

`kind` The kind of configuration — either Normal, Normal Extended, or Limp Home. These types are typically replaced by a nonportable constant for the given implementation.

Outputs

`configRef` Reference to a variable of type `ConfigType` into which this service will place the present configuration.

Return

Status	Description	S	E
E_OK	Service executed without error.	X	X

Function

This service obtains the current configuration of the type defined by the `kind` parameter and places it in the variable defined by the `configRef` parameter. The constants chosen by the individual implementations could affect portability of the application and should be encapsulated in a single module that is easily changed. Normal Extended configuration is only available under indirect NM, and Limp Home configuration is only available under direct NM.

Specification/Conformance Class Usage

NM type (X = Required, O = Optional)

Direct	Indirect
O	O

GetEvent()

Prototype

```
StatusType GetEvent(TaskType taskID, EventMaskRefType maskRef);
```

Inputs

`taskID` Name of the extended task that is to being queried. This is the task name exactly as it appears in the OIL configuration file.

Outputs

`maskRef` Reference to a variable of type `EventMaskType` into which the current status of the events for the task is placed. This will be a logical `OR` of the event names as they appear in the OIL configuration file.

Return

Status	Description	S	E
E_OS_ID	The task is not a valid task.		X
E_OS_ACCESS	The task is not an extended task.		X
E_OS_STATE	The task is in the SUSPENDED state. Events are not valid for tasks in the SUSPENDED state.		X
E_OK	Service executed without error.	X	X

Function

The current status of all events for the task defined by the input `taskID` are placed in the variable referenced by the `eventRef` input. The value placed here is the current state, either set or cleared, and does not indicate whether the task is waiting for the event.

Specification/Conformance Class Usage

OS Conformance Classes/Call Levels

BCC1	BCC2	ECC1	ECC2	TASK	ISR
		X	X	X	X

Hook Routines Allow

Error	Startup	Shutdown	PreTask	PostTask
X			X	X

GetInterruptDescriptor()

Prototype

```
StatusType GetInterruptDescriptor(IntDescriptorRefType descRef);
```

Inputs

None.

Outputs

`descRef` Reference to a variable of type `IntDescriptorType` into which the service places the status of all interrupt sources. If a source is enabled, the corresponding bit is set to 1; otherwise, it is set to 0.

Return

Status	Description	S	E
E_OK	Service executed without error.	X	X

Function

This service determines the status of all interrupt sources for the specific microcontroller. The result is dependent on the target hardware and should only be used within target-specific routines, such as hardware device drivers.

Specification/Conformance Class Usage

OS Conformance Classes/Call Levels

BCC1	BCC2	ECC1	ECC2	TASK	ISR
X	X	X	X	X	X

Hook Routines Allowed

Error	Startup	Shutdown	PreTask	PostTask
X			X	X

GetMessageResource()

Prototype

```
StatusType GetMessageResource(SymbolicName message);
```

Inputs

`message` Name of the message that is to be locked. This is the message name exactly as it appears in the OIL configuration file.

Outputs

None.

Return

Status	Description	S	E
E_COM_ID	The message is not a valid message.		X
E_COM_LOCKED	The message is locked by the communication component.	X	X
E_COM_BUSY	The message is already busy.	X	X
E_OK	Service executed without error.	X	X

Function

This service sets the message object defined by the input `message` to Busy. This service is used to limit access to a message whose Copy configuration has been defined as without-copy. If the message is already busy, the application should not attempt to change the data in the message object. It is recommended that `ReleaseMessageResource()` be invoked within the same function as this service. The application also must release the resource before terminating the task or entering the wait state whenever an OSEK/VDX-compliant OS is used.

Specification/Conformance Class Usage

OS/COM Conformance Classes/Call Levels

BCC1	BCC2	ECC1	ECC2	TASK	ISR
X	X	X	X	X	X*
CCCA	CCCB	CCC0	CCC1	CCC2	
	X	X	X	X	

Hook Routines Allowed

Error	Startup	Shutdown	PreTask	PostTask

GetMessageStatus()

Prototype

```
StatusType GetMessageStatus(SymbolicName message);
```

Inputs

`message` Name of the message that is to be checked. This is the message name exactly as it appears in the OIL configuration file.

Outputs

None.

Return

Status	Description	S	E
E_COM_ID	The message is not a valid message.		X
E_COM_LOCKED	The message is locked by the communication component.	X	X
E_COM_BUSY	The message is busy.	X	X
E_COM_NOMSG	The queue for a queued message is empty.	X	X
E_COM_LIMIT	At least one queued message has been lost because of a FIFO buffer overflow.	X	X
E_OK	Service executed without error.	X	X

Function

This service returns the current status of the message.

Specification/Conformance Class Usage

OS/COM Conformance Classes/Call Levels

BCC1	BCC2	ECC1	ECC2	TASK	ISR
X	X	X	X	X	X
CCCA	CCCB	CCC0	CCC1	CCC2	
	X	X	X	X	

Hook Routines Allowed

Error	Startup	Shutdown	PreTask	PostTask

GetResource()

Prototype

```
StatusType GetResource(ResourceType resID);
```

Inputs

resID Name of the resource that is to be locked. This is the resource name exactly as it appears in the OIL configuration file. If this value is the constant RES_SCHEDULER, the system is essentially operating in a non-preemptive mode.

Outputs

None.

Return

Status	Description	S	E
E_OS_ID	Requested resource is not a valid resource.		X
E_OS_ACCESS	The application has attempted to get a resource that is already locked.		X
E_OK	Service executed without error.	X	X

Function

This service allows the application to lock a resource and to enter into a critical section that will disable all other tasks that need access to the resource through the priority ceiling protocol. The corresponding call to ReleaseResource() should appear within the same function. The resource must be released prior to the task being placed in either the SUSPENDED or the WAITING state.

Specification/Conformance Class Usage

OS Conformance Classes/Call Levels

BCC1	BCC2	ECC1	ECC2	TASK	ISR
X	X	X	X	X	X

Hook Routines Allowed

Error	Startup	Shutdown	PreTask	PostTask

GetStatus()

Prototype

```
StatusType GetStatus(NetIdType netID, NetworkStatusType statusRef);
```

Inputs

`netID` Identifier of the communication network on which the status is to be reported. This is the network name exactly as it appears in the OIL configuration file.

Outputs

`statusRef` Reference to a variable of type `NetworkStatusType` into which the current status of the network is placed.

Return

Status	Description	S	E
E_OK	Service executed without error.	X	X

Function

This service obtains the current status of the network and places it in the variable defined by the `statusRef` parameter. The prototype for this function is misleading in that it appears that the variable `statusRef`
is passed by value, when in fact, according to the specification, it should be passed by reference.

Specification/Conformance Class Usage

NM type (X = Required, O = Optional)

Direct	Indirect
O	O

GetTaskID()

Prototype

```
StatusType GetTaskID(TaskRefType taskIDRef);
```

Inputs

None.

Outputs

`taskIDRef` Reference to a variable of type `TaskType` that contains the identifier of the task that is currently running. If no task is running, the variable is set to `INVALID_TASK`.

Return

Status	Description	S	E
E_OK	Service executed without error.	X	X

Function

This service provides the application with the identifier of the task that is presently running. It is intended to be used in hook routines and library functions to check the task from which it was invoked.

Specification/Conformance Class Usage

OS Conformance Classes/Call Levels

BCC1	BCC2	ECC1	ECC2	TASK	ISR
X	X	X	X	X	X

Hook Routines Allowed

Error	Startup	Shutdown	PreTask	PostTask
X			X	X

GetTaskState()

Prototype

```
StatusType GetTaskState(TaskType taskID, TaskStateRefType stateRef);
```

Inputs

`taskID` Name of the task that is to be checked. This is the task name exactly as it appears in the OIL configuration file.

Outputs

`stateRef` Reference to a variable of type `TaskStateType` into which the service will place the current state of the task identified by the input `taskID`. The value will be one of the following constants: `RUNNING`, `WAITING`, `READY`, `SUSPENDED`.

Return

Status	Description	S	E
E_OS_ID	Input `taskID` is not a valid task.		X
E_OK	Service executed without error.	X	X

Function

This service identifies the current state of the task identified by the `taskID` parameter and places this value into the variable referenced by `stateRef`. If this service is invoked by a task that can be preempted, the result could be invalid by the time it is evaluated. In this case, it is recommended that interrupts are disabled prior to invoking the service and until the result is analyzed.

Specification/Conformance Class Usage

OS Conformance Classes/Call Levels

BCC1	BCC2	ECC1	ECC2	TASK	ISR
X	X	X	X	X	X

Hook Routines Allowed

Error	Startup	Shutdown	PreTask	PostTask
X			X	X

GotoMode()

Prototype

```
StatusType GotoMode(NetIdType netID, NMModeName mode);
```

Inputs

`netID` Identifier of the communication network on which the `mode` will change. This is the network name exactly as it appears in the OIL configuration file.

`mode` The new operating mode, either `BusSleep` or `Awake`. These values can be replaced by implementation-specific constants.

Outputs

None.

Return

Status	Description	S	E
E_OK	Service executed without error.	X	X

Function

This service forces the NM component to either wake up or go to sleep.

Specification/Conformance Class Usage

NM type (X = Required, O = Optional)

Direct	Indirect
O	O

InitCMaskTable()

Syntax

```
InitCMaskTable(NetIdType netID, ConfigKindName config, ConfigRefType cmask);
```

Inputs

`netID` Identifier of the communication network to be initialized. This is the network name exactly as it appears in the OIL configuration file.

`config` The kind of configuration — either Normal, Normal Extended, or Limp Home.

`cmask` Mask of relevant nodes.

Outputs

None.

Function

This directive initializes an element of the table of relevant configuration masks. The entries in this table are used by `SelectDeltaConfig()`.

Specification/Conformance Class Usage

NM type (X = Required, O = Optional)

Direct	Indirect
O	O

InitCOM()

Prototype

```
StatusType InitCOM(void);
```

Inputs

None.

Outputs

None.

Return

Status	Description	S	E
E_OK	Service executed without error.	X	X
Other	Other Implementation-specific return values can be returned if the service does not complete successfully.		

Function

This service initializes all hardware and low-level resources that will be used by the COM component. It is typically called before starting the OS or during OS startup. It might be possible to invoke this service from within an OS task, however, all interrupts must be masked prior to invoking the service.

Specification/Conformance Class Usage

OS/COM Conformance Classes/Call Levels

BCC1	BCC2	ECC1	ECC2	TASK	ISR
X	X	X	X	X*	
CCCA	CCCB	CCC0	CCC1	CCC2	
X	X	X	X	X	

Hook Routines Allowed

Error	Startup	Shutdown	PreTask	PostTask
	X			

InitConfig()

Prototype

```
StatusType InitConfig(NetIdType netID);
```

Inputs

`netID` Identifier of the communication network to be initialized. This is the network name exactly as it appears in the OIL configuration file.

Outputs

None.

Return

Status	Description	S	E
E_OK	Service executed without error.	X	X

Function

This service is used to instruct the NM component to reset the configuration of the network to the default configuration and to restart configuration management. This service is only functional if the NM component is operating in the `NMNormal` state. The default configuration for direct NM is all nodes Absent from the network, and the default configuration for indirect NM is all nodes Present on the network.

Specification/Conformance Class Usage

NM type (X = Required, O = Optional)

Direct	Indirect
O	O

InitDirectNMParams()

Syntax

```
InitDirectNMParams(NetIdType netID, NodeIdType nodeId, TickType timerTyp,
                   TickType timerMax, TickType timerErr, TickType timerWBS,
                   TickType timerTx)
```

Inputs

`netID` Identifier of the communication network to be initialized. This is the network name exactly as it appears in the OIL configuration file.

`nodeId` Identification for the node-specific messages.

`timerTyp` Value of `TTyp` to be used.

`timerMax` Value of `TMax` to be used.

`timerErr` Value of `TError` to be used.

`timerWBS` Value of `TWaitBusSleep` to be used.

`timerTx` Value of `TTx` to be used.

Outputs

None.

Function

This directive initializes the parameters for a specific network that will operate in the direct mode of network management. There will be one of these directives for each node in a control unit operating under direct NM.

Specification/Conformance Class Usage

NM type (X = Required, O = Optional)

Direct	Indirect
O	O

InitIndDeltaConfig()

Syntax

```
InitIndDeltaConfig(NetIdType netID, ConfigKindName config, SignallingMode mode,
                   TaskRefType taskID, EventMaskType eventMask);
```

Inputs

`netID` Identifier of the communication network to be initialized. This is the network name exactly as it appears in the OIL configuration file.

`config` The kind of configuration — either Normal, Normal Extended, or Limp Home.

`mode` Mode of signaling the application — either Activation or Event.

`taskID` Name of the task that is to be activated or which owns the event(s) to be set. This is the task name exactly as it appears in the OIL configuration file.

`eventMask` Mask of the event or events to be set and associated with the task defined by the previous parameter. This parameter is only valid if the `mode` parameter is set to `Event`.

Outputs

None.

Function

This directive is used to specify how changes in the configuration of the network are to be indicated to the application. The signaling of the application occurs when the configuration of the network changes as defined by `SelectDeltaConfig()`.

Specification/Conformance Class Usage

NM type (X = Required, O = Optional)

Direct	Indirect
O	O

InitIndDeltaStatus()

Syntax

```
InitIndDeltaStatus(NetIdType netID, SignallingMode mode, TaskRefType taskID,
                   EventMaskType eventMask);
```

Inputs

`netID` Identifier of the communication network to be initialized. This is the network name exactly as it appears in the OIL configuration file.

`mode` Mode of signaling the application — either Activation or Event.

`taskID` Name of the task that is to be activated or that owns the event(s) to be set. This is the task name exactly as it appears in the OIL configuration file.

`eventMask` Mask of the event or events to be set and associated with the task defined by the previous parameter. This parameter is only valid if the `mode` parameter is set to `Event`.

Outputs

None.

Function

This directive specifies how changes in the status of the network are to be indicated to the application. Application signaling occurs when the status of the network changes as defined by `SelectDeltaStatus()`.

Specification/Conformance Class Usage

NM type (X = Required, O = Optional)

Direct	Indirect
O	O

InitIndirectNMParams()

Syntax

```
InitIndirectNMParams(NetIdType netID, NodeIdType nodeID, TickType timerTOB,
                     TickType timerErr, TickType timerWBS);
```

Inputs

`netID` Identifier of the communication network to be initialized. This is the network name exactly as it appears in the OIL configuration file.

`nodeId` Identification for the node-specific messages.

`timerTOB` Value of TOB (timeout for Observation) to be used.

`timerErr` Value of `TError` to be used.

`timerWBS` Value of `TWaitBusSleep` to be used.

Outputs

None

Function

This directive initializes the parameters for a specific network that will operate in the indirect mode of network management. There will be one of these directives for each node in a control unit that is operating under indirect NM.

Specification/Conformance Class Usage

NM type (X = Required, O = Optional)

Direct	Indirect
O	O

InitIndRingData()

Syntax

```
InitIndRingData(NetIdType netID, SignallingMode mode, TaskRefType taskId,
                EventMaskType eventMask);
```

Inputs

`netID` Identifier of the communication network to be initialized. This is the network name exactly as it appears in the OIL configuration file.

`mode` Mode of signaling the application — either `Activation` or `Event`.

`taskID` Name of the task to be activated or which owns the event(s) to be set. This is the task name exactly as it appears in the OIL configuration file.

`eventMask` Mask of the event or events to be set and associated with the task defined by the previous parameter. This parameter is only valid if the `mode` parameter is set to `Event`.

Outputs

None.

Function

This directive specifies how reception of a Ring message with data is to be indicated to the application. Application signaling occurs when a Ring message is received by the local node.

Specification/Conformance Class Usage

NM type (X = Required, O = Optional)

Direct	Indirect
O	O

InitNMScaling()

Syntax

```
InitNMScaling(NetIdType netID, ScalingParamType scaling)
```

Inputs

`netID` Identifier of the communication network to be initialized. This is the network name exactly as it appears in the OIL configuration file.

`scaling` Set of parameters used to scale the NM component for the particular network.

Outputs

None.

Function

This directive defines the scaling of the different parameters for the particular network management type on a given network. How this scaling is defined is specific to both a given implementation and the type of network management.

Specification/Conformance Class Usage

NM type (X = Required, O = Optional)

Direct	Indirect
O	O

InitNMType()

Syntax

```
InitNMType(NetIdType netID, NMType type)
```

Inputs

`netID` Identifier of the communication network to be initialized. This is the network name exactly as it appears in the OIL configuration file.

`type` The type of network management used on the network — either direct or indirect.

Outputs

None.

Function

This directive defines the type of network management used for a given network. There will be one of these directives for each of the networks connected to the controller. The type is typically defined with a constant parameter. This parameter is not defined in the standard and will probably vary between implementations.

Specification/Conformance Class Usage

NM type (X = Required, O = Optional)

Direct	Indirect
O	O

InitSMaskTable()

Syntax

```
InitSMaskTable(NetIdType netID, StatusRefType smask);
```

Inputs

`netID` Identifier of the communication network to be initialized. This is the network name exactly as it appears in the OIL configuration file.

`smask` Mask of relevant network states.

Outputs

None.

Function

This directive initializes an element of the table of relevant status masks. The entries in this table will be used by `SelectDeltaStatus()`.

Specification/Conformance Class Usage

NM type (X = Required, O = Optional)

Direct	Indirect
O	O

InitTargetConfigTable()

Syntax

```
InitTargetConfigTable(NetIdType netID, ConfigKindName config,
                      ConfigRefType target);
```

Inputs

`netID` Identifier of the communication network to be initialized. This is the network name exactly as it appears in the OIL configuration file.

`config` The kind of configuration — can be Normal, Normal Extended, or Limp Home.

`target` Target configuration.

Outputs

None.

Function

This directive initializes an element of the table of relevant configuration targets. The entries in this table are used by `SelectDeltaConfig()`.

Specification/Conformance Class Usage

NM type (X = Required, O = Optional)

Direct	Indirect
O	O

InitTargetStatusTable()

Syntax

```
InitTargetStatusTable(NetIdType netID, StatusRefType target);
```

Inputs

`netID` Identifier of the communication network to be initialized. This is the network name exactly as it appears in the OIL configuration file.

`target` Target network status.

Outputs

None.

Function

This directive initializes an element of the table of relevant status targets. The entries in this table are used by `SelectDeltaStatus()`.

Specification/Conformance Class Usage

NM type (X = Required, O = Optional)

Direct	Indirect
O	O

LeaveISR( )

Prototype

```
void LeaveISR(void);
```

Inputs

None.

Outputs

None.

Return

Status	Description	S	E
None		X	X

Function

This API service is the counterpart of `EnterISR()` and is invoked from a category 3 ISR to inform the implementation that it has completed processing all API services. This must be the last statement in a category 3 ISR and can be invoked only after `EnterISR()` has been invoked. The API service might or might not return to the ISR, depending on the implementation.

Specification/Conformance Class Usage

OS Conformance Classes/Call Levels

BCC1	BCC2	ECC1	ECC2	TASK	ISR
X	X	X	X		3

Hook Routines Allowed

Error	Startup	Shutdown	PreTask	PostTask

MessageInit()

Prototype

```
StatusType MessageInit(void);
```

Inputs

None.

Outputs

None.

Return

Status	Description	S	E
E_OK	Service executed without error.	X	X
Other	Other implementation-specific return values can be returned if the service does not complete successfully.		

Function

This is a callback function provided by the application and is invoked by the communication component from within StartCOM(). Many of the COM component API services indicate that they cannot be called until after StartCOM() is called; these services cannot be used within this function. The purpose of this callback function is to allow the application to initialize the application-specific message objects.

Specification/Conformance Class Usage

OS/COM Conformance Classes/Call Levels

BCC1	BCC2	ECC1	ECC2	
X	X	X	X	
CCCA	CCCB	CCC0	CCC1	CCC2
X	X	X	X	X

Hook Routines Allowed

Error	Startup	Shutdown	PreTask	PostTask

PostTaskHook()

Prototype

```
void PostTaskHook(void);
```

Inputs

None.

Outputs

None.

Return

Status	Description	S	E
None			

Function

This hook routine, if used, must be provided by the application and defined in the OIL configuration file as being available. The prototype for the routine in the application must be identical to the prototype here. This hook routine is called by the OS just after control of the CPU has been taken from a task and just prior to the task transitioning from the `RUNNING` to the `READY`, `WAITING`, or `SUSPENDED` state. Within this hook routine, the API service `GetTaskID()` returns the identifier of the old task. This hook routine is typically used to benchmark the application during development.

Specification/Conformance Class Usage

OS Conformance Classes

BCC1	BCC2	ECC1	ECC2
X	X	X	X

PreTaskHook()

Prototype

```
void PreTaskHook(void);
```

Inputs

None.

Outputs

None.

Return

Status	Description	S	E
None			

Function

This hook routine, if used, must be provided by the application and defined in the OIL configuration file as being available. The prototype for the routine in the application must be identical to the prototype here. This hook routine is called by the OS after a task has transitioned from the `READY` to the `RUNNING` state and just prior to giving the task control of the CPU. Within this hook routine, `GetTaskID()` returns the identifier of the new task. This hook routine is typically used to benchmark the application during development.

Specification/Conformance Class Usage

OS Conformance Classes

BCC1	BCC2	ECC1	ECC2
X	X	X	X

ReadFlag()

Prototype

```
FlagValue ReadFlag(FlagType flag);
```

Inputs

`flag` The name of the flag that is to be read. This is the flag name exactly as it appears in the OIL configuration file.

Outputs

None.

Return

Status	Description	S	E
TRUE	The conditions associated with the notification class to which this flag has been assigned have been met.	X	X
FALSE	The conditions associated with the notification class to which this flag has been assigned have not been met since the last time the flag was reset.	X	X

Function

This service queries the current state of the flag and returns whether the flag is set to `TRUE` or `FALSE`. The interpretation of the meaning of a `TRUE` flag depends on the notification class to which the flag is associated. If the conditions that would trigger that particular notification class have been met, the flag is set to `TRUE`. The flag is only reset to `FALSE` by `ResetFlag()`.

Specification/Conformance Class Usage

COM Conformance Classes

CCCA	CCCB	CCC0	CCC1	CCC2
	X	X	X	X

ReadRingData()

Prototype

```
StatusType ReadRingData(NetIdType netID, RingDataType ringRef);
```

Inputs

`netID` Identifier of the communication network that has received the Ring message. This is the network name exactly as it appears in the OIL configuration file.

Outputs

`ringRef` Reference to a variable of type `RingDataType` into which the Ring data is placed.

Return

Status	Description	S	E
E_OK	Service executed without error.	X	X
E_NotOK	Either the Ring data is not presently valid, or the logical ring is not running in a stable state.	X	X

Function

This service obtains the Ring data that was received with the last valid Ring message and places it in the variable referenced in the parameter list. This data can be read only while the local node has control of the Ring message. The prototype for this function is misleading in that it appears that the variable `ringRef` is passed by value, when in fact according to the specification it should be passed by reference.

Specification/Conformance Class Usage

NM type (X = Required, O = Optional)

Direct	Indirect
O	O

ReceiveDynamicMessage()

Prototype

```
StatusType ReceiveDynamicMessage(SymbolicName message, AccessNameRef dataRef,
                                 LengthRef lengthRef);
```

Inputs

`message` Name of the message that is to be received. This is the message name exactly as it appears in the OIL configuration file.

Outputs

`dataRef` Reference to the message data that is to be updated with the current data.

`lengthRef` Reference to a variable of type `Length` into which the length of the received message is placed.

Return

Status	Description	S	E
E_COM_ID	The message is not a valid message.		X
E_COM_LOCKED	Either the message is locked by the communication component or a with-copy message is set to Busy.	X	X
E_OK	Service executed without error.	X	X

Function

This service updates the data referenced by the input `dataRef` with the data from the message object associated with the requested message. How this data is updated depends on whether the message is accessed with- or without-copy. If the message is accessed with-copy, the data reference is filled with the data from the message object. If the message is accessed without-copy, no update of the data occurs because it already contains the proper data. The length of the data received is placed in the variable referenced by `lengthRef`.

Specification/Conformance Class Usage

COM Conformance Classes

CCCA	CCCB	CCC0	CCC1	CCC2
				X

ReceiveMessage()

Prototype

```
StatusType ReceiveMessage(SymbolicName message, AccessNameRef dataRef);
```

Inputs

`message` Name of the message that is to be received. This is the message name exactly as it appears in the OIL configuration file.

Outputs

`dataRef` Reference to the message data that is to be updated with the current data.

Return

Status	Description	S	E
E_COM_ID	The message is not a valid message.		X
E_COM_LOCKED	Either the message is locked by the communication component or a with-copy message is set to Busy.	X	X
E_COM_NOMSG	The queue for a queued message is empty.	X	X
E_COM_LIMIT	At least one queued message has been lost because of a FIFO buffer overflow.	X	X
E_OK	Service executed without error.	X	X

Function

This service updates the data referenced by the input `dataRef` with the data from the message object associated with the requested message. How this data is updated depends on whether the message is accessed with- or without-copy. If the message is accessed with-copy, the data reference is filled with the data from the message object. If the message is accessed without-copy, no update of the data occurs because it already contains the proper data. This function cannot be invoked from an ISR if it is accessing a queued message.

Specification/Conformance Class Usage

OS/COM Conformance Classes/Call Levels

BCC1	BCC2	ECC1	ECC2	TASK	ISR
X	X	X	X	X	X*
CCCA	CCCB	CCC0	CCC1	CCC2	
X	X	X	X	X	

Hook Routines Allowed

Error	Startup	Shutdown	PreTask	PostTask

ReceiveMessageFrom()

Prototype

```
StatusType ReceiveMessageFrom(SymbolicName message, AccessNameRef dataRef,
                              LengthRef lengthRef, AddressRef senderRef);
```

Inputs

`message` Name of the message that is to be received. This is the message name exactly as it appears in the OIL configuration file.

Outputs

`dataRef` Reference to the message data that is to be updated with the current data.

`lengthRef` Reference to a variable of type `Length` into which the length of the received message is placed.

`senderRef` Reference to a variable of type `Address` into which the address of the sender of the message is placed.

Return

Status	Description	S	E
E_COM_ID	The message is not a valid message.		X
E_COM_LOCKED	Either the message is locked by the communication component or a with-copy message is set to Busy.	X	X
E_OK	Service executed without error.	X	X

Function

This service updates the data referenced by the input `dataRef` with the data from the message object associated with the requested message. How this data is updated depends on whether the message is accessed with- or without-copy. If the message is accessed with-copy, the data reference is filled with the data from the message object. If the message is accessed without-copy, no update of the data occurs because it already contains the proper data. The length of the data received and the address of the sender of the data are placed in the variables referenced by `lengthRef` and `senderRef`.

Specification/Conformance Class Usage

COM Conformance Classes

CCCA	CCCB	CCC0	CCC1	CCC2
				X

ReleaseMessageResource()

Prototype

```
StatusType ReleaseMessageResource(SymbolicName message);
```

Inputs

`message` Name of the message that is to be released. This is the message name exactly as it appears in the OIL configuration file.

Outputs

None.

Return

Status	Description	S	E
E_COM_ID	The message is not a valid message.		X
E_OK	Service executed without error.	X	X

Function

This service sets the message object defined by the input `message` to `NOT_BUSY` and limits access to a message whose copy configuration has been defined as without-copy. It is recommended that `GetMessageResource()` be invoked within the same function as this service. It is also required that the application release the resource before terminating the task or entering the wait state whenever an OSEK/VDX-compliant OS is used.

Specification/Conformance Class Usage

OS/COM Conformance Classes/Call Levels

BCC1	BCC2	ECC1	ECC2	TASK	ISR
X	X	X	X	X	X*
CCCA	CCCB	CCC0	CCC1	CCC2	
	X	X	X	X	

Hook Routines Allowed

Error	Startup	Shutdown	PreTask	PostTask

ReleaseResource()

Prototype

```
StatusType ReleaseResource(ResourceType resID);
```

Inputs

`resID` Name of the resource that is to be unlocked. This is the resource name exactly as it appears in the OIL configuration file.

Outputs

None.

Return

Status	Description	S	E
E_OS_ID	Requested resource is not a valid resource.		X
E_OS_FUNC	The application has attempted to release a resource that is not locked or another resource has to be released first.		X
E_OS_ACCESS	The application has attempted to release a resource that has a lower ceiling priority than the statically assigned priority of the task or ISR that invoked the service.		X
E_OK	Service executed without error.	X	X

Function

This service allows the application to unlock a resource and to leave a critical section. The priority ceiling protocol returns the task that contains the critical section to the statically assigned priority. The corresponding call to `GetResource()` should appear within the same function. The resource must be released prior to the task being placed in either the `SUSPENDED` or the `WAITING` state.

Specification/Conformance Class Usage

OS Conformance Classes/Call Levels

BCC1	BCC2	ECC1	ECC2	TASK	ISR
X	X	X	X	X	X

Hook Routines Allowed

Error	Startup	Shutdown	PreTask	PostTask

ResetFlag()

Prototype

```
StatusType ResetFlag(FlagType flag);
```

Inputs

`flag` The name of the flag that is to be reset. This is the flag name exactly as it appears in the OIL configuration file.

Outputs

None.

Return

Status	Description	S	E
E_OK	Service executed without error.	X	X
Other	Other implementation-specific return values can be returned if the service does not complete successfully.		

Function

This service resets the state of the flag to FALSE.

Specification/Conformance Class Usage

COM Conformance Classes

CCCA	CCCB	CCC0	CCC1	CCC2
	X	X	X	X

ResumeOSInterrupts()

Prototype

```
void ResumeOSInterrupts(void);
```

Inputs

None.

Outputs

None.

Return

Status	Description	S	E
None		X	X

Function

This API service enables OS interrupts that were enabled prior to the most recent invocation of `SuspendOSInterrupts()` and identifies the end of a critical section. OS interrupts are defined as any interrupts that are serviced by a category 2 or 3 ISR. Within the critical section, no API service calls are allowed except nested calls to `SuspendOSInterrupts()` and `ResumeOSInterrupts()`. If a matching `SuspendOSInterrupts()` call is not found, the action taken is undefined by the specification. How the OS interrupts are enabled will differ between implementations and between microcontrollers. However, the effect to the application will be the same.

Specification/Conformance Class Usage

OS Conformance Classes/Call Levels

BCC1	BCC2	ECC1	ECC2	TASK	ISR
X	X	X	X	X	X

Hook Routines Allowed

Error	Startup	Shutdown	PreTask	PostTask

Schedule()

Prototype

```
StatusType Schedule(void);
```

Inputs

None.

Outputs

None.

Return

Status	Description	S	E
E_OS_CALLEVEL	Service was called from the interrupt level.		X
E_OK	Service executed without error.	X	X

Function

This service is used in non-preemptive tasks to allow cooperative multitasking by forcing the scheduler to run a higher priority task if there is one in the READY state. Although it is possible to call this service from a full-preemptive task, no action is taken.

Specification/Conformance Class Usage

OS Conformance Classes/Call Levels

BCC1	BCC2	ECC1	ECC2	TASK	ISR
X	X	X	X	X	

Hook Routines Allowed

Error	Startup	Shutdown	PreTask	PostTask

SelectDeltaConfig()

Prototype

```
StatusType SelectDeltaConfig(NetIdType netID, ConfigKindName kind,
                             ConfigHandleType hConfig, ConfigHandleType hCmask);
```

Inputs

`netID` Identifier of the communication network to be initialized. This is the network name exactly as it appears in the OIL configuration file.

`kind` The kind of configuration — can be Normal, Normal Extended, or Limp Home. These types will typically be replaced by a constant for the given implementation.

`hConfig` Handle to a target configuration that was previously defined by the directive `InitTargetConfigTable()`.

`hCmask` Handle to a configuration mask that was previously defined by the directive `InitCMaskTable()`.

Outputs

None.

Return

Status	Description	S	E
E_OK	Service executed without error.	X	X

Function

This service selects a combination of nodes on the network to be monitored and a target configuration for those nodes. When any of the nodes that are being monitored meets the target configuration, the application is signaled that a configuration has changed.

Specification/Conformance Class Usage

NM type (X = Required, O = Optional)

Direct	Indirect
O	O

SelectDeltaStatus()

Prototype

```
StatusType SelectDeltaStatus(NetIdType netID, StatusHandleType hStatus,
                             StatusHandleType hSmask);
```

Inputs

`netID` Identifier of the communication network to be initialized. This is the network name exactly as it appears in the OIL configuration file.

`hStatus` Handle to a target status that was previously defined by the directive `InitTarget-StatusTable()`.

`hSmask` Handle to a status mask that was previously defined by the directive `InitSMaskTa-ble()`.

Outputs

None.

Return

Status	Description	S	E
E_OK	Service executed without error.	X	X

Function

This service selects a target network status and a status mask that will be used to trigger an indication back to the application when the status changes. When any of the monitored network status values meet the target status, the application is notified.

Specification/Conformance Class Usage

NM type (X = Required, O = Optional)

Direct	Indirect
O	O

SelectHWRoutines()

Syntax

```
SelectHWRoutines(NetIdType netID, RoutineRefType busInit,
                 RoutineRefType busAwake, RoutineRefType busSleep,
                 RoutineRefType busRestart, RoutineRefType busShutDwn)
```

Inputs

`netID` Identifier of the communication network to be initialized. This is the network name exactly as it appears in the OIL configuration file.

`busInit` Routine to be invoked when the bus needs to be initialized. It is called once when the network is started.

`busAwake` Routine to be invoked when the bus leaves the power-down mode.

`busSleep` Routine to be invoked when the bus enters the power-down mode.

`busRestart` Routine to be invoked to restart the bus hardware in the case of a fatal bus error.

`busShutDwn` Routine to be invoked to shut down the bus hardware.

Outputs

None.

Function

This directive defines the set of routines that will be used by the network management component to control the hardware.

Specification/Conformance Class Usage

NM type (X = Required, O = Optional)

Direct	Indirect
O	O

SendDynamicMessage()

Prototype

```
StatusType SendDynamicMessage(SymbolicName message, AccessNameRef dataRef,
                              LengthRef lengthRef);
```

Inputs

`message` Name of the message that is to be sent. This is the message name exactly as it appears in the OIL configuration file.

`dataRef` Reference to the message data that is to be output.

`lengthRef` Reference to a variable of type `Length` that contains the length of the message to be sent.

Outputs

None.

Return

Status	Description	S	E
E_COM_ID	The message is not a valid message.		X
E_COM_LOCKED	Either the message is locked by the communication component or a with-copy message is set to Busy.	X	X
E_OK	Service executed without error.	X	X

Function

This service updates the message object associated with the requested message with the data referenced by the input `dataRef`. How this message object is updated depends on whether the message is accessed with- or without-copy. If the message is accessed with-copy, the data reference is copied to the message object. If the message is accessed without-copy, no update of the message object occurs because it already contains the proper data. After the data has been copied, if necessary, the COM component requests the transmission of the message depending on the transmission mode specified. The input length is sent to the lower layers of the COM component to format the network messages.

Specification/Conformance Class Usage

COM Conformance Classes

CCCA	CCCB	CCC0	CCC1	CCC2
				X

SendMessage()

Prototype

```
StatusType SendMessage(SymbolicName message, AccessNameRef dataRef);
```

Inputs

`message` Name of the message that is to be sent. This is the message name exactly as it appears in the OIL configuration file.

`dataRef` Reference to the message data that is to be output.

Outputs

None.

Return

Status	Description	S	E
E_COM_ID	The message is not a valid message.		X
E_COM_LOCKED	Either the message is locked by the communication component or a with-copy message is set to Busy.	X	X
E_OK	Service executed without error.	X	X

Function

This service updates the message object associated with the requested message with the data referenced by the input `dataRef`. How this message object is updated depends on whether the message is accessed with- or without-copy. If the message is accessed with-copy, the data reference is copied to the message object. If the message is accessed without-copy, no update of the message object occurs because it already contains the proper data. After the data has been copied, if necessary, the COM component requests the transmission of the message depending on the transmission mode specified. This function cannot be invoked from an ISR if it is accessing a queued message.

Specification/Conformance Class Usage

OS/COM Conformance Classes/Call Levels

BCC1	BCC2	ECC1	ECC2	TASK	ISR
X	X	X	X	X	X*

CCCA	CCCB	CCC0	CCC1	CCC2
X	X	X	X	X

Hook Routines Allowed

Error	Startup	Shutdown	PreTask	PostTask

SendMessageTo()

Prototype

```
StatusType SendMessageTo(SymbolicName message, AccessNameRef dataRef,
                         LengthRef lengthRef, AddressRef addressRef);
```

Inputs

`message` Name of the message that is to be sent. This is the message name exactly as it appears in the OIL configuration file.

`dataRef` Reference to the message data that is to be output.

`lengthRef` Reference to a variable of type `Length` that contains the length of the message to be sent.

`addressRef` Reference to a variable of type `Address` that contains the address of the recipient of the message.

Outputs

None.

Return

Status	Description	S	E
E_COM_ID	The message is not a valid message.		X
E_COM_LOCKED	Either the message is locked by the communication component or a with-copy message is set to Busy.	X	X
E_OK	Service executed without error.	X	X

Function

This service updates the message object associated with the requested message with the data referenced by the input `dataRef`. How this message object is updated depends on whether the message is accessed with- or without-copy. If the message is accessed with-copy, the data reference is copied to the message object. If the message is accessed without-copy, no update of the message object occurs because it already contains the proper data. After the data has been copied, if necessary, the COM component requests the transmission of the message depending on the transmission mode specified. The length and address inputs are sent to the lower layers of the COM component that format the network messages.

Specification/Conformance Class Usage

COM Conformance Classes

CCCA	CCCB	CCC0	CCC1	CCC2
				X

SetAbsAlarm()

Prototype

```
StatusType SetAbsAlarm(AlarmType alarmID, TickType start, TickType cycle);
```

Inputs

`alarmID` Name of the alarm that is to be set. This is the alarm name exactly as it appears in the OIL configuration file.

`start` The absolute value in counter ticks at which the alarm is to expire the first time.

`cycle` If this input is not `0`, then the alarm is a cyclic alarm with `cycle` ticks.

Outputs

None.

Return

Status	Description	S	E
E_OS_ID	The alarm is not a valid alarm.		X
E_OS_VALUE	Either the value of the input `start` is less than `0` or greater than the alarm base value `maxallowedvalue`, or the input `cycle` is less than `mincycle` or greater than `maxallowedvalue`.		X
E_OS_STATE	The alarm has previously been set and has not expired prior to a second attempt to set the alarm.	X	X
E_OK	Service executed without error.	X	X

Function

This service sets an alarm to expire at an absolute value of the counter to which it is assigned. When the counter reaches the value defined by the input `start`, the alarm expires. If the counter has already passed the value defined by `start`, the alarm expires only after the counter rolls over one time. If the counter is very close to the `start` value, the counter can expire prior to the OS returning from this service. Typically, this service is not used for a time-based alarm, but only for an alarm based on a position input, such as an engine crank angle. A cyclic alarm is defined if the input `cycle` is not equal to `0`. When the alarm expires, the value of the input `cycle` is added to the current alarm value and used as the next set point at which to expire. If the alarm is currently in use, this service fails. To restart an alarm that is currently in use, first invoke `CancelAlarm()`.

Specification/Conformance Class Usage

OS Conformance Classes/Call Levels

BCC1	BCC2	ECC1	ECC2	TASK	ISR
X	X	X	X	X	X

Hook Routines Allowed

Error	Startup	Shutdown	PreTask	PostTask

SetEvent()

Prototype

```
StatusType SetEvent(TaskType taskID, EventMaskType mask);
```

Inputs

`taskID` Name of the task that owns the event(s). This is the task name exactly as it appears in the OIL configuration file.

`mask` Event mask of the events that are to be set. This is a logical `OR` of the event names as they appear in the OIL configuration file.

Outputs

None.

Return

Status	Description	S	E
E_OS_ID	The task is not a valid task.		X
E_OS_ACCESS	The task is not an extended task.		X
E_OS_STATE	The task is in the `SUSPENDED` state. Events cannot be set for tasks in the `SUSPENDED` state.		X
E_OK	Service executed without error.	X	X

Function

The events defined by the input `mask` are set for the task defined by the input `taskID`. Multiple events can be set for a given task with one call to this service. If the task is in the `WAITING` state, and is waiting on one of the events that is set, the OS will move the task into the `READY` state. If the task is in the `READY` state, the event is set but no action occurs for that task until it runs again and invokes `WaitEvent()` with one of these events set. At that time, the task does not enter the `WAITING` state because the event is already set.

Specification/Conformance Class Usage

OS Conformance Classes/Call Levels

BCC1	BCC2	ECC1	ECC2	TASK	ISR
		X	X	X	X

Hook Routines Allowed

Error	Startup	Shutdown	PreTask	PostTask

SetRelAlarm()

Prototype

```
StatusType SetRelAlarm(AlarmType alarmID, TickType increment, TickType cycle);
```

Inputs

`alarmID` Name of the alarm that is to be set. This is the alarm name exactly as it appears in the OIL configuration file.

`increment` The incremental value in counter ticks relative to the current counter value at which the alarm is to expire the first time.

`cycle` If this input is not `0`, then the alarm is a cyclic alarm with `cycle` ticks.

Outputs

None.

Return

Status	Description	S	E
E_OS_ID	The alarm is not a valid alarm.		X
E_OS_VALUE	Either the value of the input `increment` is less than `0` or greater than the alarm base value `maxallowedvalue`, or the input `cycle` is less than `mincycle` or greater than `maxallowedvalue`.		X
E_OS_STATE	The alarm has previously been set and has not expired prior to a second attempt to set the alarm.	X	X
E_OK	Service executed without error.	X	X

Function

This service sets an alarm to expire at an incremental value of the counter to which it is assigned. When the counter reaches the value defined by the input `increment` plus the current value of the counter, the alarm expires. Typically, this service is used for a time-based alarm to set the next time that an action, such as a periodic task, would occur. A cyclic alarm is defined if the input `cycle` is not equal to `0`. When the alarm expires, the value of the input `cycle` is added to the current alarm value and used as the next set point at which to expire. If the alarm is currently in use, this service will fail. To restart an alarm that is currently in use, first invoke `CancelAlarm()`.

Specification/Conformance Class Usage

OS Conformance Classes/Call Levels

BCC1	BCC2	ECC1	ECC2	TASK	ISR
X	X	X	X	X	X

Hook Routines Allowed

Error	Startup	Shutdown	PreTask	PostTask

ShutdownHook()

Prototype

```
void ShutdownHook(StatusType error);
```

Inputs

`error` Error that caused the hook routine to be invoked.

Outputs

None.

Return

Status	Description	S	E
None			

Function

This hook routine, if used, must be provided by the application and defined in the OIL configuration file as being available. The prototype for the routine in the application must be identical to the prototype here. This hook routine is called by the OS after `ShutdownOS()` is invoked. If the OS is being shutdown because of an error detected by the OS, the `error` parameter will never be `E_OK`. This hook routine is not required to return to the OS unless both an OSEK/VDX OS and an OSEKTime OS coexist. Consequently, if the error is critical enough, it is possible for the application running in only an OSEK/VDX OS environment to force the application hardware to reset and attempt to resolve the issue.

Specification/Conformance Class Usage

OS Conformance Classes

BCC1	BCC2	ECC1	ECC2
X	X	X	X

ShutdownOS()

Prototype

```
void ShutdownOS(StatusType error);
```

Inputs

`error` This is the error value that is passed to the `ShutdownHook()` hook routine.

Outputs

None.

Return

Status	Description	S	E
None			

Function

This service can be called by an application to abort the OS function. Typically, this service is used by an application to switch `APPMODE`s or to indicate that a critical error has occurred and the system will need to be reset. While processing this service, the implementation calls the `ShutdownHook()` hook routine if it exists. If this hook routine returns, the resulting behavior is implementation specific. In most implementations, it will cause the system to return to the point in the application immediately after the call to `StartOS()`.

Specification/Conformance Class Usage

OS Conformance Classes/Call Levels

BCC1	BCC2	ECC1	ECC2	TASK	ISR
X	X	X	X	X	X

Hook Routines Allowed

Error	Startup	Shutdown	PreTask	PostTask
X	X			

SilentNM()

Prototype

```
StatusType SilentNM(NetIdType netID);
```

Inputs

`netID` Identifier of the communication network to be silenced. This is the network name exactly as it appears in the OIL configuration file.

Outputs

None.

Return

Status	Description	S	E
E_OK	Service executed without error.	X	X

Function

This service disables participation of the node in the network defined by the parameter. When invoked, this service forces network management to transition from the `NMActive` state to the `NMPassive` state.

Specification/Conformance Class Usage

NM type (X = Required, O = Optional)

Direct	Indirect
O	O

StartCOM()

Prototype

```
StatusType StartCOM(void);
```

Inputs

None.

Outputs

None.

Return

Status	Description	S	E
E_OK	Service executed without error.	X	X
Other	Other implementation-specific return values can be returned if the service does not complete successfully.		

Function

This service initializes all implementation-specific internal states, variables, and resources. If the callback function `MessageInit()` exists, it is invoked to initialize application-specific messages. On completion, the communication component is fully functional and ready to transmit and receive messages. If an OSEK/VDX-compliant OS is used, this service must be invoked from within a task.

Specification/Conformance Class Usage

OS/COM Conformance Classes/Call Levels

BCC1	BCC2	ECC1	ECC2	TASK	ISR
X	X	X	X	X	
CCCA	CCCB	CCC0	CCC1	CCC2	
X	X	X	X	X	

Hook Routines Allowed

Error	Startup	Shutdown	PreTask	PostTask

StartNM()

Prototype

```
StatusType StartNM(NetIdType netID);
```

Inputs

`netID` Identifier of the communication network to be started. This is the network name exactly as it appears in the OIL configuration file.

Outputs

None.

Return

Status	Description	S	E
E_OK	Service executed without error.	X	X

Function

This service starts network management on the network defined by the parameter. When invoked, this service forces network management to transition from the `NMOff` to the `NMOn` state.

Specification/Conformance Class Usage

NM type (X = Required, O = Optional)

Direct	Indirect
X	X

StartOS()

Prototype

```
void StartOS(AppModeType mode);
```

Inputs

`mode` This is the `APPMODE` in which the OS is to be started.

Outputs

None.

Return

Status	Description	S	E
None			

Function

This service is only allowed to be invoked outside of the OS. It starts the OS after the application hardware has been initialized. There may be implementation-specific restrictions that apply to how the OS starts or what must be done before starting the system. Although the specification indicates that this call does not need to return, most implementations will return after the OS has been shutdown. While processing this service, the implementation calls the `StartupHook()` hook routine if it exists.

Specification/Conformance Class Usage

OS Conformance Classes/Call Levels

BCC1	BCC2	ECC1	ECC2	TASK	ISR
X	X	X	X		

Hook Routines Allowed

Error	Startup	Shutdown	PreTask	PostTask

StartPeriodical()

Prototype

```
StatusType StartPeriodical(void);
```

Inputs

None.

Outputs

None.

Return

Status	Description	S	E
E_OK	Service executed without error.	X	X
Other	Other implementation-specific return values can be returned if the service does not complete successfully.		

Function

This API service initiates the periodic transmission of messages that are defined as either periodic or mixed transmission mode messages. It also restarts the periodic transmission of these messages after they have been stopped by `StopPeriodical()`.

Specification/Conformance Class Usage

COM Conformance Classes

CCCA	CCCB	CCC0	CCC1	CCC2
			X	X

StartupHook()

Prototype

```
void StartupHook(void);
```

Inputs

None.

Outputs

None.

Return

Status	Description	S	E
None			

Function

This hook routine, if used, must be provided by the application and defined in the OIL configuration file as being available. The prototype for the routine in the application must be identical to the prototype here. This hook routine is called by the OS after the system has been initialized and just prior to running the scheduler the first time after `StartOS()` has been invoked. The application can use this hook routine to initialize device drivers, start tasks based on the `APPMODE` that is active, or provide other application-specific initialization.

Specification/Conformance Class Usage

OS Conformance Classes

BCC1	BCC2	ECC1	ECC2
X	X	X	X

StopCOM()

Prototype

```
StatusType StopCOM(Scalar mode);
```

Inputs

`mode` This value determines how the system is shut down. At this time, the only required value in the standard is `COM_SHUTDOWN_IMMEDIATE`, in which case communication is shut down immediately and all pending communication is aborted. Other values can be supported by individual implementations.

Outputs

None.

Return

Status	Description	S	E
E_OK	Service executed without error.	X	X
Other	Other implementation-specific return values can be returned if the service does not complete successfully.		

Function

This service releases all resources used by COM and ceases all activity. It will not return until all pending COM operations are completed or successfully aborted and their resources can be released. On completion, the COM component is in a state where `StartCOM()` can be called to restart the component. If an OSEK/VDX-compliant OS is used, this service must be invoked from within a task. This service typically puts a network bus to sleep when it is not required.

Specification/Conformance Class Usage

OS/COM Conformance Classes/Call Levels

BCC1	BCC2	ECC1	ECC2	TASK	ISR
X	X	X	X	X	
CCCA	CCCB	CCC0	CCC1	CCC2	
X	X	X	X	X	

Hook Routines Allowed

Error	Startup	Shutdown	PreTask	PostTask

StopNM( )

Prototype

```
StatusType StopNM(NetIdType netID);
```

Inputs

`netID` Identifier of the communication network to be stopped. This is the network name exactly as it appears in the OIL configuration file.

Outputs

None.

Return

Status	Description	S	E
E_OK	Service executed without error.	X	X

Function

This service stops network management on the network defined by the parameter. When invoked, this service forces network management to transition from the `NMOn` to the `NMShutDown` state. After all of the activities related to shutting down the network occur, the NM component transitions into the `NMOff` state.

Specification/Conformance Class Usage

NM type (X = Required, O = Optional)

Direct	Indirect
X	X

StopPeriodical()

Prototype

```
StatusType StopPeriodical(void);
```

Inputs

None.

Outputs

None.

Return

Status	Description	S	E
E_OK	Service executed without error.	X	X
Other	Other implementation-specific return values can be returned if the service does not complete successfully.		

Function

This API service cancels the periodic transmission of messages that are defined as either periodic or mixed transmission mode messages.

Specification/Conformance Class Usage

COM Conformance Classes

CCCA	CCCB	CCC0	CCC1	CCC2
			X	X

SuspendOSInterrupts()

Prototype

```
void SuspendOSInterrupts(void);
```

Inputs

None.

Outputs

None.

Return

Status	Description	S	E
None		X	X

Function

This API service saves the current state of OS interrupts and then disables them. It identifies the start of a critical section. OS interrupts are defined as any interrupts that are serviced by an ISR of category 2 or 3. Within the critical section, no API service calls are allowed except nested calls to `SuspendOSInterrupts()` and `ResumeOSInterrupts()`. How the OS interrupts are disabled differs between implementations and between microcontrollers. However, the effect to the application will be the same.

Specification/Conformance Class Usage

OS Conformance Classes/Call Levels

BCC1	BCC2	ECC1	ECC2	TASK	ISR
X	X	X	X	X	X

Hook Routines Allowed

Error	Startup	Shutdown	PreTask	PostTask

TalkNM()

Prototype

```
StatusType TalkNM(NetIdType netID);
```

Inputs

`netID` Identifier of the communication network to be changed. This is the network name exactly as it appears in the OIL configuration file.

Outputs

None.

Return

Status	Description	S	E
E_OK	Service executed without error.	X	X

Function

This service enables participation of the node in the network defined by the parameter. When invoked, this service forces network management to transition from the `NMPassive` to the `NMActive` state.

Specification/Conformance Class Usage

NM type (X = Required, O = Optional)

Direct	Indirect
O	O

TerminateTask()

Prototype

```
StatusType TerminateTask(void);
```

Inputs

None.

Outputs

None.

Return

Status	Description	S	E
E_OS_RESOURCE	Invoking task still occupies resources and termination is not safe.		X
E_OS_CALLEVEL	Service was invoked from the interrupt level.		X
E_OK	Service executed without error.	X	X

Function

This function terminates the task that invoked the service, transferring it from the RUNNING to the SUSPENDED state. The service then forces a rescheduling of the application. All resources locked by the invoking task must be released using ReleaseResource() prior to invoking this service. This service only returns in the extended status state when an error occurs. All tasks must end with either TerminateTask() or ChainTask().

Specification/Conformance Class Usage

OS Conformance Classes/Call Levels

BCC1	BCC2	ECC1	ECC2	TASK	ISR
X	X	X	X	X	

Hook Routines Allowed

Error	Startup	Shutdown	PreTask	PostTask

TransmitRingData()

Prototype

```
StatusType TransmitRingData(NetIdType netID, RingDataType ringRef);
```

Inputs

`netID` Identifier of the communication network that has received the Ring message. This is the network name exactly as it appears in the OIL configuration file.

`ringRef` Reference to data to be placed in the data field of the Ring message when it is passed to the next consecutive node.

Outputs

None.

Return

Status	Description	S	E
E_OK	Service executed without error.	X	X
E_NotOK	Either the Ring data is not presently valid, or the logical ring is not running in a stable state.	X	X

Function

This service places the Ring data into the data field of the Ring message. This data can be updated only when the local node has control of the Ring message. The prototype for this function is misleading in that it appears that a variable is passed by value, when in fact, according to the specification, it should be passed by reference.

Specification/Conformance Class Usage

NM type (X = Required, O = Optional)

Direct	Indirect
O	O

WaitEvent()

Prototype

```
StatusType WaitEvent(EventMaskType mask);
```

Inputs

`mask` Event mask of the events to be waited for. This is a logical `OR` of the event names as they appear in the OIL configuration file.

Outputs

None.

Return

Status	Description	S	E
E_OS_ACCESS	Service was not invoked from an extended task.		X
E_OS_RESOURCE	The extended task from which the service was invoked still has resources locked.		X
E_OS_CALLEVEL	Service was invoked on the interrupt level.		X
E_OK	Service executed without error.	X	X

Function

This service checks the status of all of the events defined by the input value `mask`. If any of the events are set, the service immediately returns; otherwise, the service puts the extended task into the `WAITING` state and invokes the scheduler. The service can only be invoked from the extended task that owns the events.

Specification/Conformance Class Usage

OS Conformance Classes/Call Levels

BCC1	BCC2	ECC1	ECC2	TASK	ISR
		X	X	X	

Hook Routines Allowed

Error	Startup	Shutdown	PreTask	PostTask

Index

I

L

M

N

Embedded Systems Firmware Demystified

by Ed Sutter

November 2001 release

This is where the software meets the hardware! Understand embedded development from the ground up with this introduction to devices and concepts that include FLASH, EPROM, SRAM, DRAM, and data bus. Plus, you get firsthand experience with a working example for a very extensible firmware development platform. CD-ROM included, 224pp, ISBN 1-57820-099-7

RD3934 **$29.95**

Embedded Systems Design

A Step-by-Step Guide

by Arnold S. Berger

October 2001 release

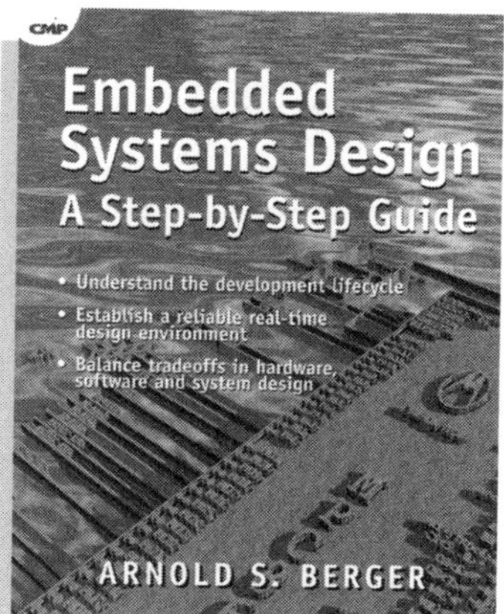

RD3689 **$34.95**

Develop embedded systems from the ground up! This primer teaches the specialized aspects of writing software in this environment that are not covered in standard coursework for software developers and electrical engineers. It traces the software and hardware methodologies and the integration of the two disciplines. 304pp, ISBN 1-57820-073-3

Find CMP Books in your local bookstore.

Order direct 800-500-6875
fax 408-848-5784

e-mail: cmp@rushorder.com
www.cmpbooks.com

What's on the CD-ROM?

Included on the CD is the entire source code for each chapter to enhance learning while studying this book. The complete OSEK/VDX standards are also included for reference. Because the standards are copyrighted material, the following copyright notice is included in the documents and reproduced here at their request.

The accompanying CD is described in more detail in Appendix B beginning on page 261 — including installation and modification of files for different OSEK/VDX environments.
